MANCHESTER
MEDIEVAL
LITERATURE
AND CULTURE

DATING BEOWULF

MANCHESTER
1824

Manchester University Press

Series editors: Anke Bernau, David Matthews and James Paz

Series founded by: J. J. Anderson and Gail Ashton

Advisory board: Ruth Evans, Patricia C. Ingham, Andrew James Johnston, Chris Jones, Catherine Karkov, Nicola McDonald, Sarah Salih, Larry Scanlon and Stephanie Trigg

MANCHESTER
MEDIEVAL
LITERATURE
AND CULTURE

Manchester Medieval Literature and Culture publishes monographs and essay collections comprising new research informed by current critical methodologies on the literary cultures of the Middle Ages. We are interested in all periods, from the early Middle Ages through to the late, and we include post-medieval engagements with and representations of the medieval period (or 'medievalism'). 'Literature' is taken in a broad sense, to include the many different medieval genres: imaginative, historical, political, scientific, religious. While we welcome contributions on the diverse cultures of medieval Britain and are happy to receive submissions on Anglo-Norman, Anglo-Latin and Celtic writings, we are also open to work on the Middle Ages in Europe more widely, and beyond.

Titles available in the series

Dating Beowulf

Studies in intimacy

Edited by
DANIEL C. REMEIN AND ERICA WEAVER

Manchester University Press

Published by Manchester University Press
Altrincham Street, Manchester M1 7JA
www.manchesteruniversitypress.co.uk

British Library Cataloguing-in-Publication Data
A catalogue record for this book is available from the British Library

ISBN 978 1 5261 3643 5 hardback
ISBN 978 1 5261 3644 2 open access

First published 2020

The publisher has no responsibility for the persistence or accuracy of URLs for any external or third-party internet websites referred to in this book, and does not guarantee that any content on such websites is, or will remain, accurate or appropriate.

Typeset
by Toppan Best-set Premedia Limited

Contents

Contributors

Christopher Abram is a member of the English department and a Fellow of the Medieval Institute at the University of Notre Dame. He works on Old English and Old Norse literature, with a special interest in poetry, religious culture, and ecocritical approaches. His most recent book, *Evergreen Ash: Ecology and Catastrophe in Old Norse Myth and Literature* (University of Virginia Press, 2019), looks at the resonances between the Norse apocalypse of Ragnarok and our own ecological crises in the twenty-first century.

Peter Buchanan is Assistant Professor of English at New Mexico Highlands University, where he teaches courses on linguistics, medieval literature, and composition. He also spends his time thinking about the relationship of the present to the past in twentieth-century literature. He lives with his wife amid a clutter of more books than can reasonably fit inside a single apartment and an impressive array of hedgehog-themed bric-a-brac.

Mary Dockray-Miller is Professor of English in the Humanities Department at Lesley University in Cambridge, MA, where she teaches undergraduate literature and humanities classes and advises the English Majors' Honor Society. She is the author of *Public Medievalists, Racism and Suffrage* (Palgrave, 2017), *The Books and the Life of Judith of Flanders* (Ashgate, 2015) and *Motherhood and Mothering in Anglo-Saxon England* (Palgrave, 2000) as well as editor of the *Wilton Chronicle* (Brepols, 2009).

Irina Dumitrescu teaches Old and Middle English literature at the Rheinische Friedrich-Wilhelms-Universität Bonn. She is the author of *The Experience of Education in Anglo-Saxon Literature* (Cambridge, 2018) and the editor of *Rumba Under Fire: The Arts of Survival from West Point to Delhi* (punctum books, 2016). She and Eric Weiskott have edited a collection of essays dedicated to Roberta Frank entitled *The Shapes of Early English Poetry: Style, Form, History* (Medieval Institute Publications, 2019).

Donna Beth Ellard is Assistant Professor of English at the University of Denver. She is the author of *Anglo-Saxon(ist) Pasts, postSaxon Futures* (punctum books, 2019) and has published in journals such as *Exemplaria*, *postmedieval*, and *Rethinking History*. Her work focuses on the haunting presence of race and empire in Anglo-Saxon studies and on the interspecies and interdisciplinary relationships between birds and humans, literary studies and the biosciences.

Roberta Frank, Marie Borroff Professor of English emerita at Yale University and University Professor emerita at the University of Toronto, has taught and written on Old English and Old Norse literature for half a century. She is now working, like Penelope at her loom, on a book about the art of early Northern poetry.

David Hadbawnik is a poet, translator, and medieval scholar. His *Aeneid* Books 1–6 was published by Shearsman Books in 2015. In 2012 he edited Thomas Meyer's *Beowulf* (punctum books), and in 2011 he co-edited selections from Jack Spicer's *Beowulf* for CUNY's Lost and Found Document series. He has published essays on poetic diction in English poetry from the medieval to the early modern period, and is a Visiting Assistant Professor at the University of Wisconsin-Eau Claire. His latest book, *Holy Sonnets to Orpheus and Other Poems*, was published by Delete Press in 2018.

Mary Kate Hurley is Assistant Professor of English at Ohio University. Her research focuses on time, translation, and community in medieval literature, and has appeared in *The Journal of English and Germanic Philology* and *Review of English Studies*, as well as in *The Politics of Ecology* (ed. Schiff and Taylor) and *American/ Medieval: Nature and Mind in Cultural Transfer* (ed. Overing and Wiethaus). With Jonathan Hsy and A. B. Kraebel, she was the co-editor of the autumn 2017 special issue of *postmedieval*, 'Thinking Across Tongues'.

Robin Norris is Chair of the Department of English Language and Literature at Carleton University, where she teaches courses on Old English, history of the language, and grammar through sentence diagramming. Her research interests include saints' lives and the litany of the saints, and with Johanna Kramer, she was one of the co-founders of the Anglo-Saxon Hagiography Society. With Rebecca Stephenson and Renée Trilling, she was one of the co-founders of the Feminist Renaissance in Early Medieval English Studies, which has been fostering new work on gender in Anglo-Saxon England since January 2016.

Mo Pareles is Assistant Professor of English at the University of British Columbia, where she holds a Hampton New Faculty Fellowship and is a member of the Oecologies Collective. She researches the mutual construction of species, sexual, and ethnic difference in medieval English religious literature. She is completing a book, *Translating Purity*, about the cultural translation of Jewish law in early medieval England, and is at work on another book project, *Time's Others*, on the roles of animal, infant, and Jewish temporalities in medieval English Christianity.

James Paz is Lecturer in Early Medieval English Literature at the University of Manchester. He is the author of *Nonhuman Voices in Anglo-Saxon Literature and Material Culture* (Manchester University Press, 2017) and the co-editor of *Medieval Science Fiction* (KCLMS, 2016). His work has also appeared in *Exemplaria*, *New Medieval Literatures*, and the *Journal of Medieval and Early Modern Studies*. His current research examines modern translations and poetic responses to Old English riddles, and he is also working on a long-term study of *cræft* in Anglo-Saxon literature.

Daniel C. Remein is Assistant Professor of English at the University of Massachusetts, Boston. His current book project concerns the aesthetics of *Beowulf* and 'Berkeley Renaissance' poets Robin Blaser and Jack Spicer, and a recent essay on eco-colonial anxiety in late Old Norse saga appears in *New Medieval Literatures*. A co-founder of the Organism for Poetic Research, he is the author of *A Treatise on the Marvelous for Prestigious Museums* (punctum books, 2018).

Benjamin A. Saltzman is Assistant Professor of English at the University of Chicago. He is the author of *Bonds of Secrecy: Law, Spirituality, and the Literature of Concealment in Early Medieval England* (University of Pennsylvania Press, 2019) and co-editor of *Thinking of the Middle Ages: Midcentury Intellectuals and the Medieval* (forthcoming from Cambridge University Press). He is beginning work on a new project about the literary and visual experience of witnessing evil, atrocity, and human suffering.

Catalin Taranu gained his PhD from the University of Leeds in 2016 and works on vernacular 'heroic' verse in Anglo-Saxon England and Carolingian Francia and on the modern uses and abuses of the early Middle Ages. He publishes and gives papers on *Beowulf*, *Maldon*, rhizomes and violence, and teaches medieval literature and Old English. He is preparing his first monograph on early medieval poetic history and is editing a volume on theories of truthfulness and historical representation in medieval history writing.

Erica Weaver is Assistant Professor of English at the University of California, Los Angeles. She is currently working on a book about the role of distraction in the development of early medieval literature and literary theory, with a related article – on medieval *enigmata* and the history of reading – in *New Literary History*. She is also co-editor, with A. Joseph McMullen, of *The Legacy of Boethius in Medieval England: The Consolation and its Afterlives* (ACMRS, 2018).

Acknowledgements

As specialists in Old English who have enjoyed the peculiar intimacy of co-editing, we may relish the idea that the editorial first-person plural pronoun of this book could have been rendered in Old English as the first-person dual pronoun 'wit' (we two). But it is just as well that the Present-Day English 'we' admits the ambiguity of collectives indeterminate in number, as this volume is the result of the labour, thought, friendship, and intellectual and political commitments of a much wider and, at times, difficult to define cadre of people. After all, the study of literature involves a wide variety of intimacies in addition to those we claim with particular texts – sometimes with persons one knows well; sometimes with persons one only corresponds with briefly, but crucially, at a propitious moment; and sometimes with larger collectives as such.

The contributors to this volume, all scholars already intimate with *Beowulf*, form one such collective. They have taken the risk of investing their time, energy, and ideas in the project of a serious book whose title announces a joke, writing with intensity, care, and a sense of adventure. We have developed a particular kind of writerly intimacy even as many of us have never met off-page. Around this immediate group, we are also especially grateful to all who have led or provoked urgent conversations and initiatives to make spaces where *Beowulf* is studied more inclusively, both within longstanding scholarly organizations and in some new groups that have formed during the gestation of this volume. We include among our contributors one of the co-founders of the organization currently known as the International Society of Anglo-Saxonists (ISAS), Roberta Frank, as well as the recent Executive Director, Robin Norris. We are grateful to both of them for their work in building community. As we go to press, we are delighted that the ISAS membership has voted to change its name to acknowledge the racist legacy embedded in the terms 'Anglo-Saxon' and 'Anglo-Saxonist', and we hope that this will prove a turning point in building a more just and open field. We recognize and thank the Medievalists of Color as an organization that has been leading the way and especially Adam Miyashiro and Mary Rambaran-Olm for their forceful critiques not only of our professional and historical monikers but also of rampant racism, misogyny, and abuse. Indeed, this volume is a direct response to related efforts to police who – and what kind of work – is welcome in the field, and we hope that it will likewise knock down doors. That said, we also openly acknowledge our own complicity in structural racism in early medieval studies. No scholars of colour appear among our contributors, and for that we are sorry.

As we think about ways to pitch in and expand the field, we also want to recognize Donna Beth Ellard's brainchild, the Islands of the North Atlantic (IONA) conferences – the first of which was held in Denver in 2017 and which Dan considers himself lucky to have been able to help plan, which are now likewise building new spaces for the kind of alternative discourses in Old English studies that this book calls for and tries to provoke. We are also both grateful to the Colloquium for Early Medieval Studies (formerly the ASSC) for providing an early intellectual home and an ongoing model of a feminist, theoretical Old English studies. The New Chaucer Society has similarly provided this early medieval work with two memorable moments: a chance for us to visit the *Beowulf* manuscript together, as it is exhibited to the public in the Treasures Room of the British Library, during the 2016 biennial congress in London and, at the 2018 congress in Toronto, an opportunity to make a pilgrimage – together with some other intrepid scholars of Old English also in attendance – to the offices of the Dictionary of Old English. These last efforts may have been more convivially than editorially focused, but they were no less important to the intimacy of the editorial process.

The conceptualization and mobilization of the volume also benefitted immensely from early support and enthusiasm from Erin Anderson, Jeffrey Cohen, Tricia Dailey, Matt Davis, Daniel Donoghue, Lara Farina, Eileen A. Fradenburg Joy, Clare Lees, Roy Liuzza, Joey McMullen, Haruko Momma, Susan Oldrieve, Gillian Overing, Robert Stanton, and Elaine Treharne. Although by the time of the first full manuscript draft Erica had moved to California, we shared Boston as an intellectual home for the early stages of the project, and we are grateful for the support of our regional medieval colleagues, as well as the Harvard English Medieval Colloquium, for making New England a great place to work on *Beowulf*.

Other friends, colleagues, teachers, students, and spouses, were all necessary and immeasurably helpful at various points in the project. Robert Kesler and Meagan Manas head the list for tolerating the strains that intimacy with an old poem can put on intimacy in the present. Others provided helpful references, critical conversation, crucial companionship in theoretical thinking, editing advice, and other sundry forms of support: Chris Baswell, Neal Bruss, Chris Chism, Jill Hamilton Clements, Taylor Cowdery, Helen Cushman, Adam Darisse, Daniel Davies, Josh Davies, Matthew Fisher, Hilary Fox, Isabel Gómez, Sarah Hamblin, Renee Hudson, Eric Jager, Ármann Jakobsson, Eleanor Johnson, Sarah Kareem, Anna Kelner, Stacy Klein, Sierra Lomuto, Deidre Lynch, Alex Mueller, Dan Najork, Anahid Nersessian, Hugh O'Connell, Arthur J. Russell, Emilio Sauri, Myra Seaman, Karl Steel, Arvind Thomas, Susan Tomlinson, Leonard Von Morzé, Audrey Walton, Nicholas Watson, Eric Weiskott, Samantha Zacher, and Jordan Zweck. We are also grateful to Kevin Killian and Peter Gizzi of the Jack Spicer Literary Estate. We were deeply saddened by Kevin's death during the final phases of the volume's production, and we hope that the Spicer material included in our introduction will mark one among the many memorials to his generosity to poets and scholars. Our especial thanks are owed to Jonathan Bellairs for his stellar assistance with copyediting at just the right time, to Jake Wilder-Smith for his terrific work on the index, and to UCLA's Division of Humanities for making their involvement possible. Last but certainly not least, we wish to thank our superb editor at Manchester University Press, Meredith Carroll, the broader Editorial Board and production team, and the anonymous readers for incisive suggestions at all stages.

This title is freely available in an open access edition thanks to the TOME initiative and the generous support of Arcadia, a charitable fund of Lisbet Rausing and Peter Baldwin, and of the UCLA Library. As scholars committed to teaching and writing in public institutions, we are incredibly grateful to Virginia Steel and Sharon Farb for working with us to include *Dating Beowulf* in this program, and we hope that this support will enable the volume to form a dating profile for readers of *Beowulf* and critics of intimacy within and beyond the immediate sphere of Old English studies.

Abbreviations

ACMRS	Arizona Center for Medieval and Renaissance Studies
ASE	*Anglo-Saxon England*
ASPR	George Philip Krapp and Elliott Van Kirk Dobbie (eds), *The Anglo-Saxon poetic records: a collective edition*, 6 vols (New York: Columbia University Press, 1931–53)
ES	*English studies*
JEGP	*Journal of English and Germanic philology*
JMEMS	*Journal of medieval and Early Modern studies*
NML	*New medieval literatures*
PMLA	*Publications of the Modern Language Association*
PQ	*Philological quarterly*
RES	*The review of English studies*

1

Getting intimate

Daniel C. Remein and Erica Weaver

'What's an old, 3000-line poem like you doing in a place like this?'

What would it mean to 'date' *Beowulf*? And what do we learn when we try? This playful pun on one of the more controversial terms in the scholarship on the poem allows a consideration of the range of intimacies generated by it as well as a conditioning of both the poem and its scholarship. Indeed, we, the editors, sincerely hope that you, the reader, considered the subtitle to this volume before picking it up. This collection of essays is in no way concerned with localizing the historical date of the composition of *Beowulf*, whether in manuscript or modern edited forms. In fact, the injunction not to address in any way the date of the poem's composition was given as a strict thematic and formal requirement to the contributors before they composed their chapters. Rather, the first part of the title of this book, *Dating Beowulf*, takes up 'dating' – that form of social and sometimes erotic interaction – as a kind of wilful and desperate anachronism whose internal and historical heterogeneity is aimed at raising the spectre of 'intimacy' with *Beowulf*, and thereby with early medieval studies broadly conceived. That is, by 'dating *Beowulf*' we mean to propose *going out with, courting, hooking up with*, etc. as a way to provocatively phrase a set of new relationships with an Old English poem.

But what kind of dating site would *Beowulf* be on anyway? The cool convenience of an app, of swiping right, a pay-to-play match-making service, or OkCupid? It would be difficult to get a date with *Beowulf* – not that function of the text that we name its hero, but the poem itself. If we take the poem's material state quite literally – the sole surviving copy in the charred manuscript held behind glass in the British Library now known as London, British Library, Cotton Vitellius MS A.xv – this is all the more true. Is that the name it puts on its Tinder account, the British Library shelf-mark

that preserves the sixteenth-century antiquarian and early owner
Robert Cotton's system for organizing his books under the busts
of Roman emperors (here, Vitellius)? Or maybe its nickname, 'the
Nowell Codex', which Kemp Malone coined in reference to the
manuscript's earliest known owner, the pioneering Old English
lexicographer Laurence Nowell (1520–76), who inscribed his name
and the date – 1563 – on the first folio? Or is *Beowulf* on Grindr?
Is 'hwæt', that famous opening word of *Beowulf* and other Old
English poems, a pick-up line, perhaps more a 'hey, girl' than a
'hark'?[1]

Kenneth Sisam once confessed that '[i]n a place far from libraries,
I have often read the text of *Beowulf* for pleasure'.[2] To which we
ask: well, Ken – what place is that exactly? And what of us who
read *Beowulf* or any other text in or maybe just near libraries, for
pleasure? Read it the 'wrong' way, and this claim comes across as
little more than awkward.[3] Plus, if it's the standard scholarly edition
of the text you are reading, the one we will be citing throughout
this volume, with its pet name 'Klaeber 4' and all those notes,[4] you
have a *de facto* library right in your hands! So this fantasy of intimacy
with *Beowulf*, of being alone with the poem 'in a place far from
libraries', free to be a caring amateur, reading 'for pleasure' far
away from an elaborate academic apparatus – well, ha. But perhaps
you're interested in a liaison with a slightly different *Beowulf*
altogether – one of the many translations and adaptations, perhaps
even the notorious computer-generated film starring Angelina Jolie?
And let's say you get a date. We know that *Beowulf* is funny, with
a knack for puns, elaborate jokes about historic feuds, and a timeless
sense of style. But is it exclusive? And anyway, that's a seriously
long-distance relationship.[5]

This brief meditation on the central pun of our title may seem
simply silly; however, each of these playful takes on our relationship to the poem raises questions about the full range of possible
intimacies and erotics in the poem itself and between the poem and
its readers. Our title is admittedly a little cheeky, but it is meant in
part as the site of an alternative discourse about the poem which aims
to open up the study of *Beowulf* and other Old English literature
to a more diverse range of voices and approaches. We thus aim
to open new trajectories in the discourse on *Beowulf*, which has
not seen a radical reconsideration, or stock-taking, of its position
and its larger set of functions within the field of literary studies
more generally for at least a decade. Indeed, no monograph or
collection of essays has intentionally engaged the study of *Beowulf*

with important developments in critical theory since Eileen A. Joy and Mary K. Ramsey's *The postmodern Beowulf: a critical casebook*, which collected scholarly contributions from the 1990s and the early 2000s and has proved a collection of continuing importance.[6]

Within Old English studies, *Dating Beowulf* responds directly to increasing calls for more feminist scholarship on early medieval texts; indeed, *The postmodern Beowulf* is the only previous volume of *Beowulf* criticism that has featured an equitable division of men and women authors. Of course, this volume also responds directly to related calls for robust alternatives to the recent revival of positivist scholarship on the date of the composition of the poem at the expense of literary and theoretical readings. Undeniably, 'dating' implies a system of understood social codes and obligations even as its incumbent emphasis on intimacy distances would-be daters from any fantasy of impersonal objectivity. In dating *Beowulf*, we thus reflect on the orientation of the field of early medieval studies as a whole towards the texts we study.

At the same time, we aim to open contemporary thought about affect to a pre-modern archive and vice versa. Indeed, we hope that affect theory and critical affect studies will benefit from this volume as a casebook of work that engages this field with an early medieval archive – not by simply extending backward the unaltered insights gleaned from the study of modernity, nor by constructing a purely linear pre-history, but by thickening and convoluting the problems and questions of the contemporary discussion. Although the closely related field of queer theory has long benefited from studies drawn from a very long history (and is very much in dialogue with our project here), affect theory and critical affect studies, as exemplified by major texts such as Lauren Berlant's *Cruel optimism* or Sianne Ngai's *Ugly feelings*, routinely consider texts from no earlier than the nineteenth century, and so remain hampered by a historically shallow archive. Scholars such as Stephanie Trigg and Thomas Prendergast have demonstrated the crucial functions of affect in modern and late medieval medievalisms, however,[7] and early medieval literature would benefit from similar sustained attention. Building on the work of early medievalists who have laid the groundwork for studies of Old English texts to contribute to affect theory,[8] *Dating Beowulf* addresses this critical lacuna, thereby seeking to fill a major gap both in medieval studies and in critical affect studies.

This introductory chapter thus seeks to get intimate with both *Beowulf* and with intimacy as a mode of critical engagement, forming a kind of dating profile that will serve as a conceptual framework for the various modes of intimacy in and with the poem that emerge throughout the volume. We will consequently delineate the difficulties and pleasures of intimacy with *Beowulf* – the philological and the speculative, the playful and serious – and how these difficulties organize themselves in an array of interrelated critical practices. Indeed, this volume coheres as a project in presenting a new set of readings both critical and personal that aim to generate new avenues of discussion for a poem too-often mired in critical impasses.

By inviting, then, an array of critical responses to and contestations of the politics, histories, affects, and sometimes even impossibilities of intimacy in and with *Beowulf*, we contend that the most basic practices and philosophical assumptions of our discipline must attend to how and why certain modes of scholarship are thought to be more or less suited to courting an Old English poem. Undeniably, even the old ways of dating *Beowulf* – for instance, philologically, metrically, historically – were, whether overtly or silently, invested in articulating the 'appropriate' methods that one could and could *not* bring to bear on Old English texts. As Roy Michael Liuzza affirms,

> I believe that the assumptions made in dating the poem, a branch of the study of Old English often regarded as ancillary, technical and perhaps a bit antique, tell us a great deal about our sometimes unspoken and unformulated critical attitudes towards Old English literary texts; each effort to date the poem contains an implicit *ars poetica*.

Indeed, 'When we talk about the dating of Beowulf we are talking about nothing less than the philosophical foundations of our discipline.'[9] So, dating *Beowulf* can be a scandalous undertaking, and getting intimate can prove tricky.

Looking for intimacy (in all the scholarly places)

What primarily constitutes intimacy? Acts (a kiss, a touch)? Knowledge (about someone)? Epistemological gestures (getting to know someone, a knowing look)? Or, apart from praxis or epistemology, a relational ontology (finding oneself caught up with, even 'stuck with' an intimate)? How would any of these possibilities condition a notion of intimacy that can speak to, and be informed by, early medieval literature? As Carissa M. Harris discerns, 'We are not accustomed to seeing the Middle Ages as intimately familiar', since, in contemporary media, '"medieval" functions as shorthand for *backwards, other. We are not like that. We are not that bad.*[10] And yet, as Harris deftly reveals, 'We are more like that than we want to admit, and our impulse to demarcate present from past, to posit ourselves as "progressive," as *not-that*, has profound implications because it elides the continuities of violence and inequality over time.'[11] It is essential to uncover our intimacy with the past, then.

Latinate in origin, the word *intimacy* only entered the English language during the early modern period, referring first to personal familiarity and then quickly developing an erotic charge in certain contexts. Indeed, the term derives from the Latin *intimus* (most inner) and originally denoted personal interiority or 'intimate thoughts' as well as exceptional closeness between 'intimates'.[12] In this sense, the intimate is always *personal* and often involves *persons*. Only later did the term develop a wider application to connections between abstract concepts. This is not to say, of course, that the intimate is a privileged realm of the human (indeed, scholars of the pre-modern have been at the forefront of studying queerly inhuman intimacies), but it does perhaps mark the ease with which our conceptualizations and readings of intimacy may relentlessly *personalize* – even when one or more of the intimate entities in question are decidedly not *persons*, or when what may be at stake in a given instance of intimacy turns less around the experience of individuals and more around questions of collectivity or the workings of normative power.

In Old English, notions of interpersonal intimacy are perhaps most apparent in the dual pronoun 'wit' (we two), but Old English also has a range of words that describe states that can involve intimacy, such as 'ferræden' (companionship or fellowship) and 'freondscipe' (friendship). Old English also has a robust vocabulary for objects of intimacy, from words for friends, lovers, and spouses, including but not limited to 'freond', 'wine', and 'gefera', to terms of endearment, such as 'dyre' (dear, precious one), 'deorling' (darling), 'leof' (beloved), and 'lufsum' (lovesome, lovable one).[13] Moreover, aristocratic society in early medieval England involved countless performances of intimacy well known to the student of *Beowulf*, from ring giving to the exchange of maxims.

Intimacy has long eluded critics of the poem, however, whether in localized textual cruces or in broader theoretical questions about the text and its world. Perhaps more than any other figure in the poem, we resemble Grendel lurking 'in þystrum' (in darkness) (87b), able to hear the music but perpetually unable to secure an invitation to the party. The 'radical reconfiguration of the interconnection of time, space, and embodiment' that, according to Gillian R. Overing, *Beowulf* offers its readers may render the poem particularly recalcitrant to any conclusive familiarity – much less intimacy, for 'the beginning student of the poem ... encounters the same difficulty as the lifelong scholar'.[14]

Even scenes in *Beowulf* that appear to centre modes of intimacy can be difficult to pin down or to schematize precisely, as for example when Overing suggests that the role of women 'in enacting the ties of kinship' in *Beowulf* is 'a task of infinite regression, a never-ending process that accurately reflects Derrida's concept of *différance*'.[15] For this reason, a seasoned critic such as James W. Earl can explicate experiences of deep intimacy with the poem, 'as if it were a dream ... as if we had dreamed it ourselves', and yet also insist that 'reading *Beowulf*, even after all these years is not like talking to an old friend'.[16] And yet, even though the poem offers itself up to questions of old friends very naturally, intimacy is rarely articulated openly as a guiding critical framework.

Many times when intimacy is invoked in places where we would expect to see it – in queer theory, affect studies, and theories of sensation or phenomenology – it functions metaphorically as a descriptor of a certain kind of intense relationship between conceptual entities rather than those of lived lives. Scholars readily discuss the intimacy of two concepts, philosophical schools, or distant times, texts, and places, but rarely focus on intimacy of the kind that exists between people – even in descriptions meant to rigorously account for factical experience itself. The phenomenologist Maurice Merleau-Ponty's famous analysis of the reversibility of flesh and world, flesh and idea, visible and invisible, '[t]he intertwining: the chiasm' – a trope of intimacy *par excellence* if there ever was one – speaks of the 'intimacy' of 'us' and the field of the visible 'as though there were between it and us an intimacy as close as between the sea and the strand'.[17] Meanwhile, Eve Kosofsky Sedgwick explores 'the intuition that a particular intimacy seems to subsist between textures and emotions',[18] with a particular instance of such an intimacy, around shame and anal eroticism in Henry James's *The art of the novel*, giving way to the traces of an intimacy between historical persons.[19]

Although the critical moves of affect theory do not turn on intimacy as such, foundational texts frequently describe the emotional effects of intimacy and its absence, for, as Nancy Yousef puts it, 'insofar as intimacy, like sympathy, designates feeling for and with another, it also admits and discloses affective expectations and disappointments – from aversion to self-abasing admiration, from gratitude to resentment, from frustration to fascination'.[20] Alternately, the terms 'intimacy' and 'intimate' often circulate, in a supporting role, around and within the analysis of specific affects and their social fields. In Sara Ahmed's groundbreaking *The promise of happiness*, for example, we hear about the 'intimacy of desire and anxiety' as taught by psychoanalysis.[21] Accordingly, intimacy provides the scene for the perniciously normative way that 'happiness makes its own horizon', in that love, which is supposed to make us happy, 'becomes an intimacy with what the other likes (rather than simply liking what the other likes) and is given on condition that such likes do not take us outside a shared horizon'.[22] Because happiness orients, as a promise, towards the future, Ahmed even figures intimacy as one crucial avenue for happiness itself: 'if happiness is what we desire, then happiness involves being intimate with what is not happy, or simply with what is not'.[23]

Indeed, intimacy signals a set of questions that organize some of the most compelling recent interventions in critical theory. Delineating her queer medieval historiography, Carolyn Dinshaw cites the influential claims of L. O. Aranye Fradenburg Joy and Carla Freccero that 'what seems crucial to a queering of historiography is not the rejection of truth for pleasure – which would only repeat the myth of their opposition – but rather the recognition of their intimacy'.[24] Here, again, the concepts of high philosophy – truth and pleasure – are mediated by 'their' intimacy, inviting us, perhaps, to consider further the question of precisely what such intimacy might consist of, or how this intimacy might relate to the intimacy of historical bodies. Consequently, a 'hermeneutics of intimacy' contends that hermeneutics – and perhaps also critique – itself *is* intimate. Our practices of reading and interpretation are not activities of distancing ourselves from our texts but of drawing them nearer. Whereas Susan Sontag famously proclaimed that 'in place of a hermeneutics we need an erotics of art',[25] then, we contend that the two are – or at least can be – one and the same, that hermeneutics and intimacy, erotics and philology all belong together.[26]

Of course, in each of these examples, an inquiry into intimacy itself is not, precisely, the point, and we do not cite them in any way as a catalogue of failures or offences. However, collectively, they do invite a fuller and more systematic assessment of intimacy as a critical term, both within each of these discourses, and as its own field for humanistic inquiry. Here, it is worth noting that all reading is an act of intimacy, since, as Daniel Boyarin notes, there is a 'pervasive association of reading in the West with the private social spaces and meanings of the erotic', as, for instance, when we read in bed.[27]

Sometimes humanists call us to lean on this intimacy. Edward Said argued that all intellectuals should be motivated by

> amateurism, the desire to be moved not by profit or reward but by love for and unquenchable interest in the larger picture, in making connections across lines and barriers, in refusing to be tied down to a specialty, in caring for ideas and values despite the restrictions of a profession.[28]

More recently, in a less Arnoldian manner, Carolyn Dinshaw has argued that '[d]efined by attachment in a detached world, amateurism in fact condenses a whole range of abjections from the normative modernist life course, including ethnicity and race, economic class, and sex and gender'.[29] Dinshaw's interest in amateurism as 'a bit queer' foregrounds the overlap between the affects and intimacies of the amateur and those assigned by twentieth-century psychology to the sexual deviant: 'immaturity, belatedness or underdevelopment, inadequate separation from objects of love, improper attachment, inappropriate loving'.[30] Which intimacies, we ask, does *Beowulf* or its world abject, and which intimacies or modes of intimacy within medieval studies are 'inappropriate' now, and why? What inappropriate loving may know something about *Beowulf*, its intimacies, its allures, or its dangers now better than any scholar, but remains unheard, dismissed as 'immature', 'not yet fully developed' (and here we think specifically of students of Old English, at all levels) – or, perhaps legitimately wronged by the field's histories of racism, misogyny, or abuse, no longer interested in the hazardous modes of intimacy that code as 'collegiality'?

Relationship status: it's complicated

No intimacy or even a critique of intimacy can be considered only from the side of the individual. No mode or instance of intimacy can offer pure, autonomous affects; it will always remain imbricated within the logics of capital and history. In Ahmed's analysis of 'the happy family', for example, heterosexual models of intimacy especially take on the charge of 'happy objects' that reproduce the form of the family on 'the assumption that happiness follows relative proximity to a social ideal'.[31] But if it is out of an analysis of contemporary texts and cinema that Ahmed's now well-known figures of the 'feminist killjoy', the 'unhappy queer', and the 'melancholic migrant' emerge as recalcitrant positions of resistance to these horizons, then it is also worth underscoring that *Beowulf* has also been the site of notably interruptive, resistant, queer intimacies in modernity. Indeed, as Toni Morrison deftly summarizes, *Beowulf* can offer 'a fertile ground on which we can appraise our contemporary world'.[32]

For example, when the queer, mid-century American poet Jack Spicer worked on a translation of *Beowulf* alongside his fellow queer poet Robin Blaser for a seminar with the Berkeley philologist Arthur G. Brodeur, the Old English poem became an unlikely node of intimacy between two men within the rhythms of a pre-Stonewall, gay, West Coast community. As Robin Blaser would later recall:

> Well, as time goes on, Jack and I will do *Beowulf* together and we work three hours a night, five nights a week, and on Friday nights we can go out to the Red Lizard. That's a queer bar. Once a week you can go out and have a big time. The rest of the time you're really doing this job, and I have my translations and Jack's of the *Beowulf*, and so on. They are better than anybody's so far, Jack's especially.[33]

Performing at once a series of intimate translations between languages, times, avocations, and subcultures, as well as the intimacy of translation itself, *Beowulf* is thus partly constitutive of a community whose intimacies simultaneously disrupt the bar scene, the philology classroom, and the world of the poem itself.

Indeed, Blaser and Spicer seem to have directly considered the complicated relationship of their mid-century, queer homosocial intimacy to the 'heroic' homosocial intimacies in the narrative of *Beowulf*. As an obscure but intimate register of this, in Spicer's notes for his *Beowulf* translation, he scrawled 'Robin – / The death of Hygelac',[34] which might seem too elliptical to be of critical interest if at the time of the seminar Brodeur had not already been at work on his *The art of Beowulf*, which argues not only that 'the defeat and death of Hygelac' (Beowulf's king) is at the heart of the poem,[35] but also that '[i]t is Hygelac who supplies the *Leitmotiv*, which is the interwoven harmony of Hygelac's death and Beowulf's love for him'.[36] An emphatic use of a conspicuous possessive adjective in a speech that Beowulf makes about King Hrethel (Hygelac's father and Beowulf's fosterer) reveals to Brodeur in a single touch the intense social and literary functions of this intimacy: 'næs ic him to life laðra owihte, / ... þonne his bearna hwylc, / Herebeald ond

Hæðcyn oððe Hygelac min' ('Never in life was I a whit less dear
to him ... than any of his children, Herebeald and Hæthcyn, or *my
Hygelac*') (2432–4).[37] Italicizing that last clause in his translation,
Brodeur maintains that within this 'strongest expression of human
feeling in the whole poem', this one phrase functions as the fulcrum
for an immense weight of intimate intensities.[38] Against this backdrop,
we might speculate that Spicer's scrawled note similarly, if frag-
mentarily, indexes the weight of working out a fraught, marginalized
intimacy.

Blaser and Spicer were never lovers, but this tiny corner of their
coterie frames crucial questions about the politics of describing
intimacy in the context of the academic humanities. 'What kind of
community is it, exactly,' asks Dinshaw, 'that consists of two people?
How can we avoid triviality and idiosyncrasy as we discuss community
formations?'[39] Despite the overwhelming homophobia of mid-century
American culture, the relative privilege of Blaser's and Spicer's
queer coterie with *Beowulf* in its midst stands, for example, in stark
contrast to the loneliness in which the mid-century Scottish poet
Edwin Morgan worked out his own intimacy with *Beowulf* while
translating the poem at the same moment. In 'Epilogue: Seven
Decades', Morgan notes how 'At thirty I thought life had passed
me by, / translated *Beowulf* for want of love. / And one night stands
in city centre lanes – / they were dark in those days – were wild
but bleak.'[40] Looking to this constellation of autobiography, loneliness,
and desire, Chris Jones observes that the poem 'reveals the other,
more surprising need that Old English fulfilled for Morgan ...
Beowulf was a palliative against the loneliness of having to live a
secret life as a gay man in Glasgow in the late 1940s.'[41]

So, intimacy has long been a part of the experience of reading
and translating *Beowulf*, with the poem itself becoming an intimate
as well as a touchstone for broader communities. But another reason
why intimacy is a particularly useful rubric for thinking about an
old poem is that it productively multiplies critical problems as well.
With a poem such as *Beowulf*, which is so often canonically situated
at the very beginning of the 'English literary tradition', intimacy
can feel both deceptively easy and especially difficult to achieve.
This multiplies the possibilities for differing kinds of intimacy with
the poem and opportunities for interpretative interventions, '[f]or
intimacy only rarely makes sense of things', as Lauren Berlant so
robustly observed.[42] Indeed, as Giorgio Agamben notes, intimacy
is at once a sensation of utmost familiarity and perpetual inaccessibility, for love is '[t]o live in intimacy with a stranger, not in order

to draw him closer, or to make him known, but rather to keep him strange, remote ... forever exposed and sealed off'.[43]

From the outset, *Beowulf* seems to resist this, with Beowulf himself assuring the Danish coast guard that nothing should be kept secret: 'Ne sceal þær dyrne sum / wesan, þæs ic wene' (There must be nothing secret, I should think) (271b–272a). 'But there are secrets in *Beowulf*, as Benjamin A. Saltzman reminds us.[44] Indeed, there is constant anxiety in the text about the failure of intimacy and the resulting atmosphere of secrecy and suspicion that enters in whenever intimacy cannot be established. In the world of the poem, every agent must be recognizable; to be anonymous, to withhold information and identity, is to pose a threat. And the very logic of secrecy itself often operates as a promise of something like intimacy (with the secret itself, with the one who delivered the secret) while delivering only its impossibility – much in the way that the engraved sword from Grendel and his mother's underwater gallery wall ultimately remains inscrutable (1687–98a). By Jacques Derrida's influential account, there is much one can do with a secret, and yet it does not exceed obscurity in the service of any intimacy but 'rather towards a solitude'.[45]

At the same time, *Beowulf* is a poem that many of us think we know well. But intimacy is tricky. Sometimes we can return to a passage that we have read many times and realize that either we are more intimate with it than we thought or that we hardly know it at all. Like many early medieval texts, the poem wavers between gossip and withholding, sometimes relying heavily on implications and raised eyebrows – a kind of 'bless her heart' digressiveness – and sometimes pointedly leaving certain things unsaid or enigmatic. When read for intimacy, however, *Beowulf*'s ellipses and litotes, its silences and hints become a kind of 'getting around the Hollywood code', fading to black, or mobilizing the 'indirect kiss' that becomes more erotic because of its misdirection. By omitting explicit references, the poem trades in a culture of discretion that relies on audiences being able to fill in the gaps, as Roberta Frank explores at greater length in her chapter in this volume. And so a 'hermeneutics of intimacy' offers a new means of relating to Old English literature, which is frequently characterized by its reticence.

Yet intimacy itself is rarely visible, or only becomes visible under certain conditions when things do not work the way they are supposed to. Berlant recognizes that 'intimacy reveals itself to be a relation associated with tacit fantasies, tacit rules, and tacit obligations to remain unproblematic. We notice it when something about it takes on a charge, so that the intimacy becomes something else, an "issue".[46] Within an academic subdiscipline, especially one as small – and yes, intimate – as Old English studies, the intimacies of the field and its members similarly become noticeable when they take on a charge and render normally 'tacit fantasies, tacit rules, and tacit obligations' more explicit. For such a subfield this 'charge' often appears when intimacies otherwise private to the field become public, or when public 'issues' intrude on the normal protocols of intimacy otherwise obscured within the relative privacy of the field. In the wake of both #femfog in 2016 and white supremacists' racist investment in an 'Anglo-Saxon' past in Charlottesville, Virginia in 2017,[47] several intimacies and their obverses that may not have been previously visible to everyone in the field became visible as such: the intimacy of hate-groups with a construction of the past that scholars may or may not find recognizable, the field's historical intimacy with misogynistic and racist ideology, and our ongoing complicities in structural racism.[48] Within this very volume for instance, we notice that not a single person of colour appears among our contributors. We thus note the ways in which intimacy can – regardless of intentions – reproduce forms of exclusion, as Benjamin A. Saltzman investigates in his chapter. Indeed, despite the intentionally international character of the list of contributors, this volume also remains largely grounded in North American discourses of Old English studies.

Of course, *Beowulf* itself also dramatizes and enacts these charges that render intimacy noticeable as a critical question. The poem presents many versions of arrivals and departures, losses and discoveries. Sometimes its guests are welcome, and sometimes they reveal the precarity of the most supposedly intimate of spaces: homes; sleeping chambers; and sites of parenting, friendship, and romantic love. There are the halls of men and the homes of figures such as Grendel, his unnamed mother, and the dragon curled around its treasures. Indeed, Grendel and his mother live in a hall, even if it is only revealed as such when its intimacy is transformed by violence and it becomes a 'niðsele' ('battle-hall' or, more bluntly, a 'violence-hall') (1513a). To the perspective of the human reader, only Beowulf's intrusion reveals that it was a 'sele' (hall) all along: an intimate, hidden retreat for mother and son – itself a place of child-rearing and domestic comforts. Even as the fight ensues, the space is described as a home, filled with heirlooms and tucked in under the bubbles. It is – or at least was – a space of safety and refuge.

Intimate relationships can prove similarly precarious. Hrothgar's great hall Heorot is finally burned by his own son-in-law: a fiery ending that is presaged even as the hall's construction is announced (67b–85). As the poem's digressions similarly underscore and as Mary Kate Hurley will explore in greater detail in the pages ahead, even the closest ties of marriage and kinship, inheritance and family heirlooms can quickly turn intrusive or hostile. It is an erotic of aftermaths. Even as Heorot is being built, we are reminded that it will burn – and thus that it has burned by the time we are reading the poem. For Beowulf, too, 'his sylfes ham' (his own home) (2325b) is melted by the heat of the dragon's 'brynewylmum' (burning flames) (2326b), constituting 'hygesorga mæst' (the greatest of mind-sorrows) (2328b) for the king whose reign – though he does not know it – is about to draw to a close. So, *Beowulf* also explores intimacies of scale: fleeting encounters and one-time transactions as much as intergenerational ties – all lasting only 'oð ðæt' (until…) to 'oð ðæt' (until…).

Similarly, we are often permitted the intimacy of hearing characters mourn, as Mary Kate Hurley, Robin Norris, and Mary Dockray-Miller explore in greater complexity in their chapters. Remembering 'min yldra mæg' (my big brother) (468a), who was killed in battle, Hrothgar achingly confides, 'se wæs betera ðonne ic' (he was better than I [am]) (469b), while the bereaved Hrethel is likened to a father mourning his hanged son in one of the poem's most heart-breakingly intimate passages (2444–62a). As the *Beowulf* poet succinctly explains, for the grieving father, 'þuhte him eall to rum / wongas ond wicstede' (it all seemed to him too spacious / the pastures and the living quarters) (2461b–2462a). After the death of the beloved if misbehaving child, no space is experienced intimately; everything is ripped open and unenclosed.

Getting physical

But even as the conceptual field of intimacy expands to necessitate such philosophizing (as well as realpolitik), intimacy remains inextricably tied to experiences of sensation. Carolyn Dinshaw's account of queer (medieval) historiography enacts what we might characterize as queerly incomplete intimacies in 'partial connections, queer relations between incommensurate lives and phenomena'.[49] These intimacies across centuries amount nevertheless to 'a history of things touching'.[50] Such 'touches' may not always be intimate touches, nor are they necessarily the touches proper to the physiology of the human organism, but neither does the latter rule out the possibility of historiographical and community-catalysing intimacies.

The intimacy of this sort of 'touch' should be apparent in considering *Beowulf* in its persistently intractable, enigmatic, and materially incomplete state. Just as the poem's brightest and most glorious halls are also some of its most precarious spaces, the precarious nature of the survival of the poem itself is difficult to forget now that its brittle pages must be reinforced by protective supports. Indeed, in literal terms, *Beowulf*'s brightest moment of all was when it was actually on fire, during the infamous 23 October 1731 Ashburnham House fire that burned much of the sixteenth-century antiquarian Robert Cotton's library. While we were both in London during the summer of 2016, we stood together in the Treasures Room of the British Library, pressing our hands to the thick glass that guards the dimly lit manuscript as these events and modern security threw the complexity – and, as North American scholars who had received institutional money for research travel, the privilege – of our intimacies with the poem, scholarly and otherwise, into high relief. Our collaboration was in its infancy, and we were then more intimate with that sealed-off manuscript than with this project, or each other's modes and rhythms of thought and work. As Ahmed notes,

> There is nothing more vulnerable than caring for someone; it means not only giving your energy to that which is not you but also caring for that which is beyond or outside your control. Caring is anxious – to be full of care, to be careful, is to take care of things by becoming anxious about their future, where the future is embodied in the fragility of an object whose persistence matters.[51]

This is especially true for a sole survivor like *Beowulf*.

Even – or perhaps especially – in the flames, however, there is intimacy to be found. The distraught librarian famously leaped from the burning library in his nightshirt, running directly from bed to the Codex Alexandrinus, which he carried out in his arms.[52] So sometimes the most precarious situations can provide the greatest opportunities for intimacies that might otherwise elude us, because they allow normative barriers to temporarily recede – as, for instance, when Wiglaf forms a heightened attachment to the dying Beowulf, in part because the other retainers have abandoned him, as Mary Dockray-Miller explores in this volume's closing chapter. One of the most intimate relationships on Earth, at least in biological terms, is that between a parasite and its host. The relationship is precarious for both parties and pernicious in its intimacy, but as Michel Serres has articulated, 'The parasite is a differential operator of change. It excites the state of the system.'[53] Non-human intimacies like this remind us that the often asymmetrical instability and power of and within the intimate relation – as a kind of catalyst or retardant, shifter or modulator of *pace* within dynamic or living systems – can modify one or more parties in ways that are existentially or biologically differentiating. Intimacy can sustain, kill, and transform beyond recognition.

The *Beowulf* manuscript preserves other kinds of codicological intimacy as well, with the poem in its current form bound amid the other texts of the 'Nowell Codex': *The Life of St Christopher*, *The Wonders of the East*, *The Letter of Alexander to Aristotle*, and *Judith*. This manuscript is also composite in another way, as the Nowell Codex itself was conjoined with another Old English manuscript in the seventeenth century, with the sole surviving copy of the Old English translation of Augustine's *Soliloquies*, a fragment of *The Gospel of Nicodemus*, *The Debate of Solomon and Saturn*, and eleven lines of a *Saint Quintin Homily* providing an additional cluster of intimates for *Beowulf*.

Moreover, the poem as we have it was copied by two scribes: one older and one younger, switching over in the middle of line 1939 – its b-verse now both a point of separation and of ultimate collaboration. Folio 172v, where the transition occurs and where the scribes' distinct styles of handwriting are still clearly visible, is thus one of *Beowulf*'s most intimate places. Community here arises out of interruption; it becomes something that disrupts larger social patterns and structures. Or, as Jean-Luc Nancy puts it, 'Incompletion is its "principle".'[54] As Overing argues, the poem's own logic of temporality, history, and corporeality 'offers a space to undo controlling distinctions between past and present temporalities; a space where moments of rupture and suspension can mutually reveal past and present perspectives, where our time can intersect with that of the poem'.[55] Moreover, such intersections are available to be *felt* by the body of a reader, for whom, 'to enter the world of *Beowulf* is to experience change at a visceral level, whether such change is temporal, spatial, or embodied'.[56]

What can be tricky, and what each of the contributors was implicitly tasked with in delineating various intimacies in and with

Beowulf, is to tease out how – with what discourses, structures, reading tactics, or theoretical manoeuvres – to render such intimacies legible. Although the intimacy of Dinshaw's 'touch' appeals to registers aside from strictly human corporeality, it is worth noting that conceiving of such touching may seem all the more difficult within Old English and Anglo-Latin texts, because they appraise the human bodily senses in historically particular ways, privileging sight within a schema very different from modern hierarchies of sense, and yet, in effect without departing from the general and long-standing Western dominance of the visual register. As Katherine O'Brien O'Keeffe forcefully articulates, sight was considered the highest sense in early medieval schematizations, while '[t]ouch, by contrast, though proper to the largest organ in the body, trails the others in statements of value or is overlooked entirely'.[57] Thus a delicate critical posture of philological intimacy is needed to tease out how Old English texts attempt to encode, generate, or harbour non-visual sensory experience and its affective functions. Here, belabouring the point that 'touch' and 'sense' invoke a broader paradigm of sensory-affective perception, we stress the need to connect work by scholars of pre-modernity in the history and theory of the emotions to those in the history of the senses.[58]

But intimacy will never be sufficient for the positivist. Such touches, as a locus of historiographical intimacy, may yield a degree of epistemological dubiousness and a partial, fragmentary, or otherwise incomplete intimacy that may resist normative modes of historiography, desire, and sexuality. Dinshaw's queer historian, we recall, may be a queer historiographical fetishist who is 'decidedly *not* nostalgic for wholeness and unity' and yet 'nonetheless desires an affective, even tactile relation to the past such as a relic provides'.[59] If the touch imbues the historiographical act with latent intimacies, positing a queer fetish as its object multiplies their complexities but also the potential for intimacies that eschew the intimate as determined by the private, the known, and the lasting, in favour of the public, the anonymous, the fleeting, the ghostly, or even the utopian, as in José Esteban Muñoz's conception of 'queer futurity'.[60] A touch can be intimate without knowing what it is that one touches or that which one is touched by, and one may or may not know more about one's intimate life through touch.

Aside from terms such as 'excessiveness'[61] or 'tension',[62] Dinshaw has left relatively untouched the precise phenomenology of such touch in its relation to intimacy with old texts, and one thing the chapters in this volume do is begin to answer that question by talking about

Beowulf from a variety of critical vantage points. But the reader will be hard-pressed to pin down a single sensation, affect, or other bodily experience proper to intimacy. Intimate feelings tend towards the vague, the slippery, the notional, even the spectral. As a limit, or perhaps paradigm, of intimacy, tactility involves that dizzying register of perceptual organization that Sedgwick sweepingly refers to as 'the whole issue of texture'.[63] Texture, Sedgwick suggests, renders the touch-er a kind of open-ended experimenter, left to post a series of questions that contribute to a general resistance to the totalization of intimacy: 'To perceive texture is never only to ask or know What is it like? nor even just How does *it* impinge on *me*? Textural perception always explores two other questions as well: How did it get that way? and What could I do with it?'[64]

So while the chapters that follow, we suggest, engage *Beowulf* intimately by perusing the texture of both the poem and our possible range of relationships to it in ways that *ask* these two questions, they will also resist providing quantifiable or stable accounts of the former, or instrumentalisable or commodifiable possibilities for the latter. As the ground of touch-sensation, texture speaks to the multiply entangled *scales* of experience, politics, economics, affect, sexuality, and so forth, on which intimacy operates: 'the sense of touch makes nonsense out of any dualistic understanding of agency and passivity; to touch is always already to reach out, to fondle, to heft, to tap, or to enfold, and always also to understand other people or natural forces as having effectually done so before oneself'.[65]

Intimacy may thus be *sensed* or experienced in/as/on the sites of textures; but this contributes directly, it would seem, to the difficulty of describing the senses (in the full semantic range of that term) of intimacy, and the recalcitrance of intimacy to totalizing accounts. And in this way, describing texture (in its elusive, interruptive, and a-systematic effects that must be tracked slowly, carefully, and closely) is not only a task well suited to the philologically trained critics of Old English who populate this volume, but also a way of describing intimacies and their risks.

Intimacy tends towards the touch within deconstructive discourses of ethics because, as Jean-Luc Nancy formulates it, it is 'touching the limit' that constitutes 'the possibility of touch itself'.[66] And for this reason, the intimacy of touch and the touch of intimacy remain disruptive and risky in such discourses in ways that both echo and differ from either more general cultural critique or Serres's account of the parasite. So it is worth noting that even patristic accounts of touch, which shaped Anglo-Saxon evaluations of the

hierarchy of bodily senses, singled out touching as an act of particular
vulnerability and danger. As O'Brien O'Keeffe helpfully summarizes,

> Theological suspicions about the sense of touch are easy to find:
> while Jerome could write to Eustochium about the spiritual touch of
> the Bridegroom [of The Song of Songs], he was unyielding on the
> dangers close by through the *fenestrae* [windows] of the senses. His
> ascending catalogue of sensory dangers is capped by carnal touch.[67]

A desire for intimacy with a poem such as *Beowulf*, with its
continuing appropriations within the horizon of fascist myth, may
run very particular risks. For Nancy, the intimacy that belongs to
'community' presents not interior secrets but mutual exteriorities,
which Nancy determines as 'sharing': 'sharing comes down to this:
what community reveals to me, in presenting to me my birth and
my death, is my existence outside myself'.[68] This sort of intimacy
is not a special case, but rather, ontologically constitutive: it turns
the question of intimacy from that of normative figures of lovers
and bourgeois privacy to the political. The worldly intimacy of
sharing is thus fundamentally interruptive of the fascist, fusional,
communal will, and, as Nancy puts it, 'community is, in a sense,
resistance itself'.[69]

Here the communal intimacy that Beowulf the warrior and king
might share in the society of dead heroes 'eager for fame' differs
markedly from the intimacy that we sense in the voice found in the
passage of *Beowulf* often referred to as the widow's lament, sung
by a woman referred to only as a 'Geatisc anmeowle' (lone Geatish
woman) (3150b) but occasionally presumed to be Beowulf's widow:[70]

> swylce giomorgyd   Geatisc anmeowle
> Biowulfe brægd   bundenheorde
> sang sorgcearig   saelðe geneahhe
> þæt hio hyre hearmdagas   hearde ondrede
> wælfylla worn   werudes egesan
> hyðo ond hæftnyd. (3150–5a)

> (just so, a lone Geatish woman drew up a grief-song
> for Beowulf; with her hair bound up,
> anxiety-ridden, she sang profusely about the future –
> that she greatly dreaded days of harm for herself,
> a glut of casualty-piles, the terror of groups of soldiers,
> trafficking and slavery).

Despite its anonymity, the texture of the voice registers an ethnically
marked, gendered being, exposed by the fusional forces of her society

to enslavement and probable rape and/or death ('hyðo ond hæftnyd') (3155a). Like the singularity of a texture that resists immediate interpolation into the totality of system or structure, intimacy with *Beowulf*, or other early medieval texts, thus requires neither a dispensing with historicism nor a supposedly exhaustive, positivist, historical narrative into which to fit the text without remainder, as the narrative of *Beowulf* itself assembles a series of remainders drawn from other poems, places, and voices.

Going home together

In order to navigate continuing critical impasses and open new directions for further study, *Dating Beowulf* thus mobilizes a range of readerly modes. While some contributors take up the kind of autobiographical literary criticism termed 'the intimate critique' by Diane P. Freedman, Olivia Frey, and Frances Murphy Zauhar,[71] others examine intimacy itself as a guiding concept for the poem, drawing on Critical Race theory, animal studies, feminist and queer theory, affect theory, and Actor-Network theory, and taking a diversity of approaches ranging between and sometimes blending traditional philological analysis and more experimental modes. All explore the various intimacies imbricated in close reading and translation.[72]

We have organized the chapters into playful clusters, though in the spirit of promiscuity their boundaries remain permeable, and many chapters could find a natural home in two or more of our thematic arrangements, which approach *Beowulf* in public, at home, and outside, before examining the poem's contact list and finally finding *Beowulf* in bed. Throughout, we have edited so that each chapter may stand alone and be read independently, but we have also shaped the volume as a unified whole, with cross-references to highlight points of particularly close contact between chapters. These clusters, in their playfulness, are also meant to suggest the simultaneous functions of the chapters collected here as both readings of *Beowulf* that will shape critical conversations and knowledge about that particular poem, and contributions to a larger theoretical conversation in the humanities – beyond medieval studies – about intimacy as a critical term and its place in fields such as affect studies, queer theory, and histories of the emotions and the senses.

Our opening section, '*Beowulf* in public', approaches the poem as from within a crowd or at a party, exploring *Beowulf*'s crowded places as well as its various publics. First, Benjamin A. Saltz-man's 'Community, joy, and the intimacy of narrative in *Beowulf*' demonstrates that intimacy's dual associations – its adjectival sense 'intimate' and its verbal sense 'to intimate' – merge in *Beowulf*'s scenes of shared storytelling. As Saltzman argues, this narrative intimacy forges not only community but also joy, particularly in Hrothgar's great hall Heorot. Turning to Grendel and Unferð, however, the chapter raises a haunting question: 'Is intimacy always dependent upon some form of exclusion?' A closing meditation centres this question for the field of Old English studies as a whole.

Roberta Frank then takes up the intimacy inherent in ambiguous allusions in '*Beowulf* and the intimacy of large parties', which asks how *Beowulf*'s many allusions to 'things offstage' invite readers to fill in the gaps. She thus seeks to get intimate with the poem's little-mentioned yet all-encompassing back stories, with *Beowulf*'s largest back story of all – the fall of the Scylding dynasty that has led the field to lovingly catalogue correspondences between *Beowulf* and later medieval Scandinavian and Icelandic texts – prompting Frank to wonder why we keep straining '[t]o hear what is not being said in *Beowulf*'. As she contends, the poem's submerged narratives beckon excavation, for '[t]he *Beowulf* poet counts on his hearers' intimacy with Scylding legend to "get it" when he means more than he says'.

Building on this interest in the poem's silences, in '*Beowulf* as Wayland's work: thinking, feeling, making', James Paz unites moving meditations on his own background as a working-class, first-generation scholar with an appeal to get to know *Beowulf*'s unseen makers: its metalworkers, embroiderers, and craftspeople of all kinds. As Paz elucidates, 'craft' provides an illuminating rubric for getting intimate with the poem, even as the poem's craftworkers – both anonymous and legendary, as in the case of Wayland – frequently prove elusive. Whereas printing and teaching *Beowulf* alongside images of Sutton Hoo overemphasizes the poem's aristocratic material culture, Paz centres the poem's skilled labourers instead.

Like many of the chapters that could feel at home in different couplings, Paz's piece transitions beautifully from the public to the personal. Fittingly, then, in the next section, we find *Beowulf* at home, with two chapters on household space both within the poem and as the poem intersects with the present. In '*Beowulf* and babies', Donna Beth Ellard searches for scenes of childbirth and infant caregiving, moving from the poem's opening description of the orphaned Scyld Scefing to think about Beowulf's own early childhood experiences. Ellard deftly reconstructs a backdrop of early medieval abandoned children, which illuminates the intimate ties shared by both Scyld and Beowulf. As she demonstrates, attending to these ties allows us as critics to push back against *Beowulf*'s seeming ambivalence and to queer our own relationships to the poem.

As with the kinds of ecological intimacies articulated above by Michel Serres, the fen next becomes a site of intimacy and domesticity, resistance and colonization for Christopher Abram – and for Grendel. In 'At home in the fens with the Grendelkin', Abram thus lets Grendel take him home to meet his mother. As he argues, the fen is thus a true home, while Heorot 'is something ecologically malevolent', 'encroaching on a landscape to which it can never belong'. In this dazzling ecological reading, Abram reveals Grendel as a figure of indigenous resistance, with Hrothgar trespassing on Grendel's domain rather than the other way around.

Abram's chapter thus transitions smoothly to the next section, on '*Beowulf* outside'. Here, the volume makes a further turn towards the ecocritical and animal, examining the pressure that the non-human places on our use of intimacy as a critical term with two chapters by Mary Kate Hurley and Mo Pareles. In 'Elemental intimacies: agency in the Finnsburg episode', Hurley turns to one of *Beowulf*'s most famous – and most intimate – digressions, focusing on the moment when the bereaved queen Hildeburh places her dead son on her own brother's funeral pyre. Drawing on Actor-Network theory, Hurley illuminates the agency of the pyre's flames, which create their own collectivity out of the failures of the human actors to do the same. The network of forces that Hurley beautifully reconstructs ultimately allows for a new reading of Hildeburh as well, revealing the queen's joy as well as her loss.

In 'What the raven told the eagle: animal language and the return of loss in *Beowulf*', Mo Pareles turns to intimacies to which the human world of the poem is not privy, measuring animal communications as threats to human modes and norms of intimacy. Bringing new perspectives from critical animal studies and eco-theory, Pareles revisits the poem's account of the Grendelkin as well as a notable instance within *Beowulf* of the so-called 'beasts of battle' trope – a traditional reference in Old English poetry to the raven, eagle, and wolf that tend to mark violent death – in which the raven is said to 'speak' with the eagle about a post-battle plunder of carrion. Pareles reads this avian intimacy as a question of translation, arguing that the poem allows 'the birds an ambiguity' which exposes the 'shadows of failure and grief' that haunt the poem's attempts at a 'portrait of a heroic culture that values homosocial intimacy'.

The section entitled '*Beowulf*'s contact list' is a little voyeuristic. Imagine these chapters as taking a peek at the poem's phone – or, perhaps, in an earlier moment, its little black book. To whom or what does *Beowulf* try to get close? What does the poem push away? Drawing on an intersectional constellation of scholars of gender, Critical Race theory, and indigenous studies, Catalin Taranu's 'Men into monsters: troubling race, ethnicity, and masculinity in *Beowulf*' follows a thread of *anxiety* as it runs through and stitches together the emotional ground of intimacies in *Beowulf*'s characters and in the poem's audiences. Taranu's argument suggests that such anxieties in *Beowulf* – and the poem's anticipation of such anxieties in its audiences – register the ways that the Welsh and Danes are racialized in early medieval English literature, and that the emotional grounds of textual intimacies are raced, gendered, and ethnicized in ways that press directly on the dynamics of abusive intimacies, racisms, and misogyny in today's professionalized humanities.

The volume renders this linkage of the affective dynamics of intimacy within *Beowulf* to the lived experience of the present perhaps even more explicitly in Robin Norris's 'Sad men in *Beowulf*', which processes the underlying misogyny of prevailing critical attitudes to displays of male sadness in the poem in relation to the emotional and sexual politics of a field marked by the ongoing operations of toxic masculinities. As Norris reveals, drawing on Richard Delgado's work on empathy, the effect of this inheritance is that, while '*Beowulf* is populated by sad men', we, as critics, 'have overlooked their emotions by focusing on the mourning of Hildeburh and the Geatish *meowle*' – one of whom, as Hurley reveals, may better be recognized for joy.

Like the above anecdote of Blaser's and Spicer's intimacies with and amid translations of *Beowulf*, David Hadbawnik's chapter, 'Differing intimacies: *Beowulf* translations by Seamus Heaney and Thomas Meyer', is a crucial demonstration of the importance of questions about how well the dynamics of textual translation can speak to the dynamics of human intimacy, and how 'extratextual' intimacies determine or allow different modes of translation. Hadbawnik pairs two of the most currently important *Beowulf* translations, which at first glance appear among the most wildly divergent, teasing out a powerful critique of customary critical and reviewing practices that (often tacitly) plot translations of *Beowulf* in terms of a false dilemma of 'fidelity' against 'creativity'.

The final section, '*Beowulf* in bed', attempts to shift and subvert assumptions about normative modes and environments of intimacy's intensities, ends, and climaxes. The chapters are thus not about the sex-acts that are explored only tangentially in the Old English poem, with the brief reference to Hrothgar withdrawing from the hall 'Wealhþeo secan, / cwen to gebeddan' (to seek Wealhtheow, the queen as a bedfellow) (664b–5a). Irina Dumitrescu instead offers us meditations on intimacy by way of considering *Beowulf*'s closest bedfellow – in very literal terms – in literary history, the Old English poem *Andreas*. Dumitrescu shows us that this other long Old English poem, sometimes maligned for what critics have characterized as heavy and clumsy borrowing from *Beowulf*, is '*Beowulf*'s most loving reader'. She thus reveals the entangled and reciprocal logics of intimacies, as *Andreas*'s borrowings of *Beowulf*'s style lead us to changed encounters with both poems.

In contrast to the intimacy of sometimes verbatim textual borrowing, Peter Buchanan's '*Beowulf*, Bryher, and the Blitz: a queer history' considers a literary-historical relationship to *Beowulf* that reveals a queerness at the heart of literary modernism, leveraged through a kitschy plaster bulldog named Beowulf in a novel of the same title by Bryher. Bryher's *Beowulf* does not, Buchanan argues, directly adapt or correspond to the Old English poem of the same name but rather performs a kind of 'historical palimpsest', returning us to an analysis of the women in the Old English *Beowulf* and the gendering of intimacy in the poem and its afterlives. A knot in the bed sheets of literary history and an important contribution to queer studies, intimacy here recalls Dinshaw's queer touch, the mutually transformative relationships of translation, and also that of the parasite that transforms the host: 'Part of the secret of Bryher's queer, feminist embrace of the medieval past lies in her refusal to take it simply as it is.'

Speaking again to the problem of sad men in *Beowulf*, whose intimacies, affects, and failures are governed by normalizing expectations for homosociality, Mary Dockray-Miller's 'Dating Wiglaf: emotional connections to the young hero in *Beowulf*' turns squarely on one of the most intimate relationships represented within the poem's narrative as it 'takes on a charge' and becomes palpable precisely as intimacy in the crosshairs of divergent gender performances. As Dockray-Miller demonstrates, Beowulf maintains the normative modes of affective intimacy in his asymmetrical relationship with his young retainer Wiglaf, who, alone among Beowulf's followers, comes to his aid in the final fight with the dragon. For Wiglaf, however, tacit models of intimacy fail, and his emotional capacities and vulnerabilities outstrip those of Beowulf's 'static, heroic masculinity'.

All told, this volume thus contends that the intimacies in *Beowulf* – textual, narrative, characterological, formal, linguistic, cultural, and so forth – escape the intimate, charged confines of an early medieval poem that will probably remain – perhaps paradoxically – anonymous and undated. In addition to addressing ongoing, crucial questions about the interpretation or function of the poem, then, these chapters ultimately give us a *Beowulf* whose relationship status will always display 'it's complicated', but which nonetheless remains available for intimate touches, rewritings, translations, mournings, trysts, hook-ups, and unworkings.

Notes

1 We thank Hilary Fox for suggesting this playful possibility.
2 Kenneth Sisam, *The structure of Beowulf* (Oxford: Oxford University Press, 1965), p. 1.
3 We would like to credit contributor Christopher Abram with a similar observation in an earlier draft of his chapter.
4 'Klaeber 4' is R. D. Fulk, Robert E. Bjork, and John D. Niles (eds), *Klaeber's Beowulf*, 4th edn (Toronto: University of Toronto Press, 2008).
5 For this particular joke, we are indebted to Robert Hanning, by way of Mary Kate Hurley.
6 Eileen A. Joy and Mary K. Ramsey (eds), *The postmodern Beowulf: a critical casebook* (Morgantown, WV: West Virginia University Press, 2006).
7 Stephanie Trigg and Thomas Prendergast, *Affective medievalism: love, abjection and discontent* (Manchester: Manchester University Press, 2018).
8 In this regard, we are especially indebted to Barbara H. Rosenwein, *Emotional communities in the early Middle Ages* (Ithaca, NY: Cornell University Press, 2006); Leslie Lockett, *Anglo-Saxon psychologies in the vernacular and Latin traditions* (Toronto: University of Toronto Press, 2011); and Alice Jorgensen, Frances McCormack, and Jonathan Wilcox (eds), *Anglo-Saxon emotions: reading the heart in Old English literature* (London: Routledge, 2015).
9 Roy Michael Liuzza, 'On the dating of *Beowulf*', in Peter S. Baker (ed.), *The Beowulf reader* (New York: Routledge, 2000), pp. 281–302, at 283, 295.

10 Carissa M. Harris, *Obscene pedagogies: transgressive talk and sexual education in late medieval Britain* (Ithaca, NY: Cornell University Press, 2018), p. 8.

11 Ibid.

12 *Oxford English Dictionary*, sv. intimate, adj. and n.

13 For a compendium of Old English terms of endearment, see Eleanor Parker, 'The language of Anglo-Saxon love' (13 February 2016), https://aclerkofoxford.blogspot.com/2016/02/the-language-of-anglo-saxon-love.html (accessed 4 June 2019).

14 Gillian R. Overing, '*Beowulf*: a poem in our time', in Clare A. Lees (ed.), *The Cambridge history of early medieval English literature* (Cambridge: Cambridge University Press, 2013), pp. 309–31, at 311–12.

15 Gillian R. Overing, *Language, sign, and gender in Beowulf* (Carbondale, IL: Southern Illinois University Press, 1990), p. 75.

16 James W. Earl, *Thinking about Beowulf* (Stanford, CA: Stanford University Press, 1994), p. 11.

17 Maurice Merleau-Ponty, *The visible and the invisible*, trans. Alphonso Lingis (Evanston, IL: Northwestern University Press, 1968), p. 130.

18 Eve Kosofsky Sedgwick, *Touching feeling: affect, pedagogy, performativity* (Durham, NC: Duke University Press, 2003), p. 17.

19 Ibid., p. 49.

20 Nancy Yousef, *Romantic intimacy* (Palo Alto, CA: Stanford University Press, 2014), p. 2.

21 Sara Ahmed, *The promise of happiness* (Durham, NC: Duke University Press, 2010), p. 47.

22 Ibid.

23 Ibid., p. 31.

24 Louise Fradenberg and Carla Freccero, 'Introduction: Caxton, Foucault, and the pleasures of history', in Louise Fradenberg and Carla Freccero (eds), *Premodern sexualities* (London: Routledge, 1996), p. xix; and see Carolyn Dinshaw, *Getting medieval: sexualities and communities pre- and postmodern* (Durham, NC: Duke University Press, 1999), p. 35.

25 Susan Sontag, *Against interpretation: and other essays* (New York: Farrar, Straus, and Giroux, 1966), p. 14.

26 For an extended philosophical consideration of these questions, see Hans Ulrich Gumbrecht, *Powers of philology: dynamics of textual scholarship* (Urbana-Champaign, IL: University of Illinois Press, 2003).

27 Daniel Boyarin, 'Placing reading: ancient Israel and medieval Europe', in Jonathan Boyarin (ed.), *The ethnography of reading* (Berkeley, CA: University of California Press, 1993), p. 19.

28 Edward Said, *Representations of the intellectual: the 1993 Reith Lectures* (New York: Vintage, 1994), p. 76.

29 Carolyn Dinshaw, *How soon is now? Medieval texts, amateur readers, and the queerness of time* (Durham, NC: Duke University Press, 2012), p. 31.

30 Ibid., pp. 30–1.

31 Ahmed, *Promise of happiness*, p. 53.

32 Toni Morrison, 'Grendel and his mother', in her *The source of self-regard: selected essays, speeches, and meditations* (New York: Alfred A. Knopf, 2019), pp. 255–62, at 255.

33 Robin Blaser, *The astonishment tapes: talks on poetry and autobiography with Robin Blaser and friends*, ed. Miriam Nichols (Tuscaloosa, AL: University of Alabama Press, 2015), p. 62.

34 Jack Spicer Papers, BANC MSS 2004/209, Bancroft Library, University of California, Berkeley, Box 26. Quoted with permission of the Jack Spicer Literary Estate. Major selections of Spicer's translation are published in David Hadbawnik and Jack Spicer (eds), *Jack Spicer's Beowulf*, Lost and Found: The CUNY Poetics Document Initiative, 2.5, Parts 1-2 (2011).

35 Arthur G. Brodeur, *The art of Beowulf* (Berkeley, CA: University of California Press, 1959), p. 77.

36 Ibid., p. 78.

37 Ibid., pp. 84–5. This is Brodeur's translation and emphasis.

38 Brodeur, *The art of Beowulf*, p. 85.

39 Dinshaw, *Getting medieval*, p. 53.

40 Edwin Morgan, *Collected poems* (Manchester: Carcanet, 1990), p. 594.

41 Chris Jones, 'While crowding memories came: Edwin Morgan, Old English and nostalgia', *Scottish literary review*, 4.2 (2012), 123–44. We thank Daniel Davies for bringing this article to our attention.

42 Lauren Berlant, 'Intimacy: a special issue', *Critical inquiry*, 24.2 (1998), 281–8, at 286.

43 Giorgio Agamben, *Idea of prose*, trans. Michael Sullivan and Sam Whitsitt (Albany, NY: State University of New York Press, 1995), p. 61.

44 Benjamin A. Saltzman, 'Secrecy and the hermeneutic potential in *Beowulf*', *PMLA*, 133.1 (2018), 36–55.

45 Jacques Derrida, *On the name*, trans. David Wood et al. (Stanford, CA: Stanford University Press, 1995), p. 30.

46 Berlant, 'Intimacy', 287.

47 For an overview of both events as they intersect with the field of Old English studies, see Rio Fernandes, 'Prominent medieval scholar's blog on "feminist fog" sparks an uproar', *The chronicle of higher education*, online, 22 January 2016, https://www.chronicle.com/article/Prominent-Medieval-Scholar-s/235014 (accessed 4 June 2019); and Josephine Livingstone, 'Racism, medievalism, and the white supremacists of Charlottesville', *The new republic*, online, 15 August 2017, https://newrepublic.com/article/144320/racism-medievalism-white-supremacists-charlottesville (accessed 4 June 2019).

48 For brief reflections, see Mary Dockray-Miller, 'Old English has a serious image problem', *JSTOR Daily*, 3 May 2017, https://daily.jstor.org/old-english-serious-image-problem (accessed 4 June 2019); Peter Baker,

'Anglo-Saxon studies after Charlottesville: reflections of a University of Virginia professor', *Medievalists of Color public discourse*, 25 May 2018, https://medievalistsofcolor.com/2018/05/ (accessed 4 June 2019); and Mary Rambaran-Olm, 'Anglo-Saxon studies, academia and white supremacy', *Medium*, 27 June 2018, https://medium.com/@mrambaranolm/anglo-saxon-studies-academia-and-white-supremacy-17c87b360bf3 (accessed 4 June 2019). Donna Beth Ellard explores these issues at greater length in her *Anglo-Saxon(ist) pasts, postSaxon futures* (Goleta, CA: punctum books, 2019).

49 Dinshaw, *Getting medieval*, p. 35.
50 Ibid., p. 39.
51 Ahmed, *Promise of happiness*, p. 186.
52 Andrew Prescott, '"Their present miserable state of cremation": the restoration of the Cotton Library', in C. J. Wright (ed.), *Sir Robert Cotton as collector: essays on an early Stuart courtier and his legacy* (London: British Library Publications, 1997), pp. 391–454. Cf. Edward Miller, *That noble cabinet: a history of the British Museum* (London: Deutsch, 1973), pp. 34–5; and Simon Keynes, 'The reconstruction of a burnt Cottonian manuscript: the case of Cotton MS. Otho A. I', *British Library journal*, xxii (1996), 113–14.
53 Michel Serres, *The parasite*, trans. Lawrence R. Schehr (Minneapolis, MN: University of Minnesota Press, 2007), p. 196.
54 Jean-Luc Nancy, *The inoperative community*, trans. Peter Conner et al. (Minneapolis, MN: University of Minnesota Press, 1991), p. 35.
55 Overing, '*Beowulf:* a poem in our time', p. 317.
56 Ibid., p. 330.
57 Katherine O'Brien O'Keeffe, 'Hands and eyes, sight and touch: appraising the senses in Anglo-Saxon England', *ASE*, 45 (2016), 105–40, at 105–6.
58 E.g. Stephanie J. Trigg and Stephanie Downes (eds), 'Facing up to the history of the emotions', special issue, *postmedieval*, 8.1 (2017); Lara Farina (ed.), 'The intimate senses: taste, touch, and smell', special issue, *postmedieval*, 3.4 (2012); Richard C. Newhauser (ed.), *A cultural history of the senses in the Middle Ages* (London: Bloomsbury, 2016). We are grateful to Arthur Russell for conversations on this topic.
59 Dinshaw, *Getting medieval*, p. 142.
60 Jose Esteban Muñoz, *Cruising utopia: the then and there of queer futurity* (New York: New York University Press, 2009), pp. 33–48.
61 Dinshaw, *Getting medieval*, p. 165.
62 Ibid., p. 171.
63 Sedgwick, *Touching feeling*, p. 13.
64 Ibid.
65 Ibid., p. 14.
66 Nancy, *The inoperative community*, p. 39.
67 O'Brien O'Keeffe, 'Hands and eyes, sight and touch', 128.
68 Nancy, *The inoperative community*, p. 26.

69 Ibid., p. 35.

70 This identification was first suggested by Moritz Heyne in his nineteenth-century translation, *Beowulf: Angelsächsisches heldengedicht* (Paderborn, 1863).

71 Diane P. Freedman, Olivia Frey, and Frances Murphy Zauhar (eds), *The intimate critique: autobiographical literary criticism* (Durham, NC: Duke University Press, 1993).

72 We are grateful to one of our anonymous readers for this observation.

Part I
Beowulf in public

2

Community, joy, and the intimacy of narrative in *Beowulf*

Benjamin A. Saltzman

1a. to make internal
1b. to make (person) intimate with (another)
2. to make known, intimate, explain, or communicate
    Dictionary of Medieval Latin from British Sources, s.v. *intimare*[1]

All great storytellers have in common the freedom with which they move up and down the rungs of their experiences as on a ladder. A ladder extending downward to the interior of the earth and disappearing into the clouds is the image for a collective experience to which even the deepest shock of every individual experience, death, constitutes no impediment or barrier.

Walter Benjamin[2]

Intimacy is etymologically bound to the medieval Latin word *intimare*, which denotes primarily a movement inwards, but also a mode of verbal communication, of making known, of announcing, of explanation. Today, these two senses are divided between, for instance, the adjective ('intimate') and the verb ('to intimate'), and when juxtaposed they seem to represent two radically antithetical phenomena. The one tends to imply internalized private reticence; the other, externalized public expression. But in *Beowulf*, these two senses of intimacy powerfully converge at moments when stories are shared and recited: moments in which knowledge is communicated through narrative and community is inwardly synthesized. It is in these moments of convergence between narrative and communal intimacy that a profound experience of joy tends to materialize in the poem.

The first such communal experience of joy is short-lived, destroyed almost as quickly as it is created. Set in motion by the construction of Heorot, the hall Grendel would eventually attack, that 'healærna mæst' (greatest of hall buildings) (78a), a space for community quickly opens up within its walls: 'ond þær *on innan* eall gedælan / geongum ond ealdum swylc him God sealde' (and there within, he shared everything with young and old, that which God had given) (71–2).[3] Within Heorot, the community is supplied and fortified by the all-encompassing gifts of God, which are shared internally ('on innan') with all those in the hall. Let us consider this communal experience to be one important form of intimacy: we might call it *communal intimacy*. Reflecting the first etymological sense described above, such communal intimacy constitutes internal coherence. Yet while such coherence seems to exist in spite of differences ('geongum ond ealdum' might imply one form of diversity, though it passes over, say, status and gender), it is often created in opposition to external forces, as we will see in a moment. This and subsequent images of community in *Beowulf* (as well as in many other Old English poems) reflect an important feature of the poem's hall culture, which, as Hugh Magennis has shown with great nuance, comes to epitomize literary conceptions of community especially as it is formed around gift giving and events of feasting and drinking.[4] Yet in Nicole Guenther Discenza's analysis, these desirable features of the hall – safety, joy, and art – are often in conflict with the hall's vulnerability to 'threats from outsiders, threats from within, and threats from time'.[5]

Emerging alongside the communal intimacy of the hall, *narrative intimacy* reflects the second etymological sense described above, as it entails the creation and sharing of knowledge and stories.[6] The naming of Heorot is a perfect example: 'scop him Heort naman / se þe his wordes geweald wide hæfde' (he assigned it the name 'Heorot', he who wields widely the power of his speech) (78b–79). The process of naming is a process of creation that takes place alongside the construction of the hall itself. The first word of this clause and its main verb ('scop', preterit of *scyppan*, here with the sense of 'to assign', but ordinarily with the sense of 'to create') evokes simultaneously the creative power of God (*Scyppend*) and of the poet (*scop*). Even as these lines emphasize the power of words, then, they remain ambiguous about who actually assigns the name to the hall: it could certainly be Hrothgar (as the context seems to suggest and scholars tend to infer), but it could also be scop or even God, given the emphasis on the power of words and the action suggested by the verb *scyppan*. Over the course of the poem, different characters – Heorot's scop, Hrothgar, Unferth, and even Beowulf himself – take up the creative power of words by narrating various stories, stories that may feel like digressions, but in fact constitute (as scholars now tend to believe) an integral part of the poem.[7] These instances of storytelling tend to coincide with moments of communal joy.

The naming of the hall thus gives way to a joyful scene, filtered through the external perspective of Grendel, the poem's first monster, as he listens from outside to the delightful sound loudly emanating from inside Heorot ('dream gehyrde / hludne in healle') (88b–89a). That sound of joy is a combination of music and storytelling: 'Þær wæs hearpan sweg, / swutol sang scopes. Sægde se þe cuþe / frumsceaft fira feorran reccan, / cwæð þæt se ælmihtiga eorðan worhte' (There was the sound of the harp, the clear song of the scop. He spoke, he who knew how to narrate the creation of humankind from long ago, said that the almighty created the world) (89b–92). To celebrate the construction of this communal space, the scop (perhaps the same one who gives Heorot its name) fittingly recites the story of the creation of the world and humanity, appearing to follow the first book of Genesis. This recitation mirrors the communal intimacy of the hall through a process of narrative intimation, in which the sharing of knowledge ('se þe cuþe ... reccan')[8] creates communal familiarity around the story itself.[9] The creative power of words thus moves from the naming of the hall ('scop him Heort naman') (78b) to the scop's narrative of creation ('swutol sang scopes') (90a) to God's creation of life itself ('life ac gesceop') (97b). All three points of narrative intimation reinforce communal intimacy.

This celebratory scene of poetic recitation concludes with the reiterated joy experienced by the community within the hall, which is quickly interrupted by Grendel's re-emergence in the poem: 'Swa ða drihtguman dreamum lifdon / eadiglice, oð ðæt an ongan / fyrene fremman feond on helle' (So these retainers lived in joy, blessedly, until one began to commit his crimes, a fiend from hell) (99–101). The reader might have even temporarily forgotten that the song of the scop and Heorot's joyous sounds have been heard by Grendel all along ('dream gehyrde') (88b). Indeed, the *Beowulf* poet sets those joys in stark relief against Grendel's marginalized perspective and dejected state of exile, even as we might imagine Grendel sharing with his mother and the other monstrous kin of Cain a different kind of intimacy unregistered by the poet. The communal and narrative intimacy within the hall is thus formed in relation to Grendel's exile, while his story is introduced into the hall through the narrative trajectory of the scop's tale of creation. Although left unstated, that tale implicitly anticipates the story of Cain and Abel, who as the children of Adam and Eve appear in Genesis shortly after the creation.

So as one spectre of Cain is anticipated by the scop's narrative, another bursts in through the door:

> siþðan him scyppen   forscrifen hæfde
> in Caines cynne –   þone cwealm gewræc
> ece drihten,   þæs þe he Abel slog;
> ne gefeah he þære fæhðe,   ac he hine feor forwræc,
> metod for þy mane   mancynne fram. (106–10)

> (since the Creator had condemned him among the kin of Cain – the eternal Lord avenged that murder, in which he slew Abel; he took no joy in that feud, but for that crime the Maker expelled him far from mankind.)

Grendel's identity as an outsider, his alienated perspective, and his disruptive intrusion into the joyful hall are explained as a consequence of Cain's fratricide, which is already subtly intimated through the scop's account of Genesis; or, if not through the scop's account, then through the *Beowulf* poet's implicit continuation of that account in the description of Grendel's lineage.[10] One way, therefore, to think about narrative intimacy as it operates here is that it creates or reinforces a community around a shared body of knowledge, but it also has the potential to disrupt that community as it introduces knowledge from the outside.

If taken further, this point raises an important question: *Is intimacy always dependent upon some form of exclusion?* Intimacy's etymological opposition to the external certainly suggests so. Moreover, when intimacy informs the nature of community, as community is often constructed and conceived around an enclosing or unifying identity within which intimacy becomes the operative feature, community and its relation to exteriority become more complicated. The dissymmetry of the Other's perspective in relation to a community's homogeneity, for example, has provoked Maurice Blanchot to examine 'whether the community … does not in the end always posit the *absence* of community'.[11] For readers of *Beowulf*, where Grendel's identity and actions are posited in relation to the community at Heorot, or for readers of, say, *The Wanderer*, which imagines community from the perspective of one who has lost it, Blanchot's logic might be especially compelling.

But community also perhaps relies on an even more fundamental externality. 'What is common', as Jean-Luc Nancy puts it, 'is the

sharing of finitude', the fact that as humans we all will face death
at some point; for Nancy, this finitude functions in the context of
community as a 'being-outside, an "outside" prior to all "inside"'.[12]
One way to approach the question, then, is through this negative
account, in which 'community is made or is formed by the retreat
or by the subtraction' of the subject.[13] In other words, community
always requires the subject to experience its own externalized
existence and singular finitude. Roberto Esposito offers a more
radical approach: community is not a form of communal ownership
or possession of some central trait, object, or similarity, not 'a
corporation in which the individuals are founded in a larger individual', but rather a voiding of subjectivity itself, as the subjects
enter into a 'common non-belonging', a giving over of the subject
to the communal: 'In the community, subjects do not find a principle
of identification nor an aseptic enclosure within which they can
establish transparent communication … They don't find anything
else except that void, that distance, that extraneousness that constitutes them as being missing from themselves.'[14] In these formulations of community, we encounter fundamental exclusion even at
the level of the individual subject.

As the formation of community can rely on mechanisms of
exteriority and, at times, exclusion, I'm reminded of work by Lauren
Berlant, who has shown how narratives of intimacy have a way of
privileging one form of life at the expense of numerous others:

> Those who don't or can't find their way in that story – the queers, the
> single, the something else – can become so easily unimaginable, even
> often to themselves. Yet it is hard not to see lying about everywhere
> the detritus and the amputations that come from attempts to fit into
> the fold … To rethink intimacy is to appraise how we have been and
> how we live and how we might imagine lives that make more sense
> than the ones so many are living.[15]

Community and narratives of intimacy can powerfully shape life,
indeed the individual lives and livability of those who experience
intimacy from within and those who experience it as abjection
from without. In *Beowulf*, then, the work of the scop seems to
reinforce communal bonds in opposition to the world outside;
and yet the scop also provides a way around that binary, as the
stories he tells can be used to imagine the perspective of others
and incorporate them into the otherwise closed communal space.
Narrative intimacy, in other words, always also has the potential to
traverse the boundaries established by those exclusive and cohesive

forces that typically animate the poem's vision of communal intimacy.

These boundaries are tested not only by Grendel's violent intrusions, but also with the arrival of Beowulf.[16] At first, Beowulf is received as a foreigner on the Danish sea-cliffs: though the coast-warden acknowledges that no troop has ever come more openly ('cuðlicor') (244a) and that he has never seen a greater warrior on earth ('Næfre ic maran geseah / eorla ofer eorþan') (247b–248a), the warden nevertheless demands to know their lineage ('frumcyn witan') (252a) in order to ensure they are not spies ('leassceaweras') (253a). Satisfied with Beowulf's response, the coast-warden leads the Geatish troop to Heorot, where Wulfgar welcomes them and announces their arrival to Hrothgar, who in turn commands that they be invited to see the assembly of kinsmen gathered together in the hall ('seon sibbegedriht samod ætgædere') (387). Speaking from within the hall, Wulfgar then summons Beowulf inside ('word inne abead') (390b). These scenes repeatedly emphasize the coherent gathering and unity (we might say, 'intimacy') of the Danes, reinforced at each of the several stages in which Beowulf and his troop are granted, with some scepticism, entrance into this intimate community and finally into Heorot itself.[17] After Beowulf enters and exchanges words with Hrothgar about Grendel's terror (the external threat), he and his troop are invited to sit on a bench inside the hall. These welcoming and inclusive gestures through which the Geats are embraced by the community at Heorot ('geador ætsomne') (491b) culminate in the appearance once again of a scop: 'Scop hwilum sang / hador on Heorote' (the clear-voiced scop sang for a while) (496b–497a). And as with the scop's song of creation in celebrating the construction of Heorot, once again communal joy ensues: 'Þær wæs hæleða dream, / duguð unlytel Dena ond Wedera' (There was the joy of heroes, a great gathering of Danes and Geats) (497b–498). *Scop* and *dream* are very much allied, as the two groups of retainers come together through this joyful experience of not only drink and feast, but also song, music, and the recitation of stories.

But this communal joy and the song of the scop are once again promptly disrupted, as Unferth unbinds his battle-rune ('onband beadurune') (501a) and launches an invective at Beowulf, calling into question his strength and courage by recounting a failed swimming contest from his youth. The figure of Unferth has vexed scholars almost as much as he himself seems vexed by Beowulf's bravery. James L. Rosier's 1962 article on the subject bolstered the predominantly negative readings of Unferth by demonstrating that the character's epithet ('Unferþ þyle') (1165b) did not merely denote a general kind of spokesman, orator, or official entertainer, but also carried a pejorative sense evocative of a more wicked role.[18] This linguistic argument has been disputed, but the underlying view of Unferth as a troubling character has been hard to shake, even in arguments that defend his vital function both in Heorot and in the narrative of the poem.[19] As Rosier puts it, though, this scene enacts a 'dramatic oscillation of joy and strife' between, for instance, the scop's joyful song and Unferth's treacherous incursion – an internal oscillation similar to that introduced by Grendel (an 'external threat'), for 'both are associated with Cain, the one by the deed of fratricide, the other in lineage; both are consigned to hell; and both disrupt the joy of the hall, Unferth by his battle-rune, and Grendel by physical assault'.[20] This particular reading of Unferth seems right, even in light of the completely divergent view, taken by Norman E. Eliason a year later, that Unferth (the *þyle*) might in fact be the very same scop who elsewhere sings such clear songs of joy.[21] This possibility is intriguing, for it suggests that the dramatic oscillation between joy and strife is actually a congruous feature of the Danish community itself, as potentially a single character utilizes narrative both to delight and to antagonize, both to cement community and to alienate an outsider.

Taken together, the two views advanced by Rosier and Eliason – in which Unferth's invective sharply turns joy into strife *and* in which this shift exemplifies a kind of communal intimacy at Heorot through storytelling – appeal to Edward B. Irving's reading of Unferth as a 'spokesman for the community of Danes', as he speaks 'for their anger, their pride, their frustrations, their xenophobia, and their honestly grateful generosity of spirit'.[22] Irving's observation is powerful not merely for its crisp realization of Unferth's purpose, but also for its recognition of the way in which community can be formed around 'negative and hidden dimensions', even dimensions that conflict with one another, even dimensions that rely on xenophobia and alienation. The dialectic of narrative and its digressive interruptions – whether recited by *scop* or *þyle* – has the unique power to move between these dimensions of intimacy; to alienate, yet to express the deep, sometimes divergent sentiments and epistemologies of a community. Irving's reading would make Unferth not so much an expression of treachery (an internal threat to the community) as, on the contrary, an assertion of that very community.

What is at stake in the Unferth episode is not only the assertion of a Danish community, but also the positioning of Beowulf within that community at a time when it is being repeatedly threatened from the outside by that unknown monster Grendel ('deogol dædhata') (275a).[23] The process of narrative recitation in the Unferth episode, even if it is clearly aggressive, is necessarily an epistemological process of vetting the figure of Beowulf – discerning him from known quantities – as he sits welcomed with wine in the midst of the hall. Unferth's sentiment is clearly aggressive, yet it is crucial that this sentiment should be manifested in the form of narrative (by telling the story of a swimming contest) as opposed to an unmediated assault (whether verbal or physical). Narrative is critical here because it allows for the possibility of inclusion by intimating Beowulf into the community, just as Grendel – perhaps not with the best outcome – is subtly intimated via Cain into the scop's earlier narrative of creation.

The effect of narrative intimacy can be seen, for example, in the way Unferth does not outright attack Beowulf by condemning his pride or disputing his courage, but begins instead with a question: 'Eart þu se Beowulf, se þe … ?' (Are you the Beowulf, who … ?) (506a). Though followed by accusations of pride ('wlence') (508a) and foolish boasting ('dolgilpe') (509a), Unferth's opening question allows Beowulf any number of different responses. He could have easily dismissed the attack ('you're drunk, Unferth, and you've clearly got the wrong guy!'), but instead Beowulf opts to present a counter-narrative: 'soð ic talige' (I shall tell the truth) (532b). Beowulf's competing account of the swimming match and his promise to defeat Grendel allows him to position himself in opposition to a more threatening outsider and thereby intimate himself into the community. That process of intimation was opened up by Unferth's narrativistic invective, giving Beowulf the opportunity to tell a narrative that not only interjects his experience into the community, but also realigns the community in opposition to the more pressing danger posed by Grendel.

This process of narrative intimation is immediately followed by further scenes of joy: 'Ðær wæs hæleþa hleahtor, hlyn swynsode, / word wæron wynsume' (There was laughter of men, making pleasant sound, the words were joyous) (611–12b). The joy in Heorot at this moment surely reflects the hopeful anticipation of Grendel's impending defeat, but it is also attached, once again, to the power of words. Accordingly, the Unferth episode is followed by Wealhðeow's gracious passing of the cup, which is followed by Beowulf's reiterated pledge of courage, at which point the scene returns, as before, to one of joyful intimacy formed around spoken words: 'Þa wæs eft swa ær *inne* on healle / þryðword sprecen, ðeod on sælum, / sigefolca sweg' (Then, afterwards as before, noble words were spoken inside that hall, the people joyful, the sounds of a victorious people) (642–4a). Restored is the joy originally celebrated in Heorot, a joy simultaneously tied both to the people inside the hall ('inne on healle') and the sounds emanating from it – a joy tied to powerful, strong, noble words ('þryðword'), which though unspecified seem to evoke the words of the scop who spoke of creation and who may have assigned Heorot its name.

To be sure, these moments of joy often accompany the anticipation or celebration of victory. As the troop returns from the mere (where Grendel has retreated, wounded and presumed dead), Beowulf's initial triumph is celebrated along a joyful journey ('gomenwaþe') (854b) with the recitation of tales:

> Hwilum cyninges þegn,
> guma gilphlæden,   gidda gemyndig,
> se ðe eal fela   ealdgesegena
> worn gemunde,   word oþer fand
> soðe gebunden;   secg eft ongan
> sið Beowulfes   snyttrum styrian
> ond on sped wrecan   spel gerade,
> wordum wrixlan. (867b–874a)

(Meanwhile, the king's thegn, filled with tales of men, mindful of songs, he who remembered so many of the ancient legends, composed different words truly bound; the man began to recite again the exploits of Beowulf, to stir up with wisdom and to rouse with skill an apt story, to weave with words.)

Even before returning to Heorot, Beowulf's victory is already being woven into the very narrative fabric that defines the communal intimacy of the Danes.[24] The binding and weaving of words – both in the poetic process described by these lines and the stylistic weaving of sounds in the lines themselves, as Megan Cavell has shown – reflects the interlacing that is such a fundamental feature of much Old English poetic composition.[25] The alliterative envelope pattern in lines 870–4 ($w - s - s - s - w$),[26] for example, produces a kind of poetic or sonic intimacy in which words and sounds internally envelop themselves, indeed are truly bound, if that is what 'soðe gebunden' is supposed to mean. Of course, envelope patterns and alliteration are common features of Old English poetry, though not always consistently applied in the same way, nor always sonically intimate as here, nor always the product of communally determined poetic principles.[27] But here, these formal techniques suggest the inclusion of Beowulf in the community of Danes as his name falls in the very centre of this alliterative envelope. This poetic process is then replicated in the narrative itself, as Beowulf's defeat of Grendel in the present is woven into the legendary narrative of Sigemund from the past, and likewise Sigemund's defeat of the dragon weaves in the anticipation of Beowulf's own dragon fight at the end of the poem.[28]

At moments like these, the repeated appearance of storytellers gives the poem a kind of rhythm that has often been noted. Scholars still refer to these stories as digressions, a slightly pejorative designation that implies separation, even though most readers follow Adrien Bonjour in accepting them as an integral feature of the poem's aesthetic.[29] In these digressions, the scop also shapes the idea of the communal by weaving the community's experiences into a longer narrative history. We see this process not only in the juxtaposition of Beowulf and Sigemund, but also in the celebration at Heorot following Grendel's defeat, a victory once again culminating in internal cohesion: 'Heorot *innan* wæs / freondum afylled' (inside, Heorot was filled with friends) (1017b–1018a).[30] And this internal cohesion is reinforced both through gift giving and, once again, through the recital of stories, this time the Finn episode:[31]

Þær wæs sang ond sweg   samod ætgædere
fore Healfdenes   hildewisan,
gomenwudu greted,   gid oft wrecen,
ðonne healgamen   Hroþgares scop
æfter medobence   mænan scolde
be Finnes eaferan. (1063–8a)

(There was song and music assembled together in the presence of Healfdene's battle-leader, the joyous-wood was played, tales often narrated, when Hrothgar's scop would perform hall-joy among the mead-benches, tell about the sons of Finn.)[32]

Elsewhere in the poem, the formulaic phrase 'samod ætgædere' tends to refer to an assembly of men (387b, 729b) or their war-gear (329b), but here the formula seems to refer either to the mingling of song and music or to a gathering of listeners enjoying those sounds of the harp. In other words, the phrase poetically joins together song and community. As we have seen, where song and community meet there is often joy, and here the joyful sound of the harp is conveyed in a kenning, '*gomen*wudu',[33] that speaks not only to the instrument itself, but also to the joyful environment in which it is found: the amusement and joy of the hall itself ('heal*gamen*'). Both the harp ('gomenwudu') and the recitation ('healgamen') produce and represent a communal joy that takes place around acts of storytelling, song, and poetry. Just as joyful sounds of community introduce the story of Finn, its end is likewise met with more communal sounds of joy: 'Leoð wæs asungen, / gleomannes gyd. Gamen eft astah, / beorhtode bencsweg; byrelas sealdon / win of wunderfatum' (The song was sung, the entertainer's tale, joyous sounds arose again, the sounds from the bench glittered, the cup-bearers gave wine from wondrous vessels) (1159b–1162a). We can see how these expressions of communal joy – wine and song, for instance – intersect with one another as they surround the act of storytelling itself; narrative intimacy is enclosed by communal intimacy.

When these events are retold by Beowulf upon his return home to Hygelac, they again demonstrate this integral connection between communal joy and storytelling, as that communal experience now becomes a new source of narrative intimacy. Beowulf's words, in other words, reiterate the poet's earlier emphasis on the affiliation between communal intimacy and narrative intimacy:

> ond we to symble   geseten hæfdon.
> *Þær wæs gidd ond gleo*;   gomela Scilding,
> felafricgende,   feorran rehte;
> *hwilum* hildedeor   hearpan wynne,
> gomenwudu *grette*,   *hwilum* gyd awræc
> soð ond sarlic,   *hwilum* syllic spell
> rehte æfter rihte   rumheort cyning;
> *hwilum* eft ongan,   *eldo gebunden*,
> gomel guðwiga   gioguðe cwiðan,
> hildestrengo;   hreðer inne weoll,
> þonne he wintrum frod   worn gemunde.
> Swa we þær *inne*   andlangne dæg
> niode naman,   oð ðæt niht becwom
> oðer to yldum. (2104–17a, italics added for emphasis)

(And we gathered at the feast. There was song and joy; the aged Scylding, well-informed, told of distant times; at times, the brave warrior played the harp with delight, touched the joyous-wood; at times, he narrated a tale, both true and sad; at times, the generous-hearted king recited a wondrous story; at times, that aged warrior, bound by old-age, told of his youth again, his battle strength; his heart welled up within him, as he, wise in winters, remembered so much. So, there inside we took our ease all day long, until another night came upon men.)

In addition to providing a more detailed account of the storytelling at Heorot following Grendel's defeat, Beowulf weaves in language from the poet's earlier description of these events. Some words and phrases are almost identical: 'worn gemunde' is used twice (870a and 2114b), and 'gomenwudu grette' (2108a) echoes 'gomenwudu greted' (1065a). Others are in parallel: 'Þær wæs gidd ond gleo' (2105a) mirrors 'Þær wæs sang ond sweg' (1063a). A few are translated into a different context: 'eldo gebunden' describes Hrothgar's age (2111b), while 'soðe gebunden' describes the binding of truth (871a). And still others correspond on a formal level: the repetition of 'hwilum' (2107a, 2108b, 2109b, 2111a) recalls a similar pattern introducing the story of Sigemund (864a, 867b, 916a). The stuff of metapoetic description, in other words, gets incorporated into Beowulf's narrative and thus the narrative of the poem itself.

This process mirrors the way in which the storyteller, in this case Hrothgar, reaches inside his own memories to produce a story that in turn incorporates the communal intimacy of the audience. The internalized welling of Hrothgar's heart ('hreðer inne weoll') (2113b), which tumultuously represents almost an eternity ('wintrum frod'), transpires into the 'we' that inhabits the interior of the hall ('we þær inne') for a finite duration of time ('andlangne dæg') that must nevertheless come to an end as night returns ('niht becwom').

Walter Benjamin was on to something. His essay lamenting the disappearance of the storyteller – who he sees as a medieval figure sacrificed to modernity's fondness for and capitalism's commodification of the novel – speaks to the way in which storytelling integrates the listener into the experience of the teller. It is, for Benjamin, an essentially communal exercise: 'The storyteller takes what he tells from experience – his own or that reported by others. And he in turn makes it the experience of those who are listening to his tale.'[34] The novelist, by contrast, 'has isolated himself' and so too has his reader, 'more so than any other reader', for in his solitude, 'the reader of a novel seizes upon his material more jealously than anyone else. He is ready to make it completely his own, to devour it, as it were.'[35] While Benjamin seems perhaps nostalgic for the vague traditions of ancient storytellers, by contrasting the alienation that accompanies the commodified novel with what existed before, with a historical phenomenon that seems also to have characterized the kind of experience that takes place around the scop in *Beowulf*, he holds up the scop as a measure of what the novel, always-already commodified, cannot do.[36] It is an event in which a storyteller such as Hrothgar or Unferth or Beowulf takes up some experience – his own or that garnered from others – and turns it into a communal experience of intimacy through narrative.[37]

For Benjamin, the storyteller thus has a pre-commodity function that offers us a post-commodity, communist horizon. This de-commodified narrative experience is Benjamin's ladder, on which the storyteller freely ascends 'into the clouds' and descends 'to the interior of the earth'.[38] It is a perplexing image, and it is not especially clear how it is meant to represent what Benjamin deems 'a collective experience'. But the storyteller's movements on the ladder somehow allow him the liberty of descending into the depths of his own memory and rendering it collective, inviting the listener to participate by in turn attempting to remember the story and integrate it into his own experience. In this way, storytelling resists the effects of death, the finitude of human life, the basis of community.[39] As the 'deepest shock of every individual experience', death 'constitutes no impediment or barrier' to the storyteller's free movement on the ladder of narrative; where for modernity 'the thought of death has declined in omnipresence and vividness', it is for Benjamin 'the sanction of everything that the storyteller can tell. He has borrowed his authority from death.'[40] This authority is vested in him not only because the stories he tells often grapple with the reality of death, but also because the process of storytelling invites listeners to remember, perpetuate, and pass along their own experience of the story, which in turn becomes a part of their own experience *qua* experience and thus the source for future expressions of what we are calling narrative intimacy.

Beowulf's return to Hygelac epitomizes this process, for not only does Beowulf integrate the celebratory storytelling of Heorot (and the language used to describe it) into his own narrative experience of events, but in doing so he also repeatedly emphasizes Hrothgar's old age ('gomela Scilding', 'eldo gebunden', 'gomel guðwiga') as he shares stories drawn from his youthful memories, bringing those stories through the temporality of the present into the immortal atemporality of narrative intimacy and the communal experience that forms around it. The stories endure, moreover, even when night descends and brings death to individuals in the hall (in this case, one particular individual, Æschere, has died at the hands of Grendel's mother); the stories endure, in other words, because both Beowulf and the *Beowulf* poet remember and retell them.

In retrospect, despite the communal joy that all of these moments of intimacy represent, they are frequently interrupted by death and killing. But although these interruptions disrupt the community, they do not constitute, as Benjamin puts it, an 'impediment or barrier' to the narrative intimacy produced by the poem's storytellers. The arrival of Grendel's mother under cover of darkness while the community sleeps and her snatching of Æschere, for instance, interrupts the earlier joyful harp and song, but the particular instance of death only gets integrated back into the narrative that Beowulf tells to Hygelac and that the *Beowulf* poet tells to his readers. This process of narrative intimation is precisely how the communal experience is formed in the face of human finitude and the 'deepest shock of every individual experience'.[41]

That is not to say that those shocks do not matter, but rather that narrative intimacy has a way of incorporating them. In fact, such rhythmic shocks of death punctuate the poem's vision of communal intimacy in a way that seems to counterbalance the joy that such intimacy celebrates in the daylight only to be destroyed as soon as the sun sets. By the end of the poem, as Beowulf prepares for his final fight against the dragon and the setting of his own life ('wælfus' [ready to be slain] (2420a)), he reflects on the narrative of his own lineage, beginning with his adoption by Hrethel as a child. The story quickly shifts to explain Hrethel's grief over the accidental death of his eldest son by the tip of his brother's arrow, imagined from the perspective of a criminal's father:

> Swa bið geomorlic   gomelum ceorle
> to gebidanne,   þæt his byre ride
> giong on galgan.   Þonne he gyd wrece,
> sarigne sang,   þonne his sunu hangað
> hrefne to hroðre,   ond he him helpe ne mæg,
> eald ond infrod   ænige gefremman. (2444–9)

> (So it is mournful for an old man to see his own son swing, young on the gallows. He shall recount a tale, a sorrowful song, when his son hangs – a comfort to ravens – and, though old and wise, he cannot provide him any help.)

Up to this point, the poem has repeatedly stressed the connection between joy and songs. But sometimes, songs and stories are unavoidably sad. By Beowulf's account, for instance, Hrothgar 'gyd awræc / soð ond sarlic' (narrated a tale, both true and sad) (2108b–2109a). Now, as Beowulf recounts how the aged Hrethel helplessly confronted his young son's execution, he acknowledges that Hrethel has no choice but to commemorate it in song with a sorrowful tale. There is no joy to be had in this scene of death, other than by the raven

– a comparison that sets the scene off from the more common images of joyful storytelling. This lack of joy is only compounded by the consequent desolation of the son's hall and the community it housed:

> Gesyhð sorhcearig   on his suna bure
> winsele westne,   windge reste
> reotge berofene;   ridend swefað,
> hæleð in hoðman;   nis þær hearpan sweg,
> gomen in geardum,   swylce ðær iu wæron. (2455–9)

(He looks sorrowfully on his son's dwelling, the wine-hall empty, the windswept home deprived of joy – the riders sleep, heroes in darkness; there is no sound of the harp, joy in the court, as there was before.)

What makes this son's death all the more devastating is the obliteration of the very symbols of communal joy: the heroes now sleeping in darkness, the sound of the harp now divorced from its usual joy, the word 'gomen' (2459a) even extracted from the kenning *gomenwudu*, and set aside in a separate line and in the past ('swylce ðær iu wæron') (2459b).

In a union typically symbolized by the hall, joy and community clearly go hand in hand. To be disconnected from such a hall, as poems such as *The Wanderer* so enthrallingly convey, is thus to experience a profoundly mournful state of isolation. But we are also frequently reminded that the physical walls of a hall can fall into ruin and its community can fall away, both easily interrupted by natural forces and death.[42] As Patricia Dailey has shown, however, poetry has a way of preserving a remnant of the subject that extends beyond the gravitational pull of the past and the erosion of the physical world in the present.[43] Songs and stories might seem inherently transient, for they are far less tangible than a wooden hall or stone buildings or a hoard of treasure, yet they have an eerily joyful way of resisting death – that shock of the individual – in their potential to form a more durable community of listeners and readers.

Indeed, Old English poets seem to have recognized this power of narrative, as the poem *Maxims I* makes quite evident: 'Longað þonne þy læs þe him con leoþa worn, / oþþe mid hondum con hearpan gretan; / hafaþ him his gliwes giefe, þe him god sealde'[44] (He longs less, who knows many tales or knows how to greet the harp with his hands; he has within himself the gift of music/joy, which God gave him). The knowledge of poems, songs, narratives, stories – however we choose to translate *leoþ* – somehow gives the individual a kind of joy that only elsewhere seems to be found either in heaven (that's for another time) or in the communal celebrations of the hall (as we have seen here). But in this aphorism, there is no hall; the tales and the harp are all that keep the individual from longing and sorrow, as the *gliw* (glee, joy, merriment, but also music) is enjoyed as a gift from God.[45] Then again, the hall is not entirely absent either. Often, the aphorisms in *Maxims I* follow one another in tenuous relation, moving from the turbulence of the ocean, for instance, to the importance of dividing up an inheritance (lines 76–9). But sometimes this apparent randomness is interrupted by a series of aphorisms that flow logically from one to the next. Accordingly, what follows this aphorism in praise of poetry is either entirely incongruous or subtly apt. I am inclined to read it as the latter, as the poetic cure for longing is followed immediately by a reflection on how miserable it is to live alone: 'Earm bið se þe sceal ana lifgan, / wineleas wunian hafaþ him wyrd geteod'[46] (Wretched is he who must live alone, fate has driven him to dwell friendless). The solution to this lonely misery, if we continue to read *Maxims I* in sequence, is to ensure that one has a brother ('betre him wære þæt he broþor ahte') (174a). But then after just a few more aphoristic detours, the poem ends with an account of the feud sprung from Cain's murder of his own brother (189–204). It seems that storytelling, after all, is perhaps the better option for combating solitude and sorrow. If Cain betokens alienation, as the *Beowulf* poet clearly suggests by drawing Grendel's marginalized lineage back to that act of fratricide, a severance of the most intimate of relationships, then it is instead the storyteller whose narrative intimacy merges into an experience of communal intimacy that can truly transform longing, loneliness, even death.

As a poem, *Beowulf* achieves this same kind of narrative intimacy from the start: 'Hwæt, we Gar-Dena in geardagum, / þeodcyninga þrym gefrunon, / hu ða æþelingas ellen fremedon' (Listen, we have heard of the glory of the kings of the Spear-Danes in days gone by, how those princes performed brave deeds) (1–3). These famed opening lines are often remarked upon for the way they incorporate the audience into the narrative of the poem.[47] Even before the figure of the scop appears in Heorot, even before his songs can animate the community there and alienate Grendel as he listens in from outside, the poet embraces the 'we' who have already heard of past glories, glories from a vague distant past ('in geardagum'), into which the audience is drawn and included: this is the narrative intimacy that lays the groundwork for the various experiences of communal joy to come.

To observe the poem's engagement with these experiences of intimacy – where narrative and community intersect – is to invite a reflection upon the ways that our own scholarly narratives and productions of knowledge have the potential to shape the field's commitment to community and inclusivity. It is often through *Beowulf* that students first encounter Old English as a language and as a field of study. From there, individual experiences differ. When I look back on my early studies, what drove me ultimately to pursue a career in this field was the warmth with which I was initially welcomed into a community of scholars, in particular the New York based Colloquium for Early Medieval Studies (formerly known as the ASSC). I expect others have had similar experiences, but I also know that many have not. It is my impression that the field as a whole and the majority of its individual members tend to welcome with enthusiasm those who share an interest in the culture and literature of early medieval England, yet some who share this interest have experienced a closed field and have not been met with the same kind of friendliness and collegiality that I for one have come to value so greatly. The unevenness of the field's collegiality is certainly changing, and it is my hope that as more students have their interests sparked by *Beowulf* and other poems, writings, and materials from the period (often through the inspiration of their teachers), they might enter the field under the same or, indeed, better circumstances than I did, warmly and enthusiastically welcomed.

This community and its friendliness ('freondum afylled') (1018a) is one of the things that I think our field, at times and especially in more recent times, does so right. And I am encouraged by the serious efforts that members of our field, both individually and institutionally, have made towards repairing and redressing past exclusionary habits and fostering a more inclusive scholarly environment, embracing the diversity of backgrounds, identities, and areas of academic interest. Yet if *Beowulf* teaches us anything, it is that the formation of community – no matter how joyous or amiable it might seem – often invites exclusion and hostility towards outsiders, sometimes subtly, sometimes blatantly, and especially in times when resources are made thin or when fears simmer up.

'The field' or 'our field', phrases I have used offhand throughout this chapter, imply collective ownership – with it communal pride and intellectual responsibility, with it the basis for potential exclusivity and alienation. But this focus on collective ownership – what is proper – as the underlying function and mechanism of community is deeply problematic, as Esposito's work has taught us.[48] Even as the very name of the field, until now commonly known as Anglo-Saxon studies, currently undergoes re-evaluation, these formulations of ownership ('a field', 'the field', but especially 'my field', 'our field') risk alienation: where do the boundaries of the field get drawn? Who gets to choose what work or scholars fall within those boundaries? Can we envision a functional field without such boundaries?[49] That re-evaluation and self-critique, that ability to create a new narrative without erasing or forgetting its history, is precisely what community can do. As 'this field' has begun to reflect more openly on its own history and is actively working to confront it, to open itself up, to raise awareness, to acknowledge flaws, to become better, I am all the more encouraged in my optimism for its future.[50]

If communal intimacy always has the potential to be exclusionary – the potential, in other words, to process internal cohesion as aggression against others – then *Beowulf* also seems to suggest that narrative has a powerful capacity to cut across this exclusionary potential. This aspect of the poem speaks, on the one hand, to the field's recent efforts at more conscientious inclusion.[51] These efforts are inadvertently being shaped by how we read this poem, a poem which in many ways is the force that connects almost every member of this community – regardless of one's department, or nationality, or seniority, or even, say, of one's relative inclination towards philological or theoretical approaches. On the other hand, the poem's depiction of narrative intimacy also speaks to larger issues about the powerful ways in which stories and narratives – domains where truth and fictionality warp and fuse – can create walls around a community to protect it from an imagined enemy and the equally powerful ways that literature and storytelling can alternatively weave in the lived experiences of those on the other side. Communal joy and communal intimacy sound so nice because they imply a happy state of inclusion. But without a radically inclusive form of narrative intimation, intimacy perpetually risks alienation; with it, a truly communal form of joy.

Notes

1 R. E. Latham and D. R. Howlett, *Dictionary of medieval Latin from British sources* (London: Oxford University Press, 1975–2013), s.v. *intimare*; I've slightly modified the form of the entry. *Intima* in the first sense is often glossed as *ingeþanc* (as a noun) and *inweard* (as an adjective).

2 Walter Benjamin, 'The storyteller: reflections on the works of Nikolai Leskov', in *Illuminations: essays and reflections*, ed. Hannah Arendt (New York: Schocken Books, 1968), pp. 83–109, at 102.

3 All quotations of *Beowulf* are from R. D. Fulk, Robert E. Bjork, and John D. Niles (eds), *Klaeber's Beowulf*, 4th edn (Toronto: University of Toronto Press, 2008) and are cited by line number. Translations are my own.

4 Hugh Magennis, *Images of community in Old English poetry* (Cambridge: Cambridge University Press, 1996), esp. pp. 60–81.

5 Nicole Guenther Discenza, *Inhabited spaces: Anglo-Saxon constructions of place* (Toronto: University of Toronto Press, 2017), p. 184.

6 I will occasionally use the term 'narrative intimation' to describe a process that produces 'narrative intimacy'. I have opted for the term 'narrative intimacy' because when the term 'intimacy' is applied to both communal and narrative events alike, we can better reflect upon the continuities between its double-edged etymology and grasp the proximity that these two concepts would have shared in early medieval discourse.

7 On the digressions, see Mary-Kate Hurley's chapter in this volume, pp. 147–63.

8 The connection between intimation and knowledge is reinforced, for instance, in at least one early medieval English glossary, where the word *intimandum* (to tell, recount, narrate) is glossed as *to cyðenne* (to know); see Jan Hendrik Hessels (ed.), *An eighth-century Latin-Anglo-Saxon glossary* (Cambridge: Cambridge University Press, 1890; repr. 2011), p. 70.

9 Brian Stock's notion of a textual community in his *The implications of literacy: written language and models of interpretation in the eleventh and twelfth centuries* (Princeton, NJ: Princeton University Press, 1983) might be useful to think with here, despite its association with the eleventh and twelfth centuries; see Nicholas Howe, 'The cultural construction of reading in Anglo-Saxon England', in Jonathan Boyarin (ed.), *The ethnography of reading* (Berkeley, CA: University of California Press, 1993), pp. 58–79. However, the scenes that I am examining in *Beowulf* depict an oral (as opposed to literate or textual) process of recitation, even as the text of *Beowulf* itself is a more textual production. On poetic communities in early medieval England, see Emily V. Thornbury, *Becoming a poet in Anglo-Saxon England* (Cambridge: Cambridge University Press, 2014), pp. 95–160.

10 Jeffrey Jerome Cohen, *Of giants* (Minneapolis, MN: University of Minnesota Press, 1999), p. 25, for example, argues that Grendel's *extimité* is realized when he 'intrudes into the narrative just as Hrothgar's scop is singing', timely given the monster's hatred for their music, 'a dynamic metaphor of their communal harmony'. See also Roberto Esposito, *Communitas: the origin and destiny of community*, trans. Timothy C. Campbell (Stanford, CA: Stanford University Press, 2009), p. 11, on the

centrality of Cain to the formation of the human community (thinking through Hannah Arendt's interpretation of Augustine).

11 Maurice Blanchot, *The unavowable community*, trans. Pierre Joris (Barrytown, NY: Station Hill Press, 1988; repr. 2006), p. 3.
12 Jean-Luc Nancy, *The disavowed community*, trans. Philip Armstrong (New York: Fordham University Press, 2016), p. 9.
13 Jean-Luc Nancy, *The inoperative community*, trans. Peter Connor et al. (Minneapolis, MN: University of Minnesota Press, 1991), pp. xxxix, 26. Indeed, for Nancy, this finitude enables the very possibility of joy, which 'has meaning and existence, only through community and as its communication' (p. 34).
14 Esposito, *Communitas*, p. 7.
15 Lauren Berlant, 'Intimacy: a special issue', *Critical inquiry*, 24.2 (1998), 281–8, at 286.
16 On the similarities between Beowulf and Grendel (e.g., both are described as 'hall-thegns', ll. 142 and 719), see Andy Orchard, *Pride and prodigies: studies in the monsters of the Beowulf-manuscript* (Cambridge: D. S. Brewer, 1995), p. 32; Cohen, *Of giants*, p. 27, notes that Beowulf 'plays the role Grendel previously enacted' in his attack of the mere.
17 For a much more nuanced reading of the numerous scenes of arrival (and departure) in the poem, see John M. Hill, *The narrative pulse of Beowulf: arrivals and departures* (Toronto: University of Toronto Press, 2008).
18 James L. Rosier, 'Design for treachery: the Unferth intrigue', *PMLA*, 77.1 (1962), 1–7.
19 Robert E. Bjork, 'Unferth in the hermeneutic circle: a reappraisal of James L. Rosier's "Design for treachery: the Unferth intrigue"', *Papers on language and literature*, 16 (1980), 133–41. See also R. D. Fulk, 'Unferth and his name', *Modern philology*, 85 (1987), 113–27, who challenges the allegorical and etymological interpretations of Unferth's name (typically construed as 'mar-peace'). Cf. Arthur Gilchrist Brodeur, *The art of Beowulf* (Berkeley, CA: University of California Press, 1959), pp. 151–5.
20 Rosier, 'Design for treachery', 7.
21 Norman E. Eliason, 'The Þyle and scop in Beowulf', *Speculum*, 38.2 (1963), 267–84.
22 Edward B. Irving, Jr, *Rereading Beowulf* (Philadelphia, PA: University of Pennsylvania Press, 1989), pp. 38, 47. For additional arguments about the centrality of Unferth's role in Hrothgar's court, see also Carol J. Clover, 'The Germanic context of the Unferþ episode', *Speculum*, 55.3 (1980), 444–68; and Michael J. Enright, 'The warband context of the Unferth episode', *Speculum*, 73.2 (1998), 297–337.
23 For more on the function of secrecy in the poem, see Benjamin A. Saltzman, 'Secrecy and the hermeneutic potential in Beowulf', *PMLA*, 133.1 (2018), 36–55.

24 The subsequent Sigemund digression likewise seems to parallel the 'sið Beowulfes' as well as his anticipated battle against the dragon at the end of the poem.

25 Megan Cavell, *Weaving words and binding bodies: the poetics of human experience in Old English literature* (Toronto: University of Toronto Press, 2016), pp. 238–3. On this formal pattern, see the seminal article by John Leyerle, 'The interlace structure of *Beowulf*', *University of Toronto quarterly*, 37.1 (1967), 1–17, at 4; on this passage and the poetic practice it imagines, see Norman E. Eliason, 'The "improvised lay" in *Beowulf*', *PQ*, 31 (1952), 171–9.

26 This pattern is observed by Cavell, *Weaving words and binding bodies*, p. 239; but Renée R. Trilling, *The aesthetics of nostalgia: historical representation in Old English verse* (Toronto: University of Toronto Press, 2009), p. 12, reads it differently: 'The integrity of the long line is thus susceptible to disruption by semantics and poetics alike, and the simultaneous assertion and disruption of wholeness is the very fabric of the Anglo-Saxon poetic form.'

27 Thornbury, *Becoming a poet*, pp. 161–83, for example, has shown how Old English metrical and alliterative practices varied by poet, particularly poets (such as the 'renovator' of *Christ and Satan*) working in isolation.

28 Trilling, *Aesthetics of nostalgia*, pp. 11–12, elegantly reads the relationship between Beowulf, Sigemund, Heremod, and the dragon as a kind of Benjaminian 'constellation' where they 'share a space in a reflective moment that invokes them all'. Moreover, we see what Trilling calls 'the aesthetics of nostalgia' operating in *Beowulf* as it 'mediate[s] between a longing for communion with ancient heroes and the recognition that their antiquity sets them apart'.

29 Adrien Bonjour, *The digressions in Beowulf* (Oxford: Blackwell, 1950); for an overview, see Robert E. Bjork and John D. Niles (eds), *A Beowulf handbook* (Lincoln, NE: University of Nebraska Press, 1997). On the place of the Finn episode in the poem, see Scott Gwara, *Heroic identity in the world of Beowulf* (Leiden: Brill, 2008), pp. 135–80, who argues that it illustrates 'grave unease over Beowulf's appointment as Hrothgar's heir' (p. 151).

30 See Roberta Frank's chapter in this volume for another take on these lines, pp. 54–72.

31 Robert E. Bjork, 'Speech as gift in *Beowulf*', *Speculum*, 69.4 (1994), 993–1022, has taught us to see the function of speeches in the poem as a kind of gift giving, which is one of the central structures of community in the poem's hall culture. We might therefore see the force of speeches enhanced by their function as gifts in a gift-giving society, or inversely the exchanging of narratives could reinforce the social function of gift giving. There is a complex web of factors that influence the structure of community in the poem; I am merely arguing that narrative intimacy is one significant factor.

32 My translation here differs from the editorial guidance of Fulk et al., *Klaeber's Beowulf*, pp. 180–1, which proposes 'Healgamen' as the subject of 'mænan scolde', and thus as an epithet for the scop. I have instead opted for the interpretation proposed by Eric Weiskott, 'Three *Beowulf* cruces: *Healgamen, Fremu, Sigemunde*', *Notes and queries*, 58.1 (2011), 3–7.

33 For a detailed study of the material and literary evidence of harps in this period, see Robert Boenig, 'The Anglo-Saxon harp', *Speculum*, 71.2 (1996), 290–320.

34 Benjamin, 'The storyteller', p. 87.

35 Ibid., pp. 87, 100.

36 It should be noted that, although Benjamin has in mind an abstracted image of medieval storytellers and the mists of oral tradition, he is almost certainly not thinking of Old English poetry or *Beowulf*.

37 Nancy, *The inoperative community*, pp. 50–1, considers the function of myth in community as 'the unique voice of the many'.

38 Benjamin, 'The storyteller', p. 102; see epigraph above for full quotation.

39 In multiple accounts, death is central to the formation of community. For example, for Nancy, *The inoperative community*, p. xvi, 'death is an experience that a collectivity cannot make its *work* or its property', so the finite singularity of the subject is what makes community ultimately impossible. On the other hand, Blanchot, *The unavowable community*, p. 9, takes that singularity as the very basis of community: 'to take upon myself another's death as the only death that concerns me, this is what puts me beside myself, this is the only separation that can open me, in its very impossibility, to the Openness of a community'. Esposito, *Communitas*, p. 13, sees the origin of community through a dark Hobbesian lens: 'What men have in common, what makes them more like each other than anything else, is their generalized capacity to be killed.' These different strains of thought share a kind of Derridean formulation, in which the irreducible experience of death – which cannot be given – is the very basis for the possibility of friendship; see Jacques Derrida, *The gift of death and literature in secret*, trans. David Wills (Chicago: University of Chicago Press, 2008), pp. 42–5; Jacques Derrida, *The politics of friendship*, trans. George Collins (New York: Verso, 1997), p. 14. On this formulation in early medieval England, see Benjamin A. Saltzman, 'Writing friendship, mourning the friend in late Anglo-Saxon *Rules of Confraternity*', *JMEMS*, 41.2 (2011), 251–91.

40 Benjamin, 'The storyteller', pp. 93, 94.

41 Ibid., p. 102.

42 This inevitability is captured not only in Hrethel's lament for the demise of his son's hall, but also in elegies such as *The Wanderer* and *The Ruin*.

43 Patricia Dailey, 'Questions of dwelling in Anglo-Saxon poetry and medieval mysticism: inhabiting landscape, body, and mind', *NML*, 8 (2006), 175–214.

44 *Maxims I*, in George Philip Krapp and Elliott Van Kirk Dobbie (eds), *The Exeter Book*, ASPR 3 (New York: Columbia University Press, 1936; repr. 2004), pp. 156–63, at 162, lines 169–71.

45 Angus Cameron, Ashley Crandell Amos, and Antonette diPaolo Healey (eds), *Dictionary of Old English: A to H* (Toronto: Dictionary of Old English Project, 2016), s.v. *gliw*.

46 *Maxims I*, lines 172–3.

47 E.g., Magennis, *Images of community*, p. 1.

48 Esposito, *Communitas*, pp. 56–7.

49 E.g., Daniel C. Remein, 'ISAS should probably change its name', paper presented at the International Congress on Medieval Studies (Kalamazoo, MI, 2017); Mary Dockray-Miller, 'Old English has a serious image problem', *JSTOR Daily*, 3 May 2017, https://daily.jstor.org/old-english-serious-image-problem (accessed 4 June 2019).

50 Yet I am reminded that intimacy's optimism does not always play out in predictable ways or ways that are necessarily good for those estranged or subjugated by a dominant narrative of intimacy; see Berlant, 'Intimacy: a special issue', 281–2 and 288: 'Intimacy was supposed to be about optimism, remember? But it is also formed around threats to the image of the world it seeks to sustain.'

51 Serious conversations took place, for example, at conferences such as 'Seafaring: an early medieval conference on the islands of the North Atlantic' at the University of Denver, organized by Donna Beth Ellard and Dan Remein (3–5 November 2016), and the International Society of Anglo-Saxonists, Biennial Meeting, at the University of Hawai'i at Mānoa, Honolulu, HI (31 July–4 August 2017).

3
Beowulf and the intimacy of large parties

Roberta Frank

> I like large parties. They're so intimate. At small parties there isn't
> any privacy.
>
> F. Scott Fitzgerald, *The Great Gatsby*[1]

Intimacy sells. So, apparently, does *Beowulf*: feature films, a TV
series, operas, graphic novels, translations, and a pride of companions
attest to its allure. Everybody, it seems, wants to date the poem,
including creationist tracts that read it as an eyewitness account of
men cohabiting with dinosaurs.[2] *Beowulf* is a flirt, alluring and ageless.
Not even the time or place of its birth is entered on online sites: the
less data, the more dates. The poem's seductive flash-forwards and
strategic withdrawals, its pitiless channel shifting and intimations
of strange doings down by the woodshed, tease and torment. Once
hooked, admirers bemoan its 'lack of steady advance',[3] disconcerting
Sprünge (leaps)[4] and *Sprunghaftigkeit* (erratic jumps),[5] its abrupt
hints, loose ends, and alarming lack of resolution. Its very coolness
attracts. (Think Lola and Professor Rath in *The Blue Angel*.) *Beowulf*
pulls hearers in a given direction, toys with them, makes them tingle
with a sense of closeness, before showing them the door. There
is an aching incompleteness to the poem's disclosures, a sense of
something almost being said. And when something is only partially
uncovered, as in a striptease, it awakens an urge to see more, to
move from what is manifest to what is kept under wraps. Intimacy
is a longing to connect with another, even with a poem.

The desire to meet is at the heart of all artfulness. Reading an
old poem is like receiving a visitor from a distant land. You try to
make sense of the stranger's words, the particular gestures and
images of the text. *The Wonders of the East* in the *Beowulf* manuscript
describes a polyglot race called the Donestre, who speak the languages
of all peoples and use this skill to lure strangers to their death:
'When they encounter someone from a foreign country, they name

him and his kinsmen with the names of acquaintances; and with false words they trick him and seize him, and after that eat all of him except for the head; and then they sit and weep over the head.'[6] Yes, small parties can go so, so wrong: guests trapped at table, immobilized, chewed over, seized upon by others as fresh meat. Films dine off this terror: *Hannibal*; *The cook, the thief, his wife and her lover*; *The discreet charm of the bourgeoisie*; *A streetcar named Desire*; Ang Lee's *Eat, drink, man, woman*; Vinterberg's *The celebration*; or any novel or play entitled *The dinner* or *The dinner party*. Avoid intimate literary soirées in particular.

Large parties, on the other hand, provide space for privacy, for bridging or at least minding the gap between bodies. At Gatsby's estate, individuals stroll, cocktails in hand, on spacious lawns criss-crossed by paths, 'through the sea-change of faces and voices and color under the constantly changing light, the swirls and eddies of strangers', meeting, separating, pausing, circling back, now moving rapidly, now at a crawl, introductions forgotten on the spot. Words waft in their wake – 'she persisted', 'butterfat', 'draining the fens', 'you don't say', 'toxic', 'recognize the ring?' 'plastics', 'believe me' – the rest muffled by the surf beating below. Imagination fills in the blanks. Eric Weiskott recently observed that much of the artistry of Old English poetry occurs in the spaces between half-lines.[7] In the caesuras formed by the separate shards of stories in *Beowulf*, time itself sometimes seems to stutter, like a song on repeat. These ruptures and fissures in the narrative appear to offer points of access, a window on to some other temporality. But an entry to what? To things that disappeared and shouldn't have? To something grimly percolating offstage?

All forms of poetic recycling – borrowing, appropriation, refer-entiality – what Freud called *Nachträglichkeit* or 'retroactive meaningfulness' – are parasitic, dependent on the existence of a body of story that audiences were expected to know. Ovid counted on his audience's familiarity with Virgil's Dido to activate multiple layers of meaning in *Heroides* 7, and the *Aeneid* was never the same again.[8] In Chaucer's *Troilus and Criseyde*, Pandarus, addressing a lovesick Troilus, quotes from a letter written by the Trojan shepherd-ess Oenone to Troilus's brother Paris (I, 652–5), after he had abandoned her for Greek Helen (Ovid's *Heroides* 5). James Simpson has noted the cunning with which Pandarus/Chaucer underlines the message's contemporaneity, saying to Troilus: 'You saw the letter that she wrote, I suppose?' (I, 656).[9] A private letter by a heartbroken wife is viewed as public property, something possibly circulating at court and available to the recipient's brother. But Pandarus's reading is also drastically foreshortened. For in the same short letter, Oenone reports the prophecy of Cassandra, sister to Paris and Troilus, concerning the coming destruction of Troy. This is the violence and catastrophe, the legendary context, with which other poetic reimaginings of Oenone's lament powerfully end: with smoke, burning fire, and everywhere the sound of armed men. Yeats sets the scene in ten syllables: 'Hector is dead and there's a light in Troy' ('The Gyres'); in another poem, a cygnine god begets 'the broken wall, the burning roof and tower / And Agamemnon dead' ('Leda and the Swan'). Elizabeth Smart writes, 'Jupiter has been with Leda … and now nothing can avert the Trojan War', confident that at least some of her readers will get the allusion to the engendering of Helen.[10] Marlowe's 'topless towers of Ilion' are still burning in twenty-first-century North America. But Heorot? Hrothulf? Halga? What have Heoroweard or Heorogar to do with us? We have heard of Myrmidons and Priam, but not of Spear-Danes or Hrothgar. The sentence 'Halga has been with Yrsa … and now nothing can avert the fall of the house of the Scyldings' no longer rings many bells.

The back story

> Thence form your Judgement, thence your Notions bring,
> And trace the Muses upward to their Spring.
>
>   Alexander Pope[11]

Beowulf opens '*We* have heard of the glory of the kings of the Spear-Danes', followed by a snapshot of the dynasty's founder, one Scyld, tugging at mead-benches, disturbing furniture, grabbing shiny objects with his fists. The light will be brighter once he reaches the top. He begets an heir; then shoves off. That's life for you. *Beowulf* has one big back story – the fall of the dynasty of Danish kings founded by Scyld – almost none of which is told 'in' the poem. The first twenty-two hundred lines of *Beowulf* fill in the early moments of this history, introducing characters as they were before the turning points that led to tragedy. Beowulf, like Aeneas, is a new hero in legend-land, meeting in his travels famous figures whose careers were just taking off: here's Ingeld, not yet married; there's Hrothulf, silent as a log; and, look, Hrethric, a mere child. We are at the *enfances* stage of the Scylding century, a time not spoken of except in *Beowulf*. 'We have heard', says the narrator, and he means it: he is going to refashion an old story that everyone knows for his own purposes. He invites his audience to serve as his agile accomplices, his co-conspirators, in breaking and entering the past, to look on when, with a torturer's pity, he puts his characters through their pre-ordained paces. The legends themselves are present in the poem chiefly as mysterious dark matter, sensed by the shadows they cast and by their gravitational pull.

For over a century and a half, a distinguished tradition in Old English scholarship has traced correspondences between *Beowulf* and the stories of the Danish Scyldings as set out in dozens of later medieval Scandinavian and Icelandic texts.[12] The same names, the same heroes, the same basic elements differently mixed and matched, appear again and again, trailing clouds of glory and a clod or two of less savoury matter as well. *Beowulf* features brief asides about three cousins: Hrethric, Hrothgar's son; Hrothulf (the North's Hrólfr Kraki), son of Hrothgar's younger brother; and Heoroweard, son of Hrothgar's older brother. In later legend, these three battle it out, with each done in by the next. But the *Beowulf* poet never mentions their conflicts, at least not directly. Hrothulf, who has been called 'the blankest' figure in the poem, will later become the greatest hero in the Scylding cycle.[13] But why is the poet so reticent about his parentage? Forgetfulness? Ineptitude? Or a crime whose name cannot be spoken? Why does Wealhtheow so pointedly express confidence in his loyalty (1180–7) before turning towards her sons? If Denmark is really as chock-full of kindness and harmony as she says, why does she task Beowulf, an outsider, with looking after her boys (1228–31)? Beowulf, taking leave of Hrothgar, gravely offers his son a haven at his own court, should the young prince 'ever determine to visit' (1836–9). Why? Was cousin Hrothulf already flexing his muscles? And why for heaven's sake did Heoroweard's father not give him that ancestral mail-shirt (2155–62)? This piece of armour is made so conspicuously absent that the cause and result of its denial demand to be recalled.

Correspondences between allusions in *Beowulf* and the Danish/Icelandic Scylding materials have haunted our handbooks since 1852.[14] Three decades earlier, the scholar and poet N. F. S. Grundtvig recognized the Scyldings of *Beowulf* as the Skjöldung rulers of early Danish story, and their legends as behind the entire first part of the poem.[15] It was another Dane, Ludvig Schröder, who in 1875 first explicated certain scenes as foretelling the fall of the

house of the Scyldings, the poem's dark backdrop.[16] Subsequent
discussions by Axel Olrik and R. W. Chambers deepened the
links. By 1951 Dorothy Whitelock was able to conclude that key
moments in Scylding history are so frequently foretold or foreseen in
Beowulf

> that it is obvious that the poet wishes them to be present in his
> hearers' thoughts as he tells his tale ... The poet describes how
> Hrothgar built a hall 'greater than the sons of men had ever heard
> of', and hints at its tragic end; he expects his audience to know that
> it was destined to see Hrothgar's strife with his own son-in-law, and
> at last to perish in flames in a war between kinfolk that put an end
> to the Scylding dynasty.[17]

Arthur Gilchrist Brodeur agreed:

> Although the poet's allusions to the dynastic quarrels of the Shieldings
> (lines 1013–19; 1162b–68a; 1180b ff.; 1219–31) concern only Hrothulf's
> usurpation and the murder of Hrethric, he and his audience must
> have known of, and borne in mind, the later attack by Heoroweard
> (Hjörvarðr) on Hrothulf (Hrólf Kraki).[18]

Marijane Osborn stressed the precociousness of the *Beowulf* poet,
whose information about the Scylding kings was far in advance of
anyone writing in Scandinavia:

> The *Beowulf* poet does not tell the full story of the Scylding dynasty;
> he merely alludes to that story, and he does so in a way suggesting
> his certainty that listeners can fill in the gaps. Today we can fill in
> those gaps only with reference to episodes of the story as they were
> told by later Scandinavian writers who probably knew nothing of
> *Beowulf*.[19]

James W. Earl detected a skeleton or two rattling in the Scylding
family closet and surmised that the Old English poet suppressed
stories involving rape or incest as too hot to handle, a kind of
self-censorship.[20] Or was the poet's deafening silence deployed to
prick or excite his audience's recall, to turn absence into presence
and thereby evoke the horror behind the curtain. To hear what is
not being said in *Beowulf* involves tapping stories from a variety
of late narratives, in full awareness that the conversation changes
over the years, that each poet or saga-teller makes the story again
in his own way.

Under the waterline

> What's past is prologue.
>
>   William Shakespeare, *The Tempest*[21]

Submerged narrative awakes, Kraken-like, in the opening lines of the poem. *Beowulf* has barely begun when we learn of the future destruction by fire of Heorot, Hrothgar's newly erected hall, and of in-law trouble waiting impatiently in the wings:

> Sele hlifade
> heah ond horngeap;   heaðowylma bad,
> laðan liges –   ne wæs hit lenge þa gen
> þæt se ecghete   aþumsweoran
> æfter wælniðe   wæcnan scolde. (81b–5)

(The hall towered, high and wide-gabled; it awaited deadly-surges, hostile flame – nor was it longer then yet that sword-hatred would awaken between son-in-law and father-in-law after deadly enmity.)

Allusions in *Beowulf* to Scylding dynastic history are set out concentrically, in a loose ring-structure, an enveloping barrow of remembrances.[22] The first incident (the fire at Heorot, 81b–83a) links up with the last (resentful Heoroweard, 2155–62), the second (the in-law feud, 83b–85) with the penultimate (the Ingeld episode, 2020–69a), and the third (young Hrethric, 1180b–1191) with the antepenultimate (Beowulf's invitation, 1836–9). Two ominous tableaux – Hrothgar and Hrothulf at drink – occupy the middle panels (1014b–1019, 1162b–1165a). Their first *tête-à-tête* precedes the recital of the battle at Finnsburg, which introduces a sad queen, newly bereft of husband, brother, and son; the second follows that poetic entertainment, marking Wealhtheow's entrance and her Pollyannish 'no-problem-here-folks' speeches: 'I am certain Hrothulf will treat our heirs kindly since we were so good to him when he was a child' (1184–7).[23] 'Be fitting in your deeds to my son, Beowulf. Here every comrade is true to the other, generous of heart, loyal to his lord; the troops are determined, the people all prepared; the rank-and-file, having drunk, do as I bid' (1226b–1231). Heartbreak will come. The queen puts a brave face on things, but history cannot be averted. The four quick references by the narrator to Danish story come before line 1169; the four incidents to which they correspond follow in reverse order and are spoken by characters in the poem who react to something they have seen or heard. The poet sets the table, then lets the help serve and clean up.

The outermost ring

> Time will say nothing but I told you so.
>
> W. H. Auden[24]

The first indication that things will not end well for the Scyldings is the narrator's statement that Heorot is destined to go up in flames (81b–83a). The timing of this conflagration is left open, perhaps to accommodate different versions of the story in circulation. In Saxo's *Gesta Danorum* (ii.7.11–12), fire imagery illuminates Heoroweard's night attack on Hrothulf, whose last stand at the royal hall was widely celebrated in the poetry of the North.[25] The *Beowulf* poet, in his final allusion to Scylding legend, dispatches Heoroweard in two and a half lines. Beowulf, presenting Hrothgar's gifts to Hygelac, announces that the Danish king wanted it known that the mail-coat in the collection was a royal heirloom, that before coming into Hrothgar's possession it had belonged to Heorogar, his older brother and predecessor on the throne. (Heorogar, the first son of Healfdene mentioned in the poem, will be the last.) For some unstated reason he refused to give the ancestral armour to his own (and loyal) son Heoroweard. As for Heoroweard, 'there he is', observes Marijane Osborn, 'in the shadows of the story, waiting for the twelfth-century *Lejre Chronicle* to develop him into a nemesis'.[26] Before handing over this battle-gear to Hygelac, Beowulf recites its genealogy in a passage rich in alliteration and half-rhymes:[27]

> Me ðis hildesceorp   Hroðgar sealde
> snotra fengel.   Sume worde het
> þæt ic his ærest ðe   est gesægde.
> Cwæð þæt hyt hæfde   Hiorogar cyning
> leod Scyldunga   lange hwile.
> No ðy ær suna sinum   syllan wolde
> hwatum Heorowearde   þeah he him hold wære
> breostgewædu.   Bruc ealles well. (2155–62)

(Hrothgar, the wise prince, gave me this battle-gear. He commanded that I should first tell you in certain words his good-will. He said that King Heorogar owned it, man of the Scyldings, for a long time. Not at all the sooner did he wish to give the breast-garment to his son, bold Heoroweard, although he was loyal to him. Enjoy all well.)

Why does the *Beowulf* poet mention Heoroweard at all? Was this prince initially passed over because he was too young? Why then didn't Hrothgar give him his father's armour when he came of age? He would have been a grown man by the time Beowulf arrived.

And where was Heoroweard during Beowulf's visit? Abroad? Sulking
in his tent? Was Hrothgar's gift to Hygelac meant to disinherit a
nephew whose resentment at this slight eventually brought the
glory of Heorot to an end? Causal connections are never made.
Key moments in the fall of the Scyldings are hinted at – and then
repressed. 'Enjoy all well', says Beowulf to Hygelac. The imperative
singular of OE *brucan*, 'to enjoy, make use of', carries ominous
overtones in *Beowulf* (the only poem in which the form occurs).
OE *bruc*, 'enjoy', is otherwise spoken only by Wealhtheow, first
when she hints to her husband that it may be time for him to do
some estate planning (1177) and again when she presents Beowulf
with a majestic neck-torque – after the narrator has reported its
quick downward trajectory (1216). When a character in *Beowulf*
says 'Enjoy', the wish seems seriously time-limited.

The second ring

> A king is history's slave.
>
>   Leo Tolstoy[28]

The poet's second allusion to the Scylding story (83b–85) concerns a
son-in-law and father-in-law conflict. We later learn more about this
feud and its chief protagonists, Ingeld and Hrothgar (2024–69a).[29]
On the basis of a piece of information picked up at the Danish
court, Beowulf supplies Hygelac with an astute political forecast.
Hrothgar has pledged his daughter to Ingeld, here prince of the
Heathobards, in the hope of settling matters. Beowulf assesses the
chances for success as nil: 'As a rule, the murderous spear will rest
idle after the fall of a people only for a little while, even though the
bride is good' (2029b–2031). Proverbs distance and depersonalize
by appealing to an authority beyond the immediate moment, by
splicing a particular situation into a universal pattern. Here Beowulf's
sentence underlines the limited capacity of the Scyldings for action
as they tread their predestined paths, fate once again stacking the
odds against human aspirations. Hrothgar will not achieve peace by
marrying off his daughter. Beowulf foresees the circumstances in
which an unnamed old warrior (the famous Starkaðr/Starcatherus
of later Scylding legend) might incite Ingeld's troops to vengeance.
A plundered ancestral Heathobard sword spotted in the possession
of a young Danish retainer will ensure that all bets are off:

Þonne bioð (ab)rocene   on ba healfe
aðsweord eorla;   (syð)ðan Ingelde
weallað wælniðas,   ond him wiflufan
æfter cearwælmum   colran weorðað. (2063–6)

(Then on both sides the oaths of men will be broken; then deadly
hostility will boil up in Ingeld, and his love for the woman will
become cooler after the seething of sorrow.)

The disaster predicted is expressed with restraint. The words *wælnið*
and *aðsweord* repeat and echo the very terms used by the poet in
his opening allusion (83b–85). The precise details of this in-law
feud remain elusive; the immediate outcome is distilled into a single
comparative adjective: 'cooler'. Will Ingeld send his bride away?
Kill her? Or will he just lose that special feeling? All semantic
gradations from somewhat chilly to fatally cold are possible. Beowulf
intimates without being specific, leaving much to an audience's
memory and imagination. Hearers fill in according to taste and
previous knowledge. Sound-effects reinforce the message.[30] The
half-lines 'weallað wælniðas' (lit. deadly-hates boil) and 'ond him
wiflufan' (and his woman-loves), joined by alliteration, are divorced
by internal half-rhymes (*weal-/wæl-* vs. *wif-/luf-*), each member of
the pair going its separate way. Images of heat and cold alliterate
(doubly) across the caesura 'cearwælmum colran weorðað', the two
half-lines linked firmly by resonant half-rhymes (*cear-/weorð-*;
-wælm/col-). Paronomasia binds the couplet (*weall-, wæl-, -wælm*)
but not the couple: Beowulf's conjectures about the future of this
marriage are acoustically buttressed. The feud will culminate with
Ingeld's defeat at Heorot, famously referred to in the Old English
poem *Widsith*.

The inner circle

Be afraid. Be very afraid.

The Fly[31]

The *Beowulf* poet counts on his hearers' intimacy with Scylding
legend to 'get it' when he means more than he says. Sometimes
ominous temporal adverbs or adverbial phrases ('at that time', 'then
still', 'for a while') do the dirty work. At the celebration following
Beowulf's victory over Grendel, the narrator twice zooms in on
two men, Hrothgar and Hrothulf, uncle and nephew, sitting at the
feast. Each tableau is a snapshot, a moment frozen in time, a minute
caught and made to stand still. Would a contemporary audience,
knowing what subsequently happened, have read the scene as we
might a painting of Judith beguiling Holofernes or of Judas nodding

at the Last Supper? The poet's description opens hopefully, but things quickly go downhill:

> Heorot innan wæs
> freondum afylled;   nalles facenstafas
> Þeod-Scyldingas   þenden fremedon. (1017b–1019)

(Heorot inside was filled with friends; *at that time* the Nation-Scyldings did *not at all* practise deceit.)

'Not at that time' does not reassure. As others have pointed out, the stressed and alliterating adverb *þenden* seems to project the end of the very concord that the poet is advertising. The *facenstafas*, 'treachery, deceit' (ON *feikenstafr*, 'baleful rune') that the Scyldings did not *then* do does double duty as a magnetic 'ye olde' sign, pointing back and due north, to a far-off past and foreign place.

The same ambiguously joyous feast and the same two kinsmen soon stagger into view again. This time the narrator (in a metre that stands out from the surrounding lines) introduces a third man into the portrait:

> Þa cwom Wealhþeo forð
> gan under gyldnum beage   þær þa godan twegen
> sæton suhtergefæderan;   þa gyt wæs hiera sib ætgædere,
> æghwylc oðrum trywe.   Swylce þær Unferþ þyle
> æt fotum sæt frean Scyldinga;   gehwylc hiora his ferhþe treowde,
> þæt he hæfde mod micel,   þeah þe he his magum nære
> arfæst æt ecga gelacum. (1162b–1168a)

(Then Wealhtheow came forward, walking under a golden torque to where the two good ones sat, nephew and paternal uncle; *then yet* was their friendship together, each true to the other. There, likewise, Unferth orator sat at the feet of the lord of the Scyldings; each of them trusted his mind, that he had great courage, though he had not been honourable to his kinsmen at swordplay.)

Then yet, still: for such little words to be effective, hearers would have had to be trained to respond to a storytelling technique so economical and so skilled in implication that the slightest hedge, the faintest trace of narrative smoke would set off an alarm. '*At that time* their kinship bonds were still together'; a reminder that Scylding family feelings will soon sour, with the additional hint that Unferth, the overreaching press secretary with a worrisome record of fratricide, will have something to do with the break. This is a

Houdini moment, a scene that has escaped by its own efforts from the confines of Scylding legend and now sits apart in deep silence. The passage above includes a long line ('sæton suhtergefæderan; þa gyt wæs hiera sib ætgædere') almost identical to one used by the *Widsith* poet of the same two individuals, as if lifted from or mimicking a phrase in a popular song or speech:[32] 'Hrothulf and Hrothgar kept *for the longest time* kinship-ties together, nephew and paternal uncle [*suhtorfædran*], after they had driven off the kindred of Wicingas and humbled Ingeld's battle-line, cut down at Heorot the glory of the Heathobards.' English tradition seems to have bestowed on Hrothulf and Hrothgar a distinctive kinship epithet: *suhtergefæderan*, 'brother's son, father's brother', a rare *dvandva-* (or copulative) compound. In the surviving corpus, this epithet is restricted to these two heroes; it is their compound and no one else's, and may have advertised something specific (and possibly unspeakable) about their family relationship.

For if early skaldic verse is any model, Anglo-Saxon audiences were primed to locate narrative meaning in a poet's kinship epithets. In stanzas attributed to the Norse poet Bragi Boddason, the great Ermanaric, king of the Goths, is designated by the epithet 'Randvér's chief-kinsman', naming the son (Randvér) he recently let swing on the gallows; the skald also refers to the Gothic king as 'Joy of Bird-Hildr [= Svanhildr]', an epithet evoking the young wife he cruelly slew at the same time. Another kinship compound, 'Erpr's bosom-brothers', identifies the avenging heroes of the tale, but solely through the sibling they had wrongheadedly killed.[33] Pointed circumlocutions like these open cracks in the frame surrounding the immediate action of the story, letting past and future in; they are condensed allusions to a legend everyone knew. Taken innocently, the epithet *suhtergefæderan*, 'brother's son, father's brother', describes an everyday kinship relation; read suspiciously, it is a mocking reminder of a particular family's disintegration.

When a few lines later Wealhtheow anxiously insists that Hrothulf will repay her and Hrothgar for their kindnesses to him when he was a child (using another antique-looking compound), that he will be good to their boys when her aged husband departs this life (1180–7), the poet is presumably counting on his audience to recall that Hrothulf did not play 'nice-nice' with his cousins before taking the throne. The narrator allows a quick glimpse of the two boys, Hrethric and Hrothmund, Beowulf by their side. Hrothmund at once vanishes from the poem, but Hrethric is mentioned one more time, in Beowulf's farewell to Hrothgar (1817–39). After pledging

military support should the Danish king ever need it, Beowulf adds
a further sweetener:

> Gif him þonne Hreþric   to hofum Geata
> geþingeð þeodnes bearn,   he mæg þær fela
> freonda findan;   feorcyþðe beoð
> selran gesohte   þæm þe him selfa deah. (1836–9)

> (If then Hrethric, child of the ruler, determines to go to the court
> of the Geats, he will be able to find many friends there; far nations
> are better visited by one excellent in himself.)

Conceivably (given the likelihood of problems with Hrethric's
succession) Beowulf is not offering the lad a junior year abroad,
but a political safe haven. The generalizing proverb that follows
is a polite compliment to both the prince and his father. Hrothgar
immediately recognizes Beowulf's diplomatic tact and praises his
indirection ('I have never heard anyone at such a young age make
arrangements more wisely', 1842b–1843). The Danish king has no
trouble translating the speaker's round-aboutness, his excruciatingly
good manners. Here, as elsewhere in *Beowulf*, strength of feeling is
conveyed by not being spoken. Intimacy is the thing with feathers that
makes your interlocutor either respond quickly with an appreciative
'I get it; I know just what you mean', or send you to a specialist.

Surfacing

> The famous
> Northern reticence, the tight gag of place
> And times
>   Seamus Heaney[34]

The secret to success in almost any relationship is knowing what
not to say. Talking to anyone not yourself is always problematic;
but, then, so is talking to yourself. There may be questions too
cutting, direct, or trivial to ask our poem, especially when its
characters sound perceptually challenged. We must show tender
solicitude for the tiniest hints and fragments of its vanished past,
the preceding and surrounding world that gave context to the poem's
utterances. So what if there are things about *Beowulf* we shall never
fully understand. Every communication is faulty, every comparison
lame, every interpretation imperfect.

A shared sense of wit or style is often the spark for an intimate relationship. The *Beowulf* poet entices with his wryness and

obliqueness, turning hearers into accomplices, companions in making meaning, if not whoopee: 'Cain did not rejoice in that crime' (= God sent him packing) (109); Grendel 'mourned not at all for his crimes' (= he was a happy camper) (136–7); 'he didn't want to sue for peace or pay wergild' (= some men prefer to eat and run) (154–8); 'nor did his death seem painful to them' (= it was party-time at Heorot) (841–2). The poem employs almost a hundred of these negations, along with a troop of adverbial down-toners: 'not much' or 'little' (= not at all), 'not many' (= none), 'not least' (= greatest), 'enough' (= many), 'seldom' (= never), 'long' (= forever), and 'often' (= always).[35] The hero early confides about his heroism: 'I don't brag about it much' (586). (Imagine dating someone who talks like this.) There is an inherent fuzziness or imprecision in such evaluations, foreshadowing the basic fact of modern physics that 'nothing can ever be measured with perfect accuracy'.[36] Peter Ackroyd, searching in Anglo-Saxon England for the origins of the English imagination, speaks of a common 'fierce reticence', a 'brevity of understatement, fading into silence'. 'Instead of asking what is "modern" about the Anglo-Saxons', he urges, 'inquire instead what is Anglo-Saxon about "the modern".'[37] Think of Edward Gibbon confiding in a footnote: 'The portrait of Athanasius is one of the passages of my history with which I am the least dissatisfied.'

Only connect

> For every image of the past that is not recognized by the present as one of its own concerns threatens to disappear irretrievably.
>
> Walter Benjamin[38]

History matters in *Beowulf*. Old Hrothgar urges Beowulf to learn from the example of Heremod, a pre-Scylding king who became pathologically greedy and violent, and had to be removed:[39]

Breat bolgen-mod   beod-geneatas,
eaxl-gesteallan,   oþ þæt he ana hwearf,
mære þeoden   mon-dreamum from.
Ðeah þe hine mihtig God   mægenes wynnum,
eafeþum stepte   ofer ealle men,
forð gefremede,   hwæþere him on ferhþe greow
breost-hord blod-reow,   nallas beagas geaf
Denum æfter dome;   dreamleas gebad
þæt he þæs gewinnes   weorc þrowade,
leod-bealo longsum. (1713–22a)

(Enraged, he cut down his table-companions, his intimate comrades, until that famous prince turned away alone from human pleasures. Although mighty God exalted him in the joys of power and strength, advanced him over all men, nevertheless a bloodthirsty breast-hoard grew in his mind; not at all did he give rings to the Danes for their glory; he endured, joyless, to suffer the pain of that struggle, a long-lasting evil to his people.)

Hrothgar's lesson in leadership suggests that the poem, when new, had something to say to its contemporaries. But what can it tell us? In a moving essay, Gillian R. Overing cites the comment in the latest edition of Klaeber's work that 'perhaps the most important audience of all is the implied (or fictional) audience that is generated by the rhetorical action of the text itself with each and every reading of it'.[40] What can be said about *Beowulf* as a poem for our time? What does it say to and for our 'now'? How does the poem's history meet ours? Is intimacy with *Beowulf* desirable or even possible? For the poem refuses to stay put.

Beowulf in its early eleventh-century manuscript is already in transition, a poem making a progress through time. Oddly named strangers move through the work at different speeds, on different trajectories, some up, some down, all under a darkening sky. Stories arrive and depart with the suddenness of a summer cloudburst. Night-inhabiting fen creatures (the past in drag) mock human aspirations. A dragon rejoices in his wall. Nicholas Howe early stressed the need to 'recognize the subtle and inescapable interactions between the historical moment at which one writes as a critic and the historical moment about which one writes'.[41] The joy of communal celebration in *Beowulf* is shadowed, front and back, by images of loss and suffering. The poem concludes with an image of the hero's gold-rich barrow standing high and broad on its headland, a guide to sailors of the future. Earlier we were presented with another powerful image, of a woman fleeing war and enslavement, stripped of gold adornments and sick at heart, 'treading foreign paths, not once but often' (3019). No one promised that intimacy with *Beowulf* would be easy.

The large parties of *Beowulf* – the three monstrous beings at the heart of the poem – publicly got their due in J. R. R. Tolkien's influential lecture of 1936.[42] This Oxford don had learned Old English early, read the poem at a young age with schoolmates, and never lost his fondness for golden treasure and coiled dragons. Some time after 1920 he began a translation of *Beowulf*, finishing it in 1926 before putting it aside (and then fiddling with it for decades).

The translation and commentary were published in 2014 by his son, Christopher.[43] Why, wondered reviewers, had Tolkien not published his '*Beowulf*' himself? Joan Acocella in *The New Yorker* imagined that he didn't do so because the poem meant so much to him; it was his lodestar, his muse, and the thought of exposing it dressed by him to all comers was disquieting: 'Perhaps, in the dark of night, he already knew what would happen: that he would never publish his beautiful "*Beowulf*," and that his intimacy with the poem, more beautiful, would remain between him and the poet – a secret love.'[44] It is not difficult to date *Beowulf*. It has shown itself liberal and generous, some might even say promiscuous, in its attachments. But to have, like Tolkien, a deep, life-long relationship with the poem and want never to let it go – this is a bonding rare and, because inevitably one-sided, strangely moving.

Notes

1 F. Scott Fitzgerald, *The Great Gatsby* (New York: Scribner, 1925), p. 49.
2 See, for example, Bill Cooper, *After the Flood: the early post-Flood history of Europe traced back to Noah* (Chichester: New Wine Press, 1993). Grendel is already a Tyrannosaurus Rex in 'Beowulf the Mighty', a 1955 one-shot from Eastern Color comic artist Bill Ely.
3 See R. D. Fulk, Robert E. Bjork, and John D. Niles (eds), *Klaeber's Beowulf and the fight at Finnsburg*, corrected reprint of 4th edn (Toronto: University of Toronto Press, 2009), p. xcv. Citations are from this edition; all translations are mine. Frederick Klaeber famously used 'Lack of steady advance' as a subtitle (3rd edn, Boston: D. C. Heath and Co., 1950), p. lvii. In 1871 Lewis Carroll in *Through the looking glass* had introduced an Anglo-Saxon messenger whose similar way of progressing down a road – forward, twist, pause, leap – drew Alice's attention.
4 Franz Joseph Mone, 'Zur Kritik des Gedichts vom *Beowulf*', in *Untersuchungen zur Geschichte der teutschen Heldensage*, vol. 1 of 2nd series of the Bibliothek der gesammten deutschen national-literatur (Quedlinburg and Leipzig, 1836), pp. 129–36, at 130.
5 Alois Brandl, 'Die angelsächsische Literatur', *Grundriss der germanischen Philologie*, ed. Hermann Paul, 2nd edn (Strassburg, 1901–09), vol. 2, pt A, pp. 941–1134, at 1005. Issued separately with the same pagination: *Geschichte der angelsächsische Literatur* (Strassburg, 1908).
6 *The wonders of the East*, no. 20: 'Þonne hy fremdes cynnes mannan geseoð, þonne nemnað hy hyne ond his magas cuþra manna naman, ond mid leaslicum wordum hy hine beswicað ond hine gefoð, ond æfter

þan hy hine fretað ealne buton þon heafde ond þonne sittað ond wepað ofer þam heafde.' For Latin and Old English texts and translation, see Andy Orchard, *Pride and prodigies: studies in the monsters of the Beowulf-manuscript* (Cambridge: D. S. Brewer, 1995), pp. 175–203, at 196–7; also R. D. Fulk (ed. and trans.), *The 'Beowulf' manuscript: complete texts and the fight at Finnsburg*, Dumbarton Oaks Medieval Library, 3 (Cambridge, MA: Harvard University Press, 2010), pp. 16–31, at 24–5.

7 Eric Weiskott, 'Old English poetry, verse by verse', *ASE*, 44 (2015), 95–130, at 113.

8 See Marilyn Desmond, *Reading Dido: gender, textuality, and the medieval 'Aeneid'* (Minneapolis, MN: University of Minnesota Press, 1994), p. 34.

9 James Simpson, 'Chaucer as a European writer', in Seth Lerer (ed.), *The Yale companion to Chaucer* (New Haven, CT: Yale University Press, 2006), pp. 55–86, at 63.

10 Elizabeth Smart, *By Grand Central Station I sat down and wept* (London: Nicholson and Watson, 1945), pp. 28–9.

11 Alexander Pope, *An essay on criticism* (London, 1711), p. 10.

12 The standard discussion of Scylding analogues is Axel Olrik, *Danmarks heltedigtning: en oldtidsstudie*. Vol. 1. *Rolf Krake og den ældre Skjoldungrække* (Copenhagen: G.E.C. Gad, 1903); translated in Axel Olrik, *The heroic legends of Denmark*, trans. Lee M. Hollander (New York: The American-Scandinavian Foundation, Oxford University Press, 1919; repr. New York: Kraus, 1971). Also R. W. Chambers, *Beowulf: an introduction to the study of the poem with a discussion of the stories of Offa and Finn*, 3rd edn, with a supplement by C. L. Wrenn (Cambridge: Cambridge University Press, 1959). See, too, Walter A. Berendsohn, *Zur vorgeschichte des Beowulf* (Copenhagen: Levin and Munksgaard, 1935) and Frederick Klaeber's editions of the poem (1922–55). Convenient translations of the Scylding material can be found in G. N. Garmonsway and Jacqueline Simpson, *Beowulf and its analogues* (New York: Dutton, 1968); in Fulk, Bjork, and Niles (eds), *Klaeber's Beowulf*, pp. 291–315; and in John D. Niles and Marijane Osborn, *Beowulf and Lejre* (Tempe, AZ: ACMRS, 2007), pp. 297–387.

13 Andy Orchard, *A critical companion to Beowulf* (Cambridge: D. S. Brewer, 2003), p. 245; Thomas A. Shippey, *Beowulf* (London: Edward Arnold, 1978), p. 32.

14 Gísli Brynjúlfsson, 'Oldengelsk og oldnordisk', *Antikvarisk tidskrift för Sverige*, 4 (1852–54), 81–143, at 130; cited by Theodore M. Andersson, 'Sources and analogues', in Robert E. Bjork and John D. Niles (eds), *A Beowulf handbook* (Lincoln, NE: University of Nebraska Press, 1997), pp. 125–48, at 130.

15 N. F. S. Grundtvig, 'Et par ord om det nys udkomme angelsaeksiske Digt', *Nyeste Skilderie af Kjøbenhavn*, 60 (1815), cols. 945–52; Thomas A. Shippey and Andreas Haarder, *Beowulf: the critical heritage* (New

York: Routledge, 1998), pp. 108–13; Marijane Osborn, 'The Lejre connection in *Beowulf* scholarship', in Niles and Osborn, *Beowulf and Lejre*, pp. 287–93, at 287–8.

16 Ludvig Schrøder, *Om Bjovulfs-drapen: efter en række foredrag på folkehöjskolen i Askov* (Copenhagen: Karl Schønberg, 1875).

17 Dorothy Whitelock, *The audience of Beowulf* (Oxford: Clarendon Press, 1951), pp. 34–5; reprinted with same pagination in Dorothy Whitelock, *From Bede to Alfred: studies in early Anglo-Saxon literature and history* (London: Variorum Reprints, 1980).

18 Arthur Gilchrist Brodeur, *The art of Beowulf* (Berkeley, CA: University of California Press, 1959), p. 77, n. 5.

19 Marijane Osborn, 'Legends of Lejre, home of kings', in Niles and Osborn, *Beowulf and Lejre*, pp. 235–54, at 235.

20 James W. Earl, 'The forbidden *Beowulf*: haunted by incest', *PMLA*, 125 (2010), 289–305.

21 William Shakespeare, *The Tempest* (London, 1611), Act II, scene i.

22 On ring composition and other mnemotechnic designs in Old English verse, see Adeline Courtney Bartlett, *The larger rhetorical patterns in Anglo-Saxon poetry* (New York: Columbia University Press, 1935), pp. 9–29; Constance B. Hieatt, 'Envelope patterns and the structure of *Beowulf*', *English studies in Canada*, 1 (1975), 249–65; H. Ward Tonfeldt, 'Ring structure in *Beowulf*', *Neophilologus*, 61 (1977), 443–62; and John D. Niles, *Beowulf: the poem and its tradition* (Cambridge, MA: Harvard University Press, 1983), pp. 152–62.

23 The word used here for 'child' (*umbor*) occurs three times in Old English, twice in *Beowulf* as part of the probable compound *umborwesende*, 'being a child' (46b, 1187a). Its etymology is uncertain: it has been linked to both Gothic *wamba*, 'womb', and Latin *umbo*, 'boss' (of a shield) as well as 'navel'. ('Child', a word peculiar to English, may be related to Gothic *kilþei*, another word for 'womb'.) See Hans Schabram, 'Bemerkungen zur etymologie von ae. *umbor* "kind"', in *Florilegium linguisticum: Festschrift für Wolfgang P. Schmid zum 70. geburtstag*, ed. Eckhardt Eggers et al. (Frankfurt: Lang, 1990), pp. 403–14.

24 W. H. Auden, 'If I could tell you', in *Collected shorter poems 1927–1957* (New York: Random House, 1967), p. 201.

25 Many commentators take these lines to allude to the Heathobard feud, either Ingeld's assault on Heorot or, in the previous generation, his father's. Chambers, in his revision of A. J. Wyatt's edition (*Beowulf with the Finnsburg Fragment* [Cambridge: Cambridge University Press, 1914], note to lines 82–5), took lines 82b–83a to be an allusion to the burning of Hrothulf's hall in the course of Heoroweard's attack (a conflagration implied by Saxo). Marijane Osborn notes that 'three different occasions for such a fire are available in the traditions, each occurring in a different generation' (Osborn, 'Legends of Lejre, home of kings', p. 252).

26 Osborn, 'Legends of Lejre, home of kings', p. 253. *Klaeber's Beowulf* unaccountably omits Heoroweard from the Danish genealogical chart, p. lii.

27 The narrator calls this brief insert a *giedd*, 'tale, (formal) speech, (enigmatic) discourse'. Its eight lines include two examples of cross-alliteration involving royal Danish names (Hiorogar, 2158; Heoroweard, 2161) and a third featuring the gift itself (*breostgewædu*, 2162). See Scott Gwara, 'Paradigmatic wisdom in the native genre *giedd* in Old English', *Studi medievali*, 53 (2012), 783–851.

28 Leo Tolstoy, *War and peace*, trans. Louise and Aylmer Maude (Ware: Wordsworth Editions, 1993), p. 479.

29 This is the same Ingeld (Hinieldus) named in the 'pagan song' to which the Anglo-Saxon poet and scholar Alcuin objected in his much-cited letter of December 796. (Epistola 81 in W. Wattenbach and Ernst Dümmler [eds], *Monumenta Alcuiniana*, Bibliotheca rerum Germanicarum [Berlin: Weidmann, 1873; repr. 1964], VI, 357). See Mary Garrison, 'Quid Hinieldus cum Christo?', in Katherine O'Brien O'Keeffe and Andy Orchard (eds), *Latin learning and English lore: studies in Anglo-Saxon literature for Michael Lapidge*, 2 vols (Toronto: University of Toronto Press, 2005), vol. 1, pp. 237–59. On the Old Norse side, see Russell Poole, 'Some southern perspectives on Starcatherus', *Viking and medieval Scandinavia*, 2 (2006), 141–66.

30 The poet's artful alliteration in this passage was noted in Orchard, *A critical companion to Beowulf*, pp. 241–2.

31 David Cronenberg and C. E. Pogue, *The fly*, directed by David Cronenberg, 20th Century Fox, 1986.

32 'Hroþwulf ond Hroðgar heoldon longest/ sibbe ætsomne suhtorfædran, / siþþan hy forwræcon Wicinga cynn / ond Ingeldes ord forbigdan, / forheowan æt Heorote Heaðobeardna þrym' (*Widsith*, lines 45–9). Cf. Shakespeare's Pistol garbling Christopher Marlowe's 'holla, ye pampered jades of Asia' as 'And hollow pampered jades of Asia'.

33 The compound here rendered 'chief kinsman' is plural in the manu-scripts; the translation 'Randvér's chief kinsmen', referring to the dynasty of the Goths, would be just as ominous. Finnur Jónsson (ed.), *Den norsk-islandske skjaldedigtning*, 4 vols (Copenhagen: Gyldendal, 1908–15), the standard edition of skaldic poetry for the past century, is being replaced by a new edition of the corpus in nine volumes. For Bragi's stanzas edited by Margaret Clunies Ross, see now Kari Ellen Gade (ed.), *Poetry from Treatises on Poetics, Part 1*, Skaldic Poetry of the Scandinavian Middle Ages 3 (Turnhout: Brepols, 2017), pp. 31–3, 36–8.

34 Seamus Heaney, 'Whatever you say say nothing', *North: poems* (New York: Farrar, Straus, and Giroux, 1975).

35 On the humorous potential of litotes in *Beowulf*, see Frederick Bracher, 'Understatement in Old English poetry', *PMLA*, 52 (1937), 915–34.

See also Roberta Frank, 'The incomparable wryness of Old English poetry', in John Walmsley (ed.), *Inside Old English: essays in honour of Bruce Mitchell* (Oxford: Blackwell, 2006), pp. 59–73; and most recently, Stephen Graham, '"So what did the Danes feel?" Emotion and litotes in Old English poetry', in Alice Jorgensen, Frances McCormack, and Jonathan Wilcox (eds), *Anglo-Saxon emotions: reading the heart in Old English language, literature and culture* (Farnham: Ashgate, 2015), pp. 75–90, and bibliography therein.

36 Murray Gell-Mann, *The quark and the jaguar: adventures in the simple and the complex* (New York: W. H. Freeman, 1994), p. 26.

37 Peter Ackroyd, *Albion: the origins of the English imagination* (London: Chatto and Windus, 2002), p. 45.

38 Thesis 5 of Walter Benjamin's 1940 *Theses on the philosophy of history*, ed. Hannah Arendt, trans. Harry Zohn, in Benjamin, *Illuminations: essays and reflections* (New York: Schocken Books, 1969), p. 255.

39 A black-garbed professor provides similar guidance on Scylding legends in the cartoon series by Claus Deleuran, *Illustreret Danmarkshistorie for folket* (Copenhagen: Ekstra Bladets Forlag, 1992), vol. 5. Hrothgar's lengthy *memento mori* advice to Beowulf is comparable to the similar reminders directed from time to time to a general in a Roman triumph – if such a tradition had existed before Tertullian publicized it; see Mary Beard, *The Roman triumph* (Cambridge, MA: Harvard University Press, 2007), pp. 85–92.

40 *Klaeber's Beowulf*, p. clxxxviii; Gillian R. Overing, '*Beowulf*: a poem in our time', in Clare A. Lees (ed.), *The Cambridge history of early medieval English literature* (Cambridge: Cambridge University Press, 2013), pp. 309–31, at 309.

41 Nicholas Howe, 'Historicist approaches', in Katherine O'Brien O'Keeffe (ed.), *Reading Old English texts* (Cambridge: Cambridge University Press, 1997), pp. 79–100, at 80.

42 J. R. R. Tolkien, '*Beowulf*: the monsters and the critics', Sir Israel Gollancz Memorial Lecture, *Proceedings of the British Academy*, 22 (1936), 245–95.

43 J. R. R. Tolkien, *Beowulf: a translation and commentary*, ed. Christopher Tolkien (Boston: Houghton Mifflin Harcourt, 2014).

44 Joan Acocella, 'Slaying monsters: Tolkien's *Beowulf*', *The New Yorker*, 2 June 2014, pp. 70–6, at 76.

4

Beowulf as Wayland's work: thinking, feeling, making

James Paz

> But send thou to Hygelac, if the war have me,
> The best of all war-shrouds that now my breast wardeth,
> The goodliest of railings, the good gift of Hrethel,
> The hand-work of Weland.
> *Tale of Beowulf*, trans. William Morris[1]

I have long been enamoured with the material culture of *Beowulf*, with the lovely and almost loving descriptions of swords, helms, cups, tapestries, coats of mail, hoards of gold. More recently, I have become intrigued by the craftworkers behind these artefacts, the carpenters, masons, weavers and embroiderers, glassworkers and leatherworkers, and especially the smiths. But what have solid, inanimate artefacts and the hard, manual labour that goes into making those artefacts got to do with intimacy? How can we think about feeling through making?

One of the challenges of this collection is to read *Beowulf* in a more personal way. Although I had not given it much thought before, this challenge made me wonder whether my own working-class background might lie behind my love for the artefactual. I am a first-generation scholar, the first in my family to attend university, let alone pursue postgraduate studies. The norm was for men to leave school at sixteen (or younger) and find a trade, which they would remain in for the rest of their lives. My entry into middle-class academia might be viewed as a 'success story' or as evidence of 'upward' social mobility, and I am grateful for the chances that have been given to me, for being able to follow pathways that were not always open to those who came before me. In many ways, I feel more at home in the library than in the workshop. The pleasure I take from reading and writing feels innate. My hands are soft, not rough and gnarled. But for working-class students and scholars, academic achievement can come at a cost. With success comes self-doubt. The sudden transition from working class to middle class, from manual labour to the life of the mind, can leave you feeling ill at ease in both social groups, an impostor caught between two worlds, a class traitor, a kind of border-walker or *mearcstapa*.[2] The language of academia, its many unwritten rules and mysterious rituals, can seem impenetrable to someone who is late to the party. You are perpetually playing catch up with those who have benefited from expensive educations or who have accumulated years of cultural capital. Equally, I do not possess the technical skills that many members of my family, past and present, possessed, and I worry that, by embracing academia and using education to 'rise above' a life of physical labour, I am tacitly endorsing an ideology that devalues the kind of work that is carried out with tools as opposed to books.

Is there a way to reconcile these two aspects of my identity? Perhaps unconsciously, I have been drawn to ideas that trouble the dichotomies of head and hand, manual and intellectual work, thinking and making. The first academic article that I published attempted to theorize things in *Beowulf*.[3] Inspired by Bill Brown's call to complicate concrete things with abstract theory (and vice versa) and by Jane Bennett's insistence on the vibrancy and agency of even the most inanimate of things,[4] I found a way not only to think about the artefacts represented in *Beowulf* but also to recognize that these things could actively shape the events of the poem. Material culture was no longer below, marginal or irrelevant to my academic study of Old English literature, but at the centre of it. I pursued this interest in my first monograph and, in the process of researching this work, found myself drawn to Tim Ingold's book on *Making*.[5] Ingold argues for a way of thinking through making in which sentient practitioners and active materials correspond with each in the generation of form. When we engage in acts of making we realize our existence as part of an active material environment, so that the craftsperson 'couples his own movements and gestures – indeed his very life – with the becoming of his materials'.[6] The craftworker does not necessarily impose a preconceived form upon raw materials but allows those materials to shape his or her thoughts. Understood in this way, craft unites manual and intellectual labour. Craft is making and thinking at the same time, hands and head, mind and materials, together.

In both popular and academic spheres, craft is experiencing one of the periodic revivals that have recurred in industrialized societies from the nineteenth century onwards.[7] While current trends for artisanal, hand-made goods could be accused of commodifying both the concept and the products of craftwork, packaging and selling everything from craft beer to home-made candles at high prices, previous craft movements were more explicitly connected to progressive politics. Contemporary 'craft' is indebted to the Arts and Crafts movement that emerged in Britain around 1880, but the so-called hipster subculture does not always share the revolutionary spirit that characterized the ideas of (among others) the famous medievalist and translator of *Beowulf*, William Morris, who looked back to the figure of the medieval craftsman as a way of advocating traditional handicrafts, positioning the beauty and pleasure of craftwork against the evils of modern industry. Morris helped to promote a picture of medieval craftsmen who had control over their labouring activity, more opportunity to exhibit individual talent, and who identified wholeheartedly with their work. As a committed socialist reformer, Morris was influenced by the Marxist notion that craft labour involves specialized processes and skills tied to particular materials, its products designed to satisfy local needs. With the transition from handicraft production to industry, both activity and product become more abstract and universal, and the relation of subject to object in work is further mediated and distanced.[8] Although Marx and Engels were critical of medieval feudalism, Morris's version of revolutionary socialism often looked back rather than forward, participating in a working-class strand of medievalism which focused on an imagined lost world of workers' rights and liberties.[9] For Morris and many others since him, myself included, craft is not only a skill but an idea that engenders intense yearning. Looking back to medieval craft and craftsmen, and promoting a return to their practices, is a way of answering a desire for a more embodied, sensual relationship with materials and tools, a more creative experience of work, and the satisfaction of shaping and constructing things from beginning to end.

We can begin to see, then, some of the ways in which craftwork might offer a more intimate understanding of makers and making. 'Solid' artefacts are constructed from active materials by sentient craftsmen whose 'hard' labour is skilled, individualized, and thoughtful. Richard Sennett defines 'craft' far more broadly than skilled manual labour, taking issue with Hannah Arendt's theory that the human mind only engages once labour is done. Rather than separating work into two domains (in one we ask 'how?' and in the other we ask 'why?') Sennett strives for a more balanced view, whereby thinking and feeling are contained within the process of making.[10] Technique need not be a mechanical activity, for craftworkers can feel fully and think deeply about what they are doing once they do it well.[11] When adopting this utopian view of craft, however, we should be careful not to downplay the difficult, painstaking, and sometimes painful labour that craftworkers carry out. The casual association of craft with pleasure or amateurish 'play' rather than 'work' can also lead to misleading assumptions about gender, in which modes of work traditionally assigned to women get dismissed as mere arts and crafts. Spinning and weaving, for instance, are often relegated to the status of hobbies or leisurely, domestic pastimes rather than professional skills. As capitalism draws clear divisions between the workplace and the household, these skills remain undervalued and underpaid.

The popular historian Alexander Langlands has attempted to explain how 'craft' acquired some of this considerable cultural baggage. Langlands recovers the lost, early English meaning of *cræft* and resurrects the ancient craftworkers who fused exquisite skill with back-breaking labour. Rather than seeing craft as a nostalgic retreat from everyday reality, Langlands suggests that a return to an older sense of *cræft* can heighten our awareness of the environment, expand our sensory experiences, and improve our interactions with materials.[12] *Cræft* is indeed an Old English word, whose meaning ranges from the power, might, or strength of body, to an art, skill, ability, or trade, to craft of mind, knowledge, or cunning.[13] In Old English usage, the term *cræft* conveys a sense of mental ability as much as physical skill. Definitions also slide between craft as talent, or even virtue, and craft as cunning.[14] In *Beowulf*, *cræft* is often used to refer to heroic strength and prowess, as when the poet praises Beowulf for controlling his God-given might (2181). At other times, it is used to express a sense of cunning or secret plotting, as when the poet admonishes those who would conspire against kinsmen (2168). *Cræft* could carry gendered connotations in Anglo-Saxon culture, too, including the familiar association between women and textile production.[15] In *Beowulf*, weaving imagery contributes to the characterization of noblewomen such as Wealhtheow, who metaphorically 'weaves peace' among the warriors through her actions (passing mead and distributing treasure) and speeches (defusing tensions and reminding men of their obligations). Unlike in modern biases, literal and symbolic weaving is not relegated to 'domestic' labour. The mead-hall is not a domestic space but a political one and, as critics such as Stacy S. Klein have pointed out, the peace-weaving metaphor demands that one redefine the place allotted to the domestic within the heroic ethos: weaving is as central to the construction of a warrior culture as weapons are.[16]

Yet if we expect *Beowulf* to fulfil the yearnings of our modern craft movements, offering us idealized images of labourers engaged in intimate, embodied acts of making and taking pleasure in their work, then we will be disappointed. On the rare occasions that skilled craftworkers do appear in the poem, they are elusive characters, their names and deeds passed over swiftly. Printed editions and translations of *Beowulf* are often accompanied by images from Anglo-Saxon material culture, and it is common practice to use items from the Sutton Hoo treasures or the Staffordshire Hoard as visual aids when teaching the poem. A helmet or sword hilt might be used to illustrate relationships among the elite, male, warrior class, while glass vessels or drinking horns might prompt discussions about the roles of aristocratic women or the nuances of gender.[17] Artefacts within the poem, and their extant counterparts outside of the poem, are made to speak about the human communities they create and sustain, but those communities constitute the upper ranks of heroic society. Traditionally, these artefacts are analysed for the ways in which they confirm bonds of loyalty between lords and retainers in a system of gift exchange, but the makers of these gifts are not afforded great significance and the agency of the things themselves is downplayed.[18] The conduct of men and women of the ruling class becomes our main focus, the purpose for putting material things on display. Treasures, weapons, and armour are brought into the foreground, but their real or imagined makers recede into the background.[19]

Scholars and teachers of *Beowulf* usually allow its aristocratic figures to take centre stage. There are good reasons for doing so, of course: they are reading *with* the poem rather than *against* it. This is what the text wants from us. For example, early in the poem, Hrothgar is given credit for conceiving and constructing Heorot. The hall enters the king's mind and so he hands down orders for anonymous 'men' from far and wide to build this great wonder. Hrothgar, not the workers, gets to name and rule in Heorot, dealing out gifts to his followers within its walls (67–81). Later on, when Beowulf and Grendel are fighting in Heorot, we are told that the building withstood their battle-rage because it had been braced and bound with the finest of smith-work: 'ac he þæs fæste wæs / innan ond utan iren-bendum / searoþoncum besmiþod' (but it was so sturdy, within and without, skilfully forged with iron bands) (773b–5a).[20] Again, these anonymous smiths are alluded to but not dwelt upon by the poet. The same is true for other kinds of craftworkers, including the unnamed embroiderers responsible for the golden wall-hangings that adorn Heorot, said to be wondrous to all who gaze upon them (991–6). Weaving metaphors might illuminate the political roles of high-ranking women in the poem, but the actual process of textile production does not warrant prolonged attention.

One reason that we tend to accept the apparent irrelevance of these smiths and other labourers is because historicism has long been the prevailing mode of *Beowulf* criticism, leading to the assumption that the text means whatever it meant to the 'original' author or audience during the historical period when the work was composed. As Chris Jones has pointed out, this explains the emphasis placed on the more traditional kind of 'dating' of the poem in *Beowulf* studies.[21] For the purposes of this chapter, at least, I would rather not date *Beowulf*. My aim is to rebuff the aristocratic ideals of the poem and instead read it with and through my own working-class identity and my interest in makers, making, and material culture. How to resist the dominant viewpoint of the poem, which fixates upon heroic exploits but dismisses skilled labourers as marginal to the main narrative? First, I will explore how the products of craftwork – vibrant materials constructed by sentient practitioners – shape the heroic culture of the poem. Noble, male warriors may be thrust to the forefront of the narrative, but their reputations and relationships could not exist without material things. Indeed, these things often play active or even subversive roles in the poem, especially in those moments when they fail, break, or misbehave. Second, I will bring the fleeting allusions to craftsmen such as Wayland the Smith to the surface of the text, examining the tensions that the text represses by keeping the makers hidden in the shadows. The figure of the smith is potentially disruptive, I argue, because smiths possess a mysterious *cræft* that gives them the power to shape heroic culture yet exist outside of it in ways that are not always available to a warrior-king such as Beowulf.

Heroes need makers to make them into heroes. While the narrative of *Beowulf* follows the adventures of the eponymous warrior, the poem also lingers over human-made things. The three monster fights that Beowulf engages in shape our understanding of the 'plot', but anyone who reads the poem closely will get caught up in its detailed descriptions of swords, helmets, mail-coats, cups, rings, and necklaces. Similarly, the abstract concept of heroism (and the ideals and emotions such as glory, bravery, honour, and loyalty that help to construct this concept) must be materialized repeatedly through artefacts. Aaron Hostetter has recently argued that, in *Beowulf*, powerful 'things' often stand in the way of the story and its actors, momentarily capturing and diverting the course of the narrative. These things 'interrupt the legend of the greatness of human deeds, in favour of a meditation on the status of the material world'.[22]

In revenge for her son's death at the hands of Beowulf, Grendel's mother attacks Heorot and slays King Hrothgar's most trusted counsellor, Æschere, leaving his severed head on display at the mere's edge as a sign of her vengeance. In the scene shortly after Beowulf, Hrothgar, and his men find Æschere's head on the cliffside, Beowulf demonstrates his worth by bravely entering the serpent-infested lake where Grendel's mother dwells. Before Beowulf enters the water, however, the poet takes the time to construct his heroism, bit by bit, artefact by artefact, through a lengthy description in which each piece of armour or weaponry is singled out, said to be skilfully made by smiths of old, and endowed with a heroic duty:

```
                Gyrede hine Beowulf
eorlgewædum,    nalles for ealdre mearn.
Scolde herebyrne    hondum gebroden,
sid ond searofah,    sund cunnian,
seo ðe bancofan    beorgan cuþe,
þæt him hildegrap    hreþre ne mihte,
eorres inwitfeng,    aldre gesceþðan;
ac se hwita helm    hafelan werede,
se þe meregrundas    mengan scolde,
secan sundgebland    since geweorðad,
befongen freawrasnum,    swa hine fyrndagum
worhte wæpna smið,    wundrum teode,
besette swinlicum,    þæt hine syðþan no
brond ne beadomecas    bitan ne meahton.
Næs þæt þonne mætost    mægenfultuma
þæt him on ðearfe lah    ðyle Hroðgares.
Wæs þæm hæftmece    Hrunting nama.
Þæt wæs an foran    ealdgestreona.
Ecg wæs iren,    atertanum fah,
ahyrded heaþoswate.    Næfre hit æt hilde ne swac
manna ængum    þara þe hit mid mundum bewand,
se ðe gryresiðas    gegan dorste,
folcstede fara.    Næs þæt forma sið
þæt hit ellenweorc    æfnan scolde. (1441b–64)
```

(Unafraid for his own life, Beowulf adorned himself with noble attire. The hand-linked battle-shirt, broad and cunningly crafted, would seek the lake-bed, for it knew how to defend his bone-coffer, so that his foe's grasp, a fiendish grip, could not harm his heart. His head was guarded by the bright helmet, which would explore the depths of the mere, the whirling waters: it was enhanced with riches, reinforced with wires, as weapon-smiths had wrought it in days of old, wondrously embellished, emblazoned with boar-images, so that afterwards neither fire-brand nor battle-sword could do it damage. Not least among his mighty supports was the weapon which Hrothgar's spokesman had lent him in his need. Hrunting was the name of that long-hilted sword, foremost of ancient heirlooms. Its edges were iron, decorated with poisonous patterns, tempered with battle-blood. Never had it betrayed any man who wielded it in war, those who had risked terrible travels, taken the field against foes. That was not the first time that it had performed a courageous deed.)

We are told that Beowulf is brave because he does not fear for his life, but this is coterminous with putting on war-gear. The reader might casually assume that the courage to enter the monster-haunted mere comes from within the hero, but, upon closer inspection, Beowulf draws each aspect of his fortitude from the external things he is putting on. It is the hand-made, skilfully crafted mail-shirt that will explore the depths of the mere (1443–4). It is the bright helmet, the wondrously decorated work of smiths from a former age, that will plunge through swirling waves and protect its wearer from weapons (1448–54). The sword Hrunting will aid the hero's strength and carry out a courageous deed, as it has done in the past (1455–64). Discussing this passage, Gillian Overing observes that each item is 'imbued with the capacity to think independently about its function, and even possesses a degree of interiority'.[23] Action and intention are attributed to these artefacts: they *cunnian* (search, venture, explore), *cunnan* (know how, have the power to), *secan* (look for, seek out), and *æfnan* (perform, execute, labour).

This scene accentuates the physical intimacy between the body of the hero and the armour he wears in battle. Flesh and metal are closely connected. Bravery and resilience are borrowed from helms, mail-coats, and swords. Yet at other times in the narrative, a sense of disconnection between warrior and weapon is conveyed. Unlike craftsmen who work with active materials through different stages of production, heroes simply inherit weapons and armour. Swords such as Hrunting and Nægling have histories that extend beyond the lifespan of an individual person and, accordingly, these things can display an agency or even willpower that is not always in sync with the will of the hero. This is especially true in the later parts of the poem.

After a gap of fifty years, Beowulf has become an aged king who must do battle with a fire-breathing dragon ravaging his kingdom. Beowulf is still depicted as a capable fighter, willing to face the dragon himself, but he is not the young warrior he once was. He depends upon ever more armoury to defeat each monster (no weapons against Grendel, two swords against Grendel's mother, two swords and a shield against the dragon) and yet experiences ever more difficulty in achieving success.[24] At the same time as appearing more physically vulnerable, Beowulf begins to appear mentally vulnerable, too. The ageing Beowulf, nearing death and sensing doom, is suddenly less assured and more anxious. When news of the dragon reaches him, Beowulf worries that he has offended God and his 'breost innan weoll / þeostrum geþoncum, swa him geþywe ne wæs' (breast surged inside him with dark thoughts, as was not his way) (2331b–2). As if in response to this unaccustomed self-doubt, Beowulf orders an all-iron shield to be made for his use (2337–41).

Beowulf remembers how he survived by his own strength in his youth. Now that he is old, he remains brave in battle but must go forth against the dragon in a mail-shirt, behind a shield (2512–24). The king is at pains to stress that the dragon's flaming breath is the only reason for his reliance on armour and weapons, but, in the speeches before his final fight, he shows an awareness of his own mortality. The solid endurance of metal artefacts stands firm against the fragility of ageing flesh. When Beowulf needs them most, however, his weapons stubbornly refuse to perform their part. In the midst of the fray, with the dragon rushing towards him, Beowulf finds that 'Scyld wel gebearg / life ond lice læssan hwile / mærum þeodne þonne his myne sohte' (The shield defended the life and body of the famous king for less time than he had intended) (2570b–2). Beowulf raises his sword, but 'Hond up abræd / Geata dryhten, gryrefahne sloh / incgelafe, þæt sio ecg gewac / brun on bane, bat unswiðor / þonne his ðiodcyning þearfe hæfde, / bysigum gebæded' (The lord of the Geats raised his arm, struck the hideously patterned one with his sword, but its blade was blunted by the bone, bit less keenly than the desperate king had need of) (2575b–80). At these crucial moments, the intimate link between warrior and weapon is sundered. Objects that Beowulf believed he could count on cease to work for him, asserting their 'thing-power' and breaking into the foreground of the narrative.[25] These things emerge as characters rather than props, exhibiting a will of their own. The shield does not meet the hero's expectations, acting in defiance of his intentions. The sword, too, does not cut as deeply as the hero desires, betraying its wielder, as it never should have.

When Beowulf throws all of his strength behind a sword stroke, we are told that 'Nægling forbærst' (Nægling broke apart) (2680b). Even though this is because the hero's hand is too strong, the poet still criticizes the blade for letting Beowulf down: 'geswac æt sæcce sweord Biowulfes' (Beowulf's sword failed him in battle) (2681b). Blame is removed from the king. Failure is attributed to the sword and shield, distracting us from the hero's flaws and transferring them on to his weapons. The narrator grants artefacts agency, even endows them with heroic characteristics, while still striving to maintain the hero's reputation. Underlying class tensions begin to surface here. Swords and shields exist to 'serve' their aristocratic wielders, and therefore material breakage or damage is represented, in moral terms, as a failure of duty. The narrator reprimands them as a haughty master might reprimand an idle or negligent servant. Conversely, if these personified weapons were to perform too well in battle – that is, if victory were ascribed to the strength of the shield or the cutting edge of the blade – then the heroic qualities embodied by Beowulf would be diminished. Ultimately, the work of the craftsman cannot be allowed to eclipse the deeds of the nobleman. Artefacts and, by extension, their makers are pitted against warriors and found wanting.

If aristocratic warriors rely on material artefacts to perform heroic deeds, they also rely on them to form bonds with one another. In perhaps the most intimate scene in the poem, a dying Beowulf sits on the edge of the barrow while Wiglaf washes his lord's wounds. Knowing that he has little time left in this world, Beowulf begins to speak:

'Nu ic suna minum   syllan wolde
guðgewædu,   þær me gifeðe swa
ænig yrfeweard   æfter wurde
lice gelenge.' (2729–32)

('Now I would give this war-gear to my son, if any heir to my body, living after me, had been granted.')

Reflecting on the son he never fathered, Beowulf suddenly takes on the role of a parent wanting to bestow material possessions on a child. The ability to pass temporal riches on to the next generation

is, of course, a privilege of the highborn. But it is hard not to feel
a pang of sympathy for the lonely hero in this moment. In the
absence of a wife and children, deserted by all but one of his followers, all that Beowulf has left are the treasures he has won. Even
the name of the one remaining loyal thegn, Wiglaf, 'the leavings
of war', evokes images of spolia. The final exchanges between
Beowulf and Wiglaf are emotive, yet these acts of touching and
looking and speaking are mediated by artefacts. It is difficult to
imagine these scenes without the presence of things. Beowulf and
Wiglaf would have nothing to gaze upon, if not for the sight of the
glittering treasure. Words would remain unspoken, if not provoked
by handfuls of gold. Memories remain unremembered, if not induced
by rituals of gift giving. The two warriors would scarcely touch
each other, if not for the unbuckling of a helmet, the passing on
of a neck-ring and mail-coat:

> Dyde him of healse   hring gyldenne
> þioden þristhydig,   þegne gesealde,
> geongum garwigan,   goldfahne helm,
> beah ond byrnan,   het hyne brucan well (2809–12)

(The bold-minded lord unclasped the golden ring from his neck,
gave it to his thegn, the young spearman, also his gold-adorned helm
and mail-coat, ordered him to use them well)

Artefacts thus shape the aristocratic culture of the poem, giving
material form to abstract ideals, imbuing warriors with bravery,
sometimes asserting their own agency in the heat of battle, but also
substantiating intimate bonds of loyalty and kinship. Despite the
omnipresence of human-made things in *Beowulf*, however, the
craftworkers themselves do not leave an impression on the poem.
Can these makers be identified? Can their narratives be uncovered?
If so, what other perspectives and viewpoints might we find embedded within the text?

For James W. Earl, *Beowulf* has its 'deep silences – so much is
left unsaid! – in which we can hardly help but read ourselves, and
out of which we draw our interpretations'.[26] As I have indicated,
the poem is usually silent about the smiths who fashioned the
wondrous weapons wielded by Beowulf. The one exception is the
character from Germanic legend, Wayland the Smith, who is at
least named and acknowledged in lines 452–5. Yet even in the case
of Wayland, the poem is largely silent about who exactly this legendary metalworker was. All we can infer is that he was some kind of

master craftsman. Fortunately, other Anglo-Saxon and Scandinavian sources are not so reticent about Wayland, so I will draw on these sources to interpret line 455. But I would also like to read an aspect of myself into this silence.

Beowulf is a poem obsessed with genealogy but, as Clare Lees argues, its focus is 'narrowly circumscribed' and works to concentrate social power in a few male hands.[27] When I read my own ancestry into the silence of line 455, however, other interpretative possibilities are forged. My grandmother on my mum's side of the family died shortly before I took up my first permanent academic post. She left behind a box of handwritten notes, letters, photographs, birth and death certificates, and a family tree sketched on a large sheet of paper. This document traced the Coles (the maiden name of my great grandmother on my mum's side of the family) back to the 1700s. Only the bare bones of names, dates, and occupations had been recorded, but the listed occupations reveal a history of black-smiths and other metalworkers on that side of the family, stretching back to Charles Coles (d. 1830), who worked as a blacksmith in Portsmouth dockyard in the early nineteenth century.[28] I mention this not to try and build a direct bridge between the smiths in my own family and those of early medieval England – a wide river of time still separates these two worlds – but to try and make some sense of my interest in the makers and workers of *Beowulf*. The positions from which we read and interpret literary texts are often informed by our political, moral, and ethical views – but they can be shaped by our personal and familial narratives, too.

For this particular reader, then, the fleeting glimpse that the *Beowulf* poet gives us into Wayland's work sparks a set of associations that are at once personal and historical, igniting memories of the recent as well as the more distant past, feelings of grief as well as intellectual curiosity. I cannot help but linger over line 455, resisting the forward momentum of the poem. *Beowulf* is famous for its so-called digressions, but, in this instance, it wants us to move on from this allusion to a smith and acquiesce with the poet's preoc-cupation with heroic exploits. But, if I may be allowed a digression of my own, I want to follow my own fascination with Wayland.

Wayland is difficult to love. He thwarts attempts to read him, nostalgically, as a pre-industrial craftsperson or, romantically, as a working-class hero. I confess to a degree of admiration for this maker who uses his craft to engineer a way out of enforced subor-dination, escaping the bonds of servitude and taking grisly revenge on his captor along the way. I also admit to a strong repulsion from this cunning manipulator, who uses and abuses others, murdering boys and raping a woman, to achieve his ends. Above all, what I find most compelling about Wayland is his subversive potential. He raises questions about the 'heroic' ethos. He slides between different social ranks. He poses problems for aristocratic fighters who would seek to dominate labourers in their service.

Taken in isolation, the allusion to *Welandes geweorc* in *Beowulf* suggests that the smith exists solely to aid aristocratic characters. The reference comes early in the narrative, when Beowulf first enters Heorot, presenting himself to King Hrothgar as a warrior worthy of defeating Grendel. Directly before Beowulf begins a speech setting out his credentials, we are told that 'on him byrne scan, / searonet seowed smiþes orþancum' (on him the mail-shirt shone, a corselet linked with a smith's cunning) (405b–6). As he concludes his speech, Beowulf himself makes it clear that this is not the work of a regular smith: 'þæt is Hrædlan laf, / Welandes geweorc' ('that is Hrethel's heirloom, Wayland's work') (454b–5a). Not yet established as a hero of epic proportions, and in need of credibility, Beowulf cites Wayland's name to firm up his own reputation. We have another example of the hero depending upon the products of the craftsperson, but, when probed further, the name *Weland* summons a more socially disruptive power, a form of *cræft* that will not be restrained by class hierarchies.

The legend of Wayland tells of a smith who lives with his two brothers and their swan-maiden wives until the otherworldly women abandon their husbands, never to return. Wayland's brothers pursue their wives, but Wayland remains behind, sitting alone and hammering red gold on his anvil. The greedy King Niðhad captures Wayland while the smith is vulnerable and severs the sinews behind his knees, hamstringing the smith to prevent him from escaping. King Niðhad imprisons Wayland on an island and forces him to work as a royal craftsman. Sleep-deprived, Wayland beats away with his hammer day and night, creating trinkets for the king. It is not long before Wayland takes revenge on Niðhad by killing the king's sons when they visit his forge. Wayland then transforms their skulls into silver goblets, their eyes into gleaming gems, their teeth into brooches, and sends the beautifully crafted artefacts, made from the body parts of the boys, to their unsuspecting family members. Later, King Niðhad's daughter, Beadohild, brings Wayland her (formerly his) golden ring to repair, but the smith gives her drugged beer and rapes her while she is unconscious, impregnating her. Finally, Wayland crafts a pair of wings from magical feathers, before rising into the air, boasting of his revenge to a distraught King Niðhad, and flying away.[29]

Wayland's story shows that a craftsman can play the leading role in a thrilling, albeit gruesome narrative. What is more, the tale in its fuller form reveals how much subversive power is packed into that formulaic phrase, *Welandes geweorc*. Whereas in *Beowulf* smiths serve kings, their handiwork bolstering heroic reputations, the legend of Wayland brings latent tensions that might have existed between rulers and makers to the surface. Here, the relationship between king and smith is fraught with hostility and resentment, abuses of power and a desire for vengeance. In the first part of the tale, Wayland shares an intimate bond with his craftwork and its products. Alone and abandoned, he makes copies of the golden ring that his swan-wife gave him in the hope that she might return some day. The repetitive labour appears to be his way of coping with heartbreak, the ring a materialization of his lost love. Then, when the smith is captured by King Niðhad, Wayland becomes alienated from his own labour, as he is forced to turn the products of his craft over to a social superior. The oppressed soon becomes the oppressor, as Wayland draws on his craft and cunning to avenge himself on his captors. Wayland repays Niðhad's greed for treasures with goblets, gems, and brooches made from his dead sons, using the craft of concealment to deceive the king. The smith uses his cunning to trick Beadohild, too, by hiding drugs in her goblet of beer and taking advantage of her unconscious state. Having been emasculated, the maimed Wayland still manages to unman King Niðhad by the end of the story. Ever the craftsman, Wayland even uses prosthesis, in the form of artificial wings, to transform and enhance his hamstrung body and escape through flight.

Wayland the Smith is a skilled worker who makes the most of his *cræft* but, in many ways, he is a far cry from the utopian ideals of the modern craft movements outlined at the beginning of this chapter. Wayland does have a certain 'revolutionary' appeal insofar as he utilizes *cræft* (both manual and mental skill) to rebel against a king. Even so, it is difficult to read Wayland as the kind of idealized medieval craftsman imagined by William Morris. Of course, the concept of *cræft* was already being redefined in a more favourable light long before the Arts and Crafts movement of the nineteenth century. It could be argued that the translations associated with King Alfred and his circle pushed the meaning of *cræft* towards the more positive connotations that it retains in modern English. According to Peter Clemoes, *cræft* was one of Alfred's favourite words.[30] Alfred saw a craft as an inborn talent to serve a moral purpose. What the talented individual needed was the wisdom to understand the appropriate end and to render the talent accordingly effective. Nicole Discenza adds that Alfred treats labour as comparable to more spiritual strivings, in that both fulfil the responsibilities given one by God.[31] For Maria Sachiko Cecire, Alfred's conception of *cræft* as a moral good anticipates the Protestant work ethic (theorized by Max Weber) in which industry serves as a form of Christian piety.[32] Wayland fits the model of individualized, inborn talent well enough, but otherwise the legendary smith's *cræft* does not really satisfy Alfred's definition of the term. Wayland is a morally ambiguous pagan figure who, rather than directing his talent towards service of the Christian God, largely uses his *cræft* for revenge and personal gain. He embodies the darker sense of craft as 'craftiness'. Wayland's subversive power derives, in part, from his ability to withhold knowledge and conceal things from his regal captors. Similarly, the *Beowulf* poet insinuates that smiths are crafty craftsmen by describing the mail-shirt worn by Beowulf, and made by Wayland, as a 'searonet seowed smiþes orþancum' (a corselet linked with a smith's cunning) (406). This description balances a sense of wonder with suspicion, for the terms *orþanc* and *searu* can be applied to devices wrought with ingenuity but also to schemes or machinations contrived with treachery.[33]

Although the work of Wayland is worn and used by figures from the heroic age, he is said to make the same things that real Anglo-Saxon smiths might have made. The status of these craftsmen in Anglo-Saxon England is revealing. In the 1997 Toller Lecture, David Hinton argued that there was often something liminal or 'other' about the smith.[34] Socially, they were able to act as intermediaries between lord and churl. This ability to communicate between social ranks could win them favour with the kings or rulers they were bound to. There is archaeological evidence suggesting that the iron-working complexes in which smiths practised their craft were kept apart, at a slight distance from living areas. Functional explanations for this would include proximity to fuel and the removal of a source of danger from fire. But it would have also had the effect of distancing smiths and their skills from everyday experience. Those who had the knowledge to change metals into artefacts may have had other powers of transformation ascribed to them, heightening the sense that when smiths poured liquid metal into moulds and produced something totally different, they were practising a closed and hidden art.[35] Wayland, of course, is a mythical rather than historical smith, but he may represent a long-standing awe towards the mysteries of metallurgy. The craft of concealment therefore gives smiths a degree of power over anyone, including a king or lord, who does not know how the 'magic' works. Through their ingenious yet secretive artifice, smiths possess the ability to shape aristocratic culture while existing beyond its bounds, dwelling in marginal locations, mediating between different social classes.

Their supposed 'powers of transformation' give smiths another advantage over heroes because they can use artifice to overcome corporeal limitations. Contemporary theories of disability see all people as dependent and vulnerable, so that, for most of us, impairment is the rule and normalcy the fantasy.[36] To some degree, we all rely upon and exist within networks made up of non-human bodies and forces. The category of the human is therefore fabricated through various materials, our bodies existing in a prosthetic ecology that forms the self. Richard H. Godden has shown that Sir Gawain, the chivalric hero of *Sir Gawain and the Green Knight*, can be read as a 'dismodern subject' who is incomplete without the prosthetic objects that shape him as a subject. Yet these prosthetics can occasionally exert an excessive thing-power, interrupting the knight's identity and reinforcing his corporeal vulnerability.[37] As we have seen, Beowulf displays a similar dependency on non-human materials in order to live up to the ideals of heroic culture. When his swords suddenly break or fail, the self-sovereignty of the warrior's body may be called into question. Such incidents create a disjunction between the heroic human subject and the non-human object, which the narrator blames for its misbehaviour, diverting our attention away from any potential flaws in the hero. The physically impaired craftsman, on the other hand, finds a way to conjoin with objects in his moment of need.

Wayland, too, is dependent and vulnerable, and more obviously disabled than Beowulf. Yet Wayland turns his 'impairments' into advantages. The smith takes ownership of his disability through acts of making: his sinews have been severed but his artificial wings make him mobile again. In this way, Wayland fits the model of transhuman disability that Julie Singer has identified in medieval texts. According to this model, disability can represent a constructive alteration of the human state. Prosthetics supplement, rather than supplant, identity.[38] Wayland's craft adds *something* to his body in order to enhance its capacities, refusing the limitations that King Niðhad has imposed upon him. Even when physically impaired

and entrapped on an island, Wayland can still outwit King Niðhad
through a combination of craft and cunning. For a hero such as
Beowulf, when his mortal body becomes enfeebled by age or illness,
the heart of his identity, his heroism, is at risk. Hrothgar says as
much in his sermon (1761–8). When weapons begin to let Beowulf
down in his old age, his physical vulnerabilities are exposed. Conversely, the smith can give new life to broken things. Even a sword
such as Nægling which fails in its heroic duty, letting its lord down
and shattering into pieces, can be melted down and reforged into
a new weapon, perhaps receiving a new name and identity.

The body of Beowulf, first young and vigorous then aged and
weary, gives the poem a linear narrative, and his death brings about
an ending. But there are numerous moments in the poem when
material things – the handiwork of smiths – interrupt the text to
give us glimpses into alternative stories and histories, redirecting
the flow of time, taking us into deeper pasts and unanticipated
futures. The neck-ring that Wealhtheow bestows on Beowulf after
he has defeated Grendel ferries us forward in time towards Hygelac's
ill-fated raid on the Frisians. The sword hilt that Beowulf retrieves
from Grendel's mother's underwater hall and hands over to Hrothgar
depicts a distant, mythic past when the Flood washed the race of
giants from the earth. The treasures buried within the dragon's
barrow have become 'lost in history' altogether, existing outside of
human society for a millennium and serving as a metonym for the
'vast grinding movement of time'.[39] It is smiths, not heroes, who
work with these vibrant materials, materials that have existed and
will endure beyond human lifespans. In *Beowulf*, Wayland's work
is a mail-coat sparkling like summer sunlight on a youthful hero's
chest. Yet when a coat of mail is given a voice in Riddle 35, it
reminds us of its previous existence beneath the dark earth: 'Mec
se wæta wong, wundrum freorig, / of his innaþe ærest cende' (The
wet earth, wondrously cold, first delivered me from her womb)
(1–2).[40] Just as material things display an agency that sometimes
diverges from the desires of the hero, so do they persist beyond
the story of his life. Their timescales make the warrior-king's great
deeds seem fleeting by comparison. In the closing lines of the poem,
Wiglaf and seven thegns retrieve the treasure that Beowulf won
from the dragon. They then bury these treasures, which 'niðhedige
men' (strife-minded men) (3165a) once took from the hoard, with
their leader. These material things must 'die' with the hero, it would
seem. However, as Beowulf is being mourned by his followers, his
virtues extolled, the poet slips in a curious remark. Beowulf may

be dead and gone but the gold under the ground 'nu gen lifað' (lives even now) (3167b).

***

Hwær sint nu þæs wisan   Welandes ban,
þæs goldsmiðes,   þe wæs geo mærost?
Forþy ic cwæð þæs wisan   Welandes ban,
forðy ængum ne mæg   eorðbuendra
se cræft losian   þe him Crist onlænð.
Ne mæg mon æfre þy eð   ænne wræccan
his cræftes beniman,   þe mon oncerran mæg
sunnan onswifan,   and ðisne swiftan rodor
of his rihtryne   rinca ænig.
Hwa wat nu þæs wisan   Welandes ban,
on hwelcum hlæwa   hrusan þeccen? [41] (*Old English Boethius,*
Meter 10, lines 33–43)

(Where now are the bones of the wise Weland,
the goldsmith, who was previously very famous?
I said the bones of wise Weland
because the skill which Christ grants to
any earth dweller cannot be lost by him.
Nor can anyone ever deprive a wretch
of his skill more easily than any man can divert
and turn aside the sun and this swift firmament
from its correct course.
Who now knows in which mound the bones
of wise Weland cover the earthen floor?)

The idea of reading *Beowulf* as Wayland's work was fuelled by my own identity and ancestry, by traces of names and occupations almost forgotten by the passage of time, by a family history of blacksmiths and other workers, at once too late and too soon for the ideals of the craft movement to be fulfilled. Academia has offered me a way up the social ladder, but not without an attendant anxiety about what is left behind, what is lost or abandoned, in the pursuit of an intellectual career, the life of the mind at the expense of the craft of the hands. I have tried to counter this sense of loss with scholarship that reconciles head and hands, thinking and feeling and making. I have interpreted *Beowulf* in a more personal way, reading with and through my own working-class background, giving greater recognition to makers and made things, resisting the aristocratic interests of the poem and instead highlighting the significance of *cræft*.

The shadowy craftsman, Wayland, is difficult to idealize, and yet that phrase, *Welandes geweorc*, invites us to rethink the dominant heroic ethos of the poem from another, marginalized point of view. It seems that Wayland was a figure who provoked mixed feelings in King Alfred and his circle, too. As with the pagan characters in *Beowulf*, the allusion to Wayland in the *Old English Boethius* may represent a continued interest in those ancestors who had been 'left behind' by the pursuit of Christian learning. Alfred's reference to the legendary smith could be taken as evidence that he did not wish to completely abandon this craftsman from the past. But the ghost of Wayland is also summoned by Alfred as a warning against the heroic pursuit of everlasting fame.[42] Wayland is but a fading memory, almost forgotten as an individual, his burial mound unlocatable. In this sense, his fate is not so different from that of a hero such as Beowulf, whose own bones have never been found. And it must be conceded that, while the wondrous work of smiths can persist throughout long ages, it too must eventually decay, as Wiglaf discovers when he enters the dragon's barrow (2754–67).

The *Old English Boethius*, however, invokes Wayland in his role as a craftsman rather than a hero. Wayland the wise goldsmith is dead and buried, but Alfred broadens his reflections out to embrace all craftsmen: the craftsperson can *never* lose their craft, nor can anyone *ever* deprive them of it. This suggests that craft is a gift that can endure beyond the loss of individual names and identities, outlasting our very bones. Craft can be passed on. Craft is what continues. Craft is what will survive of us when we are gone, and all else has vanished from memory.

Notes

1 William Morris, *The tale of Beowulf*, in *The collected works of William Morris*, vol. X (London: Longmans, 1911), ll. 452–5.

2 *Mearcstapa* is an Old English term meaning 'border-walker' which is used in *Beowulf* to describe Grendel and his mother, monstrous figures who haunt the margins of civilization. Recently, it has become the name of an organization that prioritizes the study of marginalized communities in the Middle Ages and supports and embraces scholars who themselves represent marginalized identities and communities: https://www.mearcstapa.org.

3 James Paz, 'Æschere's head, Grendel's Mother and the sword that isn't a sword: unreadable things in *Beowulf*', *Exemplaria*, 25.3 (2013), 231–51. I extend this approach to other texts and artefacts in *Nonhuman voices*

in Anglo-Saxon literature and material culture (Manchester: Manchester University Press, 2017).

4   Bill Brown, 'Thing theory', *Critical inquiry*, 28.1 (2001), 1–22; Jane Bennett, *Vibrant matter: a political ecology of things* (Durham, NC: Duke University Press, 2010).

5   Tim Ingold, *Making: anthropology, archaeology, art and architecture* (London: Routledge, 2013).

6   Ibid., p. 31.

7   Some of my thoughts about craft have been informed by a workshop I co-organized with my colleague, Anke Bernau, on 'Craft in medieval and early modern England' at the John Rylands Library, University of Manchester, 2 June 2016. I am grateful to all involved.

8   Sean Sayers, 'The concept of labour: Marx and his critics', *Science & society*, 71.4 (2007), 431–54, at 439–40.

9   See further David Matthews, *Medievalism: a critical history* (Cambridge: D. S. Brewer, 2015), pp. 56–7.

10 Richard Sennett, *The craftsman* (London: Allen Lane, 2008), p. 7.

11 Ibid., p. 20.

12 Alexander Langlands, *Cræft: how traditional crafts are about more than just making* (London: Faber, 2017).

13 See the entry for *cræft* in Angus Cameron, Ashley Crandell Amos, Antonette diPaolo Healey et al. (eds), *Dictionary of Old English*, online (Toronto: University of Toronto Press, 2016).

14 For the meaning of *craft* in Middle English, see Nicola Masciandaro, *The voice of the hammer: the meaning of work in Middle English literature* (Notre Dame, IN: University of Notre Dame Press, 2007).

15 See further Maren Clegg Hyer and Gale R. Owen-Crocker, 'Woven works: making and using textiles', in Maren Clegg Hyer and Gale R. Owen-Crocker (eds), *The material culture of daily living in the Anglo-Saxon world* (Exeter: University of Exeter Press, 2011), pp. 157–84.

16 Stacy S. Klein, *Ruling women: queenship and gender in Anglo-Saxon literature* (Notre Dame, IN: University of Notre Dame Press, 2006), p. 104.

17 See Maren Clegg Hyer, 'Material culture and teaching *Beowulf*', in Howell Chickering, Allen J. Frantzen, and R. F. Yeager (eds), *Teaching Beowulf in the twenty-first century* (Tempe, AZ: ACMRS, 2014), pp. 177–84; see also Marijane Osborn, 'Visualising the material culture of *Beowulf*', in the same volume, pp. 185–93.

18 A classic study of gift exchange in the poem is Ernst Leisi, 'Gold und Manneswert im *Beowulf*', *Anglia*, 71 (1952).

19 There have, of course, been studies of Anglo-Saxon crafts and craftsmen more generally. An examination of the archaeological evidence is given in Kevin Leahy, *Anglo-Saxon crafts* (Stroud: Tempus, 2003).

20 All references to *Beowulf* are taken from R. D. Fulk, Robert E. Bjork, and John D. Niles (eds), *Klaeber's Beowulf and the Fight at Finnsburg*, 4th edn (Toronto: University of Toronto Press, 2008) and

cited in text by line number. Translations are mine, unless indicated otherwise.

21 Chris Jones, 'From Heorot to Hollywood: *Beowulf* in its third millennium', in David Clark and Nicholas Perkins (eds), *Anglo-Saxon culture and the modern imagination* (Cambridge: D. S. Brewer, 2010), pp. 13–29, at 14–18.

22 Aaron Hostetter, 'Disruptive things in *Beowulf*', *NML*, 17 (2017), 34–61, at 35.

23 Gillian R. Overing, '*Beowulf*: a poem in our time', in Clare A. Lees (ed.), *The Cambridge history of early medieval English literature* (Cambridge: Cambridge University Press, 2013), pp. 309–31, at 325.

24 Andy Orchard, *Pride and prodigies: studies in the monsters of the Beowulf-manuscript* (Cambridge: D. S. Brewer, 1995), p. 29.

25 Bennett, *Vibrant matter*, pp. 2–4; cf. Brown, 'Thing theory', p. 4.

26 James W. Earl, '*Beowulf* and the origins of civilisation', repr. in Eileen A. Joy and Mary K. Ramsey (eds), *The postmodern Beowulf: a critical casebook* (Morgantown, WV: West Virginia University Press, 2006), pp. 259–85, at 265–6.

27 Clare A. Lees, 'Men and *Beowulf*', in Joy and Ramsey (eds), *The postmodern Beowulf*, pp. 417–38, at 431.

28 The family tree was compiled by my grandmother's cousin, Laurence Coles, and was initially based on information kept in the Hampshire Record Office, in Winchester.

29 Although I have Anglicized the names, this summary is based primarily upon the *Völundarkviða*, probably composed *c.* 900–1050. It is possible that *Völundarkviða* was produced in an area of Anglo-Saxon England under Scandinavian influence. See John McKinnell, 'The context of *Völundarkviða*', in Paul Acker and Carolyne Larrington (eds), *The Poetic Edda: essays on Old Norse mythology* (London: Routledge, 2002), pp. 198–212. That the legend of Wayland was known by the Anglo-Saxons more generally is evidenced by the carvings on the Franks Casket and by literary allusions in *Deor*, *Waldere* and, of course, *Beowulf*. For a comprehensive study of the various traditions associated with Wayland, see H. R. Ellis Davidson, 'Weland the Smith', *Folklore*, 69.3 (1958), 145–59.

30 Peter Clemoes, 'King Alfred's debt to vernacular poetry: the evidence of *ellen* and *cræft*', in Michael Korhammer, Karl Reichl, and Hans Sauer (eds), *Words, texts and manuscripts: studies in Anglo-Saxon culture presented to Helmut Gneuss* (Cambridge: D. S. Brewer, 1992), pp. 223–6.

31 Nicole Guenther Discenza, 'Power, skill and virtue in the Old English Boethius', *ASE*, 26 (1997), 81–108.

32 Maria Sachiko Cecire, '*Ban Welondes*: Wayland Smith in popular culture', in Clark and Perkins (eds), *Anglo-Saxon culture and the modern imagination*, pp. 201–17, at 205.

33 See the entries on *orþanc* and *searu* in James Bosworth and T. Northcote Toller, *An Anglo-Saxon dictionary* (Oxford, 1898), with *Supplement* by

T. N. Toller (1921) and *Revised and enlarged addenda* by A. Campbell (1972).

34 David A. Hinton, 'Anglo-Saxon smiths and myths', *Bulletin of the John Rylands Library*, 80.1 (1998), 3–22.

35 Ibid., pp. 14–15.

36 Lennard J. Davis, *Bending over backwards: disability, dismodernism and other difficult positions* (New York: New York University Press, 2002), p. 31.

37 Richard H. Godden, 'Prosthetic ecologies: vulnerable bodies and the dismodern subject in *Sir Gawain and the Green Knight*', *Textual practice*, 30.7 (2016), 1273–90.

38 Julie Singer, 'Toward a transhuman model of medieval disability', *postmedieval*, 1.1/2 (2010), 173–9.

39 Hostetter, 'Disruptive things in *Beowulf*', p. 59.

40 References to the Exeter Book are taken from Bernard J. Muir (ed.), *The Exeter anthology of Old English poetry: an edition of Exeter Dean and Chapter MS 3501* (Exeter: University of Exeter Press, 1994) and cited in the text by line number. Translations are mine.

41 Text and translation are taken from Susan Irvine and Malcolm R. Godden (eds and trans.), *The Old English Boethius* (Cambridge, MA: Harvard University Press, 2012).

42 These contrasting views of Wayland are weighed up by Paul Anthony Booth, 'King Alfred versus *Beowulf*: the re-education of the Anglo-Saxon aristocracy', *Bulletin of the John Rylands Library*, 79.3 (1997), 41–66.

Part II

Beowulf at home

5
Beowulf and babies

Donna Beth Ellard

This is the second time I have written about *Beowulf*. This is also the second time I have written about *Beowulf* in the weeks following and – now, as I revise this chapter – preceding the births of my two youngest children. *Beowulf* and babies. *Beowulf* and babies? The only easy connection I can make is alliterative. For scenes of childbirth and infant caregiving fall outside the narrative purview of the poem. Yet, in *Beowulf*'s opening lines, birth and childcare are brought to centre stage in the story of Scyld Scefing. A foundling of unknown origins, Scyld is set adrift in a boat and washes up on the shores of Daneland. Taken in by the people who live there, Scyld becomes the founder of a Danish dynasty: father of Beow and grandfather of Hrothgar. Upon his death, Scyld's body is placed in a boat then sent out into the sea, from whence he came.

Although Scyld's early childhood is marked by intentional abandonment and accidental discovery, *Beowulf* and its critics express little interest in the foundling:[1] the poem makes only passing mention of his condition as an infant, which is inserted between stories that track Scyld's rise to power and sumptuous funeral display. Such narrative inattention, some have argued, invites critics to 'write of' Scyld's origins 'in an off-hand ... manner',[2] examining him from within '[t]he motif of the hapless ... child exposed in a floating vessel ... drifting helplessly in chests, casks, tubs, bins, baskets, and oarless boats'.[3] Thus, Scyld has been linked to youthful images that evoke the shadowy hero-deity, Sceaf;[4] the biblical figures of Moses in his reed basket,[5] the ark-born son of Noah,[6] and Seth, Adam's son;[7] and a range of characters from world folklore,[8] all of whom belong to literature rather than life.

Does it matter that *Beowulf* and its critical history do not dwell on the birth, infant experiences, and childhood development of Scyld? Does it matter that critics have considered his mysterious abandonment from within the exclusive, expectant purview of fiction and folklore? Like Scyld, Beowulf comes to the Danes from the sea. He is also a child of obscure parentage. And these hazy origins enable him, perhaps, as with Scyld, to be taken into the care of others: as a child, Beowulf is fostered by the Geatish king, Hrethel; and as a young man, he is offered adoption by the Danish king, Hrothgar. In this chapter, written during the first weeks and months of my second daughter, Carmela's, life, then revised just before my third daughter, Mary Ellard, was born, I discuss the history of child abandonment and parental attachment in the early medieval North, and I consider the weight of these historical issues in relation to the fictional lives of Scyld and Beowulf. That the poem mentions yet fails to integrate Scyld's abandonment and Beowulf's orphancy within a narrative that assiduously recounts their heroic ascent is important not only to *Beowulf* but also its critics. For myself, the non-integrated childhoods of *Beowulf* have facilitated my own lack of critical care for the foundling Scyld and the orphan Beowulf. Despite being parent to a daughter, prior to the births of Carmela and Mary Ellard I had kept my research, my teaching activities, and my scholarly writing at a distance from children and, consequently, from the infant and child lives of Scyld and Beowulf. By letting *Beowulf*'s babies share narrative space with my own, I have learned to take seriously the infant lives and childhood experiences of Scyld and Beowulf and have found that, despite the poem's brief mention of them, it is not carelessness but deep ambivalence, emotional complexity, and resilience that underwrites *Beowulf*'s relationship to children. In thinking about such ambivalent concern, I attend to critics such as Lauren Berlant, making room for the ambivalently 'charged' interruptions of family life in the poem and in my criticism by recalibrating these intimacies to include babies in *Beowulf*.

Abandonment, childcare, and the early medieval North

The place of infants, children, and the family has been, in large part, an unknown and under-studied aspect of the societies and cultures of the early medieval North. In the wake of Philippe Ariès's 1962 *Centuries of Childhood*, which argued that medieval parents were generally dispassionate towards their children, medievalists began to examine the topic, and Mathew Kuefler was the first to challenge Ariès's assertions with respect to families in early medieval England.[9] Examining documentary and literary evidence, in 1991 Kuefler argued that although 'life was generally harsh, both physically and psychologically ... at least some Anglo-Saxon children enjoyed great affection ... and were treated in some instances with great love, in particular by their parents'.[10] Several years later, Sally Crawford's landmark survey, *Childhood in Anglo-Saxon England*, extended Kuefler's rebuttal of Ariès and other social historians by including visual and material evidence of children and their families during the period, concluding that 'parents did invest love and care in their children, although their ideas about nurturing children were not necessarily in accordance with our views on best practice ... however lovingly you reared a child, the purpose of your care was to produce an adult whose future was not yours to protect'.[11] Almost two decades later, Crawford's arguments are echoed and extended in the recent volume *Childhood & Adolescence in Anglo-Saxon Literary Culture*. As the first essay collection dedicated to the study of infants, children, and youth in early medieval England, many of its contributors take up Ariès once again, revisiting and revising his thesis of 'parental aloofness' as one of 'tough love'[12] and reinterpreting his 'pre-modern world of imminent dangers and high child mortality rates' as 'not necessarily a deterrent of maternal love ... but rather occasion[ing] the most necessary displays of maternal strength'.[13] Editors Susan Irvine and Winfried Rudolf take up the legacy of Ariès's arguments and the ensuing scholarly debates by acknowledging that 'the current notion of childhood [is] a modern invention, essentially a social construct'.[14] Yet, in lieu of a discussion that would stake out historical 'thens' and contemporary 'nows', Irvine and Rudolf 'assum[e] a range of childhoods ... varying in degrees of care and exploitation, emotional attachment and ludic freedom', all the while cautioning that the 'literary perspective of adults cannot ... be assumed to a be a reliable guide into a child's world. Moreover, although textual accounts can provide important evidence for conceptions of childhood in the period, they cannot be assumed to reflect accurately the socio-historical reality of Anglo-Saxon childhood and adolescence.'[15]

A sticking point in the debates between Ariès and early medieval historians is the practice of infant and child abandonment, a topic addressed in John Boswell's 1988 book, *Kindness of Strangers*.[16] In his wide-ranging discussion of legal, historical, and literary sources from early medieval Europe, Boswell discusses what he categorically articulates as 'abandonment', a term and a practice that includes killing, exposing, and selling infants and children as well as gifting them to the Church.[17] In short, abandoning a child means giving it up permanently, whether to death, fate, other adults, or an institution. As a consequence of such wide-ranging parental actions and life-or-death outcomes, Boswell makes no conclusive statements regarding the perception and frequency of child abandonment in any one particular place and time. 'In Germanic lore', he writes, 'all usually turns out happily ... Scyld becomes a great king, and is returned at his death to the sea on which he was cast as a child. But the reality is much harder to judge.'[18] As Boswell and others explain, 'prophecy, adultery, incest, illegitimacy, and jealousy',[19] gender preference,[20] deformity, and superstition[21] were among the varied reasons why wealthy and poor parents gave up their children in the early medieval North. While evidence of adoption indicates that some abandoned children were raised by friends, extended family, or 'the childless rich', Boswell argues that 'most likely the majority of them were brought up as servants' or sold into slavery.[22]

In early medieval England, few references are made to abandoned children and foundlings. The Laws of Ine and Alfred make brief mention of the practice, setting fees for the maintenance of foundlings for the first three years of their lives and identifying who should be paid *wergild* for an illegitimate child given up by his father.[23] Likewise, Bede's well-known description of a marketplace encounter between Pope Gregory and a group of *pueri Angeli* unflinchingly bears witness to child slavery, a practice associated with *nutritores* who have taken in abandoned infants, and parents who have, on account of need, sold their children. Literary examples texture these attestations. The Old English *Life of St Margaret* suggests that the infant Margaret was cast out by her family because she is a girl; and J. A. Tasioulas has argued that the 'concept of child abandonment ... provides the framework' for Riddle 9 and *Wulf and Eadwacer*, the latter of which, she explains, explores a mother's grief for her young, abandoned child.[24]

While these legal, historical, and literary references specify acts of desertion, abandonment is only a shade away from infanticide, as evidenced in Winfried Rudolf's assessment of Old English and Anglo-Latin homilies, which address mothers and young women who have – through ignorance, neglect, or intent – killed their children. While these religious texts and authors decry such *acwell[ende]* (killing) or *homicidum* (murder), Rudolf associates these 'infanticide practices' with 'the issue of child abandonment', and he suggests that such homiletic denouncements 'could indeed suggest the survival of a persistent practice in Anglo-Saxon England, even after the widespread conversion to Christianity ... [w]hether it was established pagan custom, shame of illicit unions, patriarchal bias against female offspring, or postpartum depression'.[25] Rudolf positions infanticide squarely within the conceptual range of abandonment and hypothesizes myriad reasons which might have prompted parents to let go of their children in early medieval England. By focusing his discussion on clerical voices in what is often perceived of as a lay action, Rudolf's essay points to the influence of the Church, which vocally opposed and, in some locales, criminalized the interconnected practices of abandonment and infanticide. Likewise, its reference to 'pagan practices' touches upon Boswell, who argued that, in a Christian milieu, traditional acts of and spaces for abandonment may have been redirected towards child oblation and the site of the church.[26]

In contrast, Old Norse texts and Scandinavian material culture, which reflect a society that converted to Christianity at a much later date, address abandonment more frequently. In addition to *Gunnlaugs saga*, *Hervarar saga*, *Finnboga saga*, and *Vatnsdœla saga*, which engage in open conversation regarding the topic, Sean B. Lawing writes that '[i]nfants appear to have lacked legal status in pre-Christian law – something that was gained only after an infant had been sprinkled with water (*ausa vatn*), named, or given food – and it was enough that the child was unwanted'.[27] He cites Norwegian and Icelandic Christian laws, dating from the eleventh to fourteenth centuries, which interdict infant abandonment, with the exception of deformity, arguing that '[p]hysically impaired children ... if reared, would present too great a demand on resources and in the future would be limited in providing for themselves and contributing to the community's economy'.[28] In addition to the sagas and law codes, which mention child abandonment with some frequency, archaeological evidence supports this practice as a fact of early medieval life. Archaeologists have, for several decades, discussed the possibility that infant bones found in cairns, middens, wells, and bogs should be interpreted as infanticide[29] – caused by either strangulation or passive neglect – and some have argued that the dearth of adult female graves suggests that selective female infanticide may have taken place in pre-Christian Scandinavia.[30]

Child abandonment in Europe is now uncommon, and contemporary discussions of the topic are few and tend to focus on the medical, not psychological, outcomes for the child who has been abandoned and survived.[31] Only one very recent study has considered the emotional impact on the child, arguing that, among its small sample group of adults who were abandoned as infants, found, and adopted, respondents described their 'ongoing' difficulties 'to foster and maintain relationships'.[32] They stated that 'long-term extensive internal grief … [was] a core part of their being and was ever present, even for those who had in some ways managed to navigate or contain such feelings'; and they noted 'feelings of anger and resentment … targeted at their mother figure'.[33] The study does not query the early childhood experiences of respondents, which may have contributed to their relationship difficulties and feelings of grief and anger as adults. Nor does it consider the respondents' expectations of family life, mothering, and childhood, all of which are culturally and socially determined. Absent these unaddressed factors, the language of participants and the findings of the study correspond with elements of attachment theory, a field pioneered by John Bowlby, who argued that the trauma of maternal deprivation may result in permanent, psychological consequences. Although Bowlby's original assertions have been overturned, the basic tenets of attachment remain upheld. Contemporary research continues to confirm the critical role of a primary caregiver in the development of a child's future emotional and social relationships. From the first moments of life, mother and newborn generate behaviours in one another that foster attachment. When placed skin-to-skin immediately after childbirth, the mother's body regulates her infant's temperature and respiration, soothes crying, and encourages nursing behaviours, just as the newborn baby regulates and consequently encourages the mother's attention through breastfeeding.[34] As the baby grows, crying, cooing, smiling, sucking, and grasping are signals that draw caregivers to them, 'develop[ing] clear-cut attachments with those adults … who are most likely to soothe, comfort, and protect them'.[35] In turn, these adults 'develop affectional ties with the child … called a caregiving bond'.[36] When these bonds are broken or disturbed – as a consequence of the caregiver's absence, separation, rejection, or death – this can result in a spectrum of feelings, ranging from anxiety to aggression, which can last throughout childhood into adulthood.

Medievalists have been quick to caution against biological determinism and psychosocial presentism when assessing the early developmental relationship between parents and their children. The evolutionary mechanisms that operate within infant–mother dyads do not override the social meanings of infancy and childhood, which differ across cultures and temporalities. Consequently, while historical assessments regarding attachments between early medieval parents and their children remain, to an extent, a fraught subject, recent scholarship on attitudes towards infant and child caregiving in these societies has challenged the conceptual and affective frame of 'abandonment' that research by Boswell (and, perhaps, Bowlby) has placed around certain early medieval practices. In her introduction to the recent essay collection, *Anglo-Saxon emotions*, Alice Jorgensen writes that 'we need not be bound by our everyday, culturally instilled concepts, but it is only by applying them that we can begin to critique them, and get a sense of what our evidence is showing us instead'.[37] Mary Garrison advances this statement in her discussion of child oblation, a practice of permanent separation between parent and child that occurred around the age of six. Garrison argues that 'while attachment theory and modern grief studies undoubtedly shed some light on medieval experiences of grief and [early-childhood] separation', because early English peoples participated in 'a range of non-parental child-rearing practices' such as fosterage, court education, and political hostage taking, the findings of contemporary child psychology 'need to be qualified by attention to differences in [early medieval] family structure, expectations, and social environment'.[38] Such a statement, which articulates oblation as a 'child-rearing practice', challenges it as an instance of Boswellian abandonment by inserting it within a list of acts meant to extend, rather than cut off, kinship networks between families.

Patrick Ryan's *Master–servant childhood: a history of the idea of childhood in medieval English culture* attends to the differences suggested by Jorgensen and Garrison by using the term 'household' rather than 'family' to discuss these kinship networks, which, during the medieval period, often exceeded nuclear and biological units. Ryan writes, '[a]cross the medieval period ... [b]elonging to a household was a general principle of *both* productive and affective ties'.[39] Consequently, he continues, 'growing up' in a household was physically enacted and discursively imagined as a 'master–servant relation[ship,] ... a discourse [that] carried with it a strong sense of generational responsibility, care and family devotion. It simply did not share the modern dualism' not only between public and private spheres but also 'between power and love, or the opposition between violence and empathy'.[40] After reframing the conceptual parameters of medieval childhood and caregiving such that they do not align (and are therefore not in conflict) with these 'modern dualism[s]', Ryan turns to Classical and early medieval abandonment. He cautions against evaluating these practices from within 'a romantic polarity between sentimental parental care/affections and matters of power and polarity'.[41] Then he suggests that such false distinctions

may actually run cover for connections between abandonment then
and now which we might not want to acknowledge:

> So too, Plato's and Aristotle's support for ridding the polis of deformed
> newborns was not based upon a rejection of the humanity of children
> in general, anymore than the contemporary debate over abortion is
> neatly divided between murderers and saviours of the child. Armed
> as we are with prenatal testing and hygienic abortive technologies,
> perhaps we should not be so superior when we consider the Roman
> *susceptio* – the father's power to accept or reject a newborn's entrance
> into his house. An honest look into current trends toward 'screening'
> (a telling word) for Down's syndrome *in utero* should complicate our
> moral assessment of the Spartan 'leskhe,' a council of elders, who
> had the power to inspect infant boys and remand those deemed
> defective to the 'apthetai,' [or pit].[42]

In the process of nuancing early medieval histories of childhood,
childcare, and attachment, Ryan destabilizes 'abandonment' – a
word brought into English during the fourteenth century and
retroactively applied to myriad Latin terms for parental actions. In
connecting Roman *susceptio* with prenatal 'screening', Ryan suggests
that terminology such as 'abandonment' has a preservative psychological function. Namely, that in using it, 'we' run the risk of
off-loading the modern-day semantic and moral weight of abandonment into the distant past so that 'we' do not have to recognize its
function in contemporary practices of family planning. While Ryan's
statement asks to what extent medieval histories of childhood, in
particular Boswell's study of abandonment, preclude our abilities
to perceive and admit that contemporary society continues to sanction
practices of giving up babies and children, it also, and perhaps
moreover, asks us to recognize the, at times, deep and profound
ambivalence that parents experience in relation to acts of having,
keeping, and raising a child.

Abandoning Scyld, Beowulf, and my daughters – lessons in ambivalence

Beowulf is an ambivalent poem. Its contradictory positions towards
Beowulf and the monsters, its heroic and violent displays, and its
scenes of living and dying express a position that is 'aware of
simultaneously opposing emotions toward the same object and [yet]
... able to live with it'.[43] As an organizing principle of the poem,
Beowulf's 'ambivalence does not ... reflect indecision or paralysis

but a mature step towards acknowledging a more complex world of multiple perspectives and emotional resilience'.[44]

First among the poem's many ambivalences is its position towards the infant Scyld, whose 'expos[ure] in a boat' marks him as 'the ubiquitous founding foundling' and among Boswell's marquee examples of early medieval abandonment.[45] While mention of Scyld's origins appears in the prologue of *Beowulf*, this is not the poem's narrative beginning. Rather, two short statements regarding Scyld's early childhood are deposited and displaced in vignettes that track his ascension to the Danish kingship and funereal memorialization by the Danes:

> Oft Scyld Scefing   sceaþena þreatum
> monegum mægþum   meodosetla ofteah,
> egsode eorlas,   syððan ærest wearð
> *feasceaft funden.   He þæs frofre gebad*:
> weox under wolcnum,   weorðmyndum þah,
> oð þæt him æghwylc   þara ymbsittendra
> ofer hronrade   hyran scolde,
> gomban gyldan.   Þæt wæs god cyning.
> ...
> Nalæs hi hine læssan   lacum teodan,
> þeodgestreonum   þonne þa dydon
> *þe hine æt frumsceafte   forð onsendon*
> aenne ofer yðe   umborwesende.
> Þa gyt hie him asetton   segen gyldenne
> heah ofer heafod,   leton holm beran,
> geafon on garsecg. (4–11, 43–9a; italics added for emphasis)[46]

(Often, Scyld Scefing deprived mead-benches from enemy hosts, from many peoples, terrified men, though first he was found destitute. Because of that he experienced comfort/awaited consolation: he grew under the skies, thrived in honours, until each of the neighbouring peoples over the whale-road had to submit, to yield tribute, to him. That was a good king.
...
They did not furnish him with lesser gifts, treasures of a people, than those did who in the beginning sent him forth alone over the waves as a child. Then they set a golden standard high up over his head. They let the sea take him; they gave him up to the ocean.)

In the middle of two passages that chronicle Scyld's beginning and ending moments as king of the Danes, *Beowulf* inserts brief mention of his non-Danish origins. Line 7 explains that Scyld is *feasceaft funden*: a 'forlorn', wretched', or 'destitute' foundling, who experiences *frof*, or comfort, among the Danes. Later on, line 45 reveals that Scyld is not a native son but *forð onsendon* as a young child by an unknown, plural subject, arriving in Daneland from over the sea. This account of Scyld's *frumsceaft*, or origin, textures his foundling status as one whose obscure tribal affiliations and unidentifiable homeland result from intentional abandonment or, more specifically, exposure. The poetics that generate Scyld's origin story are connected by way of subject matter and alliteration. *Frofre* and *forð*, the staves of these lines, look back to *feasceaft* and *frumsceaft*, respectively. Together, these compounds not only signal 'destitute beginnings' or 'wretched origins' for Scyld but also fold *sceaft* – a simplex referencing 1) the shaft of a spear or arrow, and 2) creation or that which is created[47] – within them. The conceptual ties between *feasceaft*, *frumsceaft*, and *sceaft* extend a micro-narrative of infant exposure and foundling past towards *Scyld Scefing*. Located amid sonic and lexical horizons that bridge a family lost and found with the weapons of war, Scyld is both the poem's narrative primogenitor and its alliterative 'creation'.

Lines 7 and 45 communicate a deep ambivalence towards Scyld's childhood. Scyld is exposed, yet discovered; he is sent from home, but arrives at another. His name carries the alliterative force of 'creation' (*frumsceaft*), infant 'destitution' (*feasceaft*), and weaponry (*sceaft*), even as these signals of originary loss, trauma, and violence are weighted against Scyld's adoptive 'comfort' (*frof*) and the promise of futurity (*forð*). Despite the poem's shifting and contradictory position towards the youngest of babes, its ambivalence towards Scyld is indicative of anything but carelessness. Rather, the emotional tension surrounding his earliest years articulates the poem's deep, unresolved concern for the baby, Scyld. And as a site of ambivalent unresolve, the particular environment of Scyld the baby opens the door for acknowledging a world of complexity, where emotional tension facilitates an emotional resilience that extends across the adult world of *Beowulf* and its alternative temporalities.

Not only are the pieces of Scyld's infancy and young childhood nested within the arc of his rise and fall from kingly power in Daneland; they are, moreover, centred within narratives that recount his adult activities, interrupting and structuring the passages that surround them. While recounting Scyld's rise to power by way of his terrifying violence, the poem steps back in time, revealing that Scyld was first found destitute. Because of 'that' – his foundling state – Scyld *frofre gebad*, a phrase that can mean 'experienced comfort' during childhood or 'awaited consolation' in the form of future martial actions that result in political successes. When the scene of his abandonment is disclosed a few lines later, these infant experiences point, with more suggestive force, towards a martial future. Amid an elaborate narrative of Scyld's funeral, the poem explores new details about his beginnings. Just as Scyld is sent forth as a baby, the Danes place his hoary body on a boat, surround it 'hildewæpnum ond heaðowædum, / billum ond byrnum' (with battle weapons and war dress, swords and mail-coats) (39–40a), and set it adrift. Scyld is sent into the sea from whence he came. He floats, unassisted and surrounded by an armoury, beyond the Danish horizon.

Does Scyld travel back in time in search of those who sent him, as a baby, from them? Is his funeral an act of post-mortem abandonment – or, more precisely, exposure – by the Danes, who off-load his hyper-martial cargo on yet another unnamed, unknown, and unsuspecting people? The emotional ambivalence and complexity that underwrites Scyld's infant and funereal send-offs temporally entangles him in the pasts and futures of multiple semi-known communities. Abandonment, fraught with the complexities of love, heartbreak, fear, and dread, launches Scyld into the sea where he floats towards unknown destinations. He carries with him the materials of military might (at the centre of which are the hazy memories of a child's life) from which springs not only the story of Scyld but also of Beowulf.

The poem's ambivalent mention of Scyld's infant abandonment and discovery loops together and entangles peoples, places, and times; and these attachments acknowledge a complex world of multiple perspectives and emotional resilience. Consequently, Scyld's story functions as a micro-narrative that operates as an open circuit which, as John Hill writes, sets the tempo for a 'large-scale, structural vie[w] of Beowulf ... [as] a poem of arrivals and departures'.[48] Scyld's story is generated by his abandonment and foundling state, a 'departure' from his biological and extra-biological kin and 'arrival' on the shores of Daneland. These movements, which separate the baby, Scyld, from his parents and immediate community, make way for adoptive kinships, both paternal and social, that are stronger, more fraught yet more tensile, perhaps, than the infant–parent dyad. Thus, as Hill argues, Scyld's circuit of childhood departure and arrival acts as a 'foundation myth'.[49] It generates 'an overall and variable narrative pulse' for Scyld's narrative of adult life and for other narratives of many other lives of the poem, generating the 'cultural model of a major battle-king'.[50] These narratives are defined by their ambivalence – their emotional complexity and resilience – and it is important to recall that Scyld's martial activities and political behaviour, which circumscribe his infant goings and comings, are consequential of these childhood movements and the unspoken emotions that attend them. Thus, Scyld's post-mortem return to the sea is a second departure that ushers in many arrivals: a succession of heirs to his Scylding dynasty, the glory of Hrothgar as architect of Heorot, and the coming of Grendel. Yet it is not until Beowulf's boat launches from Geatland and lands on the Danish coastline that another traveller departs and arrives from the sea, following the emotionally ambivalent 'pulse' of Scyld towards becoming the poem's next celebrated 'battle-king'.

Scyld and Beowulf are, in many respects, parallel figures.[51] Both travel by boat – Scyld, an infant; Beowulf, a youthful hero. Both make their way to Daneland, where they re-establish the might of the Danes. Furthermore, both experience parental abandonment that is explored via micro-narratives that interrupt, put on pause, and thereby emotionally complicate their portrayals as 'major-battle king[s]'. Of Beowulf, Hrothgar states:

> Ic hine cuðe   cnihtwesende
> wæs his ealdfæder   Ecgþeo haten
> ðaem to ham forgeaf   Hreþel Geata
> angan dohtor
> ...
>   Hwæt, þæt secgan mæg
> efne swa hwylc mægþa   swa ðone magan cende
> æfter gumcynnum,   gyf heo gyt lyfað
> þæt hyre ealdmetod   este wære
> bearngebyrdo.   Nu ic, Beowulf, þec,
> secg betesta,   me for sunu wylle
> freogan on ferhþe. (372–5a, 942b–8a)

(I knew him [Beowulf] as a youth. His once-living father was called Ecgtheow, to whom Hrethel of the Geats gave his own daughter as wife
...
Indeed, she may say, whichever of women among mankind who gave birth to that child, if she yet lives, that the Old Creator was kind to her in childbirth. Now, Beowulf, best man, I desire to love you in my mind as a son.)

Upon meeting Beowulf in Heorot, Hrothgar, a Danish king and descendant of Scyld, speaks of the Geatish warrior as a *cnihtwesende*, or youth, then proceeds to identify Beowulf's father and mother.

Hrothgar mentions his association with Ecgtheow, Beowulf's father and a figure of shadowy relations, who is possibly Geatish[52] but may be a Swede.[53] Regardless of his cultural identity, Ecgtheow, according to Hrothgar, is dead. As Beowulf's *ealdfæder*, his once-living father, Ecgtheow belongs to a former time or is no longer living.

Hrothgar not only places his father in a distant past but also deadens him, calling into question the bonds between father and son. Once Beowulf defeats Grendel, Hrothgar casts similar doubts upon the relationship between mother and son. As Hrothgar has explained previously, Beowulf's mother is the nameless daughter of Hrethel, king of the Geats. Now he questions her survival. In a half-line that brackets her identity – *seo*, or she – between the speculative, alliterating adverbs, *gyf* (if) and *gyt* (yet), Hrothgar commits Beowulf's mother to the *ealdmetod* (Old Creator) in childbirth. Such a benediction not only associates her with Beowulf's *eald*, or once-living, *fæder* (father) but also suggests the danger of childbirth, or *bearngebyrdu*, which she may not have survived. Hrothgar's prayerful statement tacitly removes Beowulf's mother from life by way of labour and delivery, acts that have always been a dangerous business. While *bearngebyrdu* is a unique self-alliterating compound that sonically attaches itself to 'Beowulf', in this line the hero's signifier is likewise bracketed by the personal pronouns *ic* (Hrothgar) and *þec* (Beowulf). Via the poetics of the line, *bearngebyrdo. Nu ic, Beowulf, þec*, Hrothgar draws the Geatish hero from a mother's womb into his own Danish, paternal orbit. As he reflects upon Beowulf's origins, Hrothgar suggests that Beowulf experiences a different shade of abandonment from that of Scyld – he is orphaned by his mother – and offers himself as an adoptive father.

While Hrothgar's statements hint at an infancy marked by abandonment, it is not until Beowulf faces death that the ambivalence associated with his early years comes into clearer focus. When the old king prepares to meet the dragon and fight his last battle, Beowulf's mind turns to a story of his childhood beginnings:

Fela ic on giogoðe   guðræsa genæs,
orleghwila;   ic þæt eall gemon.
Ic wæs syfanwintre   þa mec sinca baldor,
freawine folca   æt minum fæder genam;
heold mec ond hæfde   Hreðel cyning
geaf me sinc ond symbel,   sibbe gemunde;
næs ic him to life   laðra owihte,
beorn in burgum,   þonne his bearna hwylc,
Herebeald ond Hæðcyn   oððe Hygelac min. (2426–34)

(In youth, I survived/was saved from many war storms, times of hostility; I remember all that. I was seven winters old when the prince of treasure, the beloved lord of the people took me from my father; King Hrethel held me and kept me, gave me treasure and feast, mindful of our kinship; I was no more of a burden to him while he was alive, a man in his fortification, than any of his sons, Herebald and Hathcyn, or my Hygelac.)

At seven, Beowulf was sent from his father, Ecgtheow, to be raised by his grandfather, Hrethel, who loved him like a son. This formative memory begins with individual 'survival' or preservation by another in the face of war, hostilities, and the unspoken emotional aftershocks of such a childhood. Then it swings dramatically to the safety of a dyadic relationship between grandson and grandfather, foster son and foster father. The emotional space of this dyad is expressed in an alliterative prosody that ties together 'Hrethel's' tender acts of 'holding' and 'having' Beowulf ('heold mec ond hæfde ... Hreðel cyning') with a 'kinship' ('sibbe') that is demonstrated in the courtly acts of 'treasure and feast' ('sinc ond symbel'). As the biological bonds between father and son are broken, alternative bonds of kinship politics between Hrethel and Beowulf extend to uncles, nephews, and foster brothers. The alliterative sounds that accompany Hrethel's affection return when Beowulf names 'Herebeald ond Hæðcyn oððe Hygelac min'. This multi-generational portrait of family kindness is, however, surrounded by Beowulf's preparations for and enactment of his battle with the dragon, and temporally dislocated and displaced within an adult narrative of martial action.[54] Moreover, Beowulf's reflection upon his time spent with Hrethel, Herebald, Hathcyn, and Hygelac emerges from his own stark memory of being a child during a time of war, and the alliterative ties that knit together Beowulf's adopted family aid in its violent disassembling. Hrethel's loving embrace ('heold mec ond hæfde') (2430a) turns into a 'wearying heart' ('hreðre hygemeðe') (2442a) and a heart's sorrow ('heortan sorge') (2463b) when one of Hrethel's sons is killed, accidentally, by another. As with the micro-narrative of Scyld, Beowulf's mention of childhood 'survival' introduces an ambivalence that manages complexity in terms of emotional resilience and transtemporal entanglement.

While Beowulf has a mother and father, Hrothgar's statements echo those regarding Scyld's beginnings. Beowulf's youth, or *cnihtwesende*, recalls Scyld's *umborwesende*, or infancy. Beowulf's parentage, like that of Scyld, is neither fully known nor living, and absent these ties to family or community, both are subject to Danish adoption. Moreover, for both Scyld the foundling and Beowulf the orphan, their respective stories of destitute origins and parental losses are temporally dislocated micro-narratives inserted into the poem's larger, mostly continuous narratives of heroic becoming. For Scyld, the details of his foundling past are inserted within passages that track his terrifying rise to power and sumptuous funeral, which arms him, once again, and sends him towards another unsuspecting people. For Beowulf, becoming an orphan unfolds alongside his combat narrative against the Grendelkin and the dragon. When examined together, these inserted origins of Scyld and Beowulf interrupt their paths towards heroism and eventual kingship with childhood experiences of abandonment and orphancy, community and parental loss, all of which are not only remediated by Danish adoption but also considered 'cultural models' of heroism and 'battle-king[ship]'. These interruptions, which are managed by a deep ambivalence towards the survival, compassionate care, and parental attachments between Scyld, Beowulf, and their fathers and mothers, articulate the critical and complex role that childhood plays in the narrative lives – the arrivals and departures – of these adult men.

There is no paved or easy path to childrearing for those who are responsible for children. Yet these movements, which separate Scyld and Beowulf from their biological parents and community ties, make way for adoptive kinships, both paternal and cultural, in life as well as after death. They suggest, ever so slightly, that infant abandonment need not be perceived as neglectful, but as an act pointed towards what Garrison categorized as 'non-parental child-rearing practices' which extend, rather than cut off, family ties. Via abandonment, 'family', we may understand, exceeds the biological unit. It becomes collective, dynastic, intergenerational, and, perhaps, intercultural. It is a complexity that engages simultaneously multiple emotions, responses, ethics, and interpersonal dynamics. Conse-quently, despite the partial, unintegrated, and recursive positions at which the infant and childhood micro-narratives of Scyld and Beowulf appear in the poem, *Beowulf* does not claim the early years of these heroes and kings as founding traumas upon which the poem builds its world. In spite of Scyld's abandonment and 'destitu-tion', a 'comfort' (*frof*) follows from his foundling state. Whether we translate this comfort as an experience of Danish adoption or of warfare to come, its language does not suggest a childhood of

sadness but of warmth and love. And while Hrothgar suggests that
Beowulf's parents are no longer living, at the moment of childbirth,
the event that orphans Beowulf, he wishes Hrethel's daughter 'grace'
(*este*).

What, then, is the role of infant–parent relationships in the
poem? How does attachment theory find its place in the story?
This chapter suggests that the presence of parents and parenting,
babies and infant growth, signals an emotional narrative that is
tensely present, but its complexity remains as an unresolved and
unintegrated resilience within *Beowulf* that permits another story to
be told. It suggests that these scenes of childbirth, infant care, and
child guardianship – touched upon, but passed over – are loci where
deep and meaningful attachments develop, if not from biological
parents then from adoptive, Danish caregivers. While acknowledged
by the poem, these attachments are sidelined and exchanged for the
alternative intimacies of Scyld's conflict with neighbouring tribes and
Beowulf's combat with Grendel. Further, when these attachments
are addressed (for the anecdotes of parent–child bonds populate
all corners of the poem), it is in tragedy's rearview mirror, when
children are killed as a consequence of such violence. And yet they
are never forgotten, but return as if they were present in the very last
moments of a person's life and in a community's memorialization
of them.

As I mentioned previously, I wrote and revised this chapter in
the weeks and months after one birth and prior to another. What
I could not predict when I alighted upon the topic of child abandonment and began to research it is that I would be writing this chapter
while I was facing the very real possibility of having to abandon
my own children. After much research and preliminary close readings,
I found myself working on a draft while living in a hospital room
with Carmela, who, at two months old, was struggling to survive
after contracting infant botulism; and, as if in a terrible dream, I
revised this same chapter during weeks of ultrasounds, non-stress
tests, and doppler readings that showed Mary Ellard's signs of an
intrauterine growth restriction that threatened her viability as a
neonate. Abandonment became, for me, a real and existential concern,
and *Beowulf*'s ambivalence towards its babies suddenly felt immediate.
In the face of paediatric and neonatal specialists trained in medical
procedures, the express purpose of which is premised upon never
abandoning any baby – on never being ambivalent – my husband
and I had to consider the lives of our two infants with extreme
ambivalence. How to manage the flood of emotions associated with

preparing for the loss of a child still in utero, and yet remain understanding that some babies are not meant to – or cannot, because of genetics, biology, or the luck of the draw – live?

Ambivalence, intimacy, and babies in *Beowulf* and among its scholars

Beowulf's ambivalence towards childhoods that are marked by abandonment speaks to contemporary discussions of intimacy, a vast and sprawling topic that has fallen within the express purview of social scientists for over half a century. Intimacy is not created or sustained by a universal process, and it is understood and enacted differently in many places and times. Despite the many and diverse forms that intimacy takes, sociologists and psychologists point to two overarching activities that characterize it: 'self-disclosure and partner responsiveness'.[55] 'I express a vulnerability, and you accept or rebuff me.' Initially understood within the context of heterosexual relationships, intimacy was, until the 1990s, presumed to be limited to the private, rather than public, sphere. Yet as public–private divisions were interrogated, so were the formulations (and boundaries) of intimacy. Intimacy has been extended to include homosexual, transgendered, and interspecies relationships; and studies have articulated its presence in 'public' spheres such as the workplace, reality television shows, and forums for citizen expression. As a consequence of reframing its boundaries, intimacy is no longer understood solely as a matter of interpersonal, domestic relationships. It likewise functions as a practice of self-knowing. As Ken Plummer explains, the 'doing' of intimacy between partners in the public sphere feeds back into 'being' intimate within a family, a shift that renders intimacy no longer a functional aspect of relationships but rather one of affective fulfilment.[56]

As outlined in these terms, intimacy at work and at home stresses it as a highly pleasurable experience. Yet beginning with intergenerational family research[57] and then with parenting,[58] social scientists began to access the role that ambivalence rather than sentimentality and attachment play in parent–child relationships. As these discussions extended beyond the family unit, 'intimacy ambivalence' became recognized as a state of feeling that, according to Karen Prager, 'is built into intimate relationships',[59] whether these are enacted between couples or friends, in private or public domains. Thus, as Lauren Berlant comments, while 'in popular culture ambivalence is seen as the failure of a relation, the opposite of happiness', in actuality it is 'an inevitable condition of intimate attachment and a pleasure in its own right'.[60] The dynamic interplay between conflicting emotions such as attachment and distance, sentimental affection and coldness, are necessary to sustaining relationships and even, as Berlant writes, 'pleasure[ful]'. Yet as Berlant also understands, such pleasure is often unspoken. Her research underscores intimacy in America as a construct sustained by narratives that reach for a life of happiness and belonging even though these aspirational stories carry the weight of institutions such as marriage and family life that fail their heroes; desires that contradict formulaic notions of love, friendship, or sexuality; and the inequalities of gender and race. With respect to my own life, the medical narratives into which Carmela and Mary Ellard were placed – narratives for which I am extraordinarily grateful because they saved my daughters' lives – are aspirational stories that fit into Berlant's assessment of American intimacy. The pain and grief of a child's death are both disavowed and avoided through medical practice, discourse, and procedures. Parents who are in the position of losing, giving up on, or 'abandoning' a child must face the deep psychic gulf between what they desire and what they cannot have, and grapple with an ambivalence towards intimacy that structures *living* itself. Further, for me to make such an anecdotal statement about my personal life is to further extend the place of intimacy from the domestic to the public domain, considering the extent to which ambivalence operates here, then draws each of us back to our own family lives wherein we might reconsider childhood abandonment in a different, more complex light.

To return, finally, to *Beowulf* and its babies: if we reposition Scyld's abandonment and Beowulf's orphancy and adoption as ambivalent scenes that radiate outwards and structure other relationships in the poem's narrative world, child lives become central rather than peripheral to adult ones. If we underscore the poem's ambivalence towards children as a sign of emotional complexity, then the abandonment of Scyld and Beowulf can be repositioned not as acts of carelessness but of complex care that manifest attachments beyond the immediate purview of one's biological family and cultural community. And finally, if ambivalence underwrites and structures not only intimacy but moreover the intimate aspects of living – in domestic and public worlds – then *Beowulf*'s brief but central descriptions of babies within its families ask us to give key consideration to babies within our working environments. Not only how and when they are present in the poem but also how and when they are present in our professional lives – in the classroom, at conferences, and in our criticism.

Notes

1 Note that in contrast to scant scholarly discussions about Scyld's infant status, a robust critical tradition engages with his arrival by sea and his ship burial. Uninterested in the issue of Scyld's age, this critical tradition discusses the narrative details of his prologue in relation to source analogues, early medieval genealogies, and concerns regarding structural and artistic 'unity', often with the purpose of deciphering a possible date for the *Beowulf* poem. For an extensive summary of this scholarship, see Robert E. Bjork, 'Digressions and episodes', in Robert E. Bjork and John D. Niles (eds), *A Beowulf handbook* (Lincoln, NE: University of Nebraska Press, 1997), pp. 193–211, at 201–5.

2 Carolyn Hares-Styker, 'Adrift on the seven seas: the mediaeval topos of exile at sea', *Florilegium*, 12 (1993), 79–98, at 79.

3 R. D. Fulk, 'An Eddic analogue to the Scyld Scefing story', *RES*, 40.159 (1989), 313–22; quoted in Hares-Styker, 'Adrift on the seven seas', 79.

4 *Scef* is an Old English term that references a sheaf (of corn) or bundle. As Fulk, following Eisen, writes, *scef* has been associated with the Estonian folk-practices of keeping 'a wax image … formed to resemble a three-year-old child' in a grain bin ('An Eddic analogue', 314). The image, he continues, is meant to resemble Peko, a god of agricultural fertility, and Fulk traces the etymology of 'Pekko' from the Proto-Germanic form *beww-* to the Icelandic and Old English words for 'barley' and finally to 'the Germanic barley-figure from which he must be descended' (Fulk, 'An Eddic analogue', 314, 315). Sceaf is likewise a figure that 'may instead (or also?) have been a culture hero … who came over the water to help his future people with a new crop' (Audrey Meaney, *Scyld Scefing and the dating of Beowulf – again* [Manchester: Manchester Centre for Anglo-Saxon Studies, 1988], p. 16). See also Mercedes Salvador, 'The arrival of the hero in a ship: a common leitmotif in OE regnal tables and the story of Scyld Scefing in *Beowulf*, *Selim: journal of the Spanish Society for Medieval English Language and Literature: Revista de la Sociedad Española de Lengua y Literatura Inglesa Medieval*, 8 (1998), 205–21.

5 Gale Owen-Crocker, *The four funerals in Beowulf: and the structure of the poem* (Manchester: Manchester University Press, 2000), p. 18.

6 See Meaney, *Scyld Scefing and the dating of Beowulf*; Thomas D. Hill, 'The myth of the Ark-born son of Noe and the West-Saxon Royal Genealogical Tables', *Harvard theological review*, 80 (1987), 379–83; Daniel Anlezark, 'Sceaf, Japheth, and the origins of the Anglo-Saxons', *ASE*, 31 (2002), 13–46.

7 Kenneth Sisam, 'Anglo-Saxon Royal Genealogies', *Proceedings of the British Academy*, 39 (1953), 287–348, at 316; Anlezark, 'Sceaf, Japheth', 33.

8 Fulk, 'An Eddic analogue'; Hares-Stryker, 'Adrift on the seven seas'; and Tomoaki Mizuno, 'The divine infant coming over the waves: an Old Nordic *Mare-bito* figure', *Iris*, 23 (2002), 37–52.

9 Philippe Ariès, *Centuries of childhood: a social history of family life*, trans. Robert Baldick (New York: Vintage, 1962).

10 Mathew Kuefler, '"A Wryed existence": attitudes toward children in Anglo-Saxon England', *Journal of social history*, 24.4 (1991), 823–34, at 827, 828, 830.

11 Sally Crawford, *Childhood in Anglo-Saxon England* (Stroud: Sutton Publishing, 1999), p. 168.

12 Winfried Rudolf, 'Anglo-Saxon preaching on children', in Susan Irvine and Winfried Rudolf (eds), *Childhood & adolescence in Anglo-Saxon literary culture* (Toronto: University of Toronto Press, 2018), pp. 48–70, at 50.

13 Shu-Han Luo, 'Tender beginnings in the Exeter Book *Riddles*', in Irvine and Rudolf (eds), *Childhood & adolescence*, pp. 71–94, at 81.

14 Susan Irvine and Winfried Rudolf, 'Introduction', in Irvine and Rudolf (eds), *Childhood & adolescence*, pp. 3–14, at 8, 9.

15 Ibid., pp. 10, 11.

16 In the introduction to his book, Boswell addresses arguments made by Ariès which claim that, because a concept of childhood did not exist in pre-modern Europe, child–parent relations were 'inherently and categorically different from those in the modern West' (John Boswell, *Kindness of strangers: the abandonment of children in Western Europe from Late Antiquity to the Renaissance* [New York: Pantheon Books, 1988], p. 36). Boswell states that 'In regard to abandonment, [Volker] Hunecke wryly notes that the greatest known increase in the exposing of children occurred "at the point when, as Philippe Ariès has shown, Europe began to discover childhood"' (p. 37).

17 For Boswell, child oblation, or the practice of promising one's infant or young child to monastic life, likewise falls into this category.

18 Boswell, *Kindness*, p. 223.

19 Ibid., p. 213.

20 Carol J. Clover, 'The politics of scarcity: notes on the sex ratio in early Scandinavia', *Scandinavian studies*, 60.2 (1988), 147–88; Nancy L. Wicker, 'Selective female infanticide as partial explanation for the death of women in Viking Age Scandinavia', in Guy Halsall (ed.), *Violence and society in the early medieval West* (Woodbridge: Boydell, 1998), pp. 205–21.

21 Sean B. Lawing, 'The place of the evil: infant abandonment in Old Norse society', *Scandinavian studies*, 85.2 (2013), 133–50.

22 Boswell, *Kindness*, p. 225.

23 Felix Liebermann (ed.), *Die Gesetze der Angelsachsen*, vol. 1 (Halle: Max Niemeyer, 1903), p. 100, [26] and [27].

24 J. A. Tasioulas, 'The mother's lament: Wulf and Eadwacer reconsidered', *Medium Aevum*, 65.1 (1996), 1–14. While Tasioulas's article is referenced frequently in texts that consider the enigmatic place of *Wulf and Eadwacer* in the consideration of sex, gender, and emotions in Old English and medieval literature, her arguments regarding the poem have not been seconded. Sources that discuss infanticide include an eighth-century penitential attributed to Bede, and, possibly, Wulfstan's Homily 29. Cf. Jennifer Neville, 'Fostering the cuckoo: "Exeter Book" *Riddle 9*', *RES*, 58.236 (2007), 431–46.

25 Rudolf, 'Anglo-Saxon preaching on children', p. 60.

26 Boswell, *Kindness*, p. 228.

27 Lawing, 'The place of evil', 137.

28 Ibid., 142.

29 Wicker, 'Selective female infanticide', pp. 215–16.

30 Ibid.; Nancy L. Wicker, 'Christianization, female infanticide, and the abundance of female burials at Viking Age Birka in Sweden', *Journal of the history of sexuality*, 21.2 (2012), 245–62.

31 Lorraine Sherr, Joanne Mueller, and Zoe Fox, 'Abandoned babies in the UK – a review utilizing media reports', *Child: care, health and development*, 35.3 (2009), 419–30, at 420.

32 Lorraine Sherr, Kathryn J. Roberts, and Natasha Croome, 'Emotional distress, resilience and adaptability: a qualitative study of adults who experienced infant abandonment', *Health psychology and behavioral medicine*, 5.1 (2017), 197–213, at 202.

33 Ibid., 202, 203.

34 Jan Winberg, 'Mother and newborn baby: mutual regulation of physiology and behavior – a selective review', *Developmental psychobiology*, 47.3 (2005), 217–29.

35 David Howe, *Attachment across the lifecourse: a brief introduction* (New York: Palgrave, 2011), p. 12.

36 Ibid., p. 13.

37 Alice Jorgensen, 'Introduction', in Alice Jorgensen, Frances McCormack, and Jonathan Wilcox (eds), *Anglo-Saxon emotions: reading the heart in Old English literature, language, and culture* (Burlington, VT: Ashgate, 2015), pp. 1–18, at 4.

38 Mary Garrison, 'Early medieval experiences of grief and separation through the eyes of Alcuin and others: the grief and gratitude of the oblate', in Jorgensen, McCormack, and Wilcox (eds), *Anglo-Saxon emotions*, pp. 227–62, at 254.

39 Patrick Joseph Ryan, *Master–Servant childhood: a history of the idea of childhood in medieval English culture* (New York: Palgrave, 2013), pp. 32, 33, 83, author's italics.

118 Beowulf and babies

40 Ryan makes this argument via a series of lengthy etymological discussions that interrogate Latin, Old English, and Middle English words for boy, child, and servant, which illustrate the 'long-term thatching between terms of childhood and servitude' (*Master–Servant childhood*, p. 50).
41 Ibid., p. 83.
42 Ibid., pp. 83–4; cf. Stephen G. Post, 'History, infanticide, and imperiled newborns', *The Hastings Center report*, 18.4 (1988), 14–17, at 15.
43 D. Lorenz-Meyer, cited in Simon Biggs, 'Thinking about generations: conceptual positions and policy implications', *Journal of social issues*, 63 (2007), 695–711, at 706.
44 Ibid., 706.
45 Boswell, *Kindness*, pp. 214, 223.
46 Quotations of *Beowulf* are drawn from R. D. Fulk, Robert E. Bjork, and John D. Niles (eds), *Klaeber's Beowulf*, 4th edn (Toronto: University of Toronto Press, 2008). All Old English translations are my own.
47 Joseph Bosworth, *An Anglo-Saxon Dictionary*, ed. Thomas Northcote Toller et al., comp. Sean Christ and Ondřej Tichý (Prague: Faculty of Arts, Charles University, 2010), 'sceaft' I, II; 'sceaft' I, II.
48 John M. Hill, *Narrative pulse of Beowulf: arrivals and departures* (Toronto: University of Toronto Press, 2008), pp. 3–4.
49 Ibid., pp. 4–6.
50 Ibid.
51 For a lengthy summary, see David Clark, 'Relaunching the hero: the case of Scyld and Beowulf re-opened', *Neophilologus*, 90 (2006), 612–42.
52 Norman E. Elaison, 'Beowulf, Wiglaf and the Wægmundings', *ASE*, 7 (1978), 95–105.
53 Ruth Lehmann, 'Ecgþeow the Wægmunding: Geat or Swede?', *English language notes*, 31.3 (1994), 1–5; Erin M. Shaull, 'Ecgþeow, brother of Ongenþeow, and the problem of Beowulf's Swedishness', *Neophilologus*, 101 (2017), 263–75.
54 Richard North reminds that 'Beowulf's words on his childhood conflict with the poet's', and North emphasizes the context for these statements, 'for he is then speaking to his retinue before leaving them so that he may fight with the Dragon alone. Beowulf must convince these hand-picked Geatish warriors that he belongs to a family with experience in war.' See 'Hrothulf's childhood and Beowulf's: a comparison', in Irvine and Rudolf (eds), *Childhood & adolescence*, pp. 222–43, at 240.
55 Jean-Philippe Laurenceau et al., 'Intimacy as an interpersonal process: current status and future directions', in Debra J. Mashek and Arthur Aron (eds), *Handbook of closeness and intimacy* (Mahwah, NJ: Lawrence Erlbaum Associates, 2004), pp. 61–78, at 62.
56 Ken Plummer, *Intimate citizenship: private decisions and public dialogues* (Seattle, WA: University of Washington Press, 2003).

57 Kurt Luescher and Karl Pillemer, 'Intergenational ambivalence: a new approach to the study of parent–child relations in later life', *Journal of marriage and family*, 60.2 (1998), 413–25.

58 Rozsika Parker, 'Maternal ambivalence', *Winnicott studies*, 9 (1994), 3–17; Wendy Hollway and Brid Featherstone, *Mothering and ambivalence* (New York: Routledge, 1997).

59 Karen J. Prager, *The dilemmas of intimacy: conceptualization, assessment, and treatment* (New York: Routledge, 2014), p. 139.

60 Lauren Berlant, *The female complaint: the unfinished business of sentimentality in American culture* (Durham, NC: Duke University Press, 2008), p. 2.

6

At home in the fens with the Grendelkin[1]

Christopher Abram

In his 1914 book *Vampires and vampirism*, Dudley Wright wrote that 'there is an Anglo-Saxon poem with the title *A vampyre of the fens*'.[2] You can hardly imagine how excited I was to read this: one comes across new Anglo-Saxon poems so rarely, and rarer still are compositions with such juicy titles. *A vampyre of the fens*, with its ring of the slightly schlocky Gothick shocker, would have been an unexpectedly thrilling addition to the canon. Alas, *A vampyre of the fens* is found nowhere in the Anglo-Saxon Poetic Records (the standard edition of the Old English verse corpus), and the usual works of reference are silent on the subject. I needed more information about this mysterious text. Turning to Brian J. Frost's classic of popular vampirology, *The monster with a thousand faces*, I found some. According to Frost, *A vampyre of the fens* is an obscure (no kidding) Anglo-Saxon poem, written at the beginning of the eleventh century. This poem, he claims, marks the first appearance of a vampire in a work of pure imagination.[3]

'Pure imagination' is, of course, right, in that this poem is entirely imaginary. There is no such poem as *A vampyre of the fens*. Frost is passing on unscrutinized Wright's assertion – and there are other vampirological treatises that repeat the claim.[4] Thanks to the detective work of Eugenio Olivares Merino, we now know that the ultimate source of the idea of a lost Anglo-Saxon vampire tale is found in Charles Dickens's *Household words* magazine where, in 1855, Edmund Ollier introduced it to the world, in terms that Wright would borrow wholesale: 'There is an old Anglo-Saxon poem on the Vampyre of the Fens', he wrote.[5] Ollier was an all-purpose hack with no knowledge that we can ascertain of early medieval literature and culture – the trail ends with him, though Olivares Merino speculates that Ollier may have been influenced, probably indirectly, by a reference to *Beowulf* in Jacob Grimm's *Deutsche Mythologie*. Grimm made the connection between Grendel and a vampire for the first time in scholarship.[6] Grendel, writes Grimm, sucks blood from the veins of his victims – that much is certainly true; he does so quite explicitly in line 742b of the poem: *blod edrum dranc*.[7] In the same passage, Grimm speaks of Grendel's dwelling in swamps and marshes. And so, perhaps, 'the vampire of the fens' was born. It seems likely, therefore, that Ollier was referring to *Beowulf*, a poem that he didn't know but had heard tell of, possibly from somebody familiar with Grimm's work. Dudley Wright then gave a title to Ollier's imaginary poem, after which *The Vampyre of the Fens* became what Olivares Merino calls a 'bibliographic ghost', a false echo of a song that was never actually sung.[8]

It's a shame, because *The Vampyre of the Fens* is potentially a splendid title for the poem we know as *Beowulf*, or at least for that part of the poem that takes place in Denmark. We must always remember that the title *Beowulf*, as solid and definitive and obvious as it is, is an invention of modern antiquarianism. We have no idea what the Anglo-Saxons called this poem – or even if any of them ever read it. (The two scribes responsible for copying *Beowulf* into London, British Library, Cotton Vitellius A. xv certainly processed its text, but we might question to what extent and in what manner they were *reading* it.) Thinking about alternative titles for *Beowulf* can be a productive way of destabilizing our comfortable preconceptions about the poem. If *Beowulf* were called *A Vampyre of the Fens*, the murderous monster Grendel would appear to be more central to the narrative's design – perhaps we might even try to imagine Grendel as the poem's protagonist, rather than as an always Othered antagonist to Beowulf and the men of Heorot, which is the name given to the Danes' newly built hall, which Grendel attacks murderously. The new title can also conjure a sense of place that might be hermeneutically productive in reading the poem, leading us on a journey into a particular type of landscape – a wetland environment in which Grendel is intimately embedded.

The Old English poem *Maxims II* states that 'þyrs sceal on fenne wunian' (a *þyrs* shall [or must] live in a fen), as if this were something everybody knew:

> God sceal on heofenum,
> dæda demend.   Duru sceal on healle,
> rum recedes muð.   Rand sceal on scylde,
> fæst fingra gebeorh.   Fugel uppe sceal
> lacan on lyfte.   Leax sceal on wæle
> mid sceote scriðan.   Scur sceal on heofenum,

winde geblanden,   in þas woruld cuman.
þeof sceal gangan þystrum wederum.   þyrs sceal on fenne
    gewunian
ana innan lande.[9]

(God must be in the heavens, the judge of deeds. A door must be
on the hall, the building's open mouth. A boss must be on a shield,
firm protection for fingers. A bird must soar in the air on high. A
salmon must glide in the pool, darting about quickly. The rain must
be in the heavens, mixed with the wind, to come upon this world.
A thief must travel in dark weather. A *þyrs* must dwell in a fen, alone
in the land.)

A *þyrs* shall live in a fen: it is as much his habitat as the pond is
the salmon's or the wood is the wild boar's or the kingdom is the
king's. Such is the natural order of the world. Or perhaps we should
take *sceal* as imperative: a *þyrs* must live in a fen, where it will be
alone in the land. The fen is the space apportioned to these creatures,
whether by man, God, or fate, and they must not live anywhere
else. It would not be natural. Why? What happens when a *þyrs*
leaves the fen?

We know very well what happens, because Grendel is a *þyrs*.
Beowulf says so, in his first speech to Hrothgar: 'Ond nu wið Grendel
sceal, / wið þam aglæcan ana gehegan / ðing wið þyrse' (and now
I must seek a meeting alone with Grendel, the terrible adversary,
the *þyrs*) (424b–426a). The poem gives us no clue what a *þyrs* is – but
Grendel is one.[10] And we know, too, that Grendel conforms to type
in his habitat, whether because of his nature, by choice, or by
compulsion. Grendel's home in the fens is one of the first things
we learn about him: this information is given the very first time
that we hear the monster's name.

Swa ða drihtguman   dreamum lifdon,
eadiglice,   oð ðæt an ongan
fyrene fremman   feond on helle;
wæs se grimma gæst   Grendel haten,
mære mearcsteapa,   se þe moras heold,
fen ond fæsten;   fifelcynnes eard
wonsæli wer   weardode hwile. (99–105)

(Thus the warriors lived in joy, happily, until a fiend in hell began
to commit an atrocity. The grim guest was called Grendel, the famous
march-stepper, he who held the marshes, fen, and fastness; the
unfortunate man guarded for a time the homeland of the kindred
of monsters.)

Grendel occupies a very particular landscape: it is a border territory, a *mearc*; it is a *mor*, which it is almost impossible to persuade *Beowulf* translators is not directly equivalent to moor in modern English usage, with its windswept, hilly, and romantic *Wuthering Heights* connotations. Rather, *mor* can (and here, should) refer specifically to swampy waste ground, a morass: it is recorded as such in the Old English *Life of Guthlac*, the Old English *Hexateuch*, and in an early Aldhelmian gloss, and remains so in the moors of Somerset, ancient marshlands that have long since been drained. Although there are also Anglo-Saxon attestations of *mor* as meaning a desolate high place, to translate as 'moor' when 'marsh', 'mire', and 'morass' are available to us seems like an infelicity in this instance, since *mor* is so closely collocated with *fenn* in this passage.[11]

A *fenn* is a fen, which is to say that it is a place that is somewhat watery, somewhat muddy, pretty much flat – difficult territory to live in, unsuitable for farming, hardly land at all, but something marginal and transitory. Like all wetlands, fenland is hard to pin down, hard to categorize. As William Howarth puts it:

> We cannot essentialize wetlands, because they are hybrid and mul-
> tivalent: neither land nor water alone, they are water land; a continuum
> between terra and aqua. In rhetorical terms they are not syntax but
> parataxis, phrases placed side by side, without apparent connection,
> a term Joseph Frank used to describe spatial forms that evoke a great
> variety of response. In their wildness, wetlands dispossess readers
> of old codes and lead toward new syntax, where phrases may begin
> to reassemble.[12]

Fæsten, however, carries with it the idea of a place of security or sanctuary: somewhere that can shelter one – a home that can be a castle. Not everybody can, must, or would wish to live in the fen: it is the *fifelcynnes eard*, the home or land of a race of monsters – specifically, a race of aquatic monsters, as all occurrences of *fifel* in Old English poetry refer to creatures that live in or around bodies of water.[13] Grendel is practically and perhaps actually amphibious. His dwelling-place is underwater, or at least has to be entered via a long and arduous swim. It is difficult to get to, just as the fens have traditionally been regarded as one of the most inaccessible landscapes of England. Its remoteness and inaccessibility makes the fen a place of refuge for Grendel and his mother: as well as a *fæsten*, we hear the mere described as a *fen-freoðo* (851b), a *fen-hop* (764a), and a *mor-hop* (450a) – a 'sanctuary' and a 'refuge' twice over. The first two of these instances might be ironic, since they both refer to the fen as a sanctuary for the mortally wounded Grendel – the fen becomes the monster's resting-place, his mausoleum. Once he has left the fastness of the fens, they can no longer protect him from the likes of Beowulf, but the fens are nonetheless Grendel's true homeland, his family's *eard*. The *Dictionary of Old English* glosses the occurrence of *eard* at *Beowulf* 104b as 'habitat', which has the advantage of emphasizing the symbiotic relationship between the Grendelkin and their *oikos*, though it also runs the risk of aligning them more closely than necessary with the 'natural', the 'animal', the 'wild'.[14] Grendel returns home to his proper habitat, his real home, to die.

In other Old English poems, the *eard* is often the place one is exiled from, but for Grendel it is the place he is exiled *to* – and this place of exile becomes a new home.[15] Grendel is a *mearcstapa*, but he is not an *eardstapa* like the Exeter Book's exilic Wanderer, who is characterized by a restless rootlessness as he trudges over land and sea: deprived of a home with God or among men, Grendel and his kin have found a new *eard*, a habitat in the fens that suits them, a place which they have settled.[16] And this homeland is God-given or at least God-sanctioned: Hrothgar, the Danish king whose realm has been ravaged by Grendel's attacks, acknowledges (1724b–1726) that it is God himself who apportions *eard* to people, along with wisdom and nobility (*snyttru* and *eorlscipe*).

As it happens – and I hope this is the only characteristic I share with Grendel – the fens are also *my* homeland, my *eard*. I have lived most of my life on the edge of the low-lying, marshy plains of Lincolnshire and Cambridgeshire. (When I moved to northern Indiana, I discovered a landscape that had once been another major wetland habitat and had since been drained for agriculture; it is possible that this explains why I quickly came to feel at home there.) I am writing this chapter in Little Downham, three miles from Ely, whose magnificent cathedral, the so-called 'ship of the fens', can be seen clearly from the edge of the village. Here, we are on solid ground, rather than down in the mire itself; Downham derives its name from Old English *dun-ham*, 'hill settlement', and the older name for the village is Downham-in-the-Isle, for once upon a time we would have been surrounded here on three sides by marshland that flooded regularly in winter and remained distinctly boggy the whole year round.[17] To this day, the road between the nearby towns of Littleport and Wisbech is normally closed for weeks each winter when the Great Ouse overflows its banks and returns this part of the fens to something like its original landscape – a great silver expanse of water broken here and there by half-submerged scrub trees, populated solely by wildfowl. Little Downham, like Ely itself, is something of a 'fen-sanctuary', though not the same type of refuge as Grendel seeks; it is a place of refuge kept apart from the rest of the world by the fens that surround it, but it is also a place of refuge *from* the fens and from whatever lurks in them.

My fens are not the Anglo-Saxon fens – few British landscapes have changed as substantially over the past thousand years – but there is still a shock in hearing this landscape collocated with the abode of a monstrous race, in the possibility of an unthought-of exoticism around a bend in the road. But after the initial shock has worn off, I find myself admitting that there is still something uncanny about this corner of the world, something never quite settled or wholly stable about it. These fens are no longer wetlands, but they are still a landscape of featureless expanses, of a disorienting lack of landmarks, a landscape in which roads proceed in dead straight lines for miles before haring off at right-angles for no apparent reason. Drowning is one of the most common causes of death in road accidents around here. On a foggy night in the fens it is still quite easy to imagine Grendel creeping up the hill to the village under cover of darkness, looming out of the thick, white mist, and appearing at the window. There could well be something 'out there' in the fens, precisely because the fens still feel so powerfully 'out there' – so alien, so unwelcoming. Grendel's entrance in the poem – one of the most effectively terrifying passages in all literature, to my mind – is all the more spine-chilling when I read it in the fens, and as a fenlander. Grendel comes out of a particular landscape, and this landscape is, at least in part, what makes him what he is.

By the time we see Grendel, some seven hundred lines into *Beowulf*, we have already heard plenty about him. The narrator speaks of him, Beowulf speaks of him, Hrothgar speaks of him. We have learned of Grendel's origin among the kindred of Cain, and his ravages have been described. We have seen Heorot cleared for the night and entrusted to its new guardian, Beowulf. But for all the information we have already received about Grendel, nothing can prevent his arrival from shocking us:

> Com on wanre niht
> scriðan sceadugenga.   Sceotend swæfon,
> þa þæt hornreced   healdan scoldon,
> ealle buton anum   – þæt wæs yldum cuþ
> þæt hie ne moste,   þa metod nolde,
> se scynscaþa   under sceadu bregdan –

ac he wæccende   wraþum on andan
bad bolgenmode   beadwa geþinges.
    Ða com of more   under misthleoþum
Grendel gongan,   Godes yrre bær;
mynte se manscaða   manna cynnes
sumne besyrwan   in sele þam hean.
Wod under wolcnum   to þæs þe he winreced,
goldsele gumena   gearwost wisse,
fætum fahne.   Ne wæs þæt forma sið
þæt he Hroþgares   ham gesohte;
næfre he on aldordagum,   ær ne siþðan,
heardran hæle   healðegnas fand.
Com þa to recede,   rinc siðian,
dreamum bedæled.   Duru sona onarn,
fyrbendum fæst,   syþðan he hire folmum æthran;
onbræd þa bealohydig,   ða he gebolgen wæs,
recedes muþan.   Raþe æfter þon
on fagne flor   feond treddode,
eode yrremod;   him of eagum stod
ligge gelicost   leoht unfæger. (702b–727)

(The shadow-walker came striding in dark night. The warriors slept,
those who were supposed to guard the gabled house, all but one –
people knew that the hostile foe couldn't draw him into the shadows,
if God didn't wish it – but awake he waited, swollen-hearted, to
meet the wrathful soul in battle.

Then came from the marsh Grendel, walking under misty slopes,
bearing God's wrath. Mankind's assailant thought to seize someone
in the high hall. He waded in the shadows, beneath the clouds, until
he could perceive the men's gold-hall as clear as day, adorned with
decorations. It wasn't the first time that he had sought out Hrothgar's
home; never, before or after, in all the days of his life, did he find a
harder fortune among the hall-thegns. The warrior came travelling
to the hall, deprived of joys. The door, fast with forged bands, soon
gave way when he touched it; the evil-minded one broke open the
mouth of the hall because he was swollen with rage. Straight away
the fiend stepped on to the decorated floor: he went angrily. From
his eyes shone a light most like an unpleasant flame.)

This passage is justly famous for its terrifying affect.[18] The threefold
repetition of *com* (702b, 710a, 720a) evokes the deliberate, inexo-
rable approach of the killer, which is intercut with images of the
Danes sleeping unawares and Beowulf keeping his solitary vigil.
Grendel is initially called *sceadugenga* here, a 'shadow-walker' – one
of his most impressionistic epithets in the poem, emphasizing his

crepuscular creepiness as he advances *on wanre niht*. His arrival at Heorot is chilling regardless of where he came from, but reading *Beowulf* in a fenland setting adds a particular piquancy to lines 710–11, when we read *mor* as 'marsh': 'Þa com of more under misthleoþum / Grendel gongan, Godes yrre bær' (Then came from the marsh Grendel, walking under misty slopes, bearing God's wrath).

Those of us who dwell 'in the fens' for the most part dwell *out of* the fens, in fact, on the little patches of higher, drier ground like the isle upon which Little Downham was founded. The preponderance of settlement names ending in the *-ey* (Old English *-eg*, 'island') suffix around here – Coveney, Ramsey, Stuntney, Whittlesea, and so on – indicates as much. Before they were drained, the fens proper – the marshes themselves – were thought by outsiders largely unsuitable for human habitation, though, as Susan Oosthuizen has shown, even in the early medieval period this landscape was never entirely uninhabited, never as empty as people thought.[19] People could make their livelihoods from the fens – as fishermen or reed-cutters, perhaps – but they preferred to cluster together on the islands; they still do so today, even though arable farmland is all that separates one village from the next. The fact that Grendel comes *of more* is perhaps a special source of horror when we read about it in this precise spot, since it is the *mor* which surrounds us here. As a child, I lived on Moor Lane, a road which led down to Bardney Fen from the village of Potterhanworth near the northern extremity of the Lincolnshire fens. (I always wondered why it was called *moor* lane, since at the time I imagined moorland as being a barren upland environment.) I know what it is like to watch a winter fog-bank roll up the slopes of our modest escarpment and swallow the village's houses one by one until only the soft penumbra of electric lights are visible down the street. In the imagination, as well as in fact, mists are a climatic phenomenon that is inseparable from this type of landscape: in 1627 the cartographer John Speed wrote that, in Lincolnshire, 'the Ayre upon the East and South part is both thicke and foggy, by reason of the Fennes and unsolute grounds', an image that had sufficient traction for Shakespeare to have King Lear speak of 'fen-sucked fogs drawn by the powerful sun'.[20] Grendel is coming, coming, coming up from the fen, up the slopes, under the cover of mist and darkness. He is coming out of his space into ours.

Grendel's ability to move between worlds – from water to land, from his own monstrous parody of a hall to Heorot's all-too-human parody of a hall, perhaps from hell to earth and back, from the wilderness to civilization – is one of his most defining features, encapsulated in his being called *mearcstapa* (103a and 1348a, where Grendel's mother is included in the plural of the term). *Mearcstapa* is found only in *Beowulf*, and it is applied only to Grendel and his mother: it is not one of the many epithets shared by the monsters and the poem's hero. The *mearc* is a borderland, an area between places that manages to be something of both places at once but wholly of neither, establishing the limits of a community's conception of itself. As Lindy Brady puts it, 'More importantly than its precise location … a *mearc* connoted the space just beyond the utmost control of a society that marked the difference between "us" and "them".'[21] While the most famous *mearc*-derived place name in the British Isles is found in the so-called Marches that form the contested buffer zone between England and Wales, it is also easy to read the East Anglian fens as another *mearc*, not least because the Cambridgeshire market town of March derives its name from this term.

March is built on yet another island in the fenland swamp. It is not clear why this place in particular should be named after its liminal position when the fens are everywhere and always a liminal landscape, their borders undefined and their limits constantly shifting.[22] The route of a Roman causeway passes close to March, so perhaps it was perceived as having a position on the margins of navigable space in the area. Not too far away is found a second trace of the Romans' interactions with the fens – the Car Dyke, an 85-mile-long artificial ditch that limns the western edge of the fens. The Car Dyke can be seen as marking the limit of *terra cognita* in this part of the Roman world: a symbolic border, if not much of an actual defensive structure. March, and the *mearc*, is thus beyond the limits of the civilized, or truly civilizable, world. The landscape across which the *mearcstapan* travel in *Beowulf* is in a similar position relative to the built environment of Heorot and all it stands for. The fen in *Beowulf* is an out-space as defined by Heorot's in-space. Heorot is a centre; the fen is a periphery. We know that Heorot is not far from Grendel's home by measure of miles ('Nis þæt feor heonan / milgemearces þæt se mere standeð') (1361b–1362), but the two locations are worlds apart. The road from the coast to Heorot is *stanfah* (paved with stones) (320a) in the Roman manner, while Heorot itself is 'timbred / geatolic and goldfah' (constructed splendidly and with golden adornments) (307b–308a). These descriptions can be contrasted with the landscape evoked by

Hrothgar's fullest description of the environment that the monsters occupy:

> Hie dygel lond
> warigeað, wulfhleoþu,   windige næssas,
> frecne fengelad,   ðær fyrgenstream
> under næssa genipu   niþer gewiteð,
> flod under foldan.   Nis þæt feor heonon
> milgemearces   þæt se mere standeð;
> ofer þæm hongiað   hrinde bearwas
> wudu wyrtum fæst   wæter oferhelmað.   (1357b–1364)

(They occupy a secret land, wolf-inhabited slopes, windy headlands, a perilous fen-path, where a mountain stream goes down in mist underneath the crags, a torrent under the earth. It is not far from here, measured in miles, that the mere lies; above it hang frost-bound groves: the wood, fixed by its roots, overshadows the water.)

This passage has been controversial because it seems to collocate geographical features that we would not expect to find in a single location. The way to the monsters' home is called a *fengelad* (watery passage across a fen), and the modern English descendant of *gelad*, 'lode', is ubiquitous in the fens as a name for a dyke or other minor watercourse.[23] But there are other features in this passage that seem to suggest a different type of landscape, perhaps a coastal region. I do not think that *wulfhleoþu* (wolf-slopes) presents a particular problem: we have seen that Grendel comes up from below *misthleoþu*, and the wolfishness of these slopes now marks them out as the land of hostile outlaws,[24] without prejudice to where the mere is actually located.[25] The repeated references to *næssas* (headlands) do not seem to belong in a fenland setting, since the place-name element *-ness* is found exclusively around the sea-coasts of England, and not in the East Anglian fens. But there are promontories in the fens, those shallow islands and spurs of higher ground between them that in places allowed passage across the undrained fens without the use of a boat. For example, the small town of Ramsey, famous for its Anglo-Saxon monastic foundation, though named as if it were an island, is in fact situated on a narrow headland that projects out into the fens. Since Ramsey stands at the end of a gentle decline at an altitude of only about seventeen feet above sea level, it is hardly the sort of landscape feature we are accustomed to think of when we think of a ness; but in a fenland context, a change in elevation of only a few feet can be highly significant, as it takes one out of the mire back on to *terra firma*, or vice versa.

Fyrgenstream probably means 'mountain stream', and mountains are a landscape feature that the fens most definitely lack. Other aspects of Hrothgar's description, however, retain something more distinctively fennish. In particular, the phrase 'flod under foldan' (water under earth) conjures up an image of sodden marshland: the streams that flow down from the higher ground have to end up somewhere, and here we may imagine them seeping slowly into the swamp. And the trees overhanging the water would also suggest an inland lake, perhaps, more than a windswept coastal headland; at any rate, this landscape is indistinct, neither one thing nor another, and while this lack of definition may indicate – as several scholars have claimed – that this passage is a literary confection, or even simply 'a metaphor for terror',[26] the fens themselves are – in both reality and imagination – a landscape between other types of landscape, a landscape that confounds categorical identification. The use of the term *mere* for the body of water in question may itself be relevant to this discussion: though 'mere' is a perfectly ordinary word for a pond or lake, it was also applied, prior to their draining in the seventeenth century, specifically to the larger, permanent lagoons in the Cambridgeshire fens at (for example) Whittlesea, Ramsey, and Soham.[27] Bodies of water outside the fens can be called meres, but in these fens, it seems as though areas of standing water can *only* be called meres.

Hrothgar has more to say about Grendel's abode:

Þær mæg nihta gehwæm   niðwundor seon,
fyr on flode.   No þæs frod leofað
gumena bearna   þæt þone grund wite.
Ðeah þe hæðstapa   hundum geswenced,
heorot hornum trum   holtwudu sece,
feorran geflymed,   ær he feorh seleð,
aldor on ofre,   ær he in wille,
hafelan beorgan;   nis þæt heoru stow. (1365–72)

(There each night a fearful wonder may be seen: fire in the water. There is no one alive among the children of men so wise as to know the bottom. Though the heath-stepper, the strong-horned hart, pursued by dogs, chased a long way, might seek the forest, he would give up his life rather than go in[to the mere] to save his head: it is not a pleasant place.)

The 'hateful wonder' that Hrothgar reports, the *fyr on flode* (fire in/on the water) visible from the shore at night, has been interpreted in a way that could have a particular significance to a fenland reading of *Beowulf*. Though the interpretation has long since fallen out of fashion, William Witherle Lawrence's solution to the conundrum of what we should understand *fyr on flode* to mean takes us straight back to marshland: Lawrence regarded this peculiar luminescence as an image of a 'will o' the wisp that haunts marshy places', the result, in biological terms, of an emanation of swamp gases.[28] This phenomenon, also known as *ignis fatuus* (foolish fire), has been absorbed into folklore traditions wherever boggy ground is part of the landscape. If the *fyr on flode* were supposed to represent a will o' the wisp, it would tell us that the mere and its environs include wetlands as well as open water, as the methane thought necessary to produce *ignis fatuus* must come from substantial peat deposits. People's inability to discern the bottom of the mere could also be a consequence of a high proportion of organic matter in the water, as is typical of bogs, which have often been perceived as 'bottomless'.[29]

Similarly, the famously reluctant hart, which would rather die at the hands of its pursuers than leap into the mere, reflects the anxiety that outsiders have sometimes felt upon encountering the alien landscape of the fenland.[30] Perhaps the deer is reacting atavistically to the evil that permeates this *heoru stow*; perhaps it cannot swim; perhaps it is understandably anxious about the possibility of getting stuck in a bog. In any case, the hart does not belong there, as the epithet *hædstapa* may indicate: as a *hædstapa*, the stag properly belongs to the heath, an upland area, as well as to the *holtwudu*, the forest − another geographical feature not found in a fenland setting. *Beowulf*'s hart has a home on the heath, in an animal realm that is home neither to humans nor the likes of Grendel. The monsters belong in the mere, the *þyrs* in the fen. The Danes do not belong in any of these spaces by right or custom or nature: they believe that home is where the Heorot is, but there are limitations on where *heorots* can go, which borders they can transgress. Andy Orchard is surely correct to note that the terrified hart at the side of the mere 'cannot help but conjure images of the imperiled Danish hall, Heorot'.[31] Both the hall and its animal avatar are in the wrong place.

About the precise location of Heorot we learn relatively little in *Beowulf*; less, in fact than we learn about the landscapes in which either the Grendelkin or the dragon live. We know that Heorot is in Denmark, that it is a short march from the coast. And we know

what sort of building it is and why it was constructed, which also
tells us that Heorot has not always been there, wherever 'there' is:

Þa wæs Hroðgare   heresped gyfen,
wiges weorðmynd,   þæt him his winemagas
georne hyrdon,   oðð þæt seo geoguð geweox,
magodriht micel.   Him on mod bearn
þæt healreced   hatan wolde,
medoærn micel   men gewyrcean
þonne yldo bearn   æfre gefrunon,
ond þær on innan   eall gedælan
geongum and ealdum   swylc him God sealde,
buton folcscare   ond feorum gumena.
Ða ic wide gefrægn   weorc gebannan
manigre mægþe   geond þisne middangeard,
folcstede frætwan.   Him on fyrste gelomp,
ædre mid yldum,   þæt hit wearð eal gearo,
healærna mæst;   scop him Heort naman
se þe his words geweald   wide hæfde. (64–79)

(Then Hrothgar was given success in war, glory in battle, so that his
comrades eagerly obeyed him, until the young men grew into a large
band of young retainers. It came to his mind that he wanted to
command people to build a hall, a great mead-hall, one that people's
children will hear of forever; and there to distribute everything which
God had granted him with young and old – apart from ancestral
land and men's lives. Then – as I have heard tell – work was commanded from far and wide, from many peoples throughout the world,
to adorn the people's dwelling place. It came to pass quickly for him:
it was all finished in haste by the people, the greatest of halls; he
called it Heorot, he whose words had power far and wide.)

Heorot is a new building, inhabited for less than a generation before
Grendel's attacks begin, and destined to burn not far into the future
(83b–85). Presumably Hrothgar did not know in advance that his
chosen site lay close by a lair of monsters of the kindred of Cain;
though if he had known, he might not have cared, since Heorot
functions mostly as a symbolic monument to the price one pays for
hubris. (It certainly does not work very well as an actual stronghold
that one can defend against enemies, unless a preternaturally strong
hero turns up to do this job for one.) Heorot is a projection of
Hrothgar's power and wealth – it literally gleams with gold. But
what does it project that power onto? In a reading of *Beowulf* that
foregrounds the importance of the wetland landscape that Grendel
and his mother inhabit, I am inclined to see Heorot as encroaching

on a landscape to which it can never belong – as trying to impose a symbolic order on to an ecological order with which it is utterly incompatible. As Alfred K. Siewers puts it, 'Heorot is constructed as an island of civilization … confined and hemmed in by the powers of chaos', but perhaps strangely for an avowed ecocritic, Siewers does not problematize the binary between 'civilization' and 'chaos', which also encodes a human/nature dichotomy that is always constructed, never natural.[32] From the point of view of the 'civilized' reader, Heorot is a light shining in the darkness; Grendel is the darkness comprehending it not – not that Grendel does not understand Heorot so much as reject it, with all its noise and good cheer and stories of the God who has cast out Grendel's family, giving them as their *eard* a landscape that would be considered unfit for human habitation:

> Ða se ellengæst   earfoðlice
> þrage geþolode,   se þe in þystrum bad,
> þæt he dogora gehwam   dream gehyrde
> hludne in healle.   Þær wæs hearpan sweg,
> swutol sang scopes.   Sægde se þe cuþe
> frumsceaft fira   feorran reccan,
> cwæð þæt se ælmihtiga   eorðan worhte,
> wlitebeorhtne wang,   swa wæter bebugeð,
> gesette sigehreþig   sunnan ond monan,
> leoman to leohte   landbuendum (86–95)

(Then the *ellengæst* suffered grievously for a time – he who dwelled in darkness – when every day he heard joy, loud in the hall. There was the sound of the harp, the clear song of the *scop*. One who knew how to recount from long ago the creation of people said that the Almighty made the earth, the beautiful plain that the water surrounds; the victorious one set the sun and moon as lamps to give light to land-dwellers.)

In the creation story whose performance bothers Grendel so much, we hear that God has made the sun and moon 'leoman to leohte landbuendum' (as lamps to give light to land-dwellers) (95). But Grendel and his mother are not *land*-dwellers, and their watery home has to be illuminated by uncanny means;[33] they are benighted from the outset.

I am intrigued by the idea that Heorot is something ecologically malevolent, something alien, something out of place. It is a brilliant folly, an extravagant excrescence, the gin-palace of a nouveau-riche arriviste, a McMansion. It sticks out like a sore thumb; it is a blot on the landscape, and we know that it will not endure. Heorot is, presumably, built on the edge of the fen, or on an island in the fen; Grendel's mere is not very far from Heorot, though the paths between them can be difficult to follow. The two locations are part of the same landscape. When Grendel comes up from the *mor*, he is upon the hall almost at once. So, while Grendel trespasses in Heorot when he comes out of his marsh, the construction of Heorot might be read as an act of trespass in its own right. For the fen is Grendel's domain, as a member of the *fifelcyn*, and God's condemnation of Cain's line to exile includes the stipulation that they should be banished far from mankind: 'ac he hine feor forwræc, / metod for þy mane mancynne fram' (but the creator condemned him to exile for this crime, far from mankind) (109b–10). The construction of Heorot, this temple of bling and braggadocio, has brought mankind into close proximity with Grendel's homeland. It is Hrothgar, by this reading, who first transgresses the spatial proprieties of the region.[34] God's restraining order demands that Grendel should live far from people – but people are now *right there*, impinging on the space that is his by right. They made the first move: the Danes are the space invaders, and Grendel becomes an agent of resistance against a colonizing power.

The fens have often been a space in which resistance can be fomented. As well as offering sanctuary to those who, for whatever reason, cannot live in a 'civilized' in-space, this region has a long history as a locus of struggle against external oppression in many forms. Most famously, perhaps, in Cambridgeshire we have stories of Hereward the Wake, an exiled Anglo-Saxon nobleman who resisted Norman hegemony in the fens between Ely and Peterborough. In the doubtfully reliable narratives of Hereward's career, we see him, for example, escaping from the siege of Ely by leading his followers off the island and into the fenland's interior by secret tracks unknown to the colonialist interlopers.[35] Around 1070, this marginal landscape became for a moment a last enclave of pre-Norman England, precisely because the fens are so inaccessible to outsiders. The land there is impassable and impossible for those who have not adapted to its demands. The Normans failed in a direct assault on Ely because their warhorses and armour were too heavy for a wooden causeway across the fen to bear, for example.[36]

So, to oppressive external forces, the fens are a problem, because they harbour outlaws, freedom fighters, and monsters. This problem can only finally be solved through a wholesale redevelopment of the landscape. We might think of this in religious terms, first of all, and consider the way in which Ely Cathedral, the 'ship of the fens', looms over the marshes, prominent on its prominence, guiding travellers on to the island and sinners towards redemption. Instead of pursuing the tricksy will o' the wisp to our doom in a bog, today we can look for the light of the cathedral's great octagonal lantern to lead us to safety, to guide us home off the fen. It was the vision of the cathedral as a beacon on foggy autumn nights that first put me in mind of Heorot's relationship to Grendel's fenland – a building that symbolically imposes a new and alien value system on to the landscape. Like Heorot, Ely Cathedral appears as an island of cheer, security, and civilization in a sea of darkness – few places so close to significant human populations in the British Isles seem as dark as the fens at night.

But if this Christianization of the landscape fails to convert it from a monstrous, pagan wilderness into something a little more salubrious and easier to control, one can pursue other strategies in attempting to manage and tame the fens. One such strategy is to marginalize and stigmatize this world, emphasizing its distance from and opposition to 'civilization' by developing its associations with the supernatural, the evil, and the uncouth. Another, more radical approach to dealing with the fens, with the aim of neutralizing them as spaces in which both monstrosity and anti-hegemonic heroism can flourish, is to alter them physically: to change them into something which they never were before. This, of course, is what happened with the wholesale drainage of the fens that began in the seventeenth century. Ian Rotheram calls the drainage an act of ecocide and 'England's greatest ecological disaster',[37] and I tend to agree with him, but it appears to have worked an agricultural miracle. The Dutch engineers turned these marshes into the most fertile arable land in the United Kingdom – though, like Heorot, the modern, drained fenland will not last forever, as peat, which forms most of the subsoil base of the fens, shrinks as it dries out, diminishing the land available for farming and becoming more prone to flooding and topsoil loss through windblow.[38] The modern fens are still somewhat uncanny – it's always unnerving to drive alongside a river but beneath it at the same time, and they are dark and empty and difficult to navigate – but they are no longer wild. They are constrained, fenced in, bounded, denatured. They have, so people say, been 'reclaimed'. But reclaimed from what, or from whom? They were never ours in the first place. Drainage was an act of imperialist aggression against the land and its indigenous inhabitants, human and non-human.

It did not happen without resistance, however. There have always been figures, the true fenlanders with one foot in the water, who made their living from eeling, or cutting sedge for thatch, for whom the undrained wetlands were home and even homely, and who reacted strongly against the imposition of drainage, despite its promise of a more profitable and salubrious environment. Once such fenlander was Tiddy Mun.

Tiddy Mun is an obscure figure from Lincolnshire folklore, stories of whom were first recorded in print in 1891. The collector of the Tiddy Mun tales, M. C. Balfour, tells us that his informant was an unnamed old woman, to whom Tiddy Mun was 'a perfect reality', though he found no evidence of knowledge of the legend among her neighbours.[39] Tiddy Mun is a sort of sprite: an ordinarily benign, even protective spirit, three feet tall, who dwelled in the fen-waters of the Cars, around the Isle of Ancholme. Although his voice, sounding like the cry of the pyewipe, could sound eerie in the night time, locals saw him as an embodiment of the marshland, and credited him with controlling the height of seasonal floods – he did nobody harm until the Dutch arrived to begin delving and pumping. As the waters receded from the bogs, Tiddy Mun lost his habitat, for he had lived down in the still green water, coming out on to dry land only in the evenings, when the mist rose:

> For thee know'st, Tiddy Mun dwelt in tha watter-holes doun deep i' tha green still watter, an' a comed out nobbut of evens, whan tha mists rose. Than a comed crappelin out i'tha darklins, limpelty lobelty, like a dearie wee au'd gran'ther, wi' lang white hair, an' a lang white beardie, all cotted an' tangled together; limpelty-lobelty, an' a gowned i' gray, while tha could scarce see un thruff tha mist, an' a come wi' a sound o' rinnin' watter, an' a sough o' wind, an' laughin' like tha pyewipe screech.[40]

Of course, we don't think of Grendel as resembling a 'dearie wee au'd gran'ther' (grandfather), but Tiddy Mun's eventide progress out of the water, up through the mist, reminds me more of Grendel's approach to Heorot than many of *Beowulf*'s better-established analogues. The setting is right; the two figures both come creeping under the cover of mist and darkness. And their night-time prowlings are aligned in purpose, too; as the Dutchmen did their work, and his bog-refuges dried up, Tiddy Mun became unhappy – Dutch workers started to disappear in the darkness, never to be heard of again. In effect, Tiddy Mun turns into an ecological terrorist, attempting to drive out the alien species that means to deprive him of his home in the name of progress:

> Ay, an' for sure, it's ill comes o'crossin Tiddy Mun! For mark ma words! 'Twas first ane, syne anither o'that Dutchies wor gone, clean sperrited away! ... Tiddy Mun a'd fetted un away, an' drooned un i' tha mud holes, wheer tha hadn't drawed off all tha watter![41]

As Justin Noetzel puts it, 'Tiddy Mun is a metonym for the Fens, and the fen-landscape is a metonym for the natural world; when one piece of this chain of being is nearly destroyed, the whole system reacts and the usually paternal spirit turns vengeful.'[42] I believe that it is productive to think of Grendel as potentially a similar type of being. Tiddy Mun spirits away the Dutchmen who seek to destroy his home; Grendel devours the Danes who impose Heorot's urban sprawl and unendurable noise on to his territory, the *mearc* that had been marked out by God as being a suitable place of exile for one such as he, far from mankind.[43] Both of these spirits – for Grendel, let's not forget, is a *gæst*, among other things – can be read as attempting to defend a fenland that provides refuge for them only for as long as it is left in its natural state. Tiddy Mun will harm no one as long as his native waters are high enough. As far as we know, Grendel was dormant and harmless in his fenland exile before Heorot was built next door. The two figures only become aggressive in response to the arrival of invasive outsiders who threaten their homes with ecological disaster – with rendering their land uninhabitable, whether by the literal destruction of the landscape or the imposition of a foreign symbolic order on to it. It is natural that a *þyrs* will dwell in the fen. Grendel is not, in this story, the one who commits crimes against 'nature' – which is not to say, of course, that he does not commit crimes.

We can read Tiddy Mun and Grendel as two manifestations of a common impulse towards the rejection of foreign bodies from an established, indigenous natureculture – as protective spirits who guard their homelands against the intrusion of outsiders. In both cases, the fenland environments that are under threat are admittedly marginal, foreboding, insalubrious, and seemingly quite unhomely. But they are the proper home of their inhabitants, possessed by right and long custom. The human fenlanders and the monstrous fenlanders alike possess a kinship with the marshes that outsiders view as aberrant and abhorrent. They are adapted to their *oikos* in a way that 'civilized' people cannot understand or emulate.

Nicole Guenther Discenza argues that 'Grendel and his mother cross from their own waste, wild space into what had been ordered, civilized space, bringing chaos and destruction into the Danes' world. That is what makes wastelands so threatening.'[44] Discenza is right in her analysis, for this is what the poem *Beowulf*, which is written from and for the point of view of the 'civilized', wants us to think. But let us reverse these ideas: the Danes (in building Heorot in or close by the Grendelkin's *eard*) cross from their own ordered, civilized space into what had been the Grendelkin's own space – which was never wasteland *from the perspective of its inhabitants* – bringing a foreign (notion of) order into Grendel's world. That is what makes civilization so threatening to the natural world and to indigenous peoples whose naturecultures do not conform to the expectations of the civilized. Discenza continues:

> Grendel and later his mother come out of the wastes to attack the hall and the men in it. These attacks threaten the whole social fabric of Hrothgar's people, for community life centres upon the hall. They threaten the proper place of Heorot: proper as in property, something that the Danes possess and control; and proper in propriety.[45]

By my reading, however, Heorot threatens (and threatens first) the proper place of the Grendelkin, the *eard* that is theirs by gift of God, even if that gift is punitive. It is the only home they have.

Viewing Grendel in this way is not an exculpatory move. I do not seek to pardon Grendel's crimes against the Danes, which are real and horrifying. However, looking at Grendel's actions primarily in their ecological context complicates our understanding of his motivations in potentially productive ways. It requires us to take seriously the possibility that the suffering that the Danes inflict upon Grendel with Heorot's noise pollution is real, and really insupportable. Grendel cannot bear the 'dream ... hludne in healle' (joys ... loud in the hall) (88b–89a) that he hears pouring out of the gold-bright building. Grendel's angst arises because he is denied access to such hall-joys because of his family's banishment from the precincts of civilization. But any ecocritical interpretation will tend to be suspicious of any valorized notion of 'civilization'. Critics have tended to view the Grendelkin's own hall beneath or beyond the surface of the mere as somehow parodic of Heorot's true manifestation of civilization;[46] but the monsters' hall was there first, as far as we know, and it exists in a state of intimacy with its environment – however unpleasant that environment might be to the land-dwellers – in a way that Heorot never can. If we choose, we can read Heorot as being the parody: it is all show, no substance, a simulacrum of a heroic hall, built on dreams – the conventional human dreams of our mastery of nature, of the taming of the 'wild', of our separateness from our Others. The Danes cannot defend their hall because it is indefensible. And the Danes cannot, do not, will not try to penetrate the fenny fastness in which the Grendelkin live. They fail to comprehend how anyone could even live there, after all. But Grendel and his mother do live there, have lived there, perhaps would still be living there, had Hrothgar not decided to claim territory in the monsters' *eard*, their habitat.

We do not know where *Beowulf* – the poem – truly belongs, either in time or space. I would not use any of the foregoing interpretation as a means of locating the poem's *origin* in East Anglia or anywhere else – although Sam Newton's work on the possible East Anglian provenance of the text is by no means the least convincing of efforts to localize *Beowulf*'s production.[47] The faint traces of Grendel in the place-name record that Michael Lapidge was able to assemble would not suggest an East Anglian provenance for this figure: they cluster in western Mercia and Wessex, though Lapidge notes that place names associated with *grendel* do tend to be found in watery or marshy locales.[48] In any case, the imagined world occupied by Grendel, Hrothgar, and Beowulf is not and cannot be coterminous with the world of the people who were involved with the poem's production and reception. It is an Anglo-Saxon poem set entirely in a strange pseudo-Scandinavia, after all. If we are to use a sense of place as a way to become more intimate with *Beowulf*, we encounter the problem of not knowing where to stand or which direction to face.[49]

In their brilliant book *Landscapes of Desire*, Gillian Overing and Marijane Osborn narrate their sea-journey to Denmark in search of Heorot, or of a place where Heorot made sense to them, in what is by far the most successful psychogeographical approach to *Beowulf* yet undertaken.[50] I cannot pretend that Overing and Osborn truly transported me to a place where I felt, as a reader, that I had entered the world of *Beowulf*, however; in the absence of personal experience of those places, I got no frisson of recognition through Overing and Osborn's prose, no conviction that I would feel at home with the poem in Denmark, that it would make more sense to me if read in that context. I don't feel that I have to travel so far to feel close to *Beowulf*, to have a sense of belonging to the world of the poem: I just need to look out of the window. Overing and Osborn sought a truer and more meaningful engagement with

Beowulf in Scandinavia; I find that nowhere else in my experience do I feel as intimate with *Beowulf* as in the fens of East Anglia.

To me, *Beowulf* feels like a poem about home. It explores the nature of 'home' – where our homes are, how we build and defend them, the comfort they bring; what happens when we are far from home, homeless, exiled; what happens when we cannot maintain the boundaries by which we seek to define and protect our homes. To me, *Beowulf* also feels like a poem about *my* home. I do not mean by this to make any claim upon *Beowulf* as belonging to me or to this part of the world – I do not wish to own *Beowulf*. Reading *Beowulf* in the fens – and as if Grendel's fens were real fens, our fens, these fens – merely gives me a greater sense of spatial intimacy with the poem than I find elsewhere. This intimacy fosters, and is fostered by, a sense of Grendel and his mother as tragic protagonists rather than demonic antagonists, who are forced into monstrous reprisals by Hrothgar's oppressive (re)claiming of the Grendelkin's own, ancestral land for 'civilization'. My fens, the fens of the twenty-first century, are the product of similar processes of reclamation, of similar denaturings and displacements, of the defeat and banishment of figures like Grendel and Tiddy Mun. But the triumph of 'civilization' over the 'wild' is illusory and temporary, as the fall of Heorot shows. Eventually – and the day may not be far off – the flood defences will fail, the waters will rise, the fen's true identity will reassert itself. We land-dwellers will have to learn once again how to live in intimacy with the *fifelcynnes eard*. I propose we keep the noise down.

Notes

1 I am aware that by giving this title to my chapter I would have annoyed the late Eric Stanley, who sadly died before I finished this piece, and who devoted space in print to objecting to the use in Beowulf-scholarship of the term 'Grendelkin' for Grendel, his mother, and any other relations these two figures might have; Eric Stanley, '"A very land-fish, languageless, a monster": Grendel and the like in Old English', in K. E. Olsen and L. A. J. R. Houwen (eds), *Monsters and the monstrous in medieval Northwest Europe* (Leuven: Peeters, 2001), pp. 79–92. It is true that the term *Grendeles cyn* or its equivalent is nowhere found in the poem. Nonetheless, I find 'Grendelkin' a useful way of referring to Grendel and his mother that foregrounds the relative normality of their familial relations.

2 Dudley Wright, *Vampires and vampirism* (London: Rider, 1914), p. 150.

3 Brian J. Frost, *The Monster with a thousand faces: guises of the vampire in myth and literature* (Madison, WI: University of Wisconsin Press, 1989), p. 36.

4 M. Bunson, *The vampire encyclopedia* (New York: Crown, 1993), p. 85. Carol Senf mentions a poem on the same subject, and refers to Ollier's work, but does not give this text the title *Vampyre of the fens*: Senf, *The vampire in 19th-century English literature* (Bowling Green, OH: State University Popular Press, 1988), p. 169.

5 The reference to the poem is found in 'Vampyres', *Household words*, 11 (1855), 43. This article is unsigned in its published form, but Ollier was identified as its author by A. Lohrli, *Household words. A weekly journal conducted by Charles Dickens* (Toronto: University of Toronto Press, 1973), pp. 389–91.

6 Eugenio Olivares Merino, 'The Old English poem "A Vampyre of the Fens": a bibliographical ghost', *Miscelánea*, 32 (2005), 87–102. For the source passage, see Jakob Grimm, *Deutsche mythologie* (Göttingen: Dietrich, 1835), p. 570.

7 Throughout this chapter, the text of *Beowulf* is cited from R. D. Fulk, Robert E. Bjork, and John D. Niles (eds), *Klaeber's Beowulf*, 4th edn (Toronto: University of Toronto Press, 2008) by line number in the text.

8 Olivares Merino, 'The Old English poem "A Vampyre of the Fens"'.

9 Elliott Van Kirk Dobbie (ed.), *The Anglo-Saxon minor poems*, ASPR 6 (New York: Columbia University Press, 1942), pp. 55–7.

10 Justin T. Noetzel takes it as a given that 'demon is the most appropriate translation of the Old English *þyrs*', while admitting that the 'term is functionally flexible and can indicate monster, giant, and even wizard'; Noetzel, 'Monster, demon, warrior: St. Guthlac and the cultural landscape of the Anglo-Saxon fens', *Comitatus*, 45 (2014), 109.

11 Paul S. Langeslag argues that the meaning of *mor* in *Beowulf* is 'not immediately transparent', since he considers the terrain surrounding Grendel's mere to be mountainous in places, marshy in others. He suggests that 'mountain, elevated terrain' is both the common and poetic sense of *mor* in Old English, though he also admits that 'marsh, damp wasteland' is the term's more likely original etymology; Langeslag, 'Monstrous landscape in *Beowulf*', *ES*, 96 (2015), 122.

12 William Howarth, 'Imagined territory: the writing of wetlands', *New literary history*, 30 (1999), 520. I owe my knowledge of this article to Sarah Harlan-Haughey, *The ecology of the English outlaw in medieval literature: from fen to greenwood* (Abingdon: Routledge, 2016), p. 41.

13 Angus Cameron, Ashley Crandell Amos, Antonette diPaolo Healey et al. (eds), *Dictionary of Old English: A to H* (Toronto: Dictionary of Old English Project, 2016), s.v. *fifel*. Langeslag, 'Monstrous landscape', 123, argues that here *fifelcynnes eard* is a kenning for 'water, sea', an interpretation that I see no pressing justification for, although the formulation does indeed insist upon the wateriness of this landscape.

14 Cameron et al., *Dictionary of Old English: A to H*, s.v. *eard*. The primary meanings given for *eard* (1 and 1.a) are respectively 'dwelling-place' and

'country, region, native land'. According to the dictionary, sense 1.b.iii, specific to *Beowulf*, is 'habitat, referring to the habitat of monsters'.

15 Sarah Harlan-Haughey has recently written that 'in the Anglo-Saxon period, we see emotive and ecological connections repeatedly established between exile and wilderness, and especially fen land': *Ecology of the English outlaw*, p. 23. While I agree with Harlan-Haughey's summary, it is important to my argument that Grendel, though exiled, is no longer living the life of an exile: he has settled in his fenland environment in a way which other outlaw or exile figures never manage.

16 I like the way that Fabienne L. Michelet phrases it: 'Grendel and his mother form a small community and dwell in their own province. Hroðgar's adversary is not a perpetually wandering exile.' Michelet, *Creation, migration, and conquest: imaginary geography and sense of space in Old English literature* (Oxford: Oxford University Press, 2006), p. 50.

17 For a description of the geography of Little Downham in the Middle Ages, see Christopher Taylor, '"A place there is where liquid honey drops like dew": the landscape of Little Downham, Cambridgeshire, in the twelfth century?', *Landscape history*, 31 (2010), 5–23. Taylor's title refers to a twelfth-century poem in praise of Little Downham – which was a favoured residence of the bishops of Ely – found in the *Libellus Æthelwoldi Episcopi*, on which see Catherine A. M. Clarke, 'Place, poetry and patronage: the *Libellus Æthelwoldi* verses to Little Downham and their context', *Landscape history*, 31 (2010), 25–35.

18 On the horrifying affect of this passage, see Arthur G. Brodeur, 'Design for terror in the purging of Heorot', *JEGP*, 53 (1954), 503–13; Michael Lapidge, '"Beowulf" and the psychology of terror', in Helen Damico and John Leyerle (eds), *Heroic poetry in the Anglo-Saxon period: studies in honor of Jess B. Bessinger, Jr.* (Kalamazoo, MI: Medieval Institute Publications, 1993), pp. 373–402.

19 Susan Oosthuizen, *The Anglo-Saxon fenland* (Oxford: Windgather, 2017).

20 Quoted by E. Mansel Sympson, *Lincolnshire* (Cambridge: Cambridge University Press, 1913), p. 54; William Shakespeare, *King Lear*, Act II, scene iv, line 162. On Shakespeare's knowledge and deployment of the fens in his dramas, see Todd Andrew Borlik, 'Caliban and the fen demons of Lincolnshire: the Englishness of Shakespeare's *Tempest*', *Shakespeare*, 9 (2013), 21–51.

21 Lindy Brady, 'Echoes of Britons on a fenland frontier in the Old English *Andreas*', *RES*, 61 (2010), 672.

22 See Kelly Wickham-Crowley, 'Living on the ecg: mutable boundaries of land and water in Anglo-Saxon contexts', in Clare A. Lees and Gillian R. Overing (eds), *A place to believe in: medieval monasticism in the landscape* (University Park, PA: Pennsylvania State University Press, 2006), pp. 85–110.

23 Margaret Gelling and Ann Cole, *The landscape of placenames* (Donnington: Shaun Tyas, 2014), pp. 20–1; see also Dennis Cronan, 'Old English *gelad*: "a passage across water"', *Neophilologus*, 71 (1987), 316–19.

24 On the connection between wolves and outlawry, see Harlan-Haughey, *Ecology of the English outlaw*, pp. 24–6.

25 After reviewing the evidence of place names with the element *hlið* (none of which are found in East Anglia), Margaret Gelling concludes that the *hleoþu* found in *Beowulf* may specifically connote a 'hill with a hollow', which 'provides dead ground, and this could be a lurking place for natural or supernatural enemies'; Gelling, 'The landscape of *Beowulf*, *ASE*, 39 (2002), 8–9.

26 Richard Butts, 'The analogical mere: landscape and terror in *Beowulf*, *ES*, 68 (1987), 21. See also, for example, Harlan-Haughey, *Ecology of the English outlaw*, pp. 56–63; William Witherle Lawrence, 'The haunted mere in *Beowulf*, *PMLA*, 27 (1912), 208–45; William S. Mackie, 'The demons' home in *Beowulf*, *JEGP*, 37 (1938), 455–61; Richard J. Schrader, 'Sacred groves, marvellous waters, and Grendel's abode', *Florilegium*, 5 (1983), 76–84; Geoffrey Russom, 'At the center of *Beowulf*, in Stephen F. Glosecki (ed.), *Myth in early northwest Europe* (Tempe, AZ: ACMRS, 2007), p. 234; Langeslag, 'Monstrous landscape'.

27 On *mere* as a place-name element, see Gelling and Cole, *Landscape of placenames*, pp. 21–7. As an element in the name of a habitation, *mere* is widespread throughout England. Intriguingly, Gelling and Cole point out that many *mere* place names occur in the vicinity of Roman roads or other ancient pathways.

28 Lawrence, 'The haunted mere', 217.

29 Dianne Meredith, 'Hazards in the bog – real and imagined', *Geographical review*, 92 (2002), 319–20.

30 See Sarah L. Higley, '"Aldor on ofre," or the reluctant hart: a study of liminality in "Beowulf"', *Neuphilologische Mitteilungen*, 87 (1986), 342–53.

31 Andy Orchard, *A critical companion to Beowulf* (Cambridge: Brewer, 2003), p. 156.

32 Alfred K. Siewers, 'Landscapes of conversion: Guthlac's mound and Grendel's mere as expressions of Anglo-Saxon nation-building', *Viator*, 34 (2003), 38. Similar comments are made by Nicholas Howe, 'The landscape of Anglo-Saxon England: inherited, invented, imagined', in John Howe and Michael Wolfe (eds), *Inventing medieval landscapes: senses of place in western Europe* (Gainesville, FL: University Press of Florida, 2002), p. 106.

33 For a survey of theories attempting to explain the light sources in Grendel's lair, see Christopher Abram, 'New light on the illumination of Grendel's mere', *JEGP*, 109 (2010), 198–216.

34 Once again, this suggestion has been made by Fabienne Michelet (*Creation, migration, and conquest*, p. 50): 'what the monster really opposes

may be Hroðgar's territorial organization in Denmark, rather than the
scop's performance. The fact that the king's dominion impinges on the
areas where Grendel rules cannot be excluded, especially not when
one bears in mind that Beowulf purges both Heorot and the mere of
hostile presences, thereby extending Hroðgar's authority over areas
previously under Grendel's control.'

35 For a summary of the medieval sources for Hereward's legend, see
   John Hayward, 'Hereward the outlaw', *Journal of medieval history*, 14
   (1988), 293–304.
36 This anecdote is preserved in the twelfth-century *Liber Eliensis*. See
   Janet Fairweather (trans.), *Liber Eliensis: a history of the Isle of Ely
   from the seventh century to the twelfth* (Woodbridge: Boydell, 2005), p.
   210.
37 Ian Rotherham, *The lost fens: England's greatest ecological disaster*
   (Stroud: History Press, 2013).
38 David Hall and John Coles, *Fenland survey: an essay in landscape and
   persistence* (London: English Heritage, 1994), p. 5.
39 M. C. Balfour, 'Legends of the cars', *Folklore*, 2 (1891), 145–70. See
   also Darwin Horn, 'Tiddy Mun's curse and the ecological consequences
   of land reclamation', *Folklore*, 98 (1987), 11–15.
40 Balfour, 'Legends of the cars', 150–1.
41 Ibid., 152.
42 Justin T. Noetzel, 'Marshmen and trackless bogs: a cultural history
   of the English fens', PhD dissertation, Saint Louis University, 2014,
   p. 192.
43 As Manish Sharma points out, it is possible and fruitful to read *mearc* in
   Beowulf as always potentially bearing the double meaning of 'borderland'
   and 'sign'. The *mearc* that Grendel and his mother occupy is both a
   (literal and symbolic) liminal space and a (literal and symbolic) marker
   of their damnation. Sharma, 'Metalepsis and monstrosity: the boundaries
   of narrative structure in *Beowulf*', *Studies in philology*, 102 (2005), 265.
44 Nicole Guenther Discenza, *Inhabited spaces: Anglo-Saxon constructions
   of place* (Toronto: University of Toronto Press, 2017), p. 146.
45 Ibid.
46 Michelet, *Creation, migration, and conquest*, pp. 105–6; James F. Dou-
   bleday, 'Grendel's two halls', *Notes and Queries*, 58 (2011), 8–10.
47 Sam Newton, *The origins of Beowulf and the pre-Viking kingdom of
   East Anglia* (Cambridge: Brewer, 1993).
48 Michael Lapidge, 'Beowulf, Aldhelm, the *Liber Monstrorum* and Wessex',
   Studi medievali, 23 (1982), 179–81. The relevant charter clauses are
   also given as Appendix A.5 in the fourth edition of *Klaeber's Beowulf*,
   pp. 293–4.
49 See Alfred Hiatt, '*Beowulf* off the map', *ASE*, 38 (2009), 11–40.
50 Gillian R. Overing and Marijane Osborn, *Landscapes of desire: partial
   stories of the medieval Scandinavian world* (Minneapolis, MN: University
   of Minnesota Press, 1994).

Part III
Beowulf outside

7

Elemental intimacies: agency in the Finnsburg episode

Mary Kate Hurley

Beowulf – both the poem and its eponymous hero – is inextricable from the monsters that structure its plot. The young Beowulf fights the *mearcstapa* (border-stepper) Grendel in the hall at Heorot; after the creature's mother attacks in an uncomfortably human scene of revenge, he travels to her watery abode. There, Beowulf kills Grendel's mother with a sword made by giants and returns with Grendel's head to prove his victory. Later, when he is an old man, Beowulf will fight one more monster – a dragon – and that fight ends his life. Indeed, for all that scholarly readings of the poem have pushed back against this perception, *Beowulf* is inextricably identified with the monsters that form the core of its heroic action. And yet interspersed between these larger scenes, the poem subtly deploys other stories – often called 'digressions' – that, while diverging from the main action of the poem, serve to highlight its themes and structure.

One of the most moving of these digressions occurs between Beowulf's initial fight with Grendel and the creature's mother's attack. Hildeburh, a queen who has married outside of her own kin group in order to secure peace between Frisians and Healf-Denes, witnesses the breakdown of the peace that her marriage was supposed to ensure. In one of the most striking moments in this striking narrative, Hildeburh sets her own deceased son ('selfre sunu') (1115a) on her brother Hnæf's funeral pyre, 'banfatu bærnan, ond on bæl don / eame on eaxle' (to burn the bone vessel, and give to the fire, his uncle at his shoulder) (1116–17a).[1] As a number of critics have remarked, it is the only active moment that Hildeburh has in the poem: unable to otherwise remedy the violence she witnesses, she orders that her son's body be burned. After the momentary command, her actions change dramatically: 'ides gnornode, / geomrode giddum' (the lady mourned, mourned with songs) (1117b–1118a). Both descriptions – Hildeburh's command ('hatan') to burn her son on the pyre next to her brother and the observation that she mourns ('gnornian') with songs – are ultimately connected to mourning and its attendant work. Hildeburh, despite her prominence in the conflict between the Healf-Denes and the Frisians, takes her only real actions when she stands before the pyre. Even here, the actions she does take highlight her utter lack of power. She commands that the pyre burn her son and brother, but she has no agency in the conflict that brought them to the pyre, nor can she change the fate of either her family of origin or the family she produced in Frisia.

Yet if we focus our readerly attention differently in this digression – which is traditionally known as the 'Finnsburg episode'[2] – the scene of the funeral pyre highlights more than Hildeburh's brief moment of agency. Rather, the poem stresses the insistent agency of the elements that come together on the funeral pyre. In a description as moving as it is ghastly, the poem describes the scene: 'Hafelan multon, / bengeato burston ðonne blod ætspranc /, laðbite lices; lig ealle forswealg, / gæsta gifrost þara ðe þær guð fornam / bega folces' (The heads melted, wound-gates burst, and then blood sprang forth from the hateful-bites of the body. The flame swallowed [it] all up, that greediest of ghosts, all of those ones that battle seized from both of the peoples) (1120b–1124a). The scene of the funeral pyre emphasizes bodies reduced to objects that can be broken and consumed by the fire. The central words of the passage are 'gæsta gifrost' (greediest of ghosts), a personification that refers to the flames themselves. Implicitly, the use of the term 'gæsta gifrost' posits spirits that animate the element of fire, which accords with the *Dictionary of Old English* definition of the term *gast*.[3] On the one hand, this is clearly a poetic technique, part of the sheer beauty of this haunting moment in the poem. On the other hand – what if we took this moment of personification more seriously? What would it mean if the fire were itself an actant in the poem, creating its own kind of community – or more appropriately, collectivity – out of the failure of human beings to do the same?[4]

This chapter re-reads the Finnsburg episode of *Beowulf* as a monument both to the failure of human community and to the human interconnection with outside forces (both human and non-human) that presage and condition that failure.[5] Throughout the episode, we encounter scenes that foreground certain kinds of objects, such as lifeless human bodies and the gold meant to ensure that such corpses will be forgotten. However, the poem also foregrounds the ability of narratives, when circulated, to change the reception of both corpses and treasure.[6] The interrelationship between the bodies of the dead and the stories told about them creates a configuration of influence and agency larger than any singular human agent or intent. Put another way: this reading of the episode suggests that sometimes the poem can know what its characters cannot – that the kinds of connections, interrelations, and even losses that are the premise of human community also condition its eventual demise.

In order to make these connections, I will utilize Actor-Network theory (hereafter, ANT). By taking a complex structure – in this case, a society – and understanding it as a 'heterogeneous system',[7] ANT posits the interrelations and interdependencies of what might otherwise be understood as independent entities; consequently, 'there is no reason to assume, *a priori*, that *either* objects *or* people in general determine the character of social change or stability'.[8] By reorienting the presumed subject of analysis and granting that objects can, in certain senses and situations, have agency, ANT breaks down artificial bifurcations between the 'social' world and the 'natural' world. By deploying ANT analyses, the attentive reader can therefore better understand how non-human agents might have clear effects on the world formerly understood to include only human agents. In the case of the Finnsburg episode, ANT allows us to reconceptualize the types of groups that the poem describes. By paying special attention to the elemental intimacies of Hildeburh's plight, we can recover some of the enmeshments that condition social life – enmeshments that exceed the purely human relationships so often privileged in *Beowulf* criticism.[9] In so doing, this also allows us to recover Hildeburh's fuller context, beyond her loss of agency and beyond her mourning.

A short summary of the Finnsburg episode serves to contextualize my analysis, and to place it within the larger frame of studies of peace-weaving marriages and feud culture. By peace-weaving marriages, I refer to those marriages meant to secure political alliances with former enemies; such marriages were integral to feud culture.[10] Regardless of whether early England was a place of endemic feuding, there can be little doubt that *Beowulf* as a poem is particularly interested in the stakes of revenge-based aggression, and nowhere is that theme so prominent as in the Finnsburg episode.[11] After an unprovoked attack in which a group of Frisians (Hildeburh's family-in-law) attack the Healf-Denes (her family of origin), Hildeburh's brother Hnæf is among the dead. Her son has also died, and Hildeburh orders him placed on the pyre beside her brother, consigning them both to the fire as a measure of her grief as well as an indication of her power as queen. Because the winter has trapped the Healf-Denes in the Frisian court, Hildeburh's husband Finn (the Frisian leader) offers a place at his hall for the fugitive Healf-Denes for the duration of the long season. He promises that he will treat both Frisian and Healf-Dene equally, and from the poem's report he very much does so, as he distributes treasure to Hengest's men 'efne swa swiðe' (just as often) (1092a) as he does to his own.[12]

These rings are meant to bind together a community. Although the poem makes clear that Hengest (the leader of the Healf-Denes after the death of Hildeburh's brother) is already thinking about revenge, we have reason to believe that this network of Frisians and Healf-Denes might still hold together; however, Oslaf and Guðlaf, two of the Healf-Dene retainers, speak of the battle that took the lives of their kin, and as a result, the enmity between the Frisians and the Healf-Denes resumes. The story ends with Hildeburh mourning the death of her husband and being returned to her people by Hengest. That Hildeburh herself is accorded object-like status at the close of the episode is unsurprising. However, her role in the poem provides the episode's first indication that its interest is larger than the realm of human beings. The connection between humans and the objects they putatively use has a devastating effect on the feeble attempt made to mend a community rent by violence.

One core difference between my approach here and other readings of the Finnsburg episode is my framing of Hildeburh. Most readings of the narrative suggest that Hildeburh's most important attribute is as a 'freoðuwebbe' or peace-weaver: her role is to secure peace between rival kingdoms through marriage, but it is also doomed to failure in a way that highlights her lack of agency in the episode itself.[13] As a result, Hildeburh's actions in the poem run the risk of being interpreted as a stereotype of Old English poetic narrative, reinforcing the idea that women are always 'potentially, if not actually, the victim'.[14] Although there are multiple ways in which critics have rehabilitated Hildeburh's actions in the poem, the most crucial is by examining her role as a woman who mourns. Joyce Hill (although she does not think Hildeburh's agency is restored in what she calls 'the viewpoint of "story"') suggests that the poem reveals Hildeburh's centrality to the episode through the 'sophistication' of its response to marginalizing legendary materials. Moreover, she argues that the poet creates 'a position of ethical and imaginative importance' for the mourning queen as she puts her son and her brother on the same funeral pyre.[15] Helen Bennett extends Hill's point to examine the figure of the female mourner in *Beowulf*, a figure that she deems both 'strong and enduring', inhabiting an active rather than a passive role.[16] Although I broadly agree that reading Hildeburh as passive ignores the very real import of the actions she *does* take, my goal in reading her as a figure of reduced agency is not quite so straightforward. Although her lack of agency is partially the result of her being a woman in a patriarchal culture, I would argue that its significance is as a limit case of the poem's ongoing negotiation of the limits of human agency per se. Her lack of agency, along with that of other characters in the poem, is the result of human imbrication with agentic forces that exceed both their knowledge and their power to control.

The Finnsburg episode, appropriately, begins with the queen herself, suggesting that 'ne huru Hildeburh herian þorfte / Eotena treowe' (Nor did Hildeburh have any reason to praise the faithfulness of the Jutes) (1071–2a). By emphasizing Hildeburh's lack of action here – she does *not* have a reason to praise ('herian') the people who killed her family, and we assume she does not – the poem subtly sets up her later lack of agency in matters related to the deaths that the Jutes' untrustworthiness causes. Indeed, the poem is careful to note that she 'unsynnum wearð' (was guiltless) (1072b) in the feud. Whatever tragedy she has to endure, the poem wants its readers or listeners to know that it is not her fault.

This introduction to Hildeburh, which focuses poetic attention on both her lack of guilt and the death of her kinsmen, stands in stark contrast to her clear command before the funeral pyre later in the digression. Hildeburh's actions as a mourning queen begin to demonstrate the kinds of connections that will emerge as inherently problematic in the final parts of her story. 'The only initiatory act attributed to her' and a 'powerful but ultimately futile gesture', as Joyce Hill describes it,[17] the scene of the funeral pyre is the first – and only – indication that Hildeburh has any kind of agency in the Frisian court. Indeed, Dorothy Porter argues that the funeral pyre scene is Hildeburh's moment of resistance, her attempt to break free from the domination of the men in her life.[18] That she alone chooses the pyre for her son asserts her role as a mother and her position as guardian of her child. Yet the poem does not linger on Hildeburh's command at the pyre. Rather, it expends its force on the active role played by the fire that swallows ('forswealgan') (1122) the bodies, breaking them down to their component parts. In a powerful reading of this scene and its centrality to the Finnsburg episode, Stacy Klein suggests that the intensity of the flames and

their destructive power signify the most basic lesson that the
Finnsburg episode imparts. Violence begets violence:

> The melting heads, so securely trapped within the grasp of the fire
> and so clearly removed from their possible functions as trophies for
> signifying a clear battle-victor, emphasize that the winner in blood
> feud is neither Dane nor Frisian, but the fire itself, symbol of an
> ethos of insatiable violence that feeds on the destruction of men and
> their treasures.[19]

If we take Klein's analysis of the poem's exposition at face value,
we can argue that the fire and the ethos of violence it symbolizes
become active participants in the kinship feud. By suggesting that the
only 'winner' in blood feud is the fire, Klein emphasizes the way in
which cyclical violence becomes the condition of humans enmeshed
in kinship feud. This ethos of violence works against stabilizing the
relationship between the Healf-Denes and the Frisians.[20]

The fire – that *gæsta gifrost* – performs the work that Hildeburh
and her husband Finn could not. It brings together both Frisian
and Dane with ruthless efficiency. The two lines of descent inter-
mingle in the destruction of the bodies, in which 'Hafelan multon,
/ bengeato burston ðonne blod ætspranc' (Heads melt, wound-gates
burst, and then blood sprang forth) (1120b–1121). Making a distinction between the blood of the Frisians and that of the Healf-Denes
is as impossible as it would be to separate Hildeburh's grief for her
brother from her grief for her son. The two are enmeshed with
and by the fire – and the pyre itself highlights Hildeburh's shared
loyalty to both Frisian and Healf-Dene.

Indeed, the pyre seems almost to be a grotesque parallel to the
other place in which the Healf-Denes and the Frisians are meant
to be seen as equal – the hall where Finn distributes treasure over
the long winter during which the two groups must learn to coexist.
Finn promises to give out gold in his hall to both the Frisians and
the Healf-Denes, treating his erstwhile enemies to the same kind
of generosity that his own men expect from their king. Finn uses
gold and its distribution to try to reinterpret the enmity that lingers
on account of the unfinished battle between the two groups. He
gives out treasure 'efne swa swiðe sincgestreonum / fættan goldes
swa he Fresena cyn / on beorsele byldan wolde' (even as much
treasure, worked gold, as he would give to embolden the Frisians
in the beer-hall) (1092–4). The gold in question is, based on these
lines, usually given only to the Frisians, in order to embolden them
as they fight for their lord. Yet here the malleability of the gold's

distribution highlights the way in which it harbours very different meanings based on who is associated with it. Treasure can ensure loyalty when given to Frisian thanes, but here it is meant to make the tentative truce between Frisian and Dane more legible and, we assume, less fragile. In another sense, the gold replaces the violence that otherwise links these two opposing groups in the scene with the pyre, much as Hildeburh herself once might have done in her marriage. That the poem moves from enmity, to attempted community building, to the pyre underscores the relationship between these entities and actions through juxtaposition. That is, the gold stands in for both the violence and the fire, which are the only other things that can effectively unite Frisian and Healf-Dene. Moreover, the gold fails to adequately stand in for the value of the human lives it is meant to replace. Its proximity to the pyre, then, underscores the fire's elemental indifference to human concerns – the human lives that gold cannot bring together find final (and horrifically effective) union in flames.

This unstable relationship foregrounds the uneasiness of the truce while simultaneously highlighting the ways in which the new, temporary community of the Frisians and Healf-Denes might be destroyed. They pledge 'on twa healfa' (on both sides) (1095b) a 'fæste frioðuwære' (firm truce) (1096a), a truce that the rings and treasure Finn promises to distribute should secure. Yet the compact is based, first and foremost, on a premise of silence:

> þæt ðær ænig mon
> wordum ne worcum   wære ne bræce,
> ne þurh inwitsearo   æfre gemænden,
> ðeah hie hira beaggyfan   banan folgedon
> ðeodenlease,   þa him swa geþearfod wæs;
> gyf þonne Frysna hwylc   frecnen spræce
> ðæs morþorhetes   myndgiend wære,
> þonne hit sweordes ecg   syððan scede. (1099b–1106)

(That no man would break, by words or works, the treaty, nor through evil craft ever complain, although they followed the killer of their ring-giver, leaderless, through grievous necessity. If then any Frisian by horrible speech were to remind (them) of the murderous feud, then thereafter it would be determined by the edge of the sword.)

These lines make it clear that what can undo the work of the gold that Finn wishes to use to secure the uneasy peace is not just works, which would probably include the revenge killing of those who were part of the feud. The poem lingers on 'wordum ne worcum' and 'ne þurh inwitsearo', which respectively refer to 'words or works' and 'evil craft'. Moreover, the word *gemænan* incorporates two different semantic registers: both complaint and violation.[21] The word *gemænan* can gloss both *plangere* (which means to lament or mourn) and *coinquinare* or *violare* (both of which carry connotations of defiling and violating) in the Latin.[22] That the poem conflates the register of complaint with the register of defilement and violation suggests that words, in this context, have extreme power. In this instance, even speaking of the past as a way to complain of one's condition can violate a fragile peace. Put another way: words can undo what treasure is meant to ensure. They can do so because they change the nature of the thing they describe – as a result, they have force in the world.

That words can themselves have agency is hardly a new observation.[23] Their ability to break an alliance through circulating a competing, violent narrative is a repeated concern of *Beowulf*. Take, for example, the story that Beowulf himself tells about the young warrior who sits at a banquet with an old warrior, after the conclusion of a feud. The old warrior reminds his younger companion of the losses that have been suffered in the past, and the fact that those losses are still legible in the present. He points out the very weapon that 'þin fæder to gefeohte bær' (your father took to the fight) (2048), which is now possessed by the descendant of the warriors who killed him:

> Nu her þara banena   byre nathwylces
> frætwum hremig   on flet gæð,
> morðres gylpeð   ond þone maðþum byreð,
> þone þe ðu mid rihte   rædan sceoldest. (2053–6)

> (Now here, the child of one or another of those slayers goes boasting with ornaments on the floor, boasts of murder and bears the treasures that you, by rights, should have possession of.)

The presence of the weapon, in Beowulf's story, does not itself incite violence. When the story of how it came to its present owner circulates, however, the sword accrues a different meaning. No longer simply a sword belonging to another warrior, this weapon becomes *weaponized* – it becomes part of a larger and longer narrative of hostility that exists across time in part because of the memories that this old warrior continues to relate.[24] The past is, in a sense, reactivated through the old retainer's words. That this sequence takes place only in Beowulf's mind does not diminish its importance;

rather, the fact that Beowulf can predict such a sequence of events highlights how deeply ingrained in the culture it is.

Moreover, the poem foregrounds the power of words to change the characters' relationship to the material objects they use in the specific vocabulary used to describe the old retainer's speech: 'Manað swa on myndgað mæla gehwylce / sarum wordum' (He complains so and brings [it] to attention each time, with evil words) (2057–8a). Both *gemænan* and *searu* recur here, as they did in the description of the prohibition meant to secure peace between the Frisians and the Healf-Denes. *Searu* carries a range of connotations including 'craft, artifice, wile, deceit, stratagem, ambush, treachery, plot'.[25] What matters most in this usage, however, is the sense of deliberateness with which the old retainer incites his junior to violence. The *craft* with which he deploys his memory of the past ensures the continued enmity of the young retainer towards his counterpart in the other group. This same mechanism of remembrance is at work in the Finnsburg episode. Finn specifically forbids speaking of the violence that has conditioned this particular alliance, commanding that no one 'þurh inwitsearo æfre gemænden' (through evil craft ever complain) (1101). Both *searu* (as part of *inwitsearo*) and *gemænan*[26] are present in this injunction. The presence and deployment of 'evil craft' and 'evil words' are part of how speech mobilizes memory. The action that resurrects such losses is *gemænan*, and the complaint it signifies. Although the time period is far shorter, therefore, both the mechanism and the result are the same.

That Beowulf and Finn can both imagine worlds where such memories bring about further bloodshed highlights how commonplace it must be.[27] Indeed, the narrative notes that it is not simply the memory of past slaughters that undermines the truce. Rather, it is the inability of a few of the warriors involved to keep their memories silent. When 'wæs winter scacen, / fæger foldan bearm' (winter was gone, fair the earth's expanses) (1136b–37a), the Healf-Denes should be prepared to return to their home. Yet Hengest, leader of the Healf-Denes, 'to gyrnwræce / swiðor þohte þonne to sælade, / gif he torngemot þurhteon mihte' (thought more quickly to revenge than to a sea-journey, and whether he might bright about a bitter encounter) (1138b–40). These thoughts are specifically positioned as questions of *wræce* or vengeance.[28] Yet without the words that the truce explicitly forbade, the memories of slaughter and the longing for recompense lack force.

By mobilizing speech, Oslaf and Guðlaf provide the necessary incitement to violence: they 'æfter sæsiðe sorge mændon / ætwiton weana dæl' (complained of their grief after the sea-journey, blamed a measure of their sorrows [on it]) (1149–50a). The recurrence of *mænan*, even without the collocation of *searu*, harks back to precisely what neither man was meant to do: complain, and in complaining, violate the truce that held through the long winter. In the Finnsburg episode, as in Beowulf's story of Freawaru's marriage, the result is resumed enmity; that Oslaf and Guðlaf complain of their grief pushes Hengest into action, and he finds that 'ne meahte wæfre mod / forhabban in hreþre' (he could not his restless mind contain in his spirit/breast) (1150b–1a). The words of the two retainers, that is, have force, force that is made apparent in Hengest's violence. Neither a peace-weaving marriage nor a truce held in trust through the giving of gold could abate this violence for long.

The complaint of Oslaf and Guðlaf, and the speech that spurs Hengest to violence, is capable of creating such effects in part because of the intimacies that the Finnsburg episode generates between humans and non-humans; these intimacies alter the meanings assigned to the various non-human agents in the poem. Central to the agency of such intimacies is the mobilization of corpses to rewrite meaning. When brought into relationship with the corpses of the dead and the treasure meant to ensure community, these stories transform objects into reminders. The gold meant to buy off the memory of the violent deaths of kinsmen is qualitatively altered by its association with Oslaf and Guðlaf's angry speech. The explosive violence of the association attests to what Julia Kristeva terms the 'abject', that which the subject must forget or reject in order to maintain a coherent identity.[29] Because it defies seemingly rigid categories, the corpse highlights the capacity of the human body to be utterly non-human and yet subject to human action, memory, and interpretation. The influence of the corpses – implied by the 'sorg' of which Oslaf and Guðlaf speak – subtly modifies entities such as treasure that now serve as memorabilia of death rather than facilitators of alliance: the intimacy they signify becomes violent and unstable. Corpses may be rejected or ejected from community but remain associated with humans in collectivity. Their presence, in fact and in memory, marks a past that not only endures but also threatens the possibility of a peaceful future.

Rings and corpses thus become the ground on which the entire Finnsburg episode rests; the poem repeatedly emphasizes that these objects are unstable in meaning. Their very instability conditions the action of the poem; put another way, humans do not simply fight over the corpses of the fallen or the treasure that is meant to circulate in the hall. Rather, they fight because these objects have influence, and their unstable meanings are deployed to determine the futures that they will allow to come to pass.

In the background of each of these connections that draws together a collectivity there is another actor that needs to be accounted for. Although the poem is clearly invested in the human cost of the fighting that the Finnsburg digression describes, it also observes – however tangentially – the larger forces to which the human is connected within the poem. By carefully tracing these connections, another actor in the digression comes to the fore, one that otherwise seems a mere backdrop to the human drama of feud. Weather, it would seem, is a vital avenue of connection between the human actants in the Finnsburg digression and the natural world:

> eard gemunde,
> þeah þe ne meahte   on mere drifan
> hringedstefnan   –holm storme weol,
> won wið winde,   winter yþe beleac
> isgebinde–   oþ ðæt oþer com
> gear in geardas,   swa nu gyt deð,
> þa ðe syngales   sele bewitiað,
> wuldortorhtan weder. (1129b–1136a)

(He remembered his land, although he could not drive forth on the sea his ring-prowed vessel; the waves welled with storms, fought against the wind, locked the waves, bound with ice, until that other [season] might come, the year in the enclosure, as it now still does, the seasons still go in the hall, the glory-bright weather.)

Although earlier in the digression the poem takes pains to elaborate that 'wig ealle fornam / Finnes þegnas nemne feaum anum, / þæt he ne mehte on þæm meðelstede / wig Hengeste wiht gefeohtan' (the battle took them, few alone remained among Finn's thanes, so that he could not in the mead-hall conclude the battle with Hengest at all) (1080b–1083), it had heretofore been less clear why it was that Hengest and his men remained in the hall with Finn's thanes after the battle. In these lines, however, a larger background to the actions of humans comes into finer focus. The weather itself is the reason that Hengest finds himself stuck in Finn's hall over the long winter; waves are driven by storms and the ocean is locked in ice (*isgebinde*), until spring – noted here as 'ðæt oþer ... gear'[30] – arrives, and presumably breaks the quite literal ice. The winter itself keeps Hengest and his men in a position that will eventually lead to them rekindling the feud.

In the background, then, non-human actors are consistently modifying the behaviour of the human characters in *Beowulf* – their intimacies and conflicts – whether or not they are aware of their influence. Fire melts heads, stories modify the meaning of corpses and treasure, and even the winter's lingering effects keep Hengest and his men from escaping the fight when they cannot conclude it. What does this mean, then, for the central figure of the digression? How does this awareness of Hildeburh's connection to a network of dispersed agency help us reinterpret her actions in the narrative? Finally, is she, or is she not, made into an object by the men who surround her?

Hildeburh's strength is deeply compromised by her final appearance in the poem, and this is the crux of the question that serves as the engine for this chapter. Her final actions in the poem are not really actions at all:

> Hie on sælade
> drihtlice wif   to Denum feredon,
> læddon to leodum. (1157b–1159a)

(On the sea they carried the lord-like woman to the Danes, they led her to [her] people.)

In *Language, Sign, and Gender in Beowulf*, Gillian Overing argues that it is precisely this final moment at which Hildeburh becomes the object rather than the subject of action in the poem. Overing notes, however, that Hildeburh-as-object is not allowed the same kind of agency and transformation accorded to other objects in the text. In a poem where the exchange and possession of objects is a primary way of recalling histories and cementing group identity, as a peace-weaver, Hildeburh is not readily available for definition, by herself or others: 'the sword may recall the boast that may assure the deed … but even the gold adorning the queen will not translate *her* … her meaning as a peace-weaver is *untranslatable*'.[31] Overing's invocation of the term 'translate' raises an important point: Hildeburh's meaning, her status, and her possibilities are all irretrievable to readers of the poem precisely because her role as a facilitator of peace fails so spectacularly. Rings can promote alliances, and swords can renew revenge, but Hildeburh's work is not as active as these objects. Rather, she is seemingly moved only by the actions of others, and as the poem's audience 'we watch her as she is moved across the chessboard, given, and then taken'.[32] This reading of the role of the peace-weaver in Finnsburg removes Hildeburh from a position of agency much as her relatives remove her from the Frisian stronghold at the end of the digression.

Indeed, Hildeburh's return to the Danes after the death of her husband is neither remarkable nor unexpected. Her ties to Frisia are gone, her husband and son dead. An editorial intervention might help us better understand the stakes of her loss; earlier in the digression, the poem notes that:

> Nalles holinga   Hoces dohtor
> meotodsceaft bemearn   syþðan morgen com,
> ða heo under swegle   geseon meahte
> morþorbealo maga,   þær he[o] ær mæste heold
> worolde wynne. (1076–80a)

> (Not at all in vain did the daughter of Hoc mourn the decrees of fate when morning came, when she under the heavens had to see the deadly murders of men, there where [she] before held the greatest of the world's joy.)

If we accept an earlier editorial emendation,[33] then we are given a set of conditions that describe Hildeburh's relationship to her family of marriage. On the one hand, she was a peace pledge, married to secure an alliance between Frisians and Healf-Denes. Yet here, in Frisia, she 'ær mæste heold / worolde wynne' (before held the greatest of the world's joy) (1079b–1080a). Whatever her relationship to her family of birth, Hildeburh's *joy* is in Frisia. Taken from Frisia by the Healf-Denes, 'læddon to leodum' (led [. . .] to [her] people), she is removed from those skies under which she knew both joy and grief. For all the attention critics have paid in the past to Hildeburh's sorrow and her command of the pyre, they too often forget that that sorrow plays out against a backdrop of very real joy, without which it would have no *pathos*, and really no meaning. The shift in meaning for Hildeburh – her agency and then utter lack by the end of the poem – is similar to this initial shift in her relationship to the bodies of her son and her brother. She mourned (*bemurnan*) after they died. It is the condition of these bodies – and her connection to them – that causes mourning for Hildeburh.

Indeed, then, it is the corpses, Frisian and Dane both, that animate feud and loss throughout the episode, that spark both Hildeburh's agency and her being led, object-like, back to her people. No longer the agent of her own action, she cannot participate in the life of the community because that community has failed. Put another way, 'her meaning as peace-weaver is untranslatable' – quite literally, it cannot be carried over past the violence that destroys her people.[34] When she looks at the dead bodies that remain 'where [she] before held the greatest of the world's joy', these bodies and her association with them have changed utterly.

In reading the Finnsburg episode as a case study in Actor-Network theory, several things emerge that a more traditional critique might not foreground. First and foremost, the attention paid to human action in the poem can be usefully distributed to include non-human actors as well. The resulting reading demonstrates the imbrication of the human in a world larger than the human communities that so often dominate readings of *Beowulf*. Second, surfacing these connections allows for a deeper understanding of the poem's operation; although Old English poets might not have known about the variations in agency that characterize the New Materialism, they were not strangers to the intimacies between human beings and the environment, nor to the unstable meaning of objects meant to forge human community. Indeed, that instability is rather the point of *Beowulf*. Finally, when we fully understand the networks within which Hildeburh participates, she becomes simultaneously less than and more than the object or subject of human action. She becomes a participant in a complex network made of both human beings and the living world: the stories humans tell, the materials they help to circulate and eventually, as corpses, even become. If we can remember that Hildeburh's sorrow moves her to action not in isolation from the bodies of her kin but *because* of them, we can resurrect a fuller picture of this legendary lady. No longer simply the 'ides gnornode', she is also a woman who, for too brief a span, held joy.

Notes

1 All citations from *Beowulf* are from R. D. Fulk, Robert E. Bjork, and John D. Niles (eds), *Klaeber's Beowulf*, 4th edn (Toronto: University of Toronto Press, 2008) and cited in the text by line number. All translations from the Old English are my own.

2 For the most traditional reading of the digressions and their importance to the poem, see Adrien Bonjour, *The digressions in Beowulf* (Oxford: Oxford University Press, 1950). For a thorough reading of the Finnsburg episode in the poem, see Gale Owen-Crocker, *The four funerals in Beowulf* (Manchester: Manchester University Press, 2000). For an overview of the roles available to women in the poem, see Alexandra Hennessey Olsen, 'Gender roles', in Robert E. Bjork and John D. Niles (eds), *A Beowulf handbook* (Lincoln, NE: University of Nebraska Press, 1998), pp. 311–24.

3 Angus Cameron, Ashley Crandell Amos, Antonette diPaolo Healey et al. (eds), *Dictionary of Old English: A to H*, online (Toronto: Dictionary of Old English Project, 2016), s.v. *gast, gæst* 13, 'a natural phenomenon (fire, frost, tempest, etc.) personified as a living spirit'.

4 My interpretation of the Finnsburg episode owes much to Actor-Network theory and its understanding of collectivity as one way in which human and non-human entities might associate with one another in ways that supersede traditional ideas about agency. For a comprehensive study of collectivity and its relationship to human ideas of community, see Bruno Latour, *Reassembling the social: an introduction to Actor-Network Theory* (Oxford: Oxford University Press, 2005); Michel Callon, 'Some elements of a sociology of translation: domestication of the scallops and the fishermen of St Brieuc Bay', in John Law (ed.), *Power, action, and belief: a new sociology of knowledge?* (New York: Routledge, 1986), pp. 196–233; and John Law, 'Notes on the theory of actor-network: ordering, strategy and heterogeneity', *Systems practice*, 5.4 (1992), 379–93.

5 Major readings of Hildeburh's role in the Finnsburg episode include Jane Chance, *Woman as hero in Old English literature* (Syracuse, NY: Syracuse University Press, 1986); Gillian Overing, *Language, sign, and gender in Beowulf* (Carbondale, IL: Southern Illinois University Press, 1990); and Stacy Klein, *Ruling women: queenship and gender in Anglo-Saxon literature* (South Bend, IN: University of Notre Dame Press, 2006).

6 On community formation via storytelling, see also Benjamin A. Saltzman's chapter in this volume, pp. 31–53.

7 Law, 'Notes on the theory of actor-network', 381.

8 Ibid., 383.

9 This project bears thematic and critical similarities to Jeffrey Cohen and Lowell Duckert's recent work in *Elemental ecocriticism*. See their 'Introduction: eleven principles of the elements', in Cohen and Duckert (eds), *Elemental ecocriticism: thinking with earth, water, air, and fire* (Minneapolis, MN: University of Minnesota Press, 2015), especially p. 5.

10 On this point, see John D. Niles, who defines feud culture as 'a culture of self-perpetuating, revenge-driven cycles of violence', in 'The myth of the feud in Anglo-Saxon England', *JEGP*, 114.2 (2015), 163–200, at 164.

11 Indeed, John D. Niles has recently argued (with others) that feud culture in Anglo-Saxon England itself has been overstated. Most importantly, he notes that, 'While only some critics have argued that the *Beowulf* poet aims to undermine the ideal of heroic vengeance, all readers are likely to agree that the poem gives a powerful account of the disasters that can accompany acts of either unprovoked or retaliatory violence' (ibid., 166).

12 For an alternative configuration of who lives and who dies in this particular feud, see Alfred Bammesburger, 'Hildeburh's son', *Notes and queries*, 53.1 (2006), 14–17.

13 Notable recent exceptions beyond those mentioned here include Peter S. Baker, *Honor, violence, and exchange in Beowulf* (Cambridge: D.S. Brewer, 2013), and Leonard Neidorf, 'Hildeburh's mourning and *The Wife's Lament*', *Studia Neophilologica*, 89.2 (2017), 197–204. Baker in particular lodges a fascinating study of the genesis and understanding of the term *freoðuwebbe* – noting its absence in general from the OE corpus's discussion of various women in marriages in the midst of feud, he attributes its genesis to nineteenth-century Anglo-Saxonists' racist and sexist views of the proper role of women in the poem.

14 Joyce Hill, '"Þæt wæs geomuru ides!" A female stereotype examined', in Helen Damico and Alexandra Hennessey Olsen (eds), *New readings on women in Old English* (Bloomington, IN: Indiana University Press, 1990), pp. 235–47, at 244.

15 Ibid., p. 244.

16 Helen Bennett, 'The female mourner at Beowulf's funeral: filling the blanks / hearing the spaces', *Exemplaria*, 4.1 (1992), 35–50, at 35.

17 Hill, '"Þæt wæs geomuru ides!"', 241.

18 'Through this action', Porter suggests, 'Hildeburh emphasizes that her son is *hers*, not her husband's.' See Dorothy Porter, 'The social centrality of women in *Beowulf*: a new context', *The heroic age*, 5 (2001), www.heroicage.org/issues/5/porter1.html (accessed 5 June 2019). Leonard Neidorf has recently suggested that, following Alexandra Hennessy Olsen and J. M. Hill, we can read Hildeburh as 'a woman whose suffering is in the end compensated by the murder of Finn, and whose experience parallels that of the Danes listening to the episode, who suffered at the hands of Grendel and have finally been compensated by his death' ('Hildburh's mourning', 203). Although Neidorf's point is well taken – indeed, Finn's death would compensate Hildeburh for the death of her son – two points seem important to raise here. First, Finn is also Hildeburh's husband, which suggests that her position in this matter is somewhat complex. Second, the Danes may well *feel* compensated by the death of Grendel, but it certainly does not bear out in the narrative that such compensation has lasting ramifications.

19 Klein, *Ruling women*, p. 94.

20 For a reading of Hildeburh's role as a peace pledge or peace-weaving woman who fails, see Chance, *Woman as hero*. See also Peter Buchanan's chapter in this volume, pp. 279–303, for a fuller discussion of Wealhtheow as a peace-weaver.

21 Joseph Bosworth, *An Anglo-Saxon dictionary: based on the manuscript collections of the late Joseph Bosworth*, ed. Thomas Northcote Toller (Oxford: Clarendon Press, 1898), s.v. *gemænan*, iii and iv.

22 R. K. Ashdowne, D. R. Howlett, and R. E. Latham (eds), *Dictionary of medieval Latin from British sources* (Oxford: British Academy, 2018), s.v. *'plangere'*, *coinquinare, violare* 1.

23 See, for example, J. L. Austin, *How to do things with words* (Cambridge, MA: Harvard University Press, 1975). Austin's approach privileges the linguistic function of perlocutionary and elocutionary force, focusing most prominently on the idea of the speech-act, which can only achieve its end if certain preconditions for its use are met. By contrast, the actor-network model of narrative circulation functions sociologically rather than linguistically, and posits stories as actants in the social world, and thus as capable of modifying the behaviour of human actors in a narrative.

24 For a variant view of the passage, see John M. Hill, 'Social milieu', in Bjork and Niles (eds), *A Beowulf handbook*, pp. 255–70.

25 Bosworth, *An Anglo-Saxon dictionary*, s.v. *searu*. For additional discussion of 'craft' in *Beowulf*, see James Paz's chapter in this volume, pp. 73–96.

26 For a fuller consideration of how we might understand this verb, see R. D. Fulk, 'Six cruces in the Finnsburg fragment and episode', *Medium Aevum*, 74.2 (2005), 191–204.

27 For readings of feud and violence in *Beowulf*, see Baker, *Honor, exchange, and violence*; Scott Gwara, *Heroic identity in the world of Beowulf* (Leiden: Brill, 2008); J. M. Hill, 'The ethnopsychology of the in-law feud and the remaking of group identity in *Beowulf*', *PQ*, 78.1 (1999), 97–123.

28 Bosworth, *An Anglo-Saxon dictionary*, s.v. *wræce*.

29 Julia Kristeva, *The powers of horror: an essay on abjection* (New York: Columbia University Press, 1982). I am not the first scholar of *Beowulf* to make a connection between Kristeva's notion of the abject and *Beowulf* (or Old English literature more generally). For a different take on the relationship between the two, see Paul Acker, 'Horror and the maternal in *Beowulf*', *PMLA*, 121.3 (2006), 702–16. Jeffrey Jerome Cohen extends his meditation on the abject to *The Wanderer* and *The Ruin* in the first chapter of his *Of giants: sex, monsters, and the Middle Ages* (Minneapolis, MN: University of Minnesota Press, 1999).

30 Here, *gear* is used in the sense of 'season', a specific period of chronological time. This usage in *Beowulf* is one of the paradigmatic attestations of this sense of *gear*. See Cameron et al. (eds), *Dictionary of Old English*, s.v. *gear* D.1.b.

31 Gillian R. Overing, *Language, sign, and gender*, p. 85. (Carbondale, IL: Southern Illinois University Press, 1990), p. 85.

32 Ibid., p. 86.

33 The emendation is by the editors of *Klaeber's Beowulf*, but see the discussion in Overing, *Language, sign, and gender*, p. 189, n. 1079b. The editors make the emendation because the main point of the passage is the sorrow of the daughter of Hoc – Hildeburh herself.

34 Overing, *Language, sign, and gender*, p. 85.

8

What the raven told the eagle: animal language and the return of loss in *Beowulf*[1]

Mo Pareles

Whatever its flaws, Old English literature continues to rebuke the humanist narcissism that denies non-human animals possession of symbolic language. Like us, the early English knew that in singing, birds speak. As Susan Crane notes, at least one strain in medieval Western European thought held that birds composed 'a society with a metaphoric relation to human society, in which birdsong fills the function of human language',[2] and recent critics have heard welcome eruptions of interspecies intercourse in the avian voices of Old English literature.[3] In this vein of ecocritical optimism, I too read in the bird language of *Beowulf* a profound moment of interspecies connection. But I argue that within *Beowulf* the human is excluded from and indeed denigrated by the intimacy of wild creatures; when birds gossip about human corpses, this intimacy thematises the breakdown of socially embedded human knowledge.

Beowulf is an ideal site for those creatures and readers drawn to dire human straits, since far from a celebration of heroic achievement, the poem is a relentless chronicle of human failures. The most abject and notorious of these include queens' failures to weave peace; fathers' failures to protect and avenge their sons; Danes' failures to defend themselves; pagans' failures to communicate with the divine and achieve salvation; human failure to control objects and make things work, as in the cases of both swords and gold; Beowulf's failure to ensure peace and security for his people; and the ultimate failure of the heroic ideal of lordship, which impossibly requires both wise statecraft and martial recklessness. *Beowulf*'s poetics of human disappointment and disaster deserves endless study. Mary Kate Hurley suggests that the avian encounter near the poem's end might provide a form of recuperation to *Beowulf*'s 'endlessly failing human communities'.[4] This chapter, while inspired by Hurley's provocation, strikes a more pessimistic note. It focuses on one crucial form of human failure in *Beowulf* – the failure of human knowledge enclosed in the homosocial bond of intimacy through which communication passes – and reveals that this bond endures in the realm of animal intimacy, where raven, wolf, and eagle triumph over the human.

This chapter begins with a moment of human loss. The murder of Æschere, the Danish king Hrothgar's *runwita* (knower of secrets, elsewhere interpreted as confidant, soul mate, and reader of runes, a point to which we shall return), severs a crucial past relation within which human meaning is made. As I shall argue, and as Thomas Meyer's experimental translation makes particularly explicit, when the Avenger[5] mutilates and kills Æschere, the total subordination of beasts is part of what is lost. Hrothgar's move to recuperate this loss through the conventional idiom of mourning – vengeance – involves, as an addendum to the eulogy, an anthropocentric remaking of the landscape as oral map. In the second movement of this chapter, I discuss a future intimacy, that of raven and eagle, in which beastly knowledge triumphs over human capacities for translation, for meaning making, for vengeance, and even for bodily integrity. In keeping with its focus on translation, the chapter reads translations of *Beowulf* as interpretations and as literature in their own right.

How animals convey meaning

Critical animal studies, the field that deconstructs human exceptionalism, has proven extremely congenial to Old English studies, prompting questions about non-human and post-human subjectivity, the maintenance of the human–animal boundary, and the costly constitution of the human in Anglo-Saxon culture. These inquiries track a larger 'animal turn' within medieval studies[6] and an ecocritical strain within early medieval studies.[7] Birds have drawn particular attention within medieval animal studies: not only the avian figures of the Exeter Book, but also the Bayeux Tapestry birds, the arguing pair of *The Owl and the Nightingale*, Chaucer's debating birds, and other medieval English textual fowls are provocative figures of animal language and knowledge transmission.[8] Peggy McCracken notes that in *Yonec*, Marie de France positions the speaking hawk as a figure who can communicate with humans, and yet who retains a store of untranslated (untranslatable?) knowledge.[9] Bird language often retains this sort of remainder, as we shall see.

In medieval literature and visual culture, non-human animals convey meaning through diverse methods; for instance, as visual images alone they ornament (e.g. the 'wyrmfah' [serpent-patterned] sword [1698a]),[10] provide visual allegory in religious images, take on narrative function in visual storytelling (e.g. the beasts of the Bayeux Tapestry, or the birds of the Illustrated Old English Heptateuch), act as emblems for human groups or gods, and behave as graphs attached to phonemes (e.g., the u-rune, *ur* [aurochs or wild ox]). Animal bodies are, as Nicole Shukin has perceptively noted, the material substrate of human communication:[11] they provided bones and skin on which to write, feathers that carried ink, and at times ink as well. They were also messengers and informers – both fictive and real. And they provided the symbolic language, allegorical symbols, and characters for human-authored literature, including the word-stock for place and human names (e.g. 'Dæghrefn' [Day-raven] [2501b], whom Beowulf kills in battle, and 'Earna Næs' [Eagles' Nest] [3031b], where Beowulf's failed war-band finds his and the dragon's dead bodies) and for kennings ('ganotes bæð' [gannet's bath, i.e. sea] [1861b]). Birds bear a disproportionate burden in this cluster of signifying roles, since they have a particular relationship to language: they are the messengers between humans, between non-human species, and between the mundane world and the divine. And they can have a particularly strong metonymic relation to violent death, especially in *Beowulf*, where the most tragic form of human death is described as 'hrefne to hroðre' (pleasure for the raven) (2448a).

Within this critical environment, it is worth paying a bit more attention to an avian speech-act at the end of *Beowulf*. Wiglaf's messenger to Beowulf's people, the Geats, announces Beowulf's death and predicts a brutal invasion once the Swedes hear of his passing. He concludes a harrowing series of predictions with avian speech: 'se wonna hrefn / ... / earne secgan, hu him æt æte speow, / þenden he wið wulf wæl reafode' (the dark raven ... will tell the eagle how he surpassed him in eating, when he with the wolf laid waste to the slain) (3024a–7). I argue that this moment of inter-avian intimacy denigrates not only the slain human body, the fighting and agential body reduced here to morsels of warm meat for the pleasure of birds, but also the intimate human relations that, in the oral culture of the poem, provide the conduit for human knowledge production.

Homosociality and knowledge

In elite homosocial cultures, including both the warrior culture of *Beowulf* and the monasticism that probably produced the text, love and knowledge are transmitted through the same intimate bonds.[12] David M. Clark demonstrates the importance of the homosocial bond in *Beowulf* and, in Old English literature generally, the 'utter wretchedness of being alone ... without a brother warrior'.[13] A friend or lord is necessary for material and martial survival (as many of the exiles in the elegies point out) and for the sharing of joy and sorrow; Beowulf seems to mean all of this when he tells his lord, uncle, and foster brother Hygelac, 'Gen is eall æt ðe / lissa gelong' (All delight still depends on you) (2149b–50a).[14] A companion is necessary, too, for that currency that relates to all other aspects of emotional and physical survival in an oral culture: knowledge. As Benjamin A. Saltzman observes in his contribution to this volume, evoking the multiple senses of *intimare*, intimacy is the medium for the culture's stories and values.

That knowledge occurs only in relation,[15] and that the most intimate form of human relation in this culture is (in theory) the elite homosocial pair, provide the conditions for the tragedy at the chronological heart of the poem: the death of King Hrothgar's 'hæleþa leofost' (most loved warrior) (1296b), 'aldorþegn' (senior thane) (1308a), and 'deorestan' (dearest) (1309a) companion, Æschere, at the Avenger's hands. We meet Æschere, killed in Hrothgar's hall after Beowulf's triumph over Grendel, only posthumously:

Ne frin þu æfter sælum! Sorh is geniwod
Denigea leodum: dead is Æschere,
Yrmenlafes yldra broþor,
min runwita ond min rædbora,
eaxlgestealla ðonne we on orlege
hafelan weredon, þonne hniton feþan,
eoferas cnysedan. Swylc scolde eorl wesan,
æþeling ærgod, swylc Æschere wæs. (1322–9)

(Don't you ask about happiness. For the Danish people, sorrow is made new. Æschere is dead – Yrmenlaf's older brother, my knower of secrets and my counsellor, comrade in arms, when we guarded our heads in battle, when armies crashed and struck the boars. As a man ought to be, a fine prince, so Æschere was.)

This royal grief, framed first as the entire people's, is also deeply personal to the king. Æschere's role in Hrothgar's life, as presented in these few lines, is capacious: he is the companion of his youth, dear friend, essential advisor. Hrothgar seems to describe him, indeed, as an extension of the lordly body, grieving, 'nu seo hand ligeð, / se þe eow welhwylcra wilna dohte' (now the hand that gave

you every good lies at rest) (1343b–4). This is the 'hand' of a
ring-giver, liberally distributing social goods, and thus behaves
functionally as Hrothgar's own hand; in Hrothgar's grief, it is also
the source of 'welhwylcra wilna' (*every* good). I have translated
runwita more or less literally as 'knower of secrets', but that is not
to say that I know what it means. The word appears only twice in
Old English, here and in *Guthlac*, where it refers to the dying saint:
'Ða se wuldormaga worda gestilde, / rof runwita' (then this steward
of heaven's glory, steadfast wise man, rested from speech) (1094–5).[16]
It may mean that Æschere was a confidant, the keeper of Hrothgar's
secrets – this role belongs to the intimacy of homosocial friendship.
It may mean, additionally or instead, that he imparted secrets to
Hrothgar – that their relationship was a vehicle for kingly wisdom.
James Paz, exploiting the connections of both *run-* and *ræd-* to
writing and knowledge, makes the intriguing argument that within
this oral culture, Æschere was the man who read, guarded, and
interpreted secret knowledge for Hrothgar and his people.[17]

Hrothgar's outpouring of grief represents an intimate as well as
a public loss. The moment of death is, as David Halperin notes,
the moment of ultimate intimacy for a heroic couple (a hero and
his companion), equivalent to consummation for a heterosexual
couple.[18] There is no stigma to a grief so intense that it seems to
erase all joy – Beowulf's location of his entire happiness in Hygelac
recalls such a statement. Yet this is meant to be a death in battle,
with one companion ideally dying in the other's arms. This pair
has grown too old to make such a death likely, yet it is not impossible.
Although the young Beowulf in fact survives his uncle in battle,
the elderly Beowulf will die in heroic manner in the company of
Wiglaf, who expresses an unfulfilled wish to die alongside him
(2650–2). Grendel's mother, the Avenger, smashes the fantasy of a
battlefield death and all of its comforting androcentric implications:
homosociality, patriarchal kinship, control over animals as symbols,
the legibility of blood, the meaningfulness of human suffering.
Meyer's translation makes clear what is lost:

> What we shared:
>
> secrets stomping feet
> battles arms swinging
>
> slashed boar emblems   blood
> heads split wide open   noise
>   gone!

A bitch's bare hands crushed
that model man. Somewhere now
a beast's lips suck the bloody
stump of Yrmenlaf's brother[19]

The initial couplets, undisrupted by verticality or capitalization, enclose what is lost: the lack of differentiation, of what never had to be differentiated or separated previously. Here are the unnamed (and perhaps even unremembered) secrets shared by these two (as well as the capacity to keep and unlock secrets), the youthful limbs moving joyfully and in sync, the violence against the enemy, framed first as the destruction of his animal symbolism (the 'slashed boar emblems' on warriors' helmets) and then as the graphic invasion of his body. Perhaps this final recollection tips the scale, the memory of broken heads too much in this moment of violence, for here the topography shifts. As the vertical interrupts, so too do the graphemes and poetics of hierarchy, the complete sentences, the need for plans, the rage. For here, in the reality of violence against the one Hrothgar loves, is also the reality of the monster – not a flat 'emblem' but an agent with a body and motives that Hrothgar tries to atomize, sexualize, chop away: '[a] bitch's bare hands', 'a beast's lips'.

When translating the poem's omniscient descriptions of the Avenger, Meyer renders her appropriately formidable and sovereign; for example, 'se ðe floda begong / heorogifre beheold hund missera' (the one who, predatory, had held the water's course for a hundred half-years) (1497b–98) is rendered as 'that terrible mother of floods, / those deep regions' guardian for a hundred seasons'.[20] In Hrothgar's angry, grieving voice, he translates her in terms of misogyny and dehumanization. This should not be seen as a literal translation, but as a succinct amplification of Hrothgar's claims that the Grendelkin are monstrous, bestial, wicked, and have no right to hold territory or avenge death.[21] Thus the vulgarity 'a bitch's bare hands' draws not only on the Old English lines this most directly translates ('handbanan / wælgæst wæfre' (a barehanded killer, a nimble, murdering visitor) (1330–1) but also on the Avenger's ambiguous relation to the human: apparently a woman, she lives among wolves and mothers a monster; she is, in some way, vulpine, a 'brimwylf' (sea-wolf) (1506a); her powerful body can slaughter without weapons, but she uses a knife. The capacious semantic range of 'bitch', with the particular capacity of that word to flicker across species boundaries and moral categories, encompasses the poem's association of Grendel's mother with maternity outside the patriarchial human order and with feminine perversity within it. And it makes explicit the alignment of Grendel's mother with the bestial world once so easily sliced through.

Grendel's mother gets away from Hrothgar, conceptually and physically; it is his friend, still whole in his mind ('that model man', 'Yrmenlaf's brother') who has in fact been reduced to parts ('bloody / stump'). And it is necessary, too, to blame Beowulf, which is really to blame Grendel:

> in revenge for that hard grip
> of yours, the life torn from
> that mother's son, that monster
> who raided this hall & claimed
> the lives of some of my best
>
> warriors. I'm told two *things*
> can be seen to prowl the nearby
>
> borderlands, a male & female[22]

Here, though, Hrothgar gets into ontological difficulties, for this beast-woman, monster's mother, acts from motives he understands well: she subscribes wholeheartedly to the culture of kin vengeance that governs the poem's other actors.[23] And so his enraged vision of her is not coherent; he overdetermines her as dehumanized 'beast', humanized 'mother', ambiguous 'bitch'; he tries again: 'two *things*'. And, as if he has no other knowledge about the Grendelkin, 'a male & female'. Yet he has already revealed that he knows much more: their relationship, her mourning. This is where he turns from a description of his enemy to a plan of attack. Perhaps it is safer territory for him, although his account is little more coherent.

Intertwined with Hrothgar's intense personal grief is nostalgia for the symbolic mastery over the animal world that he enjoyed with his *runwita*. While some critics have reduced nearly all animals in medieval literature to the symbolic and typological, the 'boar emblems' of Hrothgar's elegy are rare in presenting animal as pure symbol: the very narrowest type of those beasts that Gilles Deleuze and Félix Guattari call 'State animals', images and archetypes around which a political identity coalesces.[24] They hearken to the strange description of Grendel's mother's horrifying powers as inferior 'be wæpnedmen / þonne … / sweord swate fah swin ofer helme / ecgum dyhttig andweard sireð' (to men's, when … a bloodstained sword, strong in its edges, cuts through the swine on an opposite helmet) (1284b–7).[25] Graphic, man-made, representative not of the beast it depicts but of the men who travel under its sign, this boar is made (from a Danish perspective, at least) to be cracked along with the shields it embosses, to be slashed with swords, to bear the humiliation and loss of the ones who carry it and to reflect, in humiliation, the glory of the men who violate it. Such violence can be inscribed on real animals, too, but while the monsters (voiceless but for their cries) are slaughtered, the bragging birds use their voices and their motility to triumph discursively over the dead bodies of humanity.

For the human characters of Old English literature, intimacy is a key site of knowledge production. Exiles, disoriented from the sources of meaning that governed their lives, produce new under-standing in solitary relation to God. The heathen Danes, in unwitting one-sided relation with a divine that does not exist, cannot find the source of their misery. Hrothgar, failing to strike a mutual chord in Beowulf, is rendered mute. In bragging, gossip, and threats, histories and futures emerge. That different histories work in different relationships is not inherently a problem in *Beowulf* – on the contrary, as Rosemary Huisman demonstrates of Beowulf's retellings of the battle with Grendel's mother, it is a design feature.[26] The more pertinent issue for these characters, demonstrated poignantly in the Lay of the Last Survivor (2247–65), which narrates the loss of an entire people, is that when there are no relationships, history is threadbare and cannot bring forth a future. As Nicholas Howe has observed, 'the gift of history' – knowledge about neighbouring lands, ledgers of battle debts incurred and paid, and examples of successful and failed rule – is 'more precious than gold or horses' in the world of *Beowulf*.[27]

Secrecy/Hrothgar's map

The poem's ideology operates in part, as Saltzman and Alexandra Bolintineanu note, through the open discussion of secrets. In particular, this is how it makes its monsters. As Bolintineanu observes, *Beowulf* redeploys the 'men ne cunnon' / 'god ana wat' (people do not know / only God knows) trope, which occurs throughout Old English literature to refer to eschatological matters and other divine mysteries, to talk about the details of the Grendelkin's lives, thus, as she says, 'signal[ing] the utter alterity of the monsters'.[28] Saltzman notes that secrecy is in fact key to the poem's entire epistemology, but 'human agency is often inadequate both to the act of concealment … and to the act of discovery (Grendel is concealed by night; his

traces can be examined only in the morning)'.[29] This secrecy allocates
power not only to those who understand the unknown, but also to
those who, standing outside the inner gates of knowledge, understand
what is unknown or secret.

The secrecy of the landscape is, for Hrothgar, a crucial aspect
of his territorial claims and strategies. Hrothgar turns immediately
from his grief to present to Beowulf an 'oral map', in Daniel C.
Remein's terms,[30] of the mere and a description of its inhabitants in which contradictions and lacunae in human knowledge are
features, not bugs:

Ic þæt londbuend,   leode mine,
selerædende   secgan hyrde,
þæt hie gesawon   swylce twegen
micle mearcstapan   moras healdan,
ellorgæstas.   Ðæra oðer wæs,
þæs þe hie gewislicost   gewitan meahton,
idese onlicnæs;   oðer earmsceapen
on weres wæstmum   wræclastas træd,
næfne he wæs mara   þonne ænig man oðer;
þone on geardagum   Grendel nemdon
foldbuende;   no hie fæder cunnon,
hwæþer him ænig wæs   ær acenned
dyrnra gasta.   Hie dygel lond
warigeað wulfhleoþu,   windige næssas,
frecne fengelad,   ðær fyrgenstream
under næssa genipu   niþer gewiteð,
flod under foldan.   Nis þæt feor heonon
milgemearces   þæt se mere standeð;
ofer þæm hongiað   hrinde bearwas,
wudu wyrtum fæst   wæter oferhelmað.
Þær mæg nihta gehwæm   niðwundor seon,
fyr on flode.   No þæs frod leofað
gumena bearna   þæt þone grund wite. (1345–67)

(I have heard the land's inhabitants, my people, the hall counsellors,
say that they saw two such large border-walkers guarding the moors,
foreign spirits. One of these was, insofar as they could know for sure,
in the form of a woman. The other, wretched, walked the paths of
exile in the shape of a man, except that he was bigger than any other
man; in the old days, the people living there called him Grendel.
They do not know his father, or whether any were born before him
among hidden spirits. They hold this secret land – wolf-hills, windy
headlands, dangerous fen-path – where the mountain stream flows
down into dark abysses, water under the earth. It is not far from

here in miles that the mere stands; over it hangs a frosty grove, a
hard-rooted forest hangs over the water. There at night anyone can
see a sinister marvel: fire on the water. Among the children of men
there lives none wise enough that he knows the [mere's] bottom.)

Hrothgar turns here to the medium with which he is most comfortable
– the (somewhat synthetic, in this case) bond of masculine intimacy
– to communicate a litany of secret knowledge. Hrothgar speaks
of 'dyrnra gasta' (hidden spirits) and 'dygel lond' (secret land), and
gestures ostentatiously, as Bolintineanu observes, to the unreliable
links in the chain of his knowledge: he has heard people say that
one of the monsters was 'þæs þe hie gewislicost gewitan meahton,
/ idese onlicnæs' (insofar as they could know for sure, in the form
of a woman), embedding the apparent fact of this monster's woman-
hood in the unreliability of second-hand knowledge and witness
doubt, with room to distinguish between appearance and ontology.
He notes that his informants do not know Grendel's fatherhood
and lineage, 'no hie fæder cunnon, / hwæþer him ænig wæs ær
acenned / dyrnra gasta' (they do not know his father, or whether
any were born before him among hidden spirits), nor do they, or
anyone alive, have personal knowledge of the mere's bottom: 'No
þæs frod leofað / gumena bearna þæt þone grund wite' (Among the
children of men there lives none wise enough that he knows the
[mere's] bottom).[31]
    Yet Hrothgar demonstrates no uncertainty about who rightfully
possesses this wild territory or the right to speak about it: 'Ic þæt
londbuend, leode mine, / selerædende secgan hyrde' (I have heard
the land's inhabitants, my people, the hall counsellors, say). By
defining the 'londbuend' as 'leode mine', he lays an ironclad transitive
claim to the land that the mysterious creatures (thus) wrongfully
guard; by making the inhabitants' testimony intelligible in the hall
and by speaking this from Heorot, he affirms Heorot as the proper
clearing house for information about them. The claim that it is
impossible to trace Grendel's lineage, or discover whether he is
first-born, thus becomes intelligible not as lack but as positive
assertion: a negation of the Grendelkin's land rights. The archive
that has its raw materials in the wilderness (the sights of monsters,
of frightened animals, of eerie wonders) acquires meaning within
the processing logic of the hall, where narrative undergirds possession, just as in the world of *Beowulf* all stories about the world
of creation, of men and women, of non-human animals and of
good and evil, acquire intelligibility only by retelling in the hall.

It is standard to assume that the 'mere', because of its name and its function as the home of outlaws (among other reasons), is located in a fen of the sort known to Anglo-Saxons; fens were productive and provocative cultural locations precisely because they were inhospitable to agriculture and thus large-scale settlement. As Andy Orchard and others have noted and as Christopher Abram explores in this volume, however, the Grendelkin's territory is a highly idiosyncratic wetland, with a diverse range of topographical elements, flora, and fauna (including, for instance, wolves and sea-monsters) that 'can scarcely be harmonised'.[32] As such, it is hardly representational, yet its very unlikeliness seems to amplify the features that attracted hermits such as Guthlac and monastic communities to the East Anglian wilderness with which this passage is often associated. As Sarah Harlan-Haughey observes, the fens offer 'a retreat from normative topographies, from normative human lifestyles'.[33]

This map is what the ecocritic Bruce Braun calls an 'environmental imaginar[y]', a vision of the land divided into socially intelligible zones, including different forms of so-called wilderness.[34] As Braun notes, all wilderness is co-produced by the natural and the social; there is no pristine, uninhabited land until someone needs *terra nullius*. So, too, with the wilderness outside Heorot's gates, which must be wild – that is, its known inhabitants must be portrayed as incapable of holding territory, as Fabienne Michelet argues, for the purposes of the Danish succession's land claims.[35] The oral map is gloriously incongruous in its details, combining for instance uplands and lowlands in a single monstrous landscape. Yet it is nonetheless naked in its intentions – to place the monsters firmly outside the bounds of human civilization and to entice Beowulf to murder Grendel's mother, who has killed Hrothgar's companion. Thus, when Hrothgar gestures repeatedly in this passage towards things that no one knows, he is not humbly indicating the limits of human knowledge, but rather constructing a landscape of secrets for the benefit of a man who likes to find what is untouched and unknown, and kill it. The intimacy between Hrothgar and Beowulf, a shadow of the lost intimacy between lord and *runwita*, takes studied ignorance as its currency.

What the raven said to the eagle: birds in translation

If, as Saltzman observes, 'Beowulf posits a past against the limits of human knowledge and the limits of its own narrative', its animal

world makes the future equally epistemologically threatening.[36] Bestial
intimacy, expressed in shared enjoyment of and secret knowledge
about human bodies, emerges among the ominous group of predators
whose appearance signals the end of Geatish happiness. Raven,
eagle, and wolf are, in Francis P. Magoun's trope, the 'beasts of
battle' who show up in Old English, Old Norse, and arguably
Middle High German literature where violent death is expected.[37]
Although most scholars, including critical animal studies scholars
such as Donna Beth Ellard, see these beasts primarily as symbolic
figures in a human drama, Joseph Harris notes 'the attribution of
voice and even of language to the beasts' in many of their itera-
tions.[38] Yet this boast, as R. D. Fulk, Robert E. Bjork, and John
D. Niles observe, is the only Old English 'conversation' among
the beasts of battle,[39] and only its outline reaches human ears, at
the triple remove of space, time, and voice. That is, the speech
appears before it is spoken, presumably at a physical distance from
where it is spoken, and in the voice of a human being who does not
attempt to approximate it closely. This third remove, that of voice,
is itself a multiple remove – the poet translates into Old English the
words of the Geatish messenger, who is translating bird language
into his own dialect of Old Norse. Indeed, he indirectly reports
the raven's words – not actually the words themselves, but only
the topic of the bird's conversation. Implied here is a pan-avian
language; if the raven and eagle speak their own dialects, these
are mutually intelligible. There is no attempt, as so often when
humans describe birdsong, to approximate any specific sounds.
Moreover, this difference in voice emerges in part from temporal
difference, since the foretold future of the Geats is the ever-receding
distant past of the poet, scribes, and readers; and as Robert Stanton
observes,

> Imagining the sounds made by nonhuman animals involves grappling
> with extinction, species development, domestication, and breeding
> practices over the course of a thousand to fifteen hundred years; it
> is an open question whether a domesticated pig in the year 900
> sounded more like a present-day pig than any English speech from
> 900 resembles any English spoken today.[40]

The details of the message are, in fact, fairly ambiguous, and
even the simple paraphrase gives rise to a number of possible
interpretations. In Roy Liuzza's verse translation, for instance, 'the
dark raven, / greedy for carrion, shall speak a great deal, / ask the
eagle how he fared at his feast / when he plundered corpses with

the wolf'.[41] Here, the eagle is the agent, the raven only his interlocutor, and the questioning implies that there is plenty of carnage for seconds. The ambiguity of *wið* (a preposition that can mean, among other things, both 'with' and 'against') demonstrates what else the human reader has no access to: the level of intimacy, the kind of relations between birds and wolves. Can birds and wolves speak over, maybe about, our dead bodies? Do they have mutually intelligible dialects? What else might they talk about over a meal of our flesh? Despite its potential polysemy, *wið* in Beowulf usually indicates an adversarial relationship (see lines 113, 144, 152, *inter alia*).[42] Yet even in the context of warfare or strife it can still take a cooperative meaning; for example, '[Grendel] sibbe ne wolde / wið manna hwone mægenes Deniga' ([Grendel] would never make peace with any of the Danes) (154b–5), where it aids a negative reference to peace that underlines the hostile mood. Liuzza interprets the word as indicating cooperation between the scavengers. Can we, too, imagine the wolf and the raven as intimate partners in anthropophagous passion, egging each other on, worrying at the same corpses with beaks and claws and teeth, and finally resting to tally the number of still-warm bodies they consumed; or can we imagine them only as rivals, the raven snatching pieces of flesh from the wolf's jaws, the wolf swiping at the raven with her already bloodied claws?

Translators and critics have struggled to interpret the nature of these intimacies: raven and eagle, raven and wolf. The answer depends, in turn, on interpreting the speech so narrowly withheld from human comprehension. As Mary Kate Hurley notes, the verb *reafian* (plunder, lay waste), which attaches elsewhere in *Beowulf* to the actions of warriors, 'suggests that human plunder can be equated – at least lexically – with the plundering of carrion eaters'.[43] Thus, in Meyer's experimental translation, the raven is making a battle boast: 'The greedy raven will have tales / to tell the eagle of feats shared / with the wolf on slaughter's field.'[44] In this interpretation, bird and wolf are allies in what to them are honourable feats on the battlefield, kills to be 'shared' between them, tales to be shared abroad.[45] J. R. R. Tolkien sees the meaning of *wið* quite differently, translating this line as 'the dusky raven gloating above the doomed shall speak many things, shall to the eagle tell how it sped him at the carrion-feast, when he vied with the wolf in picking bare the slain'.[46] These options are not mutually exclusive: the raven and wolf may have met as strangers and before long become friendly competitors, engaged in tugs of war over bodies snapping at the joints. In times of abundance, it is possible to be generous to one's erstwhile enemies. In both cases, the framing of this speech as battle-boast rewrites the field of battle as an arena for beastly victory, with human bodies the spoils of war. This is knowledge that counts in the culture of birds of prey, worth sharing with a companion in the same way that Beowulf shares with Hrothgar his battle victories and his knowledge of the Heathobardish loot.

Ultimately, this brief and partial moment of knowledge-in-relation intervenes to devastating effect in the anthropomorphic world of the poem. The raven who crows victoriously over the slain Geats has accrued associations of battle-joy (1801) and the despair of unavenged mourning (2448) before this final appearance in the poem. In Gillian Overing's well-known argument establishing metonymy as the dominant sign system of *Beowulf*, one potent example is the glorious necklace that 'weighs like a millstone on the narrative'; arriving at a moment of triumph, it links that moment to the bitterness of past and future by participating, along with the poem's other significant rings and cups, in an endless dance of mutual reference.[47] So too does the figure of the raven bring the joy of earlier victory into tragically ironic inversion at Beowulf's death. Yet this joy is not entirely inverted, for the raven's own jubilation, and that of his comrades, continues unabated; nor is the helplessness of grief abated, since it will pass into the possession of the surviving Geats. The beasts of battle provide a counterpoint of vitality and abundance to Geatish death and poverty. While the Geats will go hungry, the beasts of battle can brag about their gorging. Where the Geats were subjects of battle-knowledge, now they are objects. And while all of this is too distant from the human observer to be independently verifiable, the selectively omniscient voice of the poem affirms its truth-value: 'Swa se secg hwata secggende wæs, / laðra spella; he ne leag fela / wyrda ne worda' (So the man was telling evil news; he did not mislead much in words or deeds) (3028a–30). In other words, he did not mislead them at all.

Bird language in translation

It is difficult for humans to parse and taxonomize avian language. Harris lightly distinguishes between 'voice and even … language' in the case of the birds of battle, but the problem with any distinction between voice and speech, or between what Harris calls 'sublinguistic cries' and exclamations that count as speech (e.g., in English, 'Oh!') is that it is almost always impossible for an outsider to accurately determine; hence the very common descriptions of foreign speech as meaningless babble, equivalent to infant babble or animal noise (which are not necessarily themselves sublingual categories).[48] Moreover, it is based on a logocentric and Eurocentric view of language that pre-emptively evacuates sound quality (tone, pitch, accent) of the capacity to convey symbolic meaning, despite the evidence that it does so in every spoken language and, indeed, the fact that more than a billion humans speak a tonal language as their first tongue. Recent work on avian and particularly corvid intelligence has demonstrated that anthropocentric definitions of intelligence and of communication can operate only via logocentric tautology; (one particular strand of) human self-consciousness defines as intelligent only entities that engage in the abstract, rational processes that produce these exclusions.[49] As Laurie Shannon notes, in the Cartesian logic that classified non-human animals as machines, 'Speaking only counts if it is speaking to us and in our language.'[50] In this Enlightenment frame, the only thought that exists is the one that can be communicated to and understood by rational (educated, adult, white, Western, male, modern) human interlocutors. Nonetheless, avian scientists have demonstrated that birds, which are not evolutionarily close to humans, are intelligent to a degree that even humans can begin to comprehend.[51]

I follow Ellard in noticing the importance of Ælfric's *Grammar* to discussions of bird language; I am particularly interested in how he has altered his source. He begins with a discussion of *vox* (speech or voice), the auditory basis of spoken language:

> Omnis vox aut articulata est aut confusa. articulata est, quae litteris conprehendi potest; confusa, quae scribi non potest ... ælc stemn is oððe andgytfullic oððe gemenged. andgytfullic stemn is, þe mid andgyte bið geclypod, swaswa ys *arma uirumque cano* ic herige þa wæpnu and ðone wer. gemenged stemn is, þe bið butan andgyte, swylc swa is hryðera gehlow and horsa hnægung, hunda gebeorc, treowa brastlung et cetera.[52]

> (All voice is either meaningful or mixed. What has meaning is called meaningful voice, as in *I sing of arms and the man*, I praise arms and the man. Mixed voice is what is without sense, such as the lowing of oxen and neighing of horses, barking of dogs, rustling of trees, etc.)

As so frequently in Ælfric's work, small alterations to his sources prove philosophically significant.[53] Ælfric begins with a Latin excerpt that derives from Isidore, and explicates it in Old English, borrowing heavily from Priscian, in a way that entirely changes both Isidore's and Priscian's categories.

Isidore distinguishes, as Karl Steel notes, between human *vox articulata* ('articulated' voice) and non-human *vox confusa* ('confused' voice); the first 'scribi potest' (can be written), while the second cannot.[54] Ælfric's main source for the *Grammar*, the *Excerptiones de Prisciano* (which includes material from Priscian, Isidore, Donatus, and others) renders Isidore's thesis as four separate but presumably overlapping types of sound: 'articulata, inarticulata, litterata, inlitterata' ('articulate and inarticulate, those expressible in writing and those inexpressible in writing'). The *Excerptiones* explains these as follows:

> Articulate speech is that which is pronounced in connected fashion, that is, joined with some meaning in the mind of the one who speaks, such as 'I sing arms and the man.' Opposite to this is inarticulate speech, which is uttered without the influence of the mind, such as whistles or groans. These cannot be written even though they can be understood. Speech expressible in writing is that which can be written without conveying meaning, such as *coax* and *cra*. Speech inexpressible in writing is that which can be neither written nor understood, such as a noise or bellow or the like.[55]

Articulate speech is the speech of men; not only does it require 'mind' and intention, but its exemplary subject is men and their weaponry. More than in Isidore's accounting, and far more than in Ælfric's, such speech relies on a binary relation, a disavowal, for its definition; the 'mind[less]' sounds of inarticulate voice can be interpreted by the skilled listener, but there is no intellect crafting their message – they are sounds of the body. The third set includes nonsense syllables – manipulations of known phonemes without the intention to produce a message – and (as evidenced in the happy accident of *coax*) words in barbarian languages, whose meaning it is not necessary to know. The final category is the province of noise-making things. It is not entirely clear where bird and other non-human animal cries fit into this schema – as the carnal sounds of inarticulate speech? the transcribable nonsense of speech expressible in writing? the final category of abject sounds that might as well be silence? – and perhaps it is precisely this problem, among others, that prompts Ælfric's reworking of these categories.

Ælfric is perfectly happy to translate the Latin he incorporates into his Old English writings, even if this intimate mingling (as in '*arma uirumque cano* ic herige þa wæpnu') creates redundancy for Latinate readers, although he does not always do so. Instead of translating Isidore's division between *vox articulata* and *vox confusa* as a matter of what can be written and what cannot, or glossing it in a way that preserves or extends the definition, he recasts the distinction as one of sense. Yet as Ellard notes, the flagrantly improper binary he chooses as gloss – 'gemenged stemn' (mixed voice), which also describes Ælfric's own hybrid writing, versus 'andgytfullic stemn' (meaningful voice) – functions as acknowledgement of animal language.[56] Although Ælfric describes hybrid speech as 'butan andgyte' (without sense), the very appellation indicates that it *is* meaningful – just not to humans, who cannot separate the static from the noise and parse the signals into information. It is, Ellard observes, 'a semiotics that cannot be translated'.[57] That Ælfric renders the difference of animal language into a problem of translation, rather than of writing, may also indicate a recognition of the fragility of the Isidorean binary, for humans can and do transcribe birdsong.[58] It also, certainly, reflects the abbot's habitual preoccupation with the question of translation. To my mind, it is more appropriate to Old English literary culture, where the questions of what is known and what can be said are inextricably bound up with questions of translation.

Translatability is not, however, the only criterion for meaning as represented in Old English. Although Shannon understates the anthropocentrism of medieval European Christian culture,[59] there is still a crucial difference between these early medieval understandings of bird language and later reductions of bird language to the mechanical. It is not the case that sense that humans cannot understand is no sense at all. As I have argued, the speech of raven to eagle derives its sinister power in part from the fact that humans cannot directly translate its details. Its 'mixed' character – the intimate mixing of what humans can know and what they can never know – is the ideal form for its terrifying rebuke of the possibility of human survival through relation.

Ellard compellingly depicts *The Phoenix* and the Exeter Book bird riddles, the core of Old English literature's avian imaginary, in terms of a 'vernacular ecosystem' that enfolds birdsong/speech into Anglo-Saxon translation. This produces a hopeful reading that illuminates the connections between 'avian intelligence' and (post) human spirituality.[60] Similarly, Jonathan Hsy finds in Anglo-Saxon taxonomies of birdsong an interspecies 'bilingualism': 'an intimate partnership that bridges species boundaries and language difference'.[61] *Beowulf* takes quite a different approach, approximating meaning but not sounds, and allowing the birds an ambiguity that triumphs over human comprehension.

Conclusion: the return of loss

Although *Beowulf* is, ostensibly, the portrait of a heroic culture that values homosocial intimacy, it is also incapable of imagining this intimacy without the shadows of failure and grief. We learn of the king's companion only in elegy; we perceive him only as a bloodied, disembodied head and in the image of the king's grief. Yet I do not suggest that we pursue this homosocial loss through the lens of what is now called queer mourning, grief for what has been rendered conventionally ungrievable. While it is not sufficiently significant to some modern queer readings to merit much analysis – Æschere does not, for instance, appear at all in Clark's or in Allen J. Frantzen's speculations on same-sex love in *Beowulf*[62] – Hrothgar's love is culturally intelligible and therefore this loss can be avenged with all available resources. Vengeance is primary, as Beowulf reminds Hrothgar, among what Judith Butler calls the 'cultural conventions' of mourning through which grief may be acknowledged and expunged in this world.[63] Hence the frustrated griefs of this poem, when those who cannot avenge find shame or depression their constant companions. In the act of violence itself, and in the acts of planning, coaxing, and bragging that precede it and boasting that follow, human bodily integrity is affirmed, homosocial cohesion restored, and supremacy over the wide and terrible non-human world temporarily regained.

Avian confidences bring the cycle of loss to a new beginning. When the raven and the eagle share a boast over human corpses, they are not only recapitulating the poem's paradigmatic moment of human helplessness, when a man past the age of strength watches the raven slowly delight in the body of his dear one and realizes the world is too much for him. Nor are they, to speak in more detached terms, only liberating avian life and language from their accustomed yoke of symbolism. They are also forging, and recounting, interspecies connections to which human intelligence is not privy, speaking a language that humans cannot even hear, much less accurately translate. They are making human flesh the material substrate of this non-human culture – our ravaged bones and bodies, our severed bonds, the fuel for animal knowledge and thought.

Notes

1 I presented portions of this chapter in 2017 in the UBC English Faculty Research Series and at the Medieval Association of the Pacific

Conference, and I am grateful to the organizers and participants, particularly Robert Rouse. I would also like to thank Peter Cole, Allen Fulghum, Mary Kate Hurley, Daniel Remein, Benjamin Saltzman, Erica Weaver, the anonymous Manchester University Press readers, and the many colleagues and students who have discussed these ideas with me and shared their own.

2 Susan Crane, *Animal encounters: contacts and concepts in medieval Britain* (Philadelphia, PA: University of Pennsylvania Press, 2012), p. 121.

3 Donna Beth Ellard, 'Going interspecies, going interlingual, and flying away with the phoenix', *Exemplaria*, 23.3 (2011), 268–92; Jonathan Hsy, 'Between species: animal–human bilingualism and medieval texts', in Catherine Batt and René Tixier (eds), *Booldly bot meekly: essays on the theory and practice of translation in the Middle Ages in honour of Roger Ellis* (Turnhout: Brepols, 2018), pp. 563–79; Robert Stanton, 'Mimicry, subjectivity, and the embodied voice in Anglo-Saxon bird riddles', in Irit Ruth Kleiman (ed.), *Voice and voicelessness in medieval Europe* (New York: Palgrave Macmillan, 2015), pp. 29–43.

4 Mary Kate Hurley, 'Ravens, wolves, and a different *Beowulf*', *In the middle*, 17 May 2011, http://www.inthemedievalmiddle.com/2011/05/ravens-wolves-and-different-beowulf.html (accessed 5 June 2019).

5 I use this appellation for Grendel's mother, whose proper name the poem does not reveal, in the spirit of the naming tradition that has given us such Old English poetic protagonists as the Wanderer, the Seafarer, the Last Survivor, et al. As Jana K. Schulman notes, *wrecend* (avenger) (1256) is the poem's first description of this adversary. Desire for vengeance is the constant core of her otherwise highly ambiguous character. See Jana K. Schulman, 'Monstrous introductions: "ellengæst" and "aglæcwif"', in Jana K. Schulman and Paul E. Szarmach (eds), *Beowulf at Kalamazoo: essays on translation and performance* (Kalamazoo, MI: Medieval Institute Publications, 2012), pp. 69–92, at 79.

6 See, for instance, in English and French medieval studies alone, a flurry of monographs and essay collections since 2010: *inter alia*, Peggy McCracken, *In the skin of a beast: sovereignty and animality in medieval France* (Chicago: University of Chicago Press, 2017); Alice M. Choyke and Gerhard Jaritz (eds), *Animaltown: beasts in medieval urban space* (Oxford: BAR Publishing, 2017); John Allan Mitchell, *Becoming human: the matter of the medieval child* (Minneapolis, MN: University of Minnesota Press, 2014); Carolynn Van Dyke (ed.), *Rethinking Chaucerian beasts* (New York: Palgrave Macmillan, 2012); Crane, *Animal encounters*; Karl Steel, *How to make a human: animals and violence in the Middle Ages* (Columbus, OH: Ohio State University Press, 2011).

7 See, for instance, in Old English studies, Heide Estes, *Old English literary landscapes: ecotheory and the Anglo-Saxon environmental imagination* (Amsterdam: Amsterdam University Press, 2017); Della Hooke, *Trees in Anglo-Saxon England: literature, lore and landscape* (Woodbridge:

Boydell and Brewer, 2010); and Alfred Kentigern Siewers, *Strange beauty: ecocritical approaches to early medieval landscape* (New York: Palgrave Macmillan, 2009).

8 See especially Gale R. Owen-Crocker, 'Squawk talk: commentary by birds in the Bayeux Tapestry?', *ASE*, 34.1 (2005), 237–54; Carolynn Van Dyke, 'Touched by an owl? An essay in vernacular ethology', *postmedieval*, 7.2 (2016), 304–27; Lesley Kordecki, *Ecofeminist subjectivities: Chaucer's talking birds* (New York: Palgrave Macmillan, 2011); Emma Gorst, 'Interspecies mimicry: birdsong in Chaucer's "Manciple's Tale" and *The Parlement of Fowles*', *NML*, 12 (2010), 147–54; Seeta Chaganti, 'Avian Provocation: Roosters and Rime Royal in Fifteenth-Century Fable', *Exemplaria*, 29.4 (2017), 314–30.

9 Peggy McCracken, 'Translation and animals in Marie de France's *Lais*', *Australian journal of French studies*, 46.3 (2009), 206–18, esp. 211.

10 All *Beowulf* extracts in Old English are from R. D. Fulk, Robert E. Bjork, and John D. Niles (eds), *Klaeber's Beowulf and the fight at Finnsburg*, 4th edn (Toronto: University of Toronto Press, 2008) and are cited by line. All translations from Old English are my own unless otherwise noted.

11 Nicole Shukin, *Animal capital: rendering life in biopolitical times* (Minneapolis, MN: University of Minnesota Press, 2009). As Shukin's analysis suggests, elite cultural production has often required the forcible extraction of ideological and material value from non-human and human bodies; vellum is an unusually durable artefact of one such extraction history.

12 See especially C. Stephen Jaeger, *Ennobling love: in search of a lost sensibility* (Philadelphia, PA: University of Pennsylvania Press, 1999), pp. 59–81.

13 David M. Clark, *Between medieval men: male friendship and desire in early medieval English literature* (Oxford: Oxford University Press, 2009), p. 130.

14 See Clark, *Between Medieval Men*, pp. 132–3.

15 I draw the notion of knowledge arising from relationship largely from Leanne Betasamosake Simpson, 'Land as pedagogy: Nishnaabeg intelligence and rebellious transformation', *Decolonization: indigeneity, education & society*, 3.3 (2014), 1–25. The pedagogy Simpson advocates is, however, based on feminism, non-violence, and Indigenous resurgence. To read Simpson alongside *Beowulf*, as my students do, is to reflect on two visions of cultural futurity – one radical and hopeful, the other doomed.

16 Jane Roberts (ed.), *The Guthlac poems of the Exeter Book* (Oxford: Clarendon Press, 1979), p. 116.

17 James Paz, 'Æschere's head, Grendel's mother, and the sword that isn't a sword: unreadable things in Beowulf', *Exemplaria*, 25.3 (2013), 231–51, esp. 235–6.

18 David M. Halperin, 'Heroes and their pals', in *One hundred years of homosexuality: and other essays on Greek love* (New York: Routledge, 1990), pp. 75–87, at 79. See Allen J. Frantzen, *Before the closet: same-sex love from Beowulf to Angels in America* (Chicago: University of Chicago Press, 1998), p. 95, for further discussion of Halperin's concepts in *Beowulf*.

19 Thomas Meyer, *Beowulf: a translation* (New York: punctum books, 2012), p. 123.

20 Ibid., p. 134. Note that the pronoun *se* (he, the one), used here and in line 1260, is masculine, while *seo* (she) is used elsewhere for the same character. Gender fluidity, even in a mother, is hardly scandalous in 2019, but like other translators of his century, Meyer prefers uniformly feminine language for this character.

21 See the original: 'Wearð him on Heorote to handbanan / wælgæst wæfre; ic ne wat hwæder / atol æse wlanc eftsiðas teah, / fylle gefrecnod' (He was done for in Heorot by a barehanded killer, a nimble, murdering visitor. I do not know where that terrible one returned, emboldened by the feast, glorying in evil meat) (1330–3a).

22 Meyer, *Beowulf*, p. 123.

23 See Schulman, 'Monstrous introductions', p. 79.

24 Gilles Deleuze and Félix Guattari, *A thousand plateaus: capitalism and schizophrenia*, trans. B. Massumi (London: Athlone Press, 2004), p. 240.

25 On this passage, see M. Wendy Hennequin, 'We've created a monster: the strange case of Grendel's mother', *ES*, 89.5 (2008), 503–23, at 506; and Renée R. Trilling, 'Beyond abjection: the problem with Grendel's mother again', *Parergon*, 24.1 (2007), 1–20, at 10–12.

26 Rosemary Huisman, 'The three tellings of Beowulf's fight with Grendel's mother', *Leeds studies in English*, 20 (1989), 217–47, esp. 217–18. For a catalogue of discrepancies in Beowulf's battle-boasts, as well as a contrasting perspective on their meaning, see Dana M. Oswald, '"Wigge under wætere": Beowulf's revision of the fight with Grendel's mother', *Exemplaria*, 21.1 (2009), 63–82.

27 Nicholas Howe, *Writing the map of Anglo-Saxon England: essays in cultural geography* (New Haven, CT: Yale University Press, 2008), pp. 154–5.

28 Alexandra Bolintineanu, 'Declarations of unknowing in *Beowulf*', *Neophilologus*, 100.4 (2016), 631–47, esp. 638–43, at 643.

29 Benjamin A. Saltzman, 'Secrecy and the hermeneutic potential in *Beowulf*', *PMLA*, 133.1 (2018), 36–55, at 49–50.

30 Daniel C. Remein, 'Introduction: locating *Beowulf*', in Meyer, *Beowulf*, pp. 5–34, at 14, 21. Remein draws this concept from Gillian R. Overing and Marijane Osborn, *Landscape of desire: partial stories of the medieval Scandinavian world* (Minneapolis, MN: University of Minnesota Press, 1994), p. 11.

31 Bolintineanu, 'Declarations of unknowing', 639–41.

32 Andy Orchard, *Pride and prodigies: studies in the monsters of the Beowulf-manuscript* (Toronto: University of Toronto Press, 2003), p. 42.

33 Sarah Harlan-Haughey, *The ecology of the English outlaw in medieval literature: from fen to greenwood* (New York: Routledge, 2016), p. 47.

34 Bruce Braun, *The intemperate rainforest: nature, culture, and power on Canada's west coast* (Minneapolis, MN: University of Minnesota Press, 2002), p. 8.

35 Fabienne Michelet, *Creation, migration, and conquest: imaginary geography and sense of space in Old English literature* (Oxford: Oxford University Press, 2006), p. 28.

36 Saltzman, 'Secrecy', 38.

37 Francis P. Magoun, Jr, 'The theme of the beasts of battle in Anglo-Saxon poetry', *Neuphilologische Mitteilungen*, 56.2 (1955), 81–90.

38 Ellard, 'Going interspecies', 273; M. S. Griffith, 'Convention and originality in the Old English "beasts of battle" typescene', *ASE*, 22 (1993), 179–99; Joseph Harris, 'Beasts of battle, south and north', in Charles D. Wright, Frederick M. Biggs, and Thomas N. Hall (eds), *Source of wisdom: Old English and early medieval Latin studies in honour of Thomas D. Hill* (Toronto: University of Toronto Press, 2007), pp. 3–25, esp. p. 11.

39 Fulk, Bjork, and Niles (eds), *Klaeber's Beowulf*, p. 263, n. 3024b–3027.

40 Robert Stanton, 'Bark like a man: performance, identity, and boundary in Old English animal voice catalogues', in A. Langdon (ed.), *Animal languages in the Middle Ages* (New York: Palgrave, 2018), pp. 91–111, at 91.

41 Roy Liuzza, *Beowulf: a new verse translation* (Peterborough, Ont.: Broadview Press, 2000), p. 145.

42 See Saltzman's comments on 'ambiguous *wið*' in line 1880 and his argument, drawing on Leslie Lockett's work, that 'Hroðgar's secrecy burns *against* his blood ("born wið blode")' in 'a kind of affective torment'. Saltzman, 'Secrecy', 42–4, emphasis mine.

43 Mary Kate Hurley, *Translation Effects: Language Time and Community in Medieval England* (Athens, OH: Ohio University Press, forthcoming), n.p.

44 Meyer, *Beowulf*, p. 243.

45 On the beasts of battle as human types, see Estes, *Anglo-Saxon literary landscapes*, pp. 131–3.

46 J. R. R. Tolkien, *Beowulf: a translation and commentary, together with Sellic Spell*, ed. Christopher Tolkien (New York: Houghton Mifflin Harcourt, 2014), p. 101.

47 Gillian R. Overing, *Language, sign, and gender in Beowulf* (Carbondale, IL: Southern Illinois University Press, 1990), pp. 51–2.

48 Harris, 'Beasts of battle', p. 11.

49 See, for instance, Alphonso Lingis, 'Understanding avian intelligence', in Laurence Simmons and Philip Armstrong (eds), *Knowing animals* (Boston: Brill, 2007), pp. 43–56; D. Abram, 'The discourse of the birds', *Biosemiotics*, 3.3 (2010), 263–75; Nathan J. Emery, 'Cognitive ornithology: the evolution of avian intelligence', *Philosophical transactions of the Royal Society B*, 361 (2006), 23–43.

50 Laurie Shannon, *The accommodated animal: cosmopolity in Shakespearean locales* (Chicago: University of Chicago Press, 2013), p. 15.

51 On the difficulties of using human intelligence to assess avian intelligence, see for instance Frans de Waal, *Are we smart enough to know how smart animals are?* (New York: Norton, 2016); Jennifer Ackerman, *The genius of birds* (New York: Penguin, 2016). On producing non-anthropocentric classifications for animal language, see Zhanna Reznikova, *Studying animal languages without translation: an insight from ants* (New York: Springer International, 2006).

52 *Ælfrics Grammatik und Glossar: Text und Varianten*, ed. Julius Zupitza (Berlin: Max Niehans Verlag, repr. 1966 [1880]), p. 4, ll. 3–16.

53 See, for instance, Mo Pareles, 'Jewish heterosexuality, queer celibacy? Ælfric translates the Old Testament priesthood', *postmedieval*, 8 (2017), 292–306.

54 *PL* 82:89B; English translation is Karl Steel's in 'Medieval muteness', *In the middle*, 25 April 2016, www.inthemedievalmiddle.com/2016/04/medieval-muteness.html (accessed 5 June 2019).

55 David W. Porter (ed.), *Excerptiones de Prisciano* (Cambridge: D.S. Brewer, 2002), pp. 44–5. English translation is Porter's.

56 Ellard, 'Going interspecies', 277. I am grateful to Dan Remein for his observation that Ælfric is himself a source of 'gemenged stemn'.

57 Ibid., 277.

58 On the literary life of transcribed bird sounds in pre-Conquest England, see Steel, 'Medieval muteness'; Stanton, 'Bark like a man'; Hsy, 'Between species'; and Eric Lacey, 'Birds and words: aurality, semantics and species in Anglo-Saxon England', in Simon C. Thomson and Michael D. J. Bintley (eds), *Sensory perception in the medieval West* (Turnhout: Brepols, 2016), pp. 75–98.

59 See Crane, *Animal encounters*, p. 175, n. 14; Karl Steel, 'First space; then, maybe, time: on Laurie Shannon's *Accommodated Animal* and the heterogeneous then', *Upstart: a journal of English Renaissance studies*, 7 November 2013, https://upstart.sites.clemson.edu/Reviews/accomodated_animal/accomodated_animal.xhtml (accessed 5 June 2019).

60 Ellard, 'Going interspecies', 281, 289.

61 Hsy, 'Between species', 567, 578.

62 Clark, *Between medieval men*, pp. 130–43; Frantzen, *Before the closet*, pp. 92–8.

63 Judith Butler, *Bodies that matter: on the discursive limits of 'sex'* (New York: Routledge, 1993), p. 236.

Part IV
Beowulf's contact list

9

Men into monsters: troubling race, ethnicity, and masculinity in *Beowulf*

Catalin Taranu

Sometimes we find the deepest intimacy not in sex, friendship, communal joy, or grief, but in shared anxiety. It is a subtler, though no less powerful, kind of togetherness, communed less overtly through sideways glances, heavy silences, nervous laughter. As such, it subtends 'emotional communities' that are harder to trace in texts such as *Beowulf*, notorious for how opaque their emotional language has become to us.[1] Perceiving anxiety in others is difficult primarily because the people subjected to it can often find it hard to articulate it, or may even be unaware that they are experiencing it. At times, the strongest clue to its existence is the effort people make to deny it.

Anxiety is protean, too: it can take forms as mundane as being ashamed or embarrassed and as vivid as full-blown panic or inexplicable bursts of rage. It can coalesce into cultural anxieties or moral panics or it can take the shape of a brief, individual episode.[2] Yet I suggest that, apart from the joy of reading and listening, it is anxiety that gathered so many audiences around *Beowulf* for so long a time. The purpose of this chapter, then, is to probe some of the points in the poem that trouble certain audiences in order to understand the ways in which these communities function emotionally in relation to the text. In particular, I pursue this work of emotional archaeology by tracing anxieties around masculinity, ethnicity, and race that found their expression in *Beowulf* – and that different audiences have projected on to it, first in Beowulf's sexualized encounter with Grendel's mother and then in the Grendelkin's broader connection to tensions between Anglo-Saxons and indigenous Britons and, later, the Danes.

Gender, race, and ethnicity are too intimately entwined to focus on any one of these aspects in isolation, for as Geraldine Heng remarks, 'the ability of racial logic to stalk and merge with other hierarchical systems – such as class, gender, or sexuality' allows race to function as class, 'ethnicity', religion, or sexuality.[3] In the following, I fix my gaze particularly on emotional communities made up of men, not because I assume that *Beowulf* is in any way fit reading for men only, or that its audiences were or are made up mostly of men.[4] Yet it is in the ways in which men read the poem through the ages that I find a fascinating and hitherto unexplored pervasive pattern of conjoined anxiety and aspirational projection, which in its turn provides significant clues to cultural and social change in the twenty-first as much as in the eighth or eleventh centuries, especially with regard to how gender, race, and ethnic belonging are constructed.

My chapter begins with two central premises: 1) we can detect anxieties related to masculinity, race, and ethnicity in the ways men behave in and read *Beowulf*, and 2) these anxieties are almost always interconnected in complex ways, so that our focus needs to be intersectional. This is why Critical Race theory (CRT) and Indigenous Studies can help us see that *Beowulf* could be read as relating to both the racialized Britons and Danes at different historical moments. Indeed, whether or not we fix a date, I argue that we need to account for the emotional life of the poem as it circulated before, within, and beyond its early eleventh-century manuscript. Who would have read *Beowulf* at different points in time and space? How would they have related and reacted to it? What made successive textual and emotional communities come back to the same text again and again?

If reader-response theory has taught us anything, it is that different audiences do not read the same text.[5] Thus, even if *Beowulf* were to remain a stable text for three hundred years, it is unrealistic to presume that, say, a Mercian 720s audience and a 1030s Wessex one would have read the poem in the same ways. The cultural horizons, the social and political circumstances, the textual expectations of these audiences differed greatly, no matter how much the label 'Anglo-Saxon England' that we use for both settings and for everything in between might elide the discrepancies. As Stephen Harris reminds us, the 'Anglo-Saxon' of the age of Bede is not the same as the 'Anglo-Saxon' of the age of Alfred, and 'whenever we speak of their stories, we are actually talking about two different theys'.[6] Reconstructing the emotions felt in each of these cases provides a fuller understanding of intimacy in anxiety that I argue was an important, though largely overlooked, dimension of *Beowulf* in its early medieval socio-emotional context. This involves allowing oneself to become troubled by the poem and by the ways it is read, while perhaps troubling the readers of this chapter in the process.

Indeed, the social and emotional mechanics of these anxieties are similar across a millennium-wide expanse of time, as seen in the current resurgence of medievalism in new nationalisms, racism, men's rights activism, and the involvement of medievalist scholars in or against these movements.[7] The different groups of men gathering around *Beowulf* at different points in time and space have quite a bit to say to each other, and in this chapter I place the anxieties which these very different audiences project on to and find expressed in the poem in a dialogue where they can productively illuminate each other. *Beowulf* has always been a site of both utopia and anxiety for communities of men who desire an ethnically pure, hypermasculine mythical origin, as well as the dangers inherent in such a project.

Despite the historical, ethnographic, or sociopolitical data *Beowulf* may contain, it makes sense to treat it as a collective fantasy. *Beowulf* thus exists in a ludic space in which the anxieties, beliefs, and desires of different textual and emotional communities are toyed with, allowed to measure against each other, and brought to their ultimate consequences within the safe space of a mythical past that is always just out of reach.[8] Emotionally, the poem acts as a distant screen on which the anxieties and desires of the audiences were projected, worked through, and thus potentially exorcised. Adopting Derek Neal's argument about high medieval romance, I argue that *Beowulf* functions like a dream that 'solve[s] problems and deal[s] with conflicts that are too difficult for conscious life', or, to use John Niles's terms, as 'a form of play' that 'not only gives voice to a given mentality or worldview, but is also in which issues of worldview are precisely what are at stake'.[9]

Angling for anxieties: a method

One need not go very far to find anxiety in *Beowulf*. It is present throughout the text, expressed in Old English words ranging from general terms from the semantic field of sadness or trouble such as *cearu* (sorrow, anxiety), *sorh* (care, anxiety, sorrow, grief, affliction, trouble), *murnan* (to be sad, be anxious, to mourn), and *meornan* (to care, feel anxiety, trouble oneself about anything) to the more specific or contextually connoting anxiety-words such as *bysgu* (business, labour, care, toil, difficulty, trouble, affliction, anxiety) and *wea* (woe, misery, evil, affliction, trouble, anxiety). 'þæt ys sio fæhðo ond se feondscipe, / wælnið wera, ðæs ðe ic [wen] hafo / þe us seceað to Sweona leoda' (such is the adversity and the enmity, / the slaughterous hate of men, which is why I am anxious / that the Swedish folk will seek us) (2999–3001). Here Wiglaf, the lone faithful retainer who returns to Beowulf's side during his fight with the dragon, provides an example of one of the great causes of anxiety in the poem, and more specifically, to the Geats who were the audience for the unfolding drama of Beowulf's demise: tribal and personal enmity and their accompanying causes and effects – choosing loyalty to one's kin over one's lord, the compulsion towards vengeance, rash words, the hot-headedness of young warriors' unmanly (or too manly) behaviour, monsters. Indeed, it seems that the general mood in the heroic world of the poem is that of anxiety interrupted by brief calms and timid celebrations of victory (during which, however, gloomy songs foreshadowing future anxiety are often sung).

Nonetheless, this is not the kind of anxiety that is the primary object of this chapter. In the example above, 'anxiety' is used to translate a range of words with loosely connected meanings, ranging from 'distress' to 'trouble', 'woe', and 'fear' proper. Yet just as 'sadness' is not equivalent to 'depression', (localized) 'fear' or (generalized) 'apprehension' is not the same as 'anxiety'. In psychology and psychiatry, anxiety has been defined as 'an unpleasant state of inner turmoil, often accompanied by nervous behaviour, such as pacing back and forth, somatic complaints, and rumination', or as 'a feeling of uneasiness and worry, usually generalized and unfocused as an overreaction to a situation that is only subjectively seen as menacing'.[10] While I am not claiming to diagnose anxiety disorders in Old English texts, it is in this more precise sense that I will use anxiety henceforth. Furthermore, I am more interested in the anxieties experienced by the poem's diverse audiences than by its characters. These anxieties can be reconstructed from clues within *Beowulf* corroborated with the different sociocultural horizons and constellations of texts in which the poem was read.

Nervous laughter: wrestling with monsters

Indeed, some anxieties might have been less context-dependent and more pervasive for early medieval audiences of *Beowulf*. Rather than the straightforward anxiety occasioned by the pervasive doom and gloom in the poem, I will now consider a moment that is troubling in a more oblique fashion. During Beowulf's fight with Grendel's mother, an embarrassing episode occurs. After he has pulled her to the floor and she has grabbed him, he falls on his back while Grendel's mother sits astride him, having pulled her short sword: 'Ofsæt þa þone selegyst, ond hyre seaxe geteah, / brad ond brunecg, wolde hire bearn wrecan, / angan eaferan' (then she sat on the hall-guest and drew her short *seax*, broad and burnished, she wanted to avenge her son, her only child) (1545–7a). For Beowulf this is a position that is at once dangerous and embarrassing, and for my purposes, one that makes not only him, but, as Fred Robinson noticed, scholars and students alike uncomfortable.

In a 1994 article, Robinson asked the question 'Did Grendel's Mother Sit on Beowulf?', and argued that this was not the only way that the Old English of the passage could be construed. His motivation for reconsidering the translation is that 'like the students in our classes, the translators of the poem ... are often uncomfortable with the meaning which the glossaries stipulate for *ofsittan*. To avoid the comic indignity of Beowulf's being sat upon, they fudge the verb's meaning in artful ways.'[11] Yet, as Dana Oswald argues, in order to use her weapon effectively, Grendel's mother must be on the same level as Beowulf, and since he is on the floor, the choreographic logic of the scene requires her to be on top of him.[12]

What reactions would men in an Anglo-Saxon audience have had to this scene? Vicarious fear for the hero's life is one possible response, comic embarrassment would have been another, or both emotions at the same time. Oswald suggests that Beowulf's passive posture, however temporary, is alarming because of the resulting gender instability, which is what makes students and translators uncomfortable.[13] Thus, Beowulf being topped by Grendel's mother is not so much comic, as Robinson suggests, but alarming, and the nervous laughter it can provoke in audiences (both modern and medieval) is a response to a deeper anxiety that this situation brings out in men, especially men who define themselves according to the scripts of hegemonic masculinity. In Oswald's terms, 'Beowulf is at the mercy of a phallic woman who ... symbolically castrates [him] ... even if her blade never pierces his body.'[14] Whether one agrees with the psychoanalytical description of the situation or not, it is clear from Robinson's account of modern reactions to this disquieting situation (the first time in the poem when Beowulf's life seems to be genuinely endangered) that it has been perceived at least by some audiences as uncomfortably comic. The scene is certainly narrated in such a way as to resemble sexual intercourse, as other scholars have previously remarked, and as such, it 'plays out anxieties about female sexuality' while also illustrating anxieties about Beowulf's own sexual identity.[15] While rolling around on the floor of Grendel's mother's cave, Beowulf is described as 'beadwe heard' (battle-hard) (1539a) and 'þa he gebolgen wæs, / feorhgeniðlan' (then he was swollen [or enraged] by the life-enemy) (1539b–1540a). Although these also work as combat metaphors, the whole episode has been described as 'a lengthy erotic *double entendre* riddle fused into a longer narrative poem', employed purposefully to paint Beowulf as full of a very masculine vigour, but also as a sexually engaged combatant.[16]

But there is more at work here than discomfort about forbidden erotic impulses. Beowulf's masculine authority in this sexually charged battle is called into question not only by his near-defeat by Grendel's mother, but also by his problematic relationship to swords.[17] The possession of weapons, especially swords, is closely related to masculine identity in Anglo-Saxon culture.[18] One of the main Old English terms for 'man', *wæpnedmann*, and a variety of compounds signifying the male sex attested copiously from royal wills to vernacular poetry testify to the understanding of 'weapon' as a metaphorical penis in the most pragmatic sense: *wæpnedcild* (male child), *wæpnedhealf* (male line) etc.[19] Hence, taking up Stacy Klein's question, in a world in which 'masculinity hinges so crucially on martial exploits, what happens when a woman takes up arms and subsequently acquits herself with great élan?'[20] By taking up weapons, Grendel's mother is 'appropriating and revising masculine identity and acting as phallic mother, which demands a response similarly laden with sexual overtones'.[21]

On the other hand, what happens to the masculinity of a man when his sword fails in a medieval honour-based culture constructed around war making? Anxiety ensues, especially when the hyper-masculine hero has his weapons repeatedly break down – most disastrously in his final fight with the dragon. The first instance is in his attempt to stab Grendel's mother (though Grendel himself being impenetrable to weapons can be counted as the first time his sword is useless), when his sword completely fails him – it is simply unable to penetrate her flesh. This forces Beowulf to take up 'a phallus that belongs not to men, but to giants', which Oswald sees as an 'ephemeral and external excess that demonstrates his own profound impotence', since the masculine authority by which he eventually manages to kill Grendel's mother is not his own, but instead is prosthetic.[22]

It is understandable why this scene in particular would have provoked the anxiety of early medieval men, and why it continues to trouble students and scholars alike to this day. The male protagonist (and in their identification with him, male audiences, too) finds himself 'at the mercy of a "phallic woman", monstrous because overstepping the boundaries of gender and of sexuality'.[23] The nervous laughter that it might have provoked may be seen as both a sign of deep-seated anxieties about masculine identity and an occasion for deeper male bonding in the intimacy of a shared anxiety. Recent research on the cognitive science of emotions argues that laughter is an essential behaviour for helping to de-escalate negative emotional experiences as well as a social emotion that increases the willingness of people sharing a laugh to disclose intimate information.[24] While the cause for this nervous laughter lies in the uncomfortable recognition of the eroticism of the encounter between the hero and the monster, the anxieties it points to are deeper than that. This reasoning can and should be extended to racial alterity. The Grendelkin were conceivably the focus of anxieties about race and ethnicity, which connect to those about gender in troubling ways.

Ellorgæstas: guests in their homeland

The *Beowulf* poet calls Grendel and his mother *mearcstapan* ('border-wanderers') (104a and 1348a). While metaphorically they straddle the boundaries of gender and humanity, they also occupy a liminal space in the fens.[25] It is a marshy place not suited for agriculture or animal rearing and hence a space for which the people ruling the land would have no use. The two monsters are also described as *ellorgæstas* (1349a), usually translated as 'alien ghosts'. In virtually all editions of *Beowulf* the aesc (æ) on *ellorgæstas* has been interpreted as a long vowel, making *gæst* mean 'ghost' or 'spirit' rather than 'guest', as a short aesc would make it. Of course, there is no way of telling from the manuscript – the Anglo-Saxons did not use macrons to mark long vowels in vernacular manuscripts. Neither is the context always helpful – sometimes the monstrous enemies are ironically called 'guests' (thus the water monster at 1441a or the dragon at 2074b). At the same time, *gæst* can also mean 'stranger', if not 'enemy' – a guest is, of course, a stranger and can easily turn out to be an enemy, and the anxiety about this potential of guests to turn inimical is pervasive in *Beowulf*. It is significant that two of the three examples from the Bosworth-Toller entry showcasing this second (apparently contradictory) meaning of short-aesc *gæst* (basic meaning 'guest') are taken from *Beowulf*, where it is used to describe Grendel (102a) and the dragon (2312a). It is not hard to imagine that an oral performer could have played on the quasi-homonymy of *gæst* and *gǣst* as well as the semantic sliding between the threatening and the benign senses of the former word to underscore the blurring of the lines between them in everyday life.[26]

My point is that Grendel and his mother would have been seen not necessarily as demonic, but as troublesome guests populating the edges of the territory inhabited by the Danes. She is, after all, 'idese onlicnes' (in the likeness of a woman) (1351a), while he is 'on weres wæstmum' (in the form of a man) (1352a). She also avenges her son as any human kinsman would, and they are the descendants of Cain, who was, however evil, a human. Thus, *ellorgæstas* could be translated as 'guests from elsewhere'. There is some irony in that they are acknowledged as indigenous to the land ('land-dwellers in days of old' had seen them, 1354a–1355a), and yet they are now dwelling on its edges, discursively pushed to the margins of humanity and gender in the process and described as 'guests from elsewhere'.[27]

More precisely, I suggest that Grendel and his mother could have been the focus for Anglo-Saxon audiences projecting anxieties about their relationship to the autochthonous Britons and, at a later stage, to the Danes. As Stephen Harris reminds us, in 'literary negotiations of communities', foreigners and outsiders are often depicted as monstrous or as 'fearsome variations on existing creatures', being somehow recognizable by the very 'terror of fear' that 'they strike in humankind' ('quae maximum formidinis terrorem humano generi incutiunt', as the author of the eighth-century *Liber monstrorum* puts it).[28] This can happen just as readily when it comes to a conquering population negotiating its relationships to indigenous people.

The semantic linkage between 'native Briton' and 'slave' is unsurprising for any student of Anglo-Saxon England: both meanings are equally well exemplified in the Bosworth-Toller for the Old English word *wealh*, and often it is not clear at all that the Anglo-Saxons writing, reading, or hearing the word would have cared to make a distinction. As John Tanke points out, 'the violence which makes a slave out of a Welsh person parallels the violence in language which makes one say "slave" when one means "Welsh" and "Welsh" when one means "slave"', thus making *wealh* a word 'whose usage dramatizes its meaning: it is a word from whose otherness there is no escape'.[29] Nina Rulon-Miller brought to light the constellation in which the few Welsh personae to appear in the Exeter Book riddles are placed – it consists of oxen, the concepts of yoking or fettering, dark skin, and the borderland.[30] For instance, in Riddle

72, an ox tended by a 'sweart hyrde' (dark herdsman) – compare the 'sweart ond saloneb' (black and dark-faced) servant in Riddle 49 – is 'bunden under beam' (bound under yoke) and treads the 'mearcpaþas Walas' (the paths on the Welsh march). In Riddle 12, swarthy Welsh men are tightly fettered with ox-leather bonds, and a dark Welsh woman works on an object made of ox-hide. Rulon-Miller proposes as the most likely solution to Riddle 52 'yoke of oxen led by a female slave', since the riddle subjects are associated with binding as well as with a female Welsh slave or 'Wale'.[31] The association with oxen is thus quite transparent: both Britons and oxen are perceived in the riddles as servile creatures, physically or socially fettered, even if not all *wealhas* are slaves. But their description as 'dark-skinned', coupled with their association to animality, points to their essential otherness, with the potential of sliding into something that is so different to the ideal audience of the riddles as to be almost inhuman.[32]

The derogatory connotations attached to *wealh* or the adjective *wilisc* are plentifully attested, from 'shameful person' to 'bad servant', while Ælfric equates *weala win* with *crudum uinum* (rough, inferior wine) and has a sinner speak *wealode mid wordum* ('strangely', 'impudently').[33] These associations survive in present-day British slang words such as 'to welsh' (to cheat) and 'welsher' (an untrustworthy person).[34] As Ryan Craig and Victoria Davis demonstrate, such discursive practices are not divorced from material realities and are often used to reinforce and sustain material inequity by creating 'a reality in which it is reasonable for a few to control and to possess the material at the sacrifice of the well-being of others'.[35]

The first written occurrence of *wealh* is already a juridical one, appearing in the seventh-century *Laws of Ine*, where the 'inferior social position' of the Britons in Anglo-Saxon England was made law.[36] In Ine's laws that deal with *wergeld*, the free *wealh* is 'accorded only half the value of his English counterpart', while in laws concerning oaths, 'a man charged with stealing or harbouring stolen cattle had to produce an oath of sixty hides if he were accused by a *wealh*, whereas if the accuser were English the oath required was doubled'.[37] In what Alexander Woolf describes as a 'long drawn-out process of economic decline', individual Britons would have 'found themselves drifting into Anglo-Saxon households, as slaves, hangers-on, brides and so forth, but they would have come into these communities as one among many'.[38]

In this society, the assimilating Britons may well have been seen as 'guests from elsewhere' (while obviously indigenous) in the

Anglo-Saxon households or communities that integrated them as
people belonging to a different category – socially and ethnically,
but also perhaps racially. Indeed, the Britons are treated as racial
others in both Felix's *Vita Guthlaci* and *Guthlac A*. As Jeffrey
Jerome Cohen argues, 'Guthlac's colonization of the demons'
cherished home' (the Fenlands, much like the home of the Grendelkin) not only 're-enacts in miniature the dispossession of that
very territory' by the Germanic tribes settling there in the fifth
century but also enacts a border war taking place on the other side
of the kingdom, in which Guthlac himself had been involved as a
young warrior.[39]

In a chapter entitled in the Old English translation 'Hu þa deofla
on brytisc spræcon' (How the devils spoke in Brittonic), the *Vita
Guthlaci* narrates that just as the Welsh are invading Mercia from
the west during the reign of King Coenred, in the Fens a crowd
of demons 'impersonates a band of British marauders and sets fire
to Guthlac's dwelling, attacking him with spears'.[40] Guthlac chants
a psalm and the demon-Britons vanish 'velut fumus' (like smoke),
potentially a symbolic parallel to the 'powerful and attractive group
fantasy' of a Mercian 'manifest destiny' entitling it to conquer
British lands while their inhabitants simply vanished.[41]

It is not too great a stretch of the imagination to think of early
audiences of *Beowulf* perceiving the interactions of its protagonist
and the Grendelkin in very similar terms. Felix reports that Guthlac
himself listened to what was probably heroic poetry in seventh-
century Mercia; so, adapting a thought experiment of James Earl,
if we imagine him as a reader of *Beowulf*, the othering of the Britons
as demons in his hagiographies can be understood as participating
in an already extant discourse in which the indigenous population
was represented symbolically as monstrous fen-dwellers.[42] By the
time the Exeter Book riddles were inscribed in their extant forms,
when the Welsh kingdoms no longer posed an immediate military
threat and the Britons on Anglo-Saxon territories had been integrated
as slaves, servants, or brides, this discourse could have developed
into a condescending (rather than outright monsterizing) linkage
of the *wealhas* with animality, bondage, and dark skin.

Of course, Guthlac probably did not actually read *Beowulf*, but
his life realistically was one of the social trajectories an Anglo-Saxon
nobleman's life could take. Audiences in 730s Mercia could perhaps
have related to *Beowulf* and *Vita Guthlaci*, and their understanding
of and emotional reaction to either of them would have been coloured
by the other.[43] If, as Cohen argues, both lives of Guthlac are 'suffused

with colonial desires, displacing into religious history a version of the engagement that was then occurring as martial history',[44] then so is *Beowulf*; only here the colonial desire is projected on to a narrative that probably began its life as folktale conjoined to legendary histories of pre-migration time, rather than on to hagiography.

Similarly to how Felix offers up the Britons as a common enemy against which he defines a presumably homogeneous Anglo-Saxon race (Angles and Saxons are not differentiated in the *Vita*), the *Beowulf* poet creates a sense of superior moral solidarity among its readers and listeners who share the political values of Hrothgar and Beowulf, regardless of ethnicity or regional sense of identity, as long as they oppose the descendants of Cain, who are radically dehumanized. As Craig Davis argues, in *Beowulf*, the primal ethnic dichotomy is not 'between Dane and Heathobard or Geat and Swede, but between royalist and renegade, human and monster, Sethite and Cainite'.[45]

I suggest that this is about more than ethnic difference, however: while the poet conveys a keen sense of ethnic differences among tribes which to us are mere names, there is an uncrossable gulf between all of these ethnicities taken together (however inimical to each other) and the *cyn* of the Cain-descended ghost-guests. Thus, Anglo-Saxon audiences of *Beowulf*, whether in early eighth-century Mercia or tenth-century Wessex, would have conceivably read this monsterization of the indigenous dwellers of the Danish fens as an opportunity to transcend ethnic and regional differences through their own cultural experience (however dim) of othering the Britons as inhuman enemies against which a pan-racial Anglo-Saxon identity could emerge. This need not have been a self-conscious judgement, but an affective response consonant with an entire discourse that was itself part of a network of power relations legally expressed in the apartheid instated by the *Laws of Ine*.

In this respect, *Beowulf* fulfilled not just a need for a search for origins, but also a desire for a trans-ethnic or even (as I argue in the next section) racial sense of identity. Those whom we are accustomed to call 'Anglo-Saxons' (itself an anachronistic concept levelling a five-century period and a region with significant local specificities into an ahistorical notion) were definable primarily by their military allegiance and by regional identity, and early medieval English sources themselves seem to be uncertain how to define their ethnic belonging.[46] Until the emergence of early West Saxon as a literary language (most probably in the decades around AD 700), even among the Germanic-speaking groups, 'there was no cohesive sense of shared English identity and significant dialect variation',[47] until Alfred the Great and his successors started referring to themselves as kings of the *Angli Saxones, Angolsaxones, Anglosaxones,* or *Angulsaxones*.[48] The only position afforded to the Britons in this uncertain but wished-for sense of trans-regional and trans-ethnic identity was that of abject Other. Reactions to *Beowulf* and *Vita Guthlaci* would have fed on this uneasiness about ethnic and racial identity.

These anxieties about indigeneity and establishing an opposing trans-ethnic (almost racial) sense of identity always intersected with anxieties about masculinity: after all, *Beowulf* is not a poem about all Danes, Geats, or, obliquely, Anglo-Saxons or even Mercians, but about a particular class of men, associated by their aristocratic rank and their lords. What unifies the male war-bands of different ethnicities is 'a certain ethic of warrior behaviour', or in other terms, a hegemonic masculinity.[49] Hence, regional or ethnic difference is not an issue if you are a male aristocrat fighting the monsterized ancient dwellers of the land.

And yet, just as Guthlac's recognition of the *brytisc* language and his haunting by the Welsh-speaking demons point to troubling internal differences, so does Beowulf's participation in monstrosity haunt the poem, so that his final mutilation of the bodies of the Grendelkin brings to mind a history of violence against the Britons. At least some members of the Anglo-Saxon male audiences of *Beowulf* would have shared these conjoined anxieties about gender, race, and ethnicity in the intimacy of listening to the poem together. Their emotional reactions could have included a sense of cathartic jubilation at the erasure of the monstrous bodies and an anxiety that they were able to exorcize by projecting it on to figures of abjection such as the Grendelkin or the demonic Britons.

Crushing the *laðan cynnes*: on Anglo-Saxon race, again

When the dragon comes spewing flames over the land of the Geats at the end of the poem, the poet remembers how Beowulf 'æt guðe forgrap Grendeles mægum, / laðan cynnes' (in battle crushed Grendel's kin, the hated race) (2353–4a). As Oswald remarks, this use of the plural recalls Beowulf's use of the plural *feondum* (foes) in his first telling of the fight, and that not just Grendel is exterminated, but his whole 'race': 'the feud can only be ended when the audience is absolutely assured that no grendelkin remain'.[50] I have so far used the term 'race' to describe both the Britons in the imaginary of Anglo-Saxon ethnic difference and the Grendelkin, but in this section I focus on the issue of how productive the use of this word is, considering its problematic baggage as well as its connection to gender.[51]

In his doctoral thesis investigating the Old English vocabulary of ethnic and racial belonging, Christopher Roberts finds two different concepts of identity, one based on physical or generic similarities – usually denoted with the lexemes *cynn* (sort, kind) and *mægð* (family) – and one based on social categories, consisting of the terms *leode* (people, tribe) and *þeod* (people, nation), each of which are frequently related to social concepts such as place, authority, and collective name.[52] *Leode* seems to have originally connoted 'a smaller group tied to an abstract sense of place and generic leadership', while *þeod* probably connoted 'a group under the power of a larger authority in control of a named territory'.[53] Both are used in *Beowulf* for naming all the tribal or ethnic groups (for instance, 'Geata leode' at 1213b, or 'fremde þeod' at 1691b). *Cyn* is reserved for families ('cynnes Wægmundinga') (2813b–2814a), the species of animals that God created (97b–98a), humanity ('moncynn') (164b *et passim*) and the grouping made up of Grendel, his mother, and Cain (107a). When the Danish coast guard asks Beowulf for his group's identity (244a–257b), he responds by saying first that they are 'of man-kind' ('we synt gumcynnes') (260a), secondly that they are of the tribe or people of the Geats ('Geata leode') (260b), and only then that they are Hygelac's hearthmates and that his father is Ecgþeow (261a–263b).

There is no clear taxonomy here, and at times metrical and alliterative reasons could have led the poet to use one of them rather the other. Roberts's model still applies, but the translation of *cyn* in the case of Cain's *cyn*, of which Grendel and his mother are the last survivors, needs to be problematized. It is not conceived simply as a family or a lineage, although that, too, is part of the concept. They are certainly not a *leod* or *þeod* – the separation between them and any other tribal or ethnic grouping in the poem is greater than any difference among the latter. Still, they are not simply unthinking beasts, like the water monsters that Beowulf fights on his way to Grendel's hall. They are human, descended from Cain and separated from humanity because of sinfulness. Still, the Grendelkin look like humans, are intelligent, feel rage at being left out of the human community of Heorot, have human-like social structures that predicate revenge for one of their own, and live in a hall (an inversion of Heorot though it may be).

Thus, if race is usually used to describe 'a group whose boundaries are relatively difficult to cross', and ethnicity 'a group with relatively porous boundaries', then both the Grendelkin and the Britons of the Anglo-Saxon imaginary of Beowulf and the lives of Guthlac form a race.[54] The use of the term 'race' in any pre-modern context has been criticized, for Anglo-Saxon England in particular.[55] Of course, modern terms such as 'race' and 'ethnicity' do not correspond exactly to the variety of Latin and Old English words they are used to translate. But in the case at hand, to translate the *cyn* to which Grendel, his mother, and Cain belong to as either 'family'/'kin' or 'tribe' would be disingenuous because it would erase the possibility that is certainly present in the text for Anglo-Saxon audiences to relate to the Grendelkin as their culture did to the Britons. As Geraldine Heng argues, the refusal to use 'race' when discussing medieval phenomena

> de-stigmatizes the impacts and consequences of certain laws, acts, practices, and institutions in the medieval period, so that we cannot name them for what they are, nor can we bear adequate witness to the full meaning of the manifestations and phenomena they install. The unavailability of race thus often colludes in relegating such manifestations to an epiphenomenal status.[56]

Used in this understanding, 'race' does not have to be equated to any presumably biological difference between groups of people (in the way it is popularly used). Rather, in Heng's definition, 'race' is 'a structural relationship for the articulation and management of human differences, rather than a substantive content', or in other words, 'a repeating tendency, of the gravest import, to demarcate human beings through differences among humans that are selectively essentialized as absolute and fundamental, in order to distribute positions and powers differentially to human groups'.[57]

According to this definition, the Britons are clearly racialized in the Anglo-Saxon imaginary, belonging to a system of racial categorization in which several categories intersected: bodily distinction (Britons described repeatedly as *sweart* [dark]), language (Welsh as demonic speech in Guthlac or as incomprehensible gibberish in Ælfric), and social status (according to the *Laws of Ine* and the economic consequences thereof, also evident in the very term *wealh* and its entire lexical field of derogatory connotations). While I am not claiming that the Grendelkin are present in the poem due to a self-conscious choice of the poet to represent the indigenous people the Germanic tribes found in England, I suggest that some

Anglo-Saxon audiences would have perceived them (emotionally, if not discursively) as monstrous echoes of their real-life relationships with both the Britons and, later, the Danes.

Critical Race theory (CRT), from which I derive my frame of interpretation here, was originally developed to address the specific needs of the African-American community along a 'black–white' binary, which, while not similar to the relationship between the Britons and the invading Germanic tribes, is useful for understanding how groups are constructed discursively 'within a social space and held there by institutional practice'.[58] As other race theorists have recently proposed, the dynamics of racialization are protean and work differently, for instance, for Native Americans than for African-Americans. Thus, a framework such as TribalCrit, developed by Bryan M. J. Brayboy, is meant to emphasize Indigenous peoples' racialized experience of colonization, which 'is not just an experience of racial oppression', but 'primarily an experience of territorial oppression'.[59] In the light of the devolution of the sociopolitical and economic status of the Britons, this offers a particularly helpful model through which to understand the indigenous experience of the colonized *wealhas*.

Ryan Craig and Victoria Davis argue that 'the practices to bring Indigenous peoples into the fold of Whiteness' (being sent to boarding schools, converted to Christianity, forced to switch from collective to individualized forms of land ownership) were in fact strategies for acquiring their land and resources.[60] While no similar concerted effort to turn the Britons into Anglo-Saxons took place in early medieval England, this seems to have happened over time due to the racialization instated legally, economically, and discursively, as well as symbolically through such texts as *Beowulf* and *Vita Guthlaci*.

Giant women and haunting Danes: race and gender around *Beowulf*

As I have argued throughout this chapter, novel anxieties could be projected on to what was already a focus for racialized abjection, namely, Grendel and especially his mother, in new sociopolitical (and manuscript) contexts. As we have seen, connections to sociopolitical developments in Anglo-Saxon England may serve as clues to layers of emotional response to the poem. Consider Helen Damico's interpretation of Fitt II of *Beowulf* (characterized by Klaeber as 'Grendel's Reign of Terror') as a poetic rendering of the series of Danish attacks on England in the early eleventh century, paralleling the more poetic account of the same events in the C-text of the Anglo-Saxon Chronicle.[61] Putting other kinds of dating aside, Damico's argument details one possible act of reception, wherein an element of the poem (Grendel as a terrifying character rampaging around the Danish countryside) could provide a screen on to which early eleventh-century audiences projected their own anxieties about Danish attacks on England. If Grendel and his mother could become a focus for anxieties about Welsh indigeneity, they could certainly fulfil a similar role for Danish invasion. What is more, Kathryn Powell argued that the *Beowulf* manuscript as we have it, probably written during the latter part of the reign of Æthelred the Unready, displays a new preoccupation with the tension between (not always good) rulers and foreigners, which would have been particularly relevant in the context of the Viking raids.[62]

Indeed, for an early eleventh-century audience, *Beowulf* was now part of a novel textual constellation, which included *The Letter of Alexander to Aristotle* and *The Wonders of the East*. Many of the clashes with foreigners depicted in the other works in the manuscript would have been reminiscent of recent events in England such as the St Brice's Day massacre of 1002. This was when, according to the Anglo-Saxon Chronicle, 'the king [Æthelred] commanded that all the Danish men who were among the English be slain'.[63] A necessary caveat is that the order was probably directed only against those Danes who had recently settled in various parts of England, whether as traders or mercenaries, not against those with Danish ancestry.[64] Yet, as Eileen Joy remarks, this was not an isolated event, the racialized violence of the attacks being part of a larger discourse seeking to instate 'bodily purity through the elimination of supposedly impure elements'.[65] A charter of 1004 from the monastery of St Frideswide at Oxford records that a group of Danes,

> who had 'sprung up' in England like 'cockle amongst the wheat,' had been forced to flee to the barred church, the doors and bolts of which they broke by force to get inside, and once securely settled there, an angry mob of their neighbors set fire to the church, apparently burning the Danes inside, along with 'its ornaments and books'.[66]

Anglo-Saxons reading with these recent events in mind might have reacted differently to *Beowulf* as a result. In the senses proposed above, the Danes became racialized, if not as part of a long history of structural oppression, at least in the Anglo-Saxon imaginary at the turn of the eleventh century. In reading and listening to this new *Beowulf*, Anglo-Saxons would have celebrated (and been haunted by) the erasure of the racialized abjected bodies of the race of Grendel, who once again became the focus for shared anxieties about race, ethnicity, and masculinity.

Notes

1 Frances McCormack, Jonathan Wilcox, and Alice Jorgensen (eds), *Anglo-Saxon emotions: reading the heart in Old English language, literature, and culture* (Farnham: Ashgate, 2015). For emotional community, see Barbara H. Rosenwein, *Emotional communities in the early Middle Ages* (Ithaca, NY: Cornell University Press, 2006), pp. 2, 24–5.

2 For discussions on the ways in which anxiety recombines with shame, and on how crucial shame is to the experience of homosociality, see Adam Frank and Eve Kosofsky Sedgwick (eds), *Shame and its sisters: a Silvan Tomkins reader* (Durham, NC: Duke University Press, 1995), pp. 6, 147–60; and Eve Kosofsky Sedgwick, *Touching feeling: affect, pedagogy, performativity* (Durham, NC: Duke University Press, 2003), pp. 35–121. I am grateful to Daniel Remein for pointing me towards this illuminating work.

3 Geraldine Heng, 'The invention of race in the European Middle Ages I: race studies, modernity, and the Middle Ages', *Literature compass*, 8.5 (2011), 258–74, at 262. See also Heng's magnum opus, *The invention of race in the European Middle Ages* (Cambridge: Cambridge University Press, 2018).

4 For a classic refutation of this masculinist approach to *Beowulf*, see Clare Lees, 'Men and *Beowulf*', in Clare Lees (ed.), *Medieval masculinities: regarding men in the Middle Ages* (Minneapolis, MN: University of Minnesota Press, 1994), pp. 129–48.

5 Wolfgang Iser, *From reader response to literary anthropology* (Baltimore, MD: Johns Hopkins University Press, 1989).

6 Stephen Harris, *Race and ethnicity in Anglo-Saxon literature* (London: Routledge, 2003), p. 35.

7 The issues are vast, interconnected, and wide-reaching – for a few points of entry see https://www.chronicle.com/article/Prominent-Medieval-Scholar-s/235014; https://www.insidehighered.com/news/2017/09/19/one-professors-critique-another-divides-medieval-studies; and https://www.salon.com/2017/11/30/alt-right-catches-knight-fever-but-medieval-scholars-strike-back/ (all accessed 5 June 2019).

8 Catalin Taranu, 'The making of poetic history in Anglo-Saxon England and Carolingian Francia', PhD dissertation, University of Leeds, 2016, p. 4.

9 Derek Neal, *The masculine self in late medieval England* (Chicago: University of Chicago Press, 2008), p. 10; John D. Niles, 'Reconceiving *Beowulf*: poetry as social praxis', *College English*, 61 (1998), 143–66, at 146. See also James W. Earl's view of *Beowulf* as a dream screen in

his *Thinking about Beowulf* (Stanford, CA: Stanford University Press, 1994), pp. 129–36.

10　Martin E. P. Seligman, Elaine F. Walker, and David L. Rosenhan, *Abnormal psychology* (New York: Norton, 2001), p. 275; Chrissoula Stavrakaki and Yona Lunsky, 'Depression, anxiety and adjustment disorders in people with intellectual disabilities', in Nick Bouras and Geraldine Holt (eds), *Psychiatric and behavioural disorders in intellectual and developmental disabilities* (Cambridge: Cambridge University Press, 2007), pp. 113–30, at 113.

11　Fred C. Robinson, 'Did Grendel's mother sit on Beowulf?', in Malcolm Godden, Douglas Gray, and Terry Hoad (eds), *From Anglo-Saxon to Early Middle English* (Oxford, Clarendon, 1994), pp. 1–7, at 2.

12　Dana Oswald, *Monsters, gender and sexuality in medieval English literature* (Woodbridge: D. S. Brewer, 2010), p. 95.

13　Ibid., p. 96.

14　Ibid.

15　Jane Chance, *Woman as hero in Old English poetry* (Syracuse, NY: Syracuse University Press, 1986), p. 102; Shari Horner, 'Voices from the margins', in Eileen Joy and Mary Ramsay (eds), *The postmodern Beowulf: a critical casebook* (Morgantown, WV: West Virginia University Press, 2006), pp. 467–500, at 485; Oswald, *Monsters*, p. 94.

16　Glenn Davis, 'The Exeter Book riddles and sexual idiom', in Nicola McDonald (ed.), *Medieval obscenities* (York: York Medieval Press, 2006), pp. 39–54, at 50; Oswald, *Monsters*, p. 94.

17　Oswald, *Monsters*, p. 95.

18　See Gillian Overing's chapter on swords and signs in *Language, sign, and gender in Beowulf* (Carbondale, IL: Southern Illinois University Press, 1990), pp. 33–67.

19　Edward Christie, 'Self-mastery and submission: holiness and masculinity in the lives of Anglo-Saxon martyr-kings', in P. H. Cullum and Katherine J. Lewis (eds), *Holiness and masculinity in the Middle Ages* (Cardiff: University of Wales Press, 2004), pp. 143–57, at 152.

20　Stacy S. Klein, 'Gender', in Jacqueline Stodnick and Renée Trilling (eds), *A handbook of Anglo-Saxon studies* (Oxford: Wiley-Blackwell, 2012), pp. 39–54, at 41.

21　Oswald, *Monsters*, p. 93.

22　Ibid., pp. 84, 99.

23　Ibid., p. 96.

24　Sophie Scott, 'The social life of laughter', *Trends in the cognitive sciences*, 18 (2014), 618–20; Oriana Aragón, 'Dimorphous expressions of positive emotion', *Psychological science*, 26 (2015), 59–273.

25　For further discussion of their place in the fens, see Christopher Abram's chapter in this volume, pp. 120–46.

26　Carolyn Anderson argued for the semantic indeterminacy of the two words in her '*Gæst*, gender, and kin in *Beowulf*: consumption of the boundaries', *The heroic age*, 5 (2001), www.heroicage.org/issues/5/ Anderson1.html (accessed 5 June 2019).

27 See also Alfred K. Siewers, 'Landscapes of conversion: Guthlac's mound and Grendel's mere as expressions of Anglo-Saxon nation-building', *Viator*, 34 (2003), 1–39.

28 Harris, *Race and ethnicity*, p. 12; Andy Orchard, *Pride and prodigies: studies in the monsters of the Beowulf-manuscript* (Cambridge: D. S. Brewer, 1995), pp. 87–8.

29 John W. Tanke, '*Wonfeax wale*: ideology and figuration in the sexual riddles of the Exeter Book', in Britton J. Harwood and Gillian R. Overing (eds), *Class and gender in early English literature: intersections* (Bloomington, IN: Indiana University Press, 1994), pp. 21–39, at 24.

30 Nina Rulon-Miller, 'Sexual humor and fettered desire in Exeter Book Riddle 12', in Jonathon Wilcox (ed.), *Humour in Anglo-Saxon literature* (Cambridge: Cambridge University Press, 2000), pp. 99–126, at 117.

31 Ibid.

32 See also Heng, *The invention of race*.

33 Rulon-Miller, 'Sexual humor', pp. 115–16.

34 Ibid., p. 114; Debby Banham, 'Anglo-Saxon attitudes: in search of the origins of English racism', *European review of history*, 2 (1994), 143–56, at 155.

35 Ryan Craig and Victoria Davis, '"The only way they knew how to solve their disagreements was to fight": a textual analysis of Native Americans before, during, and after the Civil Rights movement', in Prentice T. Chandler (ed.), *Doing race in social studies: critical perspectives* (Charlotte, NC: Information Age Publishing, 2015), pp. 89–125, at 100. On Welsh slavery, see David A. E. Pelteret, *Slavery in early mediaeval England: from the reign of Alfred until the twelfth century* (Woodbridge: Boydell and Brewer, 1995).

36 Margaret Lindsay Faull, 'The semantic development of Old English *wealh*', *Leeds studies in English*, 8 (1975), 20–44, at 20–1; quoted in Rulon-Miller, 'Sexual humor', p. 114.

37 Ibid.

38 Alexander Woolf, 'Apartheid and economics in Anglo-Saxon England', in Nick Higham (ed.), *Britons in Anglo-Saxon England* (Woodbridge: Boydell and Brewer, 2007), pp. 115–29, at 129.

39 Jeffrey J. Cohen, *Medieval identity machines* (Minneapolis, MN: University of Minnesota Press, 2003), pp. 142, 143.

40 Ibid., p. 143.

41 Bertram Colgrave (ed. and trans.), *Felix's Life of Saint Guthlac* (Cambridge: Cambridge University Press, 1956), pp. 109–10; and Cohen, *Identity machines*, p. 144.

42 Earl, *Thinking about Beowulf*, pp. 175–87.

43 Colgrave, in *Guthlac*, p. 19, argues for a date of 730–40 for the text.

44 Cohen, *Identity machines*, p. 144.

45 Craig R. Davis, 'Redundant ethnogenesis in *Beowulf*', *The heroic age*, 5 (2001), www.heroicage.org/issues/5/Davis1.html (accessed 5 June 2019).
46 Susan Reynolds, 'What do we mean by "Anglo-Saxon" and "Anglo-Saxons"?', *Journal of British Studies*, 24 (1985), 395–414, at 403–4.
47 Woolf, 'Apartheid', 127. See also John Hines, 'The becoming of the English: identity, material culture and language in early Anglo-Saxon England', *Anglo-Saxon studies in archaeology and history*, 7 (1994), 49–60.
48 Harris, *Race and ethnicity*, p. 10; Reynolds, 'What do we mean?', 398.
49 Cf. Lees, 'Men and *Beowulf*', p. 140.
50 Oswald, *Monsters*, p. 111.
51 See Cord Whitaker, 'Race-ing the dragon: the Middle Ages, race and trippin' into the future', *postmedieval*, 6 (2015), 3–11, the introduction to a special issue of *postmedieval*, 'Making Race Matter in the Middle Ages', where he argues that we need to take for granted that the Middle Ages were raced in complex ways, and to start unravelling them.
52 Christopher M. Roberts, 'The form, aspect, and definition of Anglo-Saxon identity: a study of medieval British words, deeds, and things', PhD dissertation, Arizona State University, 2013, p. 119.
53 Roberts, 'The form, aspect, and definition of Anglo-Saxon identity', p. 120.
54 Harris, *Race and ethnicity*, p. 1.
55 William C. Jordan, 'Why "race"?', *JMEMS*, 31 (2001), 165–74; and Asa Simon Mittman, 'Are the "monstrous races" races?', *postmedieval*, 6.1 (2015), 36–51. For other critiques of the use of race for the medieval period, see Kwame Anthony Appiah, 'Race', in Frank Lentricchia and Thomas McLaughlin (eds), *Critical terms for literary study* (Chicago: University of Chicago Press, 1990), pp. 274–87; Etienne Balibar, 'Election / Selection', keynote plenary for the University of California Humanities Research Institute conference *tRACEs: Race, Deconstruction, Critical Theory*, https://vimeo.com/album/1631670/video/25691025 (accessed 5 June 2019).
56 Heng, 'Invention of race', 265.
57 Ibid., 268, 267.
58 Craig and Davis, '"The only way they knew how to solve their disagreements"', p. 99.
59 Ibid. For TribalCrit, see also Bryan McKinley Jones Brayboy, 'Toward a Tribal Critical Race Theory in education', *The urban review*, 37 (2005), 425–46, and Brayboy, 'Tribal Critical Race Theory: an origin story and future directions', in Marvin Lynn and Adrienne D. Dixson (eds), *Handbook of Critical Race Theory in education* (New York: Routledge, 2013), pp. 88–100. For CRT in general, see Richard Delgado and Jean Stefancic, *Critical Race Theory: an introduction* (New York: New York University Press, 2012).
60 Craig and Davis, '"The only way they knew how to solve their disagreements"', p. 99.

61 Helen Damico, 'Grendel's reign of terror: from history to vernacular epic', in Daniel Anlezark (ed.), *Myths, legends and heroes: essays on Old Norse and Old English literature in honour of John McKinnell* (Toronto: University of Toronto Press, 2011), pp. 148–66, at 150.

62 Kathryn Powell, 'Meditating on men and monsters: a reconsideration of the thematic unity of the *Beowulf* manuscript', *RES*, 57 (2006), 1–15, at 6.

63 Harry August Rositzke (ed.), *The C-Text of the Old English Chronicles* (Bochum-Langendreer: Heinrich Pöppinghaus, 1940), pp. 55–6, quoted in Eileen A. Joy, 'The signs and location of a flight (or return?) of time: the Old English Wonders of the East and the Gujarat Massacre', in Jeffrey Jerome Cohen (ed.), *Cultural diversity in the British Middle Ages: archipelago, island, England* (New York: Palgrave Macmillan, 2008), pp. 209–29, at 222.

64 Simon Keynes, *The diplomas of King Æthelred the Unready, 978–1016: a study in their use as historical evidence* (Cambridge: Cambridge University Press, 1980), p. 204.

65 Joy, 'Signs and location', p. 222.

66 Dorothy Whitelock (ed.), *English historical documents I, c. 500–1042*, 2nd edn (New York: Oxford University Press, 1979), p. 591, quoted in Joy, 'Signs and location', p. 222.

10

Sad men in *Beowulf*

Robin Norris

The ink spilled defining weeping as women's work in *Beowulf* far exceeds the volume of their tears. We have made too much of the summary line at the opening of the Finnsburh episode declaring Hildeburh a 'geomuru ides' (sad woman) (1075b) as 'meotodsceaft bemearn' (she mourned over the decree of fate) (1077a).[1] At the funeral she directs for her son and brother, 'ides gnornode, / geomrode giddum' (the woman mourned with songs) (1117–18).[2] Likewise, according to her editors, a Geatish *meowle* sings at Beowulf's funeral (3150b).[3] What can be read of the manuscript here includes 'giomorgyd' (song of mourning) (3150a) and 'sorgcearig' (sorrowful) (3152a). Indeed, these women are sad, but they are also surrounded by sad men.

Meanwhile, we have averted our tearless eyes from the mourning men who populate the poem. We may question how the Anglo-Saxons read this history of their continental ancestors, or why Christian scribes recorded it, but we do not question our own cathexis of the Anglo-Saxon hero with a stiff upper lip. Instead, we read the evidence through the lens of our own confirmation bias. As I argue in this chapter, we have made Beowulf a paragon of the heroic code without asking whose gender norms we expect him to uphold. We have done the same in our readings of the other poems we call heroic, such as *The Wanderer*. Early in the poem, the speaker claims:

> Ic to soþe wat
> þæt biþ in eorle   indryhten þeaw,
> þæt he his ferðlocan   fæste binde,
> healde his hordcofan,   hycge swa he wille.
> Ne mæg werig mod   wyrde wiðstondan,
> ne se hreo hyge   helpe gefremman.
> Forðon domgeorne   dreorigne oft
> in hyra breostcofan   bindað fæste. (11–18)[4]

(I know for a fact that it is a noble custom in a nobleman to bind up his spirit-locker, hold his heart-coffer, whatever he might think. A weary mind cannot withstand wyrd and a disturbed mind doesn't help. Therefore those eager for glory often bind whatever's dreary in their breast-coffer.)

But despite the nobility of this prescription, he goes on to disclose the dreary contents of his spirit-locker over the next 100 lines. In order to argue that this noble custom must have ruled the emotional lives of Anglo-Saxon men, we have cherry-picked the Wanderer's tree, blinded to the forest of his lament.

Likewise, we continue to be possessed by the Germanic spirit conjured by the Roman historian Tacitus, who famously wrote, 'Weeping and wailing they put away quickly: sorrow and sadness linger. Lamentation becomes women: men must remember', and we cling to this statement as applicable to the Anglo-Saxons, despite the fact that he was writing about continental tribes in 98 CE.[5] Moreover, Christopher Krebs calls the *Germania* 'a mosaic of Greek and Roman stereotypes, arranged by a writer who most likely never went north of the Alps'; these mourning women and repressed men 'are in many ways typical representatives of the northern barbarian, sketched within the Greek and Roman ethnographical tradition by ... a Roman in Rome for Romans'.[6] Not only does Tacitus present mourning as women's work, but in this same passage he notes that Germanic peoples avoid both ostentation in burial and 'the difficult and tedious tribute of a monument', an attitude that would seem to prohibit Beowulf's treasure-bedecked pyre and cliffside barrow, were he a reliable source. Tacitus also gives us the word *comitatus*, which is still used to encapsulate the relationship between an Anglo-Saxon leader and his thanes.[7] According to the *Oxford English Dictionary*, the word is first attested in English in 1875 as Victorian historians thought through the roots and the nature of the English nobility.[8] In the twentieth century, according to Krebs, members of the SS memorialized Tacitus's depiction of the *comitatus* by 'wear[ing] this German motto engraved on their [belt] buckles: Meine Ehre heißt Treue (My honour is called loyalty)'.[9]

Medievalists have rejected the Nazi fetishization of Germanic identity, and we have begun to critique the Victorian construction of imperial Englishness, but we have left unchallenged the 'Victorian and modern views on masculinity [that] have influenced the critical reception and interpretation of male tears in the corpus of Old

English literature', as Kristen Mills argues; 'examples of weeping men are often ignored or viewed as aberrant, while instances of women's weeping are taken as normative behaviour'.[10] In response to this tendency, in the first section of this chapter I would like simply to acknowledge the many sad men who inhabit *Beowulf*: the catalogue below serves as a monument. Even the main characters of the poem experience sorrow – both King Hrothgar and the hero himself, as I will explain. Moreover, Beowulf also demonstrates empathy for the sorrow of others, and in the conclusion of the chapter I will discuss Beowulf's empathy and its limits, and the limits of empathy in light of the current challenges facing the field presently known as Anglo-Saxon studies.

Sad men

Beowulf is famously structured by four funerals, all conducted primarily by men.[11] Clearly Hildeburh and the Geatish *meowle* have plenty of male company, but whereas we see these two women mourning only in a funereal context, and only in two of the four rites, we see ample evidence of male sorrow at all four funerals and throughout the poem. The men who bury the legendary hero Scyld Scefing at sea have 'geomor sefa, / murnende mod' (a sad and mourning mind) (49b–50a).[12] After the funeral of Hildeburh's son and brother Hnæf, the lordless Danes are twice labelled with a compound using *wea*, 'woe', which Britt Mize translates as 'the trauma-remnant' ('þa wealafe') (1084a and 1098a).[13] Two men named Guðlaf and Oslaf decide to kill Finn after 'sorge mændon, / ætwiton weana dæl' (speaking of their sorrow and attributing blame for their portion of woes) (1149b–50a). It is the sight of a sword that sparks this conversation, and the afterlife of arms that leads to the third funeral in *Beowulf*, the so-called lay of the last survivor, whom the narrator calls 'weard winegeomor' (a guardian mourning his friends) (2239).[14] After he utters his twenty-line elegy (2247–66), the narrator adds:

Swa giomormod   giohðo mænde
an æfter eallum,   unbliðe hwearf
dæges ond nihtes,   oð ðæt deaðes wylm
hran æt heortan. (2267–70a)

(Thus one [remaining] after all [the others], sad of mind, spoke of sorrow, [then] turned joyless day and night until death's welling touched him at heart.)

Grieving until the end of his days, the last survivor becomes a lordless wanderer, sharing the fate that befalls the Geats following Beowulf's death.

It is his funeral, the fourth and last of the poem, that is the most elaborate. It is not just the two-stage ceremony but the last five fitts of the poem that are inhabited by sad men. It was sadness that motivated Wiglaf, another 'wealaf', to help Beowulf fight the dragon, for 'weoll / sefa wið sorgum' (his mind welled with sorrows) (2599b–600a).[15] Wiglaf is the only one of Beowulf's men to join him in the fight, and when he explains this decision to his companions, the narrator adds the summary line: 'him wæs sefa geomor' (his was a sad mind) (2632b). Wiglaf takes Beowulf's death 'earfoðlice' (with difficulty) (2822a), and he is 'sarigferð' (sad at heart) (2863a) when he reports the news to his companions. He sends a messenger to those awaiting the outcome, who are similarly 'modgiomor' (sad at heart) (2894b). The messenger describes Wiglaf to them as holding 'higemæðum heafodwearde' (a mind-wearying death-watch) (2909) over the bodies of the king and the dragon. He then predicts that neither nobleman nor maiden will wear treasure; instead they will experience exile, 'geomormod' (sad of mind) (3018a).[16] When the messenger's work is done, the company goes 'unbliðe' (joyless) (3031a) and 'wollenteare' (with gushing tears) (3032a) to see the body.

'Lyt ænig mearn' (Little did anyone mourn) (3129b) to gather the treasure that will soon be burned and buried, but Beowulf himself is laid on the pyre by 'hæleð hiofende hlaford leofne' (men lamenting their dear lord) (3142). It is 'wigend' (warriors) (3144a) who light the fire, which is 'wope bewunden' (wound about with weeping) (3146a) as 'higum unrote / modceare mændon' (the sad ones speak of soul-sorrow in their minds) (3148b–49a). Later, after they build a barrow, twelve 'hildediore, æþelinga bearn' (battle-brave children of nobles) (3169b–70a) ride around the mound.[17] These men need to talk, and their words take the poem to its conclusion:

> woldon care cwiðan,   ond cyning mænan,
> wordgyd wrecan,   ond ymb wer sprecan;
> eahtodan eorlscipe   ond his ellenweorc
> duguðum demdon, –   swa hit gedefe bið,
> þæt mon his winedryhten   wordum herge,
> ferhðum freoge,   þonne he forð scile
> of lichaman   læded weorðan.
> Swa begnornodon   Geata leode
> hlafordes hryre,   heorðgeneatas. (3171–9)

(They wished to bewail their care and speak of their king, recite a
song and speak about the man; they considered his nobility and
highly praised his deeds of valour – as it is fitting that a man praise
his friendly lord with words, love him with their minds, when he
shall be led forth from the body. Thus the people of the Geats, the
hearth-companions, lamented their lord's fall.)

These twelve hearth-companions, Beowulf's battle-companions,
stand in for the Geatish people as a whole as they mourn for their
lord; through words, song, and praise they bewail their care and
lament his fall.

What I have demonstrated here is that *Beowulf* is populated by
sad men, though we have overlooked their emotions by focusing
on the mourning of Hildeburh and the Geatish *meowle*. In the light
of the great sorrow of the many men who participate in all four of
the poem's funerals, it is clearly inaccurate to state that weeping is
women's work in the poem. Nor is grief reserved for emasculated
men. Beowulf himself experienced a great deal of sadness in his
final days.[18] The news of his hall's burning by the dragon was
'hreow on hreðre, hygesorga mæst' (sorrow in his breast, greatest
of heart-sorrows) (2328). Wondering if he had offended God, his
'breost innan weoll / þeostrum geþoncum, swa him geþywe ne wæs'
(breast within welled with dark thoughts, as was not customary for
him) (2331b–2). Beowulf recalls many past obstacles overcome, but
now, as his unaccustomed dark thoughts continue, we realize that
he is grieving for his own imminent death, as 'him wæs geomor
sefa, / wæfre ond wælfus' (his mind was sad, restless, and ready for
death) (2419b–20a). After fighting the dragon, as he lies dying,
when he looks on the gold, Beowulf is 'gomel on giohðe' (old in
sorrow) (2793), a phrase echoed by Wiglaf when he conveys Beowulf's
last wishes to the Geats ('gomol on giohðe') (3095a).

If the critical consensus will admit a mourning man to discussion
of the poem, it is Hrothgar, but as Kristen Mills notes, 'It is a
commonplace of *Beowulf*-scholarship to observe that Hrothgar serves
as a foil to Beowulf, and thus one's interpretation of Hrothgar's
behaviour will depend largely on how one views Beowulf.'[19] If
Beowulf is the paragon of heroic masculinity, then Hrothgar must
pale by comparison. But if Beowulf is a man who experiences
sorrow himself, then we must re-evaluate our reading of Hrothgar.
First, we must understand that the sorrow of the Danish people
becomes the context for Hrothgar's own sadness. When the Danes
learn of Grendel's first attack, which takes the lives of thirty thanes,

they respond with 'wop' (weeping) (128b), 'micel morgensweg' (a great morning sound [of wailing]) (129a). The king sits 'unbliðe' (joyless) (130b), 'þolode ðryðswyð, þegnsorge dreah' (suffering and enduring strong sorrow for thanes) (131). Thus begins twelve years of suffering for Hrothgar: 'Wæs seo hwil micel: / twelf wintra tid torn geþolode / wine Scyldinga, weana gehwelcne, / sidra sorga' (It was a long time: for twelve winters, the friend of the Danes suffered grief, each woe of great sorrows) (146b–9a). Word begins to spread through 'gyddum geomore' (sad songs) (151a) about Grendel's conflict with Hrothgar, so that even Hygelac, king across the sea, later refers to Hrothgar's 'widcuðne wean' (widely known woe) (1991a). Yet the narrator continues to emphasize Hrothgar's sorrow: 'Þæt wæs wræc micel wine Scyldinga, / modes brecða' (That was great misery and heartbreak [lit. breaking of mind] for the friend of the Danes) (170–1a). And there is one last description of Hrothgar's emotional state before the narrator introduces Beowulf: 'Swa ða mælceare maga Healfdenes / singala seað; ne mihte snotor hæleð / wean onwendan' (So the son of Healfdene was agitated by continual cares; nor could the prudent man turn aside woe) (189–91a).

When Beowulf arrives, then, he touts the benefit of his services as not merely logistical but therapeutic, since he will cause Hrothgar's 'cearwylmas colran wurðaþ' (seething sorrows to become cooler) (282). When Hrothgar replies to this offer, he admits, 'Sorh is me to secganne on sefan minum / gumena ængum hwæt me Grendel hafað / hynðo on Heorote mid his heteþancum, / færniða gefremed' (It is a sorrow in my mind for me to say to anyone what Grendel has done to me in Heorot, humiliation and hostile attacks, with his thoughts of hate) (473–6). After Grendel's death, Hrothgar re-emphasizes that he had endured 'grynna æt Grendle' (grief from Grendel) (930a) without ever expecting relief from any 'weana' (woe) (933a), but relief came in the person of Beowulf, as advertised.[20] Thus, when Grendel's mother arrives, 'cearu wæs geniwod' (care was renewed) (1303b). This sentiment is repeated when Hrothgar explains to Beowulf that Æschere has died: 'Sorh is geniwod / Denigea leodum' (Sorrow is renewed for the people of the Danes) (1322b–3a). And when they find Æschere's head, 'Denum eallum wæs, / ... weorce on mode / to geþolianne' (it was painful in mind for all Danes to suffer) (1417b–19a).

How does Hrothgar himself respond to Æschere's death? The narrator tells us that he is 'on hreon mode' (in a troubled frame of mind) (1307b) and worries that God will never end his 'weaspelle'

(news of woe) (1315a). Yet when Hrothgar speaks of Æschere
to Beowulf, he begins with praise for his retainer, and ends with
the information Beowulf needs to find and kill Grendel's mother.
Hrothgar concludes this speech by promising Beowulf payment
for the feud (1380–2) – in other words by hiring Beowulf to exact
revenge. According to Erin Sebo, 'Hrothgar's mind is bent solely
on revenge and he gives Beowulf as much information as he can
to assist with the tracking and killing of Grendel's mother.'[21] It
is in this context that Beowulf gives his famous reply: 'Ne sorga,
snotor guma. Selre bið æghwæm / þæt he his freond wrece þonne
he fela murne' (Do not sorrow, wise man. It is better for anyone to
avenge his friend than to mourn much) (1384b–5), and he concludes,
'Ðys dogor þu geþyld hafa / weana gehwylces, swa ic þe wene to'
(Today have patience for every woe, as I expect you to) (1395–6),
after which Hrothgar leaps up and rides off. But a myopic focus
on Beowulf's words as evidence of the heroic code has led us too
often to extrapolate a total ban on mourning. Moreover, reading
Beowulf and Hrothgar in juxtaposition has led us to assume that
revenge is Beowulf's idea because Hrothgar has been mourning
too much, when both of these conclusions are disproven by the
textual evidence.

    Likewise, the parting of Beowulf and Hrothgar is one of the
most poignant episodes in the poem, but it is more often read
as evidence of Hrothgar's failing masculinity.[22] Bearing in mind
the fact that Hrothgar has been in constant mourning for the past
twelve years, he actually copes fairly well with Beowulf's departure.
In her reading of this scene, Leslie Lockett argues that Hrothgar
succeeds in keeping 'his intense sadness' internalized,[23] as if he
has flexed his mind-tethers 'to keep words and tears from escaping
from the breast, but at the risk of increasing the heat and pressure
inside the chest cavity'.[24] Since Hrothgar does apparently shed tears,
Kristen Mills 're-examine[s] the farewell scene in light of other
texts where the formula of a man falling on another's neck, kissing
him, and weeping occurs';[25] these parallels do not suggest 'abnor-
mality or effeminacy when men embrace, kiss, and weep during a
reunion'.[26]

    This farewell is not a definitive moment of closure but leaves
many questions open: Whose tears are falling and why? Do the two
men expect to meet again? Will they? But we cannot yield to the
mystery of poetry if we assume that we already know all the answers.
The goodbye appears on folios 173v–174r of the manuscript. It is
Beowulf's request to leave, to return to his own king, that sets the

stage for this scene, which the narrator depicts entirely from Hrothgar's perspective:

Het hine mid þæm lacum   leode swæse
secean on gesyntum,   snude eft cuman.
Gecyste þa   cyning æþelum god,
þeoden Scyldinga   ðegn betestan
ond be healse genam;   hruron him tearas
blondenfeaxum.   Him wæs bega wen,
ealdum infrodum   oþres swiðor,
þæt hie seoððan [no]   geseon moston,
modige on meþle.   Wæs him se man to þon leof
þæt he þone breostwylm   forberan ne mehte;
ac him on hreþre   hygebendum fæst
æfter deorum men   dyrne langað
beorn wið blode. (1868–80a)

(Hrothgar commanded him to go home to his people safely with these gifts, and come again soon. Then the king of good stock, the lord of the Danes, kissed the best of thanes and took him by the neck; tears fell [from/onto] him, the greying one. For the wise old man, there was expectation of two outcomes, one more likely than the other, that they would [not?] see each other afterward, emotional about meeting. The man was so dear to him that he could not forbear the breast-welling, but in his heart, firmly bound in his mind, an unspoken longing for the dear man burned in his blood.)

When Hrothgar takes Beowulf by the neck, Beowulf apparently consents, accepting if not reciprocating the embrace, and he may even kneel before the king, as does the speaker in *The Wanderer*.[27] If this is the case, then tears may well have fallen onto him from the greying one. If Beowulf is standing, however, assuming that Beowulf is taller, more erect in posture, or less stooped by age, we must consider the possibility that his tears may have fallen onto the greying one. What is clear is that Hrothgar has embraced Beowulf, and that one man touches another with that most taboo of bodily fluids, manly tears, whether a head lies on a shoulder or knee, or a face is buried in a chest. Hrothgar grants Beowulf's request to leave with a command to do so, but the *het* construction also allows Hrothgar to add his own wish that Beowulf should come again soon. Whether or not this will happen seems to be the crux of the episode.

Notice that halfway through the passage, due to damage to the top right corner of 174r, the editors have added a final -*n* to *seoððan* as well as the word *no* in line 1875.[28] The editors' note to this line begins: 'The text yields more transparent sense with the assumption of a lost negative adverb.'[29] 'After seoðða', they go on to explain, 'Thorkelin's amanuensis leaves a lengthy space, implying the loss of more than a single n.' The editors also attempt an argument on the basis of metrical parallels 'in the formally most regular poems'.[30] But both of these pieces of evidence are adduced in the interest of 'more transparent sense'. The editorial addition of *no* indicates that Hrothgar does not think he will ever see Beowulf again, which is the scenario modern readers associate with a tearful goodbye, and therefore yields 'more transparent sense' to the editors. Without *no*, however, we can assume that Hrothgar is in fact imagining a future reunion with Beowulf, which may explain why Mills has found tearful parallels in scenes of reunion. In fact, if a reunion calls for tears in Old English literature, it could be that Hrothgar is imagining this future scene of the two men 'modige on meþle' (emotional at meeting). This, then, would be the cause of Hrothgar's irrepressible 'boiling in the breast', as Lockett translates it,[31] but she also points out that Hrothgar's longing for his dear one remains unspoken, burning in his blood, firmly rooted in his 'mind-tethers'.[32]

Beowulf's empathy

What is going through Beowulf's mind at this point we do not know, but I would argue that he receives Hrothgar with empathy, as evinced by his first-person account of his journey once he returns home. His audience is yet another sad king, Hygelac, who greets him with claims of worry for the journey: 'Ic ðæs modceare / sorhwylmum seað' (I seethed with sorrow of soul and surging sorrows) (1992b–3a). As he begins to explain all that has occurred, Beowulf describes Grendel's work in the hall 'þær he worna fela / Sige-Scyldingum sorge gefremede, / yrmðe to aldre' (where he always caused the Danes so much sorrow and misery) (2003b–5a) with empathy for Hrothgar and his people. In particular, he notes that the loss of Æschere was the 'hreowa tornost' (cruellest of sorrows) (2129b) for Hrothgar, leaving him 'hreohmod' (troubled in mind) (2132a). In a seeming digression, Beowulf introduces Hrothgar's daughter Freawaru to the poem, empathetically imagining the precarious situation she is being married into as a peace-weaver, in parallel to Hildeburh's fate. He predicts that an old spearbearer, 'geomormod' (sad of mind) (2044a), with 'grim sefa' (a grim mind) (2043b), will incite revenge just as Guðlaf and Oslaf did. Unique among the humans in the poem, Beowulf's empathy extends even to the Grendelkin. It is only Beowulf who, in recounting his exploits, notes that Grendel left the hall 'modes geomor' (sad in mind) (2100a) after their fight. In fact, the narrator notes that Grendel's death did not seem 'sarlic' (painful) (842a) to them.[33] As for Grendel's mother, the narrator refers to her 'sorhfulne sið, sunu deoð wrecan' (sorrowful trip to avenge her son's death) (1278), and Beowulf echoes this in his retelling, stating that she 'siðode sorhfull' (travelled sorrowful) (2119a) to seek revenge.[34] If Beowulf can empathize with Freawaru's hypothetical sorrow and even monstrous sorrow, I have no doubt that he responded to Hrothgar with empathy in the flesh. But when faced with mourning men in Old English literature, scholars have not generally acknowledged evidence of their thoughts and feelings, nor responded with sensitivity and care to their suffering.

Despite a recent boom in empathy scholarship, even experts in the field acknowledge the term's short history and contested or multivalent meanings.[35] The word first appears in English as a borrowing from German around the turn of the twentieth century, but its current meaning is attested in 1946, and this definition was only added to the *OED* in 2014.[36] Nonetheless, the experience of empathy is a human one, rather than a recent development, as Antonina Harbus explains:

> Our understanding and empathy with the emotional complexity of the subjective experience represented in the [Old English] text [here, *Wulf and Eadwacer*] are predicated on comparable human psychological functioning shared by the creator and receiver of this text. Moreover, the apparent cross-cultural intelligibility of the text and its emotional texture points to consistency rather than variation in human apprehension of and cause for emotional pain, as well as the deep entrenchment of the reliance on poetry to represent and to engage with the emotional life.[37]

Thus, 1,000 years later, we can empathize with characters in medieval literature. But what is empathy? Richard Delgado defines it as 'the capacity to project or imagine the thoughts and feelings of another person'.[38] C. Daniel Batson explains that the term is used to refer to at least eight separate phenomena, but he synthesizes these into two aspects of empathy: knowing the internal state of another (i.e., their thoughts and feelings), and responding with sensitivity and care to their suffering.[39] Using these two criteria, we can also recognize when medieval figures such as Beowulf exhibit empathy themselves.

Harbus comments above on 'the reliance on poetry to represent and to engage with the emotional life'. Likewise, Britt Mize argues for a connection between literature and mentality for the Anglo-Saxons. 'Much Old English poetry is straightforwardly about mental states', he writes, 'but even that which is not in the ordinary sense "about" mentality still, somehow, is, returning insistently to qualities, conditions, and actions of the mind.'[40] In 2013 David Comer Kidd and Emanuele Castano argued that reading literary fiction fosters Theory of Mind in adults, and their findings were popularly reported as if reading literature increases empathy, though the study was later critiqued by other psychologists.[41] To the extent that fiction does foster empathy, it is worth wondering whether the digressions in *Beowulf* perform a similar function. After all, one of the most tragic scenes in the poem, the Finnsburh episode, is one such digression, and it must be one of the 'gyd ... soð ond sarlic' (true and painful songs) (2008–9) told at Heorot, as Beowulf recounts.

Beowulf himself gives voice to a digression within a digression when he describes the experience of a hanged man's father in the midst of his account of King Hrethel's sorrow. As Beowulf processes his dark thoughts and prepares for own death, he searches for parallels to understand his own situation and finds them in the experiences of other mourning men. First, he recalls the death of Herebeald at the hands of his brother, and its impact on their father King Hrethel, by whom Beowulf was fostered at the age of seven (2435–43 and 2462–71). This incident was 'hreðre hygemeðe' (mind-wearying to the heart) (2442a), and Hrethel 'heortan sorge / weallinde wæg' (carried welling sorrow in his heart) (2463b–4a) until it killed him. In Beowulf's own words, 'He ða mid þære sorhge, þe him sio sar belamp, / gumdream ofgeaf, Godes leoht geceas' (Then with the sorrow, the pain that befell him, he gave up the pleasures of men, chose God's light) (2468–9). Here Beowulf seems to confess that he too has chosen death in the midst of an untenable situation, but in the process he is showing empathy for the sadness of another king who was dear to him.

Within his account of this historical precedent, Beowulf introduces a hypothetical or fictional scenario featuring another mourning man: the father of a young man sentenced to hang (2444–62). This experience is 'geomorlic' (sad) (2444a) for the old man. When his son hangs, 'he gyd wrece, / sarigne sang' (he recites a sad song) (2446b–7a), not unlike Hildeburh did. Every morning he remembers his son's passing (2450). Then Beowulf offers an elegiac moment of his own creation that begins: 'Gesyhð sorhcearig on his suna bure / winsele westne, windge reste, / reotge berofene' (Sorrowful, in his son's empty chamber, he envisions the deserted hall and the windswept resting place, dreary, emptied) (2455–7a). Neither this man nor King Hrethel can avenge his son's death, and both are haunted by the loss until they choose death, for Hrethel chooses God's light (2469) and the hanged man's father takes to his bed: 'Gewiteð þonne on sealman, sorhleoð gæleð / an æfter anum; þuhte him eall to rum, / wongas ond wicstede' (Then he goes to his bed, sings one song of sorrow after another; the residence and the plains seem all too roomy to him) (2460–2a).[42] Since Beowulf has no son, it must not be the specifics of the situation but these emotions of helplessness and loss with which he empathizes.

The limits of empathy

Throughout this chapter, I have demonstrated that *Beowulf* is populated by mourning men, including the hero himself, who is in fact an exemplar of empathy towards the feelings of his fellow warriors. Why then does Beowulf seem oblivious to the fate of the Geatish people? With his death, the prophecy of the Geatish *meowle* is 'heregeongas … wælfylla worn, werudes egesan, / hynðo ond hæftnyd' (invasions, many slaughters, the terror of the troop, humiliation and captivity) (3153–5a). In denial of this reality, Beowulf consoles himself with the gold he leaves behind. One of his last wishes is to see the treasure so that he can die 'ðy seft' (more easily) (2749b). He gives thanks to God for the hoard he acquired 'for his people' (minum leodum) (2797b) and explains: 'Nu ic on maðma hord mine bebohte / frode feorhlege, fremmað gena / leoda þearfe' (Now that I have sold my old lifespan for this hoard of treasures, they will attend to the needs of the people) (2799–801a).[43] But gold is not what his people really need; they need a living lord to defend them.

   Rather than putting his people first by truly understanding their experience, Beowulf imagines what he, a noble lord, would need in this situation: namely, the wealth that enables his power in life, and failing that, the glory enabled by death. This is false empathy, for he has made the mistake of thinking that he knows what his people want.[44] Delgado's work on empathy, false empathy, and the empathic fallacy is fundamental to Critical Race Theory, and helps to elucidate the emotional crux that is the end of the poem.[45] To paraphrase Delgado, Beowulf has postulated a recipient who will like and appreciate what he would have wanted had he been in exactly that situation.[46] As a good lord, he is nonetheless 'beyond reproach',[47] and the poem itself becomes a vehicle of both his self-image and the hierarchical society that enables it. The poem, therefore, asks us to empathize with Beowulf's needs, rather than those of the Geats, who are denied the 'full due process of storytelling'.[48]

Beowulf's emotional life therefore offers two important lessons for early medievalists. First, the sorrow of both the hero and the other men of the poem, as well as the empathy Beowulf expresses for his fellow warriors, remind us that gender is culturally constructed, and that we must become aware of the filter of our own post-modern experience in order to see medieval literature on its own terms. Second, though it is based on class rather than race, Beowulf's false empathy for the Geatish people is an object lesson that is fundamental to Critical Race Theory. As Delgado explains:

> [F]alse empathy is worse than none at all, worse than indifference. It makes you over-confident, so that you can easily harm the intended beneficiary. You are apt to be paternalistic, thinking you know what the other really wants or needs. You can easily substitute your own goal for hers. You visualize what you would want if you were she, when your experiences are radically different, and your needs, too.[49]

Because 'the real kind, true empathy, is in extremely rare supply',[50] Delgado ultimately concludes by forswearing empathy altogether, arguing instead for white allyship in dismantling white supremacy. Meanwhile, when white early medievalists such as me find ourselves in sympathy with our non-white colleagues, we can question whether our empathy is false or true, and ask ourselves whether we are showing respect for the established scholarly discourse on race, citing minority voices, and – most importantly – listening to medievalists of colour, as we have been asked to do.[51]

Notes

1 The Finnsburh episode is one of the most famous digressions in *Beowulf*; the narrator recounts how the *scop* tells this story for entertainment in the hall. Hildeburh is a 'peace-weaver', a woman married off in an attempt to cement an alliance between tribes. She loses her son and brother in the same battle, and then loses her husband when they are avenged by her people. For further discussion, see below and Mary Kate Hurley's chapter in this volume, pp. 147–63. For consistency, I lean on R. D. Fulk, Robert E. Bjork, and John D. Niles's glossary in *Klaeber's Beowulf*, 4th edn (Toronto: University of Toronto Press, 2008), translating the short phrases in the first section of this chapter.

All citations to *Beowulf* are by line number from this edition, hereafter referred to as *Klaeber 4.*

2 What I object to is fetishization of Hildeburh in the service of creating a through-line from Tacitus to the Victorians to the present day, allowing us to ignore men's sadness by overemphasizing women's sorrow. The figure of the mourning woman became the focus of important feminist criticism such as Joyce Hill's 'Þæt wæs geomuru ides! A female stereotype examined', in Helen Damico and Alexandra Hennessy Olsen (eds), *New readings on women in Old English literature* (Bloomington, IN: Indiana University Press, 1990), pp. 235–47. See also Stacy S. Klein, *Ruling women: queenship and gender in Anglo-Saxon literature* (Notre Dame, IN: University of Notre Dame Press, 2006). Klein notes the presence of mourning women in other poems such as *Deor* and *The Fortunes of Men* (p. 99). She argues that the grief of Hildeburh allows readers to question and critique the heroic code, a reaction that helps to inaugurate a new, internal form of heroism, which preserves a space for the emotional lives of men.

3 See Helen Bennett, 'The female mourner at Beowulf's funeral: filling in the blanks/hearing the spaces', *Exemplaria*, 4.1 (1992), 35–50; Tauno F. Mustanoja, 'The unnamed woman's song of mourning over Beowulf and the tradition of ritual lamentation', *Neuphilologische Mitteilungen*, 68 (1967), 1–27.

4 *The Wanderer*, ed. G. P. Krapp and E. V. K. Dobbie, *The Exeter Book*, ASPR 3 (New York: Columbia University Press, 1936), pp. 134–7.

5 Tacitus, *Germania*, Loeb Classical Library 35, www.loebclassics.com/view/tacitus-germania/1914/pb_LCL035.171.xml (accessed 5 June 2019). Here is the full passage and its translation at pp. 170–1: 'Funerum nulla ambitio: id solum observatur, ut corpora clarorum virorum certis lignis crementur. struem rogi nec vestibus nec odoribus cumulant: sua cuique arma, quorundam igni et equus adicitur. sepulcrum caespes erigit: monumentorum arduum et operosum honorem ut gravem defunctis aspernantur. lamenta ac lacrimas cito, dolorem et tristitiam tarde ponunt. feminis lugere honestum est, viris meminisse.' ('In burial there is no ostentation: the single observance is to burn the bodies of their notables with special kinds of wood. They build a pyre, but do not load it with palls or spices: to each man his armour; to the fire of some his horse also is added. The tomb is a mound of turf: the difficult and tedious tribute of a monument they reject as too heavy on the dead. Weeping and wailing they put away quickly: sorrow and sadness linger. Lamentation becomes women: men must remember.').

6 Christopher B. Krebs, *A most dangerous book: Tacitus's Germania from the Roman Empire to the Third Reich* (New York: Norton, 2011), p. 49. See also Loretana de Libero, '*Precibus ac lacrimis*: tears in Roman historiographers', in Thorsten Fögen (ed.), *Tears in the Graeco-Roman world* (Berlin and New York: De Gruyter, 2009), pp. 209–34.

7 See Tacitus, *Germania*, pp. 150, 152.

8 *Oxford English Dictionary*, s.v. *comitatus*.

9 Krebs, *A most dangerous book*, pp. 46, 238.

10 Kristen Mills, 'Emotion and gesture in Hroðgar's farewell to Beowulf', in Alice Jorgensen, Frances McCormack, and Jonathan Wilcox (eds), *Anglo-Saxon emotions: reading the heart in Old English language, literature and culture* (Farnham: Ashgate, 2015), pp. 163–75, at 166.

11 Gale R. Owen-Crocker, *The four funerals in Beowulf* (Manchester: Manchester University Press, 2009).

12 Scyld himself awaited consolation for his destitute origins ('ærest wearð / feasceaft funden. He þæs frofre gebad') (6b–7), not a happy position to be in.

13 See Britt Mize's discussion of the term in *Traditional subjectivities: the Old English poetics of mentality* (Toronto: University of Toronto Press, 2013), pp. 175–81. *Klaeber 4* gives 'survivors of calamity'.

14 The last survivor voices his lament while burying the treasure of his now-extinct people in the barrow that will become the dragon's lair. The mound is later discovered by a runaway slave, who steals a golden cup in the hope of appeasing his lord, inadvertently waking the dragon and inciting its attacks. When forced to reveal the barrow, the slave is sad in mind as he leads Beowulf and his men there (2408).

15 Leslie Lockett explains the importance of welling and seething in the Anglo-Saxons' hydraulic model of the mind, our understanding of which can be distorted by a focus on mind–body dualism. See *Anglo-Saxon psychologies in the vernacular and Latin traditions* (Toronto: University of Toronto Press, 2011).

16 These dozen lines (3015–27) become an elegy for the exiled Geats that recalls the words of the last survivor.

17 These *bearn* are not minors but noblemen. The phrase is used in reference to the Danes and Geats who go to look for Æschere's body (1408) and to describe the comrades who abandoned Beowulf to the dragon (2597). The repetition of this phrase with the adjective 'battle-brave' must be deliberate and ironic.

18 Perhaps we can include his return to Geatland as an 'earm anhaga' (wretched solitary being) (2368a) after he heard the news of Hygelac's death.

19 Mills, 'Emotion and gesture', p. 164.

20 Similarly, after Grendel's mother is dead, Hrothgar reflects on the 'gyrn æfter gomene' (grief after joy) (1775) that Grendel had brought and 'modcare micel' (great sorrow of soul) (1778) that he suffered as a result. In other words, every time Beowulf delivers on the cessation of sorrow he has promised, Hrothgar remembers the twelve long years that have just come to an end.

21 Erin Sebo offers a cogent reading of this scene in '*Ne sorga*: grief and revenge in *Beowulf*', in Jorgensen, McCormack, and Wilcox (eds), *Anglo-Saxon emotions*, pp. 177–92, at 180. See also her discussion of the overemphasis on vengeance in the scholarly tradition at pp. 177–8.

22 See T. Wright, 'Hrothgar's tears', *Modern philology*, 65 (1967), 39–44; and Mary Dockray-Miller, 'Beowulf's tears of fatherhood', *Exemplaria*, 10 (1998), 1–28. A more nuanced reading of Hrothgar appears in Klein's Chapter 3: '*Beowulf* and the gendering of heroism' in *Ruling women*.

23 Lockett, *Anglo-Saxon psychologies*, pp. 82–3.

24 Ibid., p. 83.

25 Mills, 'Emotion and gesture', p. 165.

26 Ibid., p. 172. Moreover, in the hagiographic tradition that was no doubt familiar to the scribes of *Beowulf*, the generic conventions of the *uita* require a saint's followers to mourn upon their farewell; this includes Andreas, Guthlac, Martin, and even Christ. At the same time, we have not attended to the negative attitude towards sorrow exemplified by Ælfric and other Christian writers. Thus, the situation is far more complicated than our oversimplifications admit. See, for example, my 'Reversal of fortune, response, and reward in the Old English *Passion of Saint Eustace*', in Robin Norris (ed.), *Anonymous interpolations in Ælfric's Lives of Saints* (Kalamazoo, MI: Medieval Institute Publications, 2011), pp. 97–117.

27 The sleeping Wanderer dreams that 'he his mondryhten / clyppe ond cysse, ond on cneo lecge / honda ond heafod' (he embraced and kissed his lord, and laid hands and head on his knee) (41b–3a). The narrator states that in reality, the Wanderer did this 'hwilum ær in geardagum' (sometimes before in the old days) (43–4), so the dream may be a memory of the past, a present experience imagined by the dreamer, or a desired future reunion.

28 Cf. *wæs*, *breost*, and *on* supplied at the ends the next three lines in the manuscript.

29 *Klaeber 4*, p. 220.

30 Ibid.

31 Lockett, *Anglo-Saxon psychologies*, p. 83.

32 Ibid., p. 82.

33 On Grendel's monstrous lack of empathy, see Antonina Harbus, *Cognitive approaches to Old English poetry* (Cambridge: Cambridge University Press, 2012), pp. 126–9.

34 Unferth calls the swimming contest with Breca 'sorhfullne sið' (sorrowful journey) (512), and sea monsters can turn a voyage into 'sorhfulne sið' (1429a).

35 Jean Decety and William Ickes (eds), *The social neuroscience of empathy* (Cambridge, MA: MIT Press, 2009), p. vii.

36 Def. 2b: 'The ability to understand and appreciate another person's feelings, experience, etc.'

37 Harbus, *Cognitive approaches*, pp. 172–3. See also her 'Affective poetics: the cognitive basis of emotion in Old English poetry', in Jorgensen, McCormack, and Wilcox (eds), *Anglo-Saxon emotions*, pp. 19–34.

38 Richard Delgado, 'Rodrigo's eleventh chronicle: empathy and false empathy', *California law review*, 84.1 (1996), 61–100, at 68 n. 25.

39 C. Daniel Batson, 'These things called empathy: eight related but
distinct phenomena', in Decety and Ickes (eds), *The social neuroscience
of empathy*, pp. 3–15. This essay comprises the book's first section,
entitled 'What is empathy?'

40 Mize, *Traditional subjectivities*, p. 9.

41 David Comer Kidd and Emanuele Castano, 'Reading literary fiction
improves Theory of Mind', *Science*, 342 (2013), 377–80; M. E. Panero
et al., 'Does reading a single passage of literary fiction really improve
Theory of Mind? An attempt at replication', *Journal of personality and
social psychology*, 111.5 (2016), e46–e54.

42 Carol Clover calls his lament 'precisely the effect of disabled masculinity', but since Beowulf, the paragon of heroic masculinity, invents and
invokes this sad man as a parallel to his own sad situation, and since
this father's experience of grief until death seems similar to that of
King Hrethel and the last survivor, I disagree. See Clover, 'Regardless
of sex: men, women, and power in early Northern Europe', *Speculum*,
68 (1993), 363–88, at 383 n. 68.

43 This is the translation by R. M. Liuzza, who notes that the verb is
'unambiguously plural'. See *Beowulf: a new verse translation*, 2nd edn
(Peterborough, Ont.: Broadview Press, 2000).

44 See Delgado, 'Rodrigo's eleventh chronicle', 70ff.

45 See, for example, Richard Delgado and Jean Stefancic, *Critical Race
Theory: an introduction* (New York: New York University Press, 2012),
especially 'The empathic fallacy', pp. 27–9.

46 Delgado, 'Rodrigo's eleventh chronicle', 74.

47 Ibid., 78.

48 Ibid., 85.

49 Ibid., 94.

50 Ibid., 73.

51 See, for example, the comments by Jonathan Hsy and the bibliography on
race and medieval studies at http://www.inthemedievalmiddle.com/2017/06/
morevoices-citation-inclusion-and.html (accessed 5 June 2019). The
Medievalists of Color website is http://medievalistsofcolor.com. My
thanks to Eileen Joy, Dana Oswald, Mary Rambaran-Olm, and the
editors for their comments on a draft of this chapter. I am solely
responsible for any remaining errors and infelicities.

11

Differing intimacies: *Beowulf* translations by Seamus Heaney and Thomas Meyer

David Hadbawnik

A reader sits down with a book. The book contains a translation of an old poem, a poem written – or composed, passed down orally, pieced together over time, eventually copied into a manuscript, edited and printed – in a dead language, Old English. The act of reading this poem in translation is a kind of intimacy. But what kind? The reader wishes to come close to, forge a connection with, the original poem in some way. Perhaps they want to hear echoes of the sound of the dead language, its rhythms and patterns; perhaps they want to get a sense of the culture from which the poem was drawn; perhaps they want to understand how the poem makes meaning – through imagery, language, poetic effects, and concepts – and what the poem means. Perhaps they simply want to follow the narrative of the poem, which after all involves heroes, journeys, and monsters, and in the process to be entertained. This reader may have never encountered the poem before and have little or no sense of the source language from which it has been translated; or the reader may be a student of, even an expert in, that source language. The relative level of expertise and experience will certainly govern the reader's attention to and expectations for all of the above-mentioned areas of intimacy with the source text by way of the translation.

But there is a problem, related precisely to these expectations, which winds up being coded as 'fidelity' – how closely does the translation follow the word-for-word sense and meaning of the source text? – vs. 'creativity' – what kinds of liberties are taken, how 'poetic' is the translation? There is an assumption that greater accuracy with respect to the source language means a less pleasurable read – if 'pleasurable' means surprising, innovative, and poetic – while conversely, greater creativity implies a lack of fidelity to the language and literal meanings of the original text, to the point where the new text ceases to be considered a translation at all and is dismissed as an 'adaptation' or 'version' of an original. Poets who approach translation from a less than expert-level proficiency in the source language seem especially prone to having their translations damned with the faint praise of being creative at the expense of rigour and accuracy.

What these characterizations alert us to is the fact that the translator is not a neutral conduit to the source text – not a disinterested matchmaker for the reader's intimacy with the poem, but an active sort of 'Pandarus' with their own agenda, arranging not only what might be called the 'traditional' intimacies of translation outlined above, those that look back at and attempt to 'carry over' the language and sense of the source text, but also different and unexpected intimacies. In other words, the reader, in choosing one translation over another, is necessarily consenting to intimacy of a sort with the translator. The reader who seeks out a translation by a poet is, arguably, seeking these different and unexpected forms of intimacy. Intimacy with language; but perhaps with the poet's own (contemporary) language as much or more than with the old, dead language of the source. Intimacy with culture; but perhaps culture in the sense of the socio-intellectual milieu out of which the poet emerges and to which they respond, as much or more than the long-ago culture from which the poem comes down to us. Intimacy with *poetry*; but the poetry with which the poet is on intimate terms, their own poetry and the poetry that has influenced them, as much as or more than the source poem. With this in mind, I will examine Seamus Heaney's and Thomas Meyer's respective *Beowulf* translations in terms of the intimacies they forge and disclose.

The notion of 'intimacy' as applied to translation can, I argue, help break (or at least sidestep) the binary outlined above between 'accuracy' and 'creativity'. To be intimate with a given text – to have a closeness, a familiarity, a deep acquaintance, even a sort of 'intercourse'[1] – reflects an altogether different relationship than the subordinate one implied by the *'traduttore, traditore'* formula that so many critics feel compelled to grapple with, often acknowledging that 'betrayal' is a basic fact of translation.[2] In his 'poem-essay' on 'dystranslation', Chris Piuma introduces the idea of intimacy as a critical term.[3] Critiquing the idea of 'faithfulness' in translation, Piuma argues that we should instead consider 'intimacies' between texts, even taking into account the 'extratextual intimacies' (allusions, influences, and so on) that an original text already includes prior to being translated. Acknowledging that not all kinds of intimacy

are 'positive, wanted, or healthy', Piuma adds that we can still use
the idea of intimacy as a way to put the relationship between source
and translation on a more playful, equitable footing, one that offers
agency and independence to both parties.[4] Writing about translations
from Old English, Daniel Remein develops a related idea:

> translating the medieval as betrayal; as double-agency; as turning,
> the work of a turn-coat, as the work of a wolf in sheep's clothing
> – not the classical notion of a betrayal of an 'original,' not the betrayal
> of some originary Middle Ages, but one of the present. This would
> be a specifically queer betrayal, as the work of a fifth column
> embedded within the present and working on behalf of the past – a porous
> compromising of the proper which promises life mixed heterogene-
> ously and queerly with the other.[5]

Remein argues that W. H. Auden's early poem 'The Secret Agent'
is just such an act of 'queer betrayal' of the Old English poem
Wulf and Eadwacer. Auden engages the older poem through an
allusive kind of translation, one that preserves the difficulties and
ambiguities of the original rather than smoothing them out into
homogeneous, straightforward, contemporary English verse. Auden's
poem, according to Remein, is an act of 'treachery' that gleefully
inverts the 'translation as betrayal' formula, in part through a sort
of desire for the older poem that results in 'a queer mixing of times
and languages ... *a mixing of sexualities*'.[6]

Auden's own understanding of this process involved something
he called 'Literary Transference', and Remein explains Auden's
'erotic' attachment to certain poems in terms of the poet's own
experience with Freudian analysis and the intense intimacy of the
analyst/analysand relationship.[7] The practice of 'talk' in therapeutic
analysis is, I believe, a fruitful model for the translational intimacy
I am trying to describe – not only what it is, but also what it is for.
This is especially true in the '#MeToo' moment; we should not
forget that there is a complex set of relationships at work between
translator and source text, translator and reader, and so on. Leo
Bersani describes the 'impersonal intimacy of the psychoanalytic
dialogue, the intimate talk without sex', in which the analyst and
analysand 'have to endure the sexual – its conflicts, frustrations,
jealousy, the drama of misaimed desire endemic to the sexual relation',
in order to 'emerge on the other side of the sexual'.[8] The process
Bersani describes is one that risks intense closeness and desire – all
the feelings involved in an erotic relationship, without the actual
sex – for the sake of discovery, revelation, and freedom.[9]

Thinking in terms of the above-described type of intimacy can, I hope, move the conversation in a different direction than the usual binaries of accurate/creative, faithful/betraying, etc. in evaluating translations of classic poems. Instead, I would like to explore Meyer's and Heaney's different intimacies with *Beowulf* – what they risk in engaging with it and what their translations discover and reveal. What 'extratextual' intimacies does each author bring to his translation – that is to say, what *other* texts, influences, and ideas is the translation in close contact with? Heaney, an Irish poet writing in English, engages with *Beowulf* via a sort of 'postcolonial' intimacy, finding permission for a linguistic project of working through the regional vernacular, and is prompted by the poem's preoccupation with conflict and uneasy alliances to make connections with modern regional geopolitical conflicts. Meyer, meanwhile, forges a kind of 'postmodern' intimacy, marked by an intense closeness with and desire for the sound of the Old English, as well as an engagement with modernist poets who helped revive interest in elements of Old English verse.

Both of the above-mentioned approaches by Heaney and Meyer inform the issue of intimacy within the text and how such moments are handled by the translators. In other words, whereas a reader of (or listener to) the original *Beowulf* may have felt a sense of intimacy with the poem for a variety of reasons – familiarity with the stories, characters, language rhythms, etc. – a reader encountering *Beowulf* today, in modern English, will necessarily require different modes of intimacy. This last idea of intimacy is perhaps another way of asking how the translators bring the material to life, making both the horrors and joys of the poem immediate for modern readers. Perhaps, indeed, this is a quality that poet-translators at their most adventurous are especially equipped to provide, helping to remind us that early medieval readers, listeners, and poets would have encountered myriad types of intimacy (as well as challenges and difficulties) with a given poem.

The critical positioning and response to Heaney's and Meyer's respective translations displays the tension between the extremes of supposed faithfulness and unfaithful creativity, as the terms used to describe them fall along a heavily coded spectrum. Heaney's *Beowulf* is labelled 'a new verse translation' on its cover, while its back cover advertises the 'new and convincing reality' that Heaney's verse gives the epic poem.[10] Yet Heaney's translation causes an 'anxiety' among those trained in Old English who have seemed eager to show in reviews 'where Heaney gets it right or falls short'.[11] Meanwhile,

Meyer's *Beowulf*, even as it is hailed for being 'a vivid re-imagining' of the poem, has been called an 'adaptation' by some critics.[12] To some extent these responses are influenced by the markedly different publication histories of the translations. Heaney's was commissioned by Norton, 'intended to replace a scholarly prose version by E. Talbot Donaldson', and the poet worked with experts in Old English who corrected some of his translational choices.[13] Meyer, meanwhile, undertook his translation during the 1970s as part of a senior thesis project at Bard College under the direction of poet Robert Kelly; his *Beowulf* was unknown, circulating only in manuscript form, until its publication by punctum books in 2012.[14]

While the binary of accuracy vs. creativity is a vast oversimplification of actual translation theory, many critics (even those who write creatively and translate themselves) adhere to it in terms of what they seem to value in a translation. A brief overview of a few examples will suffice. At one end of the spectrum is Jorge Luis Borges, who seems willing to forgive (and even to prize) any inaccuracies of diction and content from source to target language so long as the translation is 'rethought' as he writes *'in the wake of a literature'*, that is, the rich literature of the target language.[15] Vladimir Nabokov, on the other hand, insists that

> [t]he person who desires to turn a literary masterpiece into another language, has only one duty to perform, and this is to reproduce with absolute exactitude the whole text, and nothing but the text. The term 'literal translation' is tautological since anything but that is not truly a translation but an imitation, an adaptation or a parody.[16]

These are relative extremes; yet as Lawrence Venuti writes,

> The history of translation theory can in fact be imagined as a set of changing relationships between the relative autonomy of the translated text, or the translator's actions, and two other concepts: equivalence and function. Equivalence has been understood as 'accuracy', 'adequacy', 'correctness', 'correspondence', 'fidelity', or 'identity'; it is a variable notion of how the translation is connected to the foreign text. Function has been understood as the potentiality of the translated text to release diverse effects, beginning with the communication of information and the production of a response comparable to the one produced by the foreign text in its own culture.[17]

Even in Venuti's nuanced characterization of translation theory, we discern the way in which a translation is inextricably tethered to the source text, with the latter governing the evaluation of everything from the former's language to its perceived impact in a given culture. This evaluative framework is, indeed, to some extent inevitable, if not always desirable. In Walter Benjamin's classic essay 'The Task of the Translator', he writes, 'The traditional concepts in any discussion of translations are fidelity and license', and, though he seems to want to move beyond looking at them as 'conflicting tendencies', he does not entirely do away with the concepts.[18]

The position of *Beowulf* within the 'literary polysystem' (the set of translated and original texts coexisting and valued in a given culture) of English verse is undoubtedly unique.[19] As the Old English epic poem *par excellence* – one that did not appear on the literary scene until the nineteenth or even arguably the twentieth century[20] – it poses a special challenge, but also offers a special opportunity, to translators in modern English. *Beowulf* (and, more broadly, Old English verse) is a compelling instance of a translated text 'participat[ing] actively in shaping the centre of the polysystem'.[21] As Chris Jones argues, the recovery of Old English forms, language, and rhythms was a major impetus for the 'poetic energy' of the modernist movement at the turn of the century.[22] Led by Ezra Pound, 'these poets contributed to a modernist aesthetic that is in some ways more sympathetically attuned to so-called primitive art, or to the verse of the early Middle Ages (which too is far from primitive), than to that of the Romantic or Victorian eras'.[23] In other words, Old English alliterative verse offered a key model for modernist poets in breaking out of rhyme-based iambic pentameter. As Itamar Even-Zohar writes, describing '[a] highly interesting paradox': 'translation, by which new ideas, items, characteristics can be introduced into a literature, becomes a means to preserve traditional taste'.[24] *Beowulf* manifests this paradox in interesting ways. Though it offers 'the shock of the old' to help poets in English emerge from more recent calcified trends, as noted above,[25] the 'tradition' that Old English verse helps preserve is often, if not primarily, a linguistic one, giving poets access to what they think of as pure origins in English.[26]

Heaney's linguistic intimacy

Seamus Heaney reports that an unexpected intimacy with a particular Old English word, 'þolian', acted as a 'linguistic loophole' that allowed him to find a way forward with his *Beowulf* translation. Writing at some length in his introduction about discovering the word in a glossary of the poem and recognizing it as 'thole', he writes, 'I gradually realized that it was not strange at all, for it was the word that older and less educated people would have used in the country where I grew up'.[27] The word, in both Old English and Heaney's regional vernacular, means 'to endure, suffer'.[28] Heaney recounts tracing 'thole' north into Scotland, across the water to Northern Ireland, and from there into Irish and eventually the American South, where it crops up in the poetry of John Crowe Ransom.[29] Klaeber's *Beowulf* notes the word as 'archaic – Northumbrian', so the lineage sketched by Heaney is plausible.[30] Indeed, though *Beowulf* 'was written in a standard late West Saxon poetic dialect',[31] the poem 'displays evidence of all four Old English dialects', though it is unclear at what stage in its composition or copying the linguistic strains of the poem took shape.[32] Heaney describes the permission provided by his discovery as something akin to 'illumination by philology ... *þolian* had opened my right-of-way'.[33]

The key to understanding this linguistic 'right-of-way' lies in the greater thrust of Heaney's poetry. For Heaney, the permission he takes is to explore regional vernacular, rather than to mine Old English per se for linguistic inspiration. In other words, and unlike Meyer and many of his modernist forebears, Heaney's approach to *Beowulf* has less to do with cleansing his vocabulary of the Latinate and more to do with delving deeper into terms preserved on the margins of English, a project already underway in his other translations and the larger body of his poetry. In the wake of the 'Irish Troubles' and especially after 1990, 'Heaney has continued to explore his lifelong interest in regionalism as cohering in a distinct geopolitical identity through language – specifically in Irish and English and the idioms of Hiberno-English and Ulster English'.[34] As a poet, Heaney develops a sophisticated idea of regional vernacular language offering a way for local groups to see themselves reflected in the symbolic order, clearly expanding on ideas found in Benedict Anderson's *Imagined Communities*.[35]

Heaney's perception of Old English is both paradoxical and somewhat fanciful, as his own poetry 'exhibits both resentment and admiration towards its Old English heritage'.[36] He readily partakes of the idea of Old English as a sort of origin or foundation, describing it in his introduction to *Beowulf* as a 'first stratum of the language',[37] and even seems to exaggerate the importance of Old English to his poetic influences such as Gerard Manley Hopkins and Ted Hughes. '[Fo]r Heaney', writes Jones, 'the study and translation of Old English is imagined as a form of apolitical escapism from some of the cultural divisions of his own situation.'[38] Though imaginary and fraught with contradictions, Heaney's perception of Old English – its 'foundational' status as well as its regional character in filtering through his poetic influences – is as generative as it is complex. Jones writes, 'In constructing a poetic ancestry for himself that enlists both Old English and Hopkins, Heaney wishes to construct a poetics of devolution and democratization out of their shared characteristics.'[39] The result of this construction is no less arbitrary than that arrived at by poets prior to Heaney, certainly including Pound. But this Old English-informed 'poetic ancestry' offers Heaney warrant for the politically charged regionalism that infuses his poetry.

In Heaney's introduction, he mentions his use of regional vernacular terms such as 'graith', 'harness', and 'hoked'.[40] There is a particularly interesting cluster of regional diction in Heaney's translation of part of Beowulf's account of his fight with Grendel:

> ac hyne sar hafað
> in niðgripe   nearwe befongen
> balwon bendum;   ðær abidan sceal
> maga mane fah   miclan domes
> hu him scir metod   scrifan wille. (975b–979)

> (but he the wound has
> in inescapable grip tightly seized
> deadly bond; there he must wait
> how the mighty God will decide for him.)

Heaney writes,

> He is hasped and hooped and hirpling with pain,
> limping and looped in it. Like a man outlawed
> for wickedness, he must await
> the mighty judgement of God in majesty. (975–8)

The first line and a half, in which the hero describes his victory over Grendel, shows Heaney folding together colourful terms derived from Old English as well as Scots-Irish regional vernacular.[41] There is little direct warrant for any of the alliterating words – 'hasped', 'hooped', 'hirpling', 'limping', 'looped' – in the original text. Yet, as a rhetorical flourish to close Beowulf's account of his defeat of Grendel, and a way to mimic the alliterative stress of the lines, the words fit. 'Hasp' from Old English means 'a contrivance for fastening a door or lid', and would certainly count as an archaism.[42] But 'hasp' (or 'hesp') would presumably have been known to Heaney as a regional term via Scots, in which it essentially means 'ball of yarn' and has a figurative sense: 'a confused, obscure state of affairs,

a difficult situation, quandary'.[43] It is unclear which 'hasp' Heaney
means – either works given the situation, and there is perhaps no
need to limit the possible meanings. 'Hooped' appears to be derived
from later Old English/Old Frisian 'hop', but 'hirpling' ('To move
with a gait between walking and crawling', etc.) again draws our
attention as a regional word. It appears to be 'chiefly Scottish and
northern dialect', and indeed the term seems to have fallen out of
use in English but maintained some currency in Scots.[44]

Heaney's approach responds to a difficult linguistic problem in
translating from Old into modern English: whether 'the target
language of the translation should colonize the foreign text' or 'the
foreign text should itself be allowed to colonize the host language'.[45]
Or to put it another way, whether to 'domesticate' the source language
or 'foreignize' the target language via translation.[46] In the former
approach, 'strangeness is cleansed from the source text as it passes
through the customs control of translation', while the second allows
for and even welcomes whatever strangeness results from importing
terms from the source language.[47] Given the nearly century-long
predominance of Benjamin's notion that the translator 'must expand
and deepen his language by means of the source language', it is
safe to say that some importing of disorienting 'strangeness' is
assumed and even desired in translation.[48]

Yet 'What does it mean to let the strangeness of the foreign text
affect the target language when the foreign text is also already *in*
one's language?'[49] For most contemporary translators of Old English,
including Pound, the answer has been archaism – of diction, syntax,
or both. Rejecting the alterity of archaism, Heaney opts instead for
vernacular idiom to introduce a sense of strangeness. His rendering of the verse generally features two beats per half-line and just
enough alliteration to give a feel of the original, but otherwise the
syntax and diction read as fairly standard, contemporary English.[50]
Indeed, Eagleton finds Heaney's seeming ease with rendering Old
English rhythms into colloquial English to be the strongest part
of his translation:

> This poet is so superbly in command that he can risk threadbare,
> throwaway, matter-of-fact phrases like 'of no small importance' or
> 'the best part of a day'. He has a casual way with the alliterative
> pattern of the original, which helps to strip its craft of portentous
> self-consciousness and frees up its syntax to move more nimbly.[51]

However, there is no critical consensus on the effectiveness of
Heaney's diction in the poem, and even some disagreement on how
to characterize it. Contrary to Eagleton, Remein critiques Heaney

for 'convert[ing] Old English to popular contemporary workshop verse'.[52] Daniel Donoghue, meanwhile, notes the way that Heaney's introduction and interviews on his language choices help situate the perception of the poem's diction as perhaps more heavily vernacular than it actually is; in fact, Heaney's translation is often rendered in 'Standard English' that is 'merely un-Klaeber-like', meaning that Heaney appears to deliberately break from the glossing apparatus in the definitive edited version of *Beowulf*.[53] It is this, in part, that invites the charge of 'inaccuracy' in Heaney's translation; perhaps it is ultimately an 'idiolect' that 'subtly disorients each reader'.[54] What Heaney risks in constructing this idiolect is writing 'no language'.[55] Yet the risk pays off in inviting the reader to share an intimacy with the regional vernacular – derived from his Scots-Irish background – that predominates in all of his poetry, thus drawing those readers into his postcolonial linguistic concerns. This type of intimacy sheds light on the linguistic difference and ambiguity latent in the original poem that can seem obscure, even among experts.

Thomas Meyer's 'perverse' postmodernist intimacy

Meyer's approach to poetic diction and other sound and rhythmic effects is quite different, revealing an obsession with sounds and poetic effects in the Old English. A close examination of one striking passage, provided first here with my own translation, illustrates several elements of his style:

Hæfde se goda   Geata leoda
cempan gecorone   þara þe he cenoste
findan mihte.   Fiftyne sum
sundwudu sohte.   secg wisade,
lagucræftig mon,   landgemyrcu.
Fyrst forð gewat;   flota wæs on yðum;
bat under beorge.   Beornas gearwe
on stefn stigon.   Streamas wundon,
sund wið sande.   Secgas bæron
on bearm nacan   beorhte frætwe,
guðsearo geatolic;   guman ut scufon,
weras on wilsið,   wudu bundenne.
Gewat þa ofer wægholm,   winde gefysed,
flota famiheals,   fugle gelicost,
oð þæt ymb antid   oþres dogores
wundenstefna   gewaden hæfde,
þæt ða liðende   land gesawon,

brimclifu blican,   beorgas steape,
side sænæssas;   þa wæs sund liden,
eoletes æt ende.   þanon up hraðe
Wedera leode   on wang stigon,
sæwudu sældon   syrcan hrysedon,
guðgewædo;   Gode þancedon
þæs þe him yþlade   eaðe wurdon. (205–28)

(The hero had from the Geatish people
chosen warriors that were the bravest
he might find; with fourteen others
went to the ship; he led the men,
sea-skilled man, to the shore's boundary.
Time passed; they went over waves,
boat beneath cliffs. Well-equipped warriors
stood on the prow; the water eddied,
sea on sand. The men carried
below decks gleaming prizes,
splendid armour; the men pushed off,
eager for the journey on well-made ship.
They went over the waves driven by wind,
the foamy-necked ship just like a bird,
and then after due time, on the second day
the ship with curved prow had arrived
so the sailors saw the land,
bright sea-cliffs, high peaks,
broad headlands; the sea was crossed,
their journey over. Quickly then
the Geatish warriors stepped on to land,
the ship tied up; their chainmail clanked,
their war-outfits. They thanked God
for making the sea-path easy.)

Meyer translates the passage:

He picked a company from the best men he could find.

15 sought seawood,
led to land's edge
by seawise warrior,

set keel to breakers,
left
        shore's ledge,
leapt
        churned sand.

Sea surge bore forth
    bright cargo:
weapons, trappings,
hearts keen to man
    timberbound,
wavelapped,
    windwhipped,
foamthroated bird.

        Ship floated. Sail filled.
        A day & a day prow plowed
        & crew saw bright cliffs,
        steep hills, wide beaches.

        Sea crossed. Land at last.
        Boat moored. Byrnes shook.

Weder men thanked God for an easy voyage over waves.[56]

Meyer's translation, with its narrow columns of verse sandwiched
as it were by longer, one-sentence lines at the top and bottom of
a single page, is characteristic of his approach in composing tight,
visually arresting lyrics that employ margins and negative space in
suggestive ways. Here, the shift of the narrow columns from left
to right seems meant to mimic the journey itself (as well as allude
to previous long-form modernist poems).[57] And while Meyer's
short lines appear to considerably condense the Old English, it is
worth noting that both versions fill exactly twenty-four lines. Meyer
admits that he had 'no training in Anglo-Saxon' before taking on
his translation work;[58] his major influences were modernist poets
and writers such as Pound, Basil Bunting, Gertrude Stein, Louis
Zukofsky, and Christopher Logue.[59] In terms of diction, Meyer adds
that 'translating *Beowulf* presented him with 'a real gymnasium
for trying out the possibilities of a poetic language'.[60] And for
Meyer – again influenced by modernist attitudes to English such
as those of Pound and Bunting – 'one of the most profound effects
Anglo-Saxon had on me from the beginning and to this day ... is
avoiding the Latinate'.[61]

    The persistent impression Meyer gives of further shrinking and
shortening the verse is all the more remarkable considering that
Old English already seems so dense with its colourful, figurative
compounds and kennings, and therefore confronts the translator

with an array of diverging variants in modern English.[62] As Jiří
Levý writes:

> It is a notorious fact that languages differ in the density of lexical
> segmentation of a given semantic field ... The broader the segmenta-
> tion in the source language when compared to that of the target
> language, the greater the DISPERSION OF TRANSLATION
> VARIANTS becomes ... On the contrary, the finer the lexical
> segmentation of the source language in comparison to that of the
> target language, the more limited is the dispersion of translation
> variants. *Diverging* or *converging* tendencies in choosing single lexical
> units (and of course the means of a higher order as well) are operative
> throughout the process of translating, and they are responsible for
> the ultimate relation between the source and target texts.[63]

In practice, Meyer often responds to the Old English with a
different sort of intimacy than Heaney. This intimacy is comparable
to the 'perverse' obsession with the sound of Homer's Greek that
drives poet David Melnick's 'homophonic' translation of the *Iliad*,
a project that, like Meyer's, was undertaken under the influence of
modern and postmodern poets during the 1970s.[64] Although Melnick,
unlike Meyer, did know the source language, his translation deliberately avoids syntactic or semantic sense and hews instead to
Homer's sound, with the result that he renders the poem with a
'multitude of Englishes', for example: 'Pied dapple lentoid doe cat,
the old year rain neck atom bane. / Heck, say yes, say stay, sonny.
You'd mate on pay rib bean moan.'[65] As Sean Reynolds describes
the translation, 'A relation to Homer, or, a relation *with* Homer;
one so intimate, in fact, as to be inscrutable.'[66] This relation is
styled a 'homophonic kiss', as the translator moves his mouth over
the sounds of the original poem, risking the loss of sense and inviting
fragmentation in pursuit of a perverse obsession:

> The directed 'beating' of the kissing mouth further insists upon
> hospitality to the foreign mouth: moving with it, not just duplicating,
> but complementing and completing its articulations. Keeping in mind
> also the proposed *desire* of translation, the synchronization of this
> kiss is at once a union of two mouths as well as a manifestation of
> the internal *erōs* of division.[67]

Meyer is not nearly as obsessed as Melnick, though his translation at times veers towards the intimacy of the homophonic kiss
and indulges in certain effects and sounds derived from the Old
English.

Where Heaney is led to explore the sounds and idiom of northern-Scots-Irish regional vernacular, Meyer often amplifies the sound of the Old English and moves towards a clipped diction. This is clear in the first few lines of the passage quoted above. Meyer renders 'sundwudu sohte' with the literal 'sought seawood', simply bringing the kenning over wholesale. He follows this by picking up the sound of 'secg wisade, / lagucræftig mon, landgemyrcu' (208b–209), transforming it to 'led to land's edge / by seawise warrior', using the sound of 'secg' to suggest 'edge', while 'wisade' seems to inform his compound substitution for 'lagu-cræftig', 'seawise' (which also echoes the sound of 'seawood'), and employing convergence, in Levý's terms, reducing the repetition of words for 'man' in Old English – 'secg' and 'mon' – to 'warrior'. This is one of the ways that Meyer manages to condense the Old English. Heaney, for the same lines, maintains and even increases the repetition, writing, 'the warrior boarded the boat as captain, / a canny pilot along coast and currents'.[68]

Meyer demonstrates another method of condensing the verse in the lines that follow:

> set keel to breakers,
> left
>   shore's ledge,
> leapt
>   churned sand.
> Sea surge bore forth
>   bright cargo:

After quoting Pound's *Cantos*, the next six lines consist of single-syllable words (until the last word, 'cargo') that all take a stress. The arrangement of discrete words and phrasal fragments zig-zagging across the column seems, again, meant to mimic the motion of the ship, while also offering the eye (and breath) a break from the heavy accents. The language certainly *looks* to be derived from Old English, and words such as 'shore', 'ledge', and 'churn' indeed show a Germanic/Old English etymology.[69] Further suggesting the Old English diction is the tight weave of sounds, not only alliteration but also assonance, with 'left ... ledge ... leapt', 'churned ... surge', and 'bore forth'.

Finally, with a tendency perhaps inspired by Edwin Morgan, whose *Beowulf* translation he mentions as being one of the few he admires,[70] Meyer invents and adapts a large number of compounds.

In the above passage, 'seawood' and 'seawise' have already been mentioned. Further down we find successively:

> timberbound,
> wavelapped,
>   windwhipped,
> foamthroated bird.

'Timberbound' is adapted from 'wudu bundenne' (216b), 'wave-lapped' from 'wægholm' (217a), 'windwhipped' from 'winde gefysed' (217b), and 'foamthroated' from 'famiheals' (218a); and Meyer has eliminated the comparative 'fugle gelicost' (218b) and simply made the ship a bird. Heaney, on the other hand, maintains the simile, writing, 'and foam at her neck, she flew like a bird' (218). Elsewhere, Meyer frequently invents compounds, expanding the Old English 'feond' (725b) to 'chaosfiend' in describing Grendel's approach to the hall.[71] Heaney frequently uses compounds in his original poetry, especially his verse that directly responds to Old English.[72] His *Beowulf* is not devoid of compounds, for example coining 'troll-dam' for 'Grendles magan' (1391); but compared to Meyer they are far less in evidence.

In terms of his translation's technical effects, Meyer thus points to and quotes from the modernist works out of which his poetics develops, while also displaying an oral (or aural) obsession with the sounds of Old English. The intimacy of his translation invites readers to share the experience of those sounds filtered through twentieth-century modernist poets such as Pound and others.

Intimacies within and beyond Beowulf

Heaney and Meyer bring different kinds of intimacies and go in strikingly different directions with a particularly evocative passage near the end of the poem. After Beowulf's fateful battle with the dragon in which he is mortally wounded, the Geats gather at his funeral to mourn their king. A Geatish woman is described lamenting her fallen lord and the uncertain future:

> swylce giomorgyd   Geatisc anmeowle
> [aefter Biowulfe]   bundenheorde
> sang sorgcearig   saelðe geneahhe
> þæt hio hyre hearmdagas   hearde ondrede
> wælfylla worn   werudes egesan
> hyðo ond hæftnyd.   Heofon rece swealg. (3150–5)

(so too a death-dirge a solitary Geatish woman
for Beowulf, cruelly bound,
she sang sorrowful, earnestly of fortune
that she for herself days of harm fiercely dreaded,
a multitude of slaughter-feasts, terror of troops,
rapine and bondage. Heaven swallowed the smoke.)

The woman probably does not bear any special relationship to the dead hero – she is not his widow, but a representative figure dressed for mourning and expressing the grief, worry, and uncertainty about the future appropriate to the situation. The ending of the passage, literally 'heaven smoke swallowed', is 'perhaps best read in juxtaposition ... of human suffering with a matter-of-fact observation on natural, though personified, phenomena [which] expresses the indifference of the universe to that suffering'.[73]

Heaney translates the lines thus:

A Geat woman too sang out in grief;
with hair bound up, she unburdened herself
of her worst fears, a wild litany
of nightmare and lament: her nation invaded,
enemies on the rampage, bodies in piles,
slavery and abasement. Heaven swallowed the smoke. (3150–5)

At first glance, Heaney's rendering of the passage appears fairly straightforward and conservative. Heaney uses a light alliterative touch – 'Geat ... grief' / 'hair bound ... unburdened herself' / 'worst ... wild' / 'nightmare ... nation'. He also employs caesura in all but the first line of the passage, on each side of which he skilfully manages two stresses, following the rules of Old English versification. Heaney's handling of line 3151 is especially striking: the first half of the line is badly damaged, and sense and alliteration leads Klaeber to suggest 'aefter Biowulfe', which Heaney judiciously leaves out. Yet from the compound word 'bundenheorde', Heaney fills in the first half of the line as 'with hair bound up' – the literal meaning of 'bundenheorde' – and in the second half of the line extrapolates 'she unburdened herself', which completes a chiasmic alliterative sequence and gives an approximation of the sound of 'bundenheorde'. The last line of the passage, too, is a triumph of understated accuracy. 'Slavery and abasement' sacrifice strict alliteration but maintain an assonant rhythm, and neatly match 'hýnðo ond hæftnýd', 'humiliation and captivity', while 'Heaven swallowed the smoke' is, syntax aside, quite literal for 'Heofon réce swealg'.

But there is one sequence that deviates from the straightforward feel of Heaney's version, as he ties this moment to contemporary postcolonial tensions. Heaney writes, 'a wild litany / of nightmare and lament: her nation invaded'. Of the passage Heaney remarks in his introduction,

> The Geat woman who cries out in dread as the flames consume the body of her dead lord could come straight from a late-twentieth-century news report, from Rwanda or Kosovo; her keen is a nightmare glimpse into the minds of people who have survived traumatic, monstrous events and who are now being exposed to a comfortless future.[74]

The word 'nation', indeed, while dating at least from the late medieval period in English, originally referred to a common racial or ethnic group rather than a political entity;[75] nation did not carry a sense of 'country' until at least the early modern period, and the modern nation-state arguably did not emerge until the late eighteenth or early nineteenth century.[76] While elsewhere the frequently used *leod* could be glossed 'people' or 'nation', it does not appear in this passage – the grieving woman is concerned about an invading army, but no mention is made of what collective entity or territory the army may invade.

Thus, while one could argue for the word in its original, tribal sense, Heaney clearly intends the concept of 'nation' as a sort of anachronism. Using it, Heaney breaks the backward gaze of his translation to explicitly connect with an immediate geopolitical moment: the terror of genocide around the globe and its awful aftermath. Indeed, he had already used 'nation' – more justifiably – in translating an earlier passage, in which Hrothgar addresses the about-to-depart hero (provided first with my own literal translation for context):

> Hafast þu gefered   þæt þam folcum sceal,
> Geata leodum   ond Gardenum,
> sib gemænu   ond sacu restan,
> inwitniþas,   þe hie ær drugon (1855–8)

> (You have brought about that the folk shall,
> Geatish people and Spear-Danes,
> share peace and break from strife,
> the enmity they have endured)

Heaney writes:

> What you have done is to draw two peoples,
> the Geat nation and us neighboring Danes,
> into shared peace and a pact of friendship
> in spite of hatreds we have harbored in the past. (1855–8)

Closely reading this passage, Russell argues that it should be viewed in the context of Heaney's 'regionalist, ongoing work as a potentially healing mediator between competing binaries such as abstract notions of Irish and British nationalism that have nothing to do with the lived realities of citizens in these countries'.[77] Heaney, he adds, 'read such lines through his own hopes for peace in Northern Ireland … Heaney senses that hatreds may persist, and he indicates that lingering possibility through the use of the present perfect tense.'[78] As with the linguistic intimacy that provides the impetus for Heaney's translation, with *þolian* unlocking an awareness of the connective tissue between older words and still current, regional usages throughout the English-speaking world, the many conflicts and uneasy treaties throughout *Beowulf* offer a generative sort of intimacy for author and reader alike. The connective tissue here is, of course, more like a wound: the ubiquitous violence of regional conflict. Instead of being satisfied with vividly rendering *Beowulf*'s many battles, Heaney goes out of his way to bring readers into intimate contact with contemporary regional conflicts – an uncomfortable intimacy for readers, as it persistently shatters the notion that *Beowulf* presents a distant, barbaric time. For Heaney, the focus is Northern Ireland, but the poem's figure of mourning takes on flesh and blood as an all-too-familiar type to anyone who has experienced such violence in any time, any place.

Thomas Meyer forges a completely different kind of intimacy in his translation of the 'grieving woman' passage. A glance at the several pages he devotes to it reveals his radical approach:

A woman keened:

[page break]

Sorrow binds my hair.
I outlive my lord.
Days of mourning,
months of slaughter,
seasons of terror
imprison my people.

Helpless we all.
All Midgarth rots.

[page break]

He set out now
in smoke upon the sea.[79]

Characteristically, Meyer tends to arrange the lines into short
couplets, which upon careful examination can be described as a
visual alternative to the usual rendering of alliterative lines. In
other words, each couplet represents one full line in the original,
with a line break taking the place of intra-linear caesura. Some
sounds do carry over, as in 'mourning' / 'month', which at least
offers a trace of the original's alliteration. Given the constructed
nature of modern critical editions of *Beowulf* based on the sole
surviving manuscript, there is ample justification for Meyer's
arrangement; in fact, many early print editions of Old English texts
presented half-lines in a similar way.

There are two intimacies, I argue, driving this arrangement of text.
The first, as already explored above, is Meyer's affinity for the sparse,
fragmented, modernist style introduced by Pound and perfected in
his epic *Cantos*.[80] The second is Meyer's exposure to the 'Concrete
Poetry' movement during the late 1960s. Although asserting that
the movement 'struck me as dumb, literally and figuratively. Or
too often clever and curious, risking cute',[81] Meyer admits that
Concrete Poetry also inspired him to experiment with visual effects,
particularly with his *Beowulf*: 'It's true I was fascinated by page
layout, the page as a unit, line, line break, stanza, stanza length,
essentially the drifting right hand margin, along with the recto/verso
juxtaposition. Hence my translation of *Beowulf*.'[82] The result of
this is to reveal the evolution from the rudimentary typographical
experiments of modernists such as Pound (and postmodernists such
as Robert Duncan, Charles Olson, et al.) to the more sophisticated
designs of the so-called Visual and Concrete poets – and, further,
the way in which all of them arguably connect back to the Old
English line.

Almost as striking as Meyer's visual arrangement of the text is
his narrative alteration in casting the Geatish woman's lament on
its own page, in the first person. This places the passage in the
context of Old English elegies, most obviously 'The Wife's Lament',
while also hinting at short, first-person lyric poems such as those
of Pound, H.D., and later Creeley.[83] The allusion to 'The Wife's

Lament' makes sense, as that elegy reflects the rhetorical situation of the Geatish woman in *Beowulf* writ large. As a type, she is simply a woman left alone in virtual or literal 'exile' after the death of her lord. Although Meyer does not, like Heaney, connect her grieving to that of modern women's experience of conflict and loss, the stripped-down, first-person address lends her utterance a haunting intimacy, of the type one might feel when reading a highly personal lyric poem. Coming as it does near the end of the poem, one might even momentarily imagine the woman as the suddenly revealed narrator of the entire epic. After all, in a poem that features elusive, shifting perspectives and a number of *scops* interjecting digressive songs throughout, we never really know who is telling the tale. It is at least intriguing to allow for the possibility that the tale-teller is one who 'outlives her lord', perhaps buying her very existence through weaving the story, Scheherazade-like, for her captors. The idea of a first-person female perspective is also suggested by a more recent translation by Meghan Purvis (2013), who notes in her preface that 'my translation comes from writing as a woman'. Purvis takes Meyer's lyrical intimacy one step further, structuring *Beowulf* as a 'collection-length series of poems that tell the story', offering 'many voices' as opposed to a 'single narrator'.[84]

One need not speculate about narrative possibilities, however, to argue for the significance and appropriateness of Meyer's first-person, stand-alone rendering of the Geatish woman's grief. Textually, Meyer's version fits with *Beowulf*'s often fragmented, digressive style. Arthur Brodeur, for example, in teaching the poem, once instructed his students to analyse the Finn episode – an approximately 200-line digression narrated by Hrothgar's *scop* – as if it were a modern poem standing by itself.[85] Although Brodeur largely agrees with J. R. R. Tolkien's assessment of *Beowulf* as consisting of a structurally balanced whole,[86] his suggestive instructions proved 'pedagogically transformative' for students of his who first tried their hands at translating the poem and later became major post-modern poets themselves, hinting at avenues for further experiments in long-form verse following Pound and others.[87]

More recently, James W. Earl argues for simply accepting the confusing and inconsistent elements of the poem, rather than trying to 'fill in the gaps' of passages that seem to jump around in time and space, as editors and critics have tended to do since Tolkien. Of the 'Swedish war' digressions in the second half of *Beowulf*, he writes, 'the poet seems to have gone out of his way to make this part of the poem difficult to follow'.[88] The point is that *Beowulf* criticism has gradually evolved from a seeming desire for wholeness and consistency to an acknowledgement of its fragmentary, incomplete nature, almost as if *Beowulf* itself had become postmodern alongside the critics.[89] But translations have not followed suit. To glance through almost any modern version of the poem, Heaney's included, is to encounter relatively even columns of verse (or smoothly flowing paragraphs of prose, as in Tolkien's almost century-old but recently published translation). Gaps or inconsistencies in the original are sometimes acknowledged with ellipses or discreetly flagged in notes. But to casual readers (and even beginning students) of the poem, there is little to hint at *Beowulf*'s miscellaneous nature. The intimacy introduced by Meyer's *mise-en-page* lyric arrangement of the poem repeatedly brings this element of *Beowulf* to the fore.

It is impossible to escape from the fact that in any translation one is left with two objects, which appear to be two objectively distinct texts: the original and the newly rendered version, in two distinct languages. As Reynolds writes, 'At the junction of translation, the two languages stand exposed, face to face, as though realizing their nakedness by their difference.'[90] This is perhaps the ultimate intimacy of translation. To return to Bersani's exploration of intimacy as the talk of analyst/analysand, we can imagine the two languages brought close together in a state of desire and risk, with readers allowed to share in this intimacy via the poet-translator. Both poets forge a particular intimacy with *Beowulf* – its language, its rhythms, and what could be called its cultural mystique – that reverberates throughout their poetic careers. Interestingly, for Meyer, this relationship inaugurated his career, looking back on and incorporating lessons from English and American modernist movements; for Heaney, the engagement occurred towards the end, shedding light on his original poetry written earlier in his career.

Beowulf is perhaps unique in being created over and over again by its translations – given a more whole and cohesive existence than it actually has. Heaney's translation reminds us of the linguistic variance – the marginal vernaculars – that bursts at the seams of the poem that comes down to us, belying the fantasy of unadulterated original English. His deep connection with the poem's theme of an endless cycle of conflict and reprisal, via the Irish Troubles, also serves to heighten the immediacy of *Beowulf* for contemporary readers. Heaney's postcolonial intimacy, both in terms of language and content, risks breaking with accepted ideas about accuracy in translating *Beowulf* for the sake of exposing readers to these poetic concerns explored throughout his career. Meyer's postmodern intimacy, meanwhile, alerts us to the possibility of seeing in *Beowulf* individual lyric interludes that invite readers more intimately into the space of the poem – a move that results from his filtering of the translation through his deep engagement with modern and postmodern poetic practice, but that turns out to be surprisingly appropriate to the ambiguous and challenging poem we call *Beowulf*.

Notes

1 See 'intimate', adj. and n., *OED online* (Oxford University Press, January 2018), www.oed.com/view/Entry/98506 (accessed 5 June 2019). See also Chris Piuma, 'The task of the dystranslator: an introduction to a dystranslation of the works of the "Pearl" poet', *postmedieval*, 6.2 (2015), 120–6.
2 José Ortega y Gasset, 'The misery and the splendor of translation', trans. Elizabeth Gamble Miller, in Lawrence Venuti (ed.), *The translation studies reader* (New York: Routledge, 2000), pp. 49–65, at 50. See also Roman Jakobson, 'On linguistic aspects of translation', in Venuti (ed.), *Translation studies reader*, pp. 113–19, at 118.
3 Piuma, 'The task of the dystranslator'; see also Chris Piuma, 'Dystranslation', *kadar koli*, 8 (2013), 6, in which he defines dystranslation as 'the act of translating something untranslatable … a *queer* mode of translation, one that rejoices in resisting or rejecting normative modes and models'.
4 Piuma, 'The task of the dystranslator', 122–3.
5 Daniel C. Remein, 'Auden, translation, betrayal: radical poetics and translation from Old English', *Literature Compass*, 8.11 (2011), 811–29, at 815–16.
6 Ibid., 821 (emphasis in original).
7 Ibid.
8 Leo Bersani, 'The it in the I', in Leo Bersani and Adam Phillips (eds), *Intimacies* (Chicago: University of Chicago Press, 2008), pp. 1–31, at 27.
9 Ibid., p. 28.
10 James Shapiro, 'A better "Beowulf"', *New York Times*, 27 February 2000, www.nytimes.com/books/00/02/27/reviews/000227.27shapirt.html (accessed 5 June 2019). Shapiro emphasizes Heaney's efforts to stay 'close' to the Old English while also producing 'good poetry in its own right'. See also Terry Eagleton, 'Hasped and hooped and hirpling: Heaney conquers Beowulf', *Guardian*, 3 November 1999, www.theguardian.com/books/1999/nov/03/seamusheaney (accessed 5 June 2019). Eagleton pokes holes in the notion of *Beowulf* as a receptacle for 'pure' English while also extolling Heaney's 'unique qualifications' for translating the poem.

11 Daniel Donoghue, 'The languages of *Beowulf* between Klaeber and Heaney', in Jana K. Schulman and Paul E. Szarmach (eds), *Beowulf at Kalamazoo: essays on translation and performance* (Kalamazoo, MI: Medieval Institute Publications, 2012), pp. 15–30, at 17.

12 Anthony Bale, *Beowulf* review, *Speculum*, 88.4 (2013), 1130–2. Bale calls Meyer's translation 'an exciting and vital resource', though he also notes that it is 'far from faithful to the original poem'. See also Courtney Rydel, 'Fits of imagination', *Jacket2*, 4 December 2013, https://jacket2.org/reviews/fits-imagination (accessed 5 June 2019). Rydel argues that '"collaboration" might be a better term for the interplay between the Anglo-Saxon original and Meyer's present-day English version'. See also Meghan Glass, *Beowulf* review, *Interstitial journal* (2013), https://interstitialjournal.files.wordpress.com/2013/04/glass-beowulf.pdf (accessed 5 June 2019). Glass insists on a distinction between 'translation' and 'adaptation', with Meyer's work falling into the latter category as it 'essentially seizes *Beowulf* from the medieval world of oral Old English alliterative verse and reconstructs it within the realm of modernist visual poetry'.

13 Seamus Heaney, 'Fretwork: on translating *Beowulf*', *Saltana*, 1 (2001), www.saltana.org/1/esc/91.html#.WtU_2NNuY1K (accessed 5 June 2019).

14 David Hadbawnik and Thomas Meyer, 'Interview with Thomas Meyer', in Thomas Meyer (trans.), *Beowulf* (New York: punctum books, 2012), p. 261. The author would like to acknowledge that he was the editor of the punctum edition of Meyer's *Beowulf*.

15 Jorge Luis Borges, 'The translators of *The Thousand and One Nights*', trans. Esther Allen, in Venuti (ed.), *Translation studies reader*, pp. 34–48, at 45–6.

16 Vladimir Nabokov, 'Problems of translation: "Onegin" in English', in Venuti (ed.), *Translation studies reader*, pp. 71–83, at 77.

17 Lawrence Venuti, 'Introduction', in Venuti (ed.), *Translation studies reader*, pp. 1–8, at 5.

18 Walter Benjamin, 'The task of the translator', trans. Harry Zohn, in Venuti (ed.), *Translation studies reader*, pp. 15–23, at 20–2.

19 Itamar Even-Zohar, 'The position of translated literature within the literary polysystem', in Venuti (ed.), *Translation studies reader*, pp. 192–7. Even-Zohar's argument is in some ways a response to Walter Benjamin's concept of the 'marginality' of translations: 'Unlike a work of literature, translation does not find itself in the center of the language forest but on the outside facing the wooded ridge; it calls into it without entering, aiming at that single spot where the echo is able to give, in its own language, the reverberation of the work in the alien one' (Benjamin, 'The task of the translator', p. 20).

20 See R. D. Fulk et al. (eds), *Klaeber's Beowulf*, 4th edn (Toronto: University of Toronto Press, 2009), pp. cxxii–cxxiii.

21 Even-Zohar, 'The position of translated literature', p. 193.
22 Christopher A. Jones, *Strange likeness: the use of Old English in twentieth-century poetry* (New York: Oxford University Press, 2006), p. 6. The other poets examined by Jones are W. H. Auden, Edwin Morgan, and Seamus Heaney.
23 John D. Niles, 'Old-English verse and twentieth-century poets', *Contemporary literature*, 49.2 (2008), 293–9, at 293–4.
24 Even-Zohar, 'The position of translated literature', p. 195.
25 Jones, *Strange likeness*, p. 6.
26 Allen J. Frantzen, *Desire for origins: new language, Old English, and teaching the tradition* (New Brunswick, NJ: Rutgers University Press, 1990), pp. 22–6.
27 Seamus Heaney, *Beowulf* (New York: Norton, 2000), p. xxv.
28 Fulk et al. (eds), *Klaeber's Beowulf*, p. 446. See also J. R. Hall, *A concise Anglo-Saxon dictionary*, 4th edn (Toronto: University of Toronto Press, 1960), p. 361.
29 Heaney, *Beowulf*, p. xxvi.
30 Fulk et al. (eds), *Klaeber's Beowulf*, p. 446.
31 Donoghue, 'Languages of *Beowulf*', p. 21.
32 David Crystal, *The stories of English* (New York: The Overlook Press, 2004). Crystal writes, 'The extant *Beowulf* manuscript was written probably some 250 years after it was first composed, allowing many opportunities for different dialects to manifest themselves, and for the text to display the stylistic preferences of different monastic schools or the linguistic eccentricities of individual scribes' (p. 50).
33 Heaney, *Beowulf*, p. xxvi.
34 Richard Rankin Russell, *Seamus Heaney's regions* (Notre Dame, IN: University of Notre Dame Press, 2014), p. 312.
35 Ibid., p. 313. See also Benedict Anderson, *Imagined communities: reflections on the origin and spread of nationalism* (New York: Verso, rev. edn, 2006), p. 44.
36 Jones, *Strange likeness*, p. 203.
37 Heaney, *Beowulf*, pp. xxxii–xxxiii.
38 Jones, *Strange likeness*, p. 187.
39 Ibid., p. 194.
40 Heaney, *Beowulf*, p. xxx. Jones explores Heaney's regional diction in some detail, concluding, 'the translation does not incorporate a great number of Irishisms or Ulsterisms. Most of them can be catalogued within the space of a paragraph' (*Strange likeness*, p. 230). In part this is due to the resistance that Heaney faced from the Norton editors, as noted above.
41 Eagleton, 'Hasped and hooped and hirpling'. Eagleton's otherwise positive review is critical of this passage, however; he writes, 'Lines like "He is hasped and hooped and hirpling with pain, limping and looped with it", which the young Heaney might well have written

in earnest, are really an ironic postmodern quotation, a self-parodic hint of the racket the whole poem might make if you bound yourself too grimly to its form.' See also Donoghue, 'Languages of *Beowulf*. Donoghue points out that in the poem 'the number of words with an Irish etymology is relatively small' and 'most of the idioms ... that seem dialectal are not exclusively found in Irish English' (p. 26).

42 'hasp', n., *OED online* (Oxford University Press, January 2018), www.oed.com/view/Entry/84463 (accessed 5 June 2019). See also M. Markus (ed.), *English dialect dictionary* online (Innsbruck: University of Innsbruck, 2017), http://eddonline-proj.uibk.ac.at/edd/index.jsp (accessed 5 June 2019). The *English dialect dictionary* online identifies the term as northern/Scots-Irish.

43 'hasp', n., *Dictionary of the Scots language* (University of Glasgow, January 2018), www.dsl.ac.uk/entry/snd/hesp_n2_v2 (accessed 5 June 2019); Markus (ed.), *English dialect dictionary*. The *EDD* online gives this sense of the word as unique to Scots.

44 'hirple', v., *Dictionary of the Scots language* (University of Glasgow, January 2018), www.dsl.ac.uk/entry/snd/hirple (accessed 5 June 2019); 'hirple', v., *OED online* (Oxford University Press, January 2018), www.oed.com/view/Entry/87223 (accessed 5 June 2019).

45 Jones, *Strange likeness*, p. 128.

46 Lawrence Venuti, 'Translation, community, utopia', in Venuti (ed.), *Translation studies reader*, pp. 468–88, at 468–9.

47 Jones, *Strange likeness*, p. 129.

48 Benjamin, 'The task of the translator', p. 22.

49 Jones, *Strange likeness*, p. 132.

50 Ibid. Jones writes, 'Heaney's is certainly the most idiomatic version currently available; this is both is strength and its weakness' (p. 233).

51 Eagleton, 'Hasped and hooped and hirpling'.

52 Remein, 'Auden, translation, betrayal', 813.

53 Donoghue, 'Languages of *Beowulf*, p. 26.

54 Ibid., p. 28.

55 Ibid.

56 Meyer (trans.), *Beowulf*, p. 52.

57 Daniel Remein, 'Locating *Beowulf*, in Meyer (trans.), *Beowulf*. Remein writes, 'This is of course the very effect of Meyer's pastiche of modernist long-form poems: a translation that doubles as a museum of exhibits of modernist experiment requiring its own docent. Thus ... Meyer quotes verbatim Ezra Pound's line 'set keel to breakers' ... Meyer's translation invites an archeological or geological investigation of its topography, from which uncoils a whole other set of literary histories that inescapably inhere in *Beowulf* in the present' (p. 19). Remein also notes that this and other passages recall both Charles Olson's 'Field Poetics' and 'Objectivist' approaches to poetry (p. 16).

58 Hadbawnik and Meyer, 'Interview', p. 261.

59 Ibid., pp. 262, 266, 268–9.
60 Ibid., p. 263.
61 Ibid., p. 265.
62 Remein, 'Locating *Beowulf*'. Remein discusses Meyer's tendency to condense (but in other ways expand) the Old English, comparing him to the quasi-Objectivist poet Lorine Niedecker (p. 24).
63 Jiří Levý, 'Translation as a decision process', in Venuti (ed.), *Translation studies reader*, pp. 148–59, at 152.
64 Sean Reynolds, 'Hospitality of the mouth and the homophonic kiss: David Melnick's *Men in Aïda*', *Postmodern culture*, 21.2 (2011), 295–314.
65 Ibid. In Melnick's poem, the lines are 447–8.
66 Ibid.
67 Ibid.
68 See also Jones, *Strange likeness*, p. 235: 'Heaney's verse tautens and quickens at those moments when the narrative becomes subsidiary to description', describing this passage in particular as displaying an 'almost sensuous eroticism that underscores the original's account of Beowulf's ship'.
69 'shore', n.1, *OED online* (Oxford University Press, March 2018), www.oed.com/view/Entry/178549; 'ledge', n., *OED online* (Oxford University Press, March 2018), www.oed.com/view/Entry/106892; 'churn', v., *OED online* (Oxford University Press, March 2018), www.oed.com/view/Entry/32856 (all accessed 5 June 2019).
70 Hadbawnik and Meyer, 'Interview', p. 264.
71 Meyer (trans.), *Beowulf*, p. 78.
72 Jones, *Strange likeness*, pp. 222–4.
73 Fulk et al. (eds), *Klaeber's Beowulf*, p. 270.
74 Heaney, *Beowulf*, p. xxi.
75 'nation', n.1, *OED online* (Oxford University Press, September 2016), www.oed.com/view/Entry/125285 (accessed 5 June 2019).
76 Raymond Williams, *Keywords: a vocabulary of culture and society* (New York: Oxford University Press, rev. edn, 1983), p. 213.
77 Russell, *Seamus Heaney's regions*, p. 331.
78 Ibid., p. 332.
79 Meyer (trans.), *Beowulf*, pp. 254–6.
80 Hadbawnik and Meyer, 'Interview', pp. 266–70. See also Remein, 'Locating *Beowulf*'.
81 Hadbawnik and Meyer, 'Interview', p. 270.
82 Thomas Meyer and Patrick Morrissey, 'An interview with Thomas Meyer', *Chicago Review*, 59.3 (2015), 124.
83 On H.D. and *Beowulf*, see also Peter Buchanan's chapter in this volume, pp. 279–303.
84 Megan Purvis, *Beowulf* (London: Penned in the Margins, 2013), pp. 7–8.
85 David Hadbawnik, '*Beowulf* is a hoax: Jack Spicer's medievalism', in David Hadbawnik and Sean Reynolds (eds), *Jack Spicer's Beowulf* (New

York: City University of New York, 2011), pp. 6–7. On this episode, see also see Mary Kate Hurley's chapter in this volume, pp. 147–63.

86 Arthur Brodeur, 'The structure and unity of *Beowulf*', *PMLA*, 68.5 (1953), 1183–95; J. R. R. Tolkien, '*Beowulf*: the monsters and the critics', *Proceedings of the British Academy*, 22 (1936), 245–95.

87 Daniel Remein, 'Robin Blaser, Jack Spicer, and Arthur Brodeur: avant-garde poetics, the pedagogy of Old English at mid-century, and a counterfactual critical history, or, the importance of a broadly conceived English studies department', *postmedieval*, 6.2 (2015), 174–90. Remein writes that Brodeur, despite his quasi-New Critical approach, expresses 'a desire for *Beowulf* to be in a position to matter to contemporary discussions of poetics, and so framed, to bear upon the making of poetry in the present' (p. 178).

88 James W. Earl, 'The Swedish wars in *Beowulf*', *JEGP*, 114.1 (2015), 32–60, at 35. On this backstory, see also Roberta Frank's chapter in this volume, pp. 54–72.

89 Frantzen, *Desire for origins*, p. 171: '*Beowulf* is an incomplete text, incompletely attested, and it will always be controversial. Its incompleteness is not only a conceptual problem: it is also an event.' See also Eileen Joy and Mary Ramsey (eds), *The postmodern Beowulf: a critical casebook* (Morgantown, WV: West Virginia University Press, 2007).

90 Reynolds, 'Hospitality of the mouth'.

Part V
Beowulf in bed

12

Beowulf and Andreas: intimate relations

Irina Dumitrescu

As the centuries go by, there is always a crowd before that picture, gazing into its depths, seeing their own faces reflected in it, seeing more the longer they look, never being able to say quite what it is that they see.

Virginia Woolf[1]

For years, it was not clear if *Beowulf* and *Andreas* were dating or had simply found themselves at the same restaurant, ordering the same specials. Burly, Germanic *Beowulf* and quirky, vaguely Mediterranean *Andreas* didn't seem like much of a fit, but they shared a predilection for speaking in epic formulas and collecting antiques. Anita Riedinger and Alison Powell, among other scholars, showed this was no accident: *Beowulf* and *Andreas* not only had been going steady, but like many younger lovers, *Andreas* had picked up *Beowulf*'s habits and mannerisms, even at the cost of looking awkward.[2] Rings and property, monstrous encounters, pagan practices, and ancient ruins – *Andreas* found all of these in *Beowulf*'s treasury and tried them on, with unsettling, or ridiculous, effects.

Relationships change people. Intimate encounters with poems do too. The story of Andrew and the Mermedonians was passed down in Greek and Latin before it met *Beowulf*, to say nothing of Old English prose, and most scholars agree that it was altered profoundly by its adoption of epic Anglo-Saxon vocabulary.[3] But literary influence does not travel in one direction alone. Martha Malamud has shown that Ausonius' *Cento nuptialis* outrageously alters Vergil's *Aeneid*, from which it draws; it becomes impossible to read the original epic without interference from the *Cento*'s erotic imagery.[4] *Beowulf*, too, despite being the couple's senior, is transformed through *Andreas*'s imitation. Its pagans become monstrous, as Richard North has recognized.[5] Indeed, *Andreas* reveals the darker side of *Beowulf*: the blindness of heroes, the tenuous distinctions between monsters and men, and the deathly potential of history and its artefacts. Modern scholars have recognized these too, but *Andreas*, *Beowulf*'s most loving reader, saw them first.

What might a Late Antique apostolic adventure story find to like in a tale of disastrous Scandinavian politics and bothersome monsters? Cannibals, ancient architectural features, and a fallible hero are the beginning of an answer. While *Andreas* is often described as a hagiography, its hero is not the stalwart soldier of faith one so frequently finds in Late Antique and early medieval passion narratives; any barely pubescent maiden saint found in the legendaries of Prudentius or Ælfric is tougher in the face of threats and torture. The anonymous poet of *Andreas* decorates his protagonist with heroic epithets, but they are savagely ironic. Here is a story of an apostle who is asked by God to rescue his friend Matthew from a distant Mermedonian prison, where the latter is to be slaughtered and cooked up for a cannibal's snack. Instead of dutifully obeying the Lord, Andrew complains: it is too far, he does not know the way. Christ appears to him disguised as a seafarer, complete with a boat ready to take him to the cannibal city; Andrew does not recognize his former teacher, and saintsplains the miracles of Jesus to him. These wonders include not only calming storms and healing the sick but also commanding stone statues to speak and move. One might think that observing these marvels first-hand would have convinced Andrew of his Saviour's power, but the apostle's faith turns out to be very shakable indeed. After falling asleep on the ship, Andrew awakens on the Mermedonian shore and understands his mistake. Christ appears to him again and explains that Andrew will suffer torture but not death, exhorting him to be brave in the face of suffering. Andrew releases Matthew from the prison, but once the devil incites the Mermedonians to torture him, he forgets Christ's pep talk. Instead he whines and wishes for death. At this point, even the narrator seems to need a break from the proceedings. In an authorial interruption, he describes how long – or boring – the story has been, and suggests that a wiser man might find the battles and torments in his own mind. The story finds Andrew in prison again, where he commands a column inscribed with the Ten Commandments to release a deadly flood of water. The ensuing devastation convinces the Mermedonians to convert to Christianity, at which point Andrew prepares to abandon them. Christ appears once more to this unenthusiastic apostle and convinces him to teach the people he has just baptized. So much for a hero who is described at the start of the poem as:

> anræd   ellenweorces,
> heard ond higerof,   nalas hildlata,
> gearo, guðe fram   to godes campe. (232–234)[6]

(prompt to deeds of courage, firm and strong of mind, not at all slow to fight, valiant and ready for battle in God's war.)

While *Beowulf* and *Andreas* have been spotted together for about a century and a half, they usually only prompt the question: 'Are they or aren't they?' Few critics have wondered about the nature of their intimacy. The major exception is Richard North, who, in an essay in his and Michael Bintley's edition of *Andreas*, has attempted to tease out the nuances of this strange romance. North addresses some of the best-known borrowings from *Beowulf*: the 'meoduscerwen' (serving of mead?) (1526b) doled out to the Mermedonians in the form of a deadly deluge, a play on the enigmatic 'ealuscerwen'[7] (serving of ale? terror?) (769a) served to the Danes in Heorot;[8] the way doors immediately open ('Duru sona onarn') (*A* 999b, *B* 721b) at the touch of Andrew and Grendel's hands; the narrators who have never heard of a 'cymlicor ceol' (more splendid ship) (*A* 361, *B* 38) than those of Christ and Scyld Scefing; and the treasures 'landes ond locenra beaga' (of land and linked rings) (*A* 303a, *B* 2995a) that Hygelac doles out and Andrew lacks.[9] It is hard to understand precisely what *Andreas* is doing with *Beowulf* under the book covers, but North suggests it's funny business. *Andreas* is a 'Cervantesque parody of *Beowulf*', he writes, one that mocks the Mermedonians by allusively connecting them both to Grendel and to the Scyldings.[10] Elsewhere, he and Bintley give the flip side of the argument, stating that the poet 'adopts a Beowulfian style of epic in order to undermine the values of *Beowulf* itself', noting his 'barbed references' to the *Beowulf* poet's apparently indulgent representation of heathens.[11] If *Andreas* borrows *Beowulf*'s clothing sometimes, the goal is not slavish imitation but drag.

What follows is a series of illuminations, each prompted by a moment of intimacy in a post-Anglo-Saxon work of literature. Each is a beam of light shining through tinted glass; each accentuates certain details and conceals others. The relationship between *Andreas* and *Beowulf* is shifting, enigmatic, playful. It resists simple interpretative claims. Accordingly, I use Alison Powell's rich collection of unique formulaic parallels to find points of particularly snug contact between the epics. *Andreas* is a poem fascinated by exemplarity, but instead of depicting pupils who succeed in imitating their teachers, it shows us a saint who is an imperfect copy of his divine master. Likewise, *Andreas* is a self-consciously flawed likeness of *Beowulf*, its beloved mentor. This admittedly cubist chapter is one attempt to trace the bonds in this poetic odd couple.

***

> He was not a bit like me, really; yet, as we stood leaning over my bed place, whispering side by side, with our dark heads together and our backs to the door, anybody bold enough to open it stealthily would have been treated to the sight of a double captain busy talking in whispers with his other self ... shoulder touching shoulder almost.
>
> Joseph Conrad[12]

What creates intimacy between dissimilar things? Is it enough for two poems to stand beside one another? In the Exeter Book, the verses nestled among the riddles have heightened enigmatic qualities, sometimes urging us to count them among the cryptic hundred.[13] *Andreas* and the *Fates of the Apostles*, which follows immediately on its footsteps, were once considered to be the works of a single author, even a single poem.[14] Spatial companions become other selves, individual differences blurred in their shared moment or common undertaking. Secrets join them too, private murmurs that can be heard only in closeness. Hrothgar mourns the dead Æschere by calling him 'min runwita und min rædbora, / eaxlgestealla ... þonne hniton feþan' (my confidant and my advisor, close comrade ... when the foot troops clashed) (1325–6a, 1327b), his lament recalling both the times they spent fighting on foot, shoulder to shoulder, and the quieter moments of secret advice and deep trust.

The language of closeness is a generous lender. Its terms can be taken, adapted, reshaped, and returned. So it is that the speaker of 'The Wife's Lament' imagines herself missing her 'hlaford' (lord) (6) and searching for a new 'folgað' (retinue) (9), the closeness of their marital bond best expressed through the homosocial intimacy between a liege lord and his follower.[15] In *Andreas*, the relations between student and teacher, warrior and lord, religious follower and leader, creature and Creator are tightly braided together, at the centre of this knot an intimacy beyond words. The *Andreas* poet remembers how Hygelac received the news that his nephew Beowulf, a protector of warriors but also his 'lindgestealla' (shield comrade) (1973a), had come safely home. A variation on *eaxlgestealla*, with the image that word brings up of shoulder-to-shoulder fighting, *lindgestealla* only appears in *Beowulf* and *Andreas*. *Andreas*, however, puts it in the devil's mouth, as he voices his disappointment that his little demons did such a poor job roughing up the saint: 'Hwæt wearð eow swa rofum, rincas mine, / lindgesteallan, þæt eow swa lyt gespeow?' (What happened to you, my bold warriors, my shield-companions, that you have been so unsuccessful?) (1343–4). One demon answers his father that it is difficult to deprive Andrew, that 'anhagan' (solitary being) (1351a), of his life, another devil encourages the band to fight that 'æglæcan' (formidable opponent) (1359a), to mock him about his exile ('oðwitan him his wræsið') (1358a).

The *Andreas* poet invites his readers to imagine the closeness of the devil and his hellish progeny, the demons who are at once bold warriors and cheeky children, by layering them with a a term of martial intimacy he takes from *Beowulf*. But then he flips the scene, giving us the demonic perspective: the hero is an awesome creature to be sure, but perhaps also an outcast or a monster. *Anhaga* is no rare word, but an audience member familiar with *Beowulf* might have remembered that it described its hero (2368a), a man about whom the question of exile also briefly hung. As Wulfgar pointedly remarks, 'Wen' ic þæt ge for wlenco, nalles for wræcsiðum / ac for higeþrymmum Hroðgar sohton' (I expect that you came here out of daring, not at all due to exile, but that you sought Hrothgar due to strength of heart) (338–9). That audience would be even likelier to recall the way 'æglæca' joins Grendel, his vengeful mother, the sea-creatures Beowulf fights, the dragon, as well as Beowulf himself and Sigemund.[16] The word *æglæca* is where hero and monster meet, joined in the loneliness of their uncanny strength. The *Andreas* poet saw this at work in *Beowulf*, and imagined a demonic community of warriors at arms, terrified but stirred by the invasion of a saintly villain.

***

'Blythely', quod he; 'com sytte adoun!
I telle thee upon condicioun
That thou shalt hooly, with al thy wyt,
Doo thyn entent to herkene hit.'
'Yis, syr … I shal ryght blythely, so God me save,
Hooly, with al the wit I have,
Here yow as wel as I kan.'

Geoffrey Chaucer[17]

Andreas is a poem about teaching. More precisely, it is an exploration of the various shapes the relationship between teacher and student can take. At the start of the poem, Andrew is a proselytizer, teaching the people the path to life ('leode lærde on lifes weg') (170). He is also a hypocrite who fails to believe in God's power. Later, on the boat, he teaches his followers to have faith in Christ, recalling for them the miracles Jesus performed in their presence. Christ teaches him throughout, sometimes prompting him to search his memory for the keys to spiritual succour, sometimes embodying for Andrew the example he is to follow. Later, Andrew teaches the Mermedonians, but half-heartedly, forced to return to his needy students to establish them in their new faith.[18]

The bond between teacher and student is one of faith, a plighting of troth, a promise to reveal and to attempt to understand that revelation. It is also a relation of copying, of echoing words, of occasional misunderstandings, some of them productive. The attitude of Andrew to his teacher Christ is analogous to the position of *Andreas* to *Beowulf*; both relationships follow the logic of exemplarity, and both experience the failure of that logic. Andrew is a bragging warrior but a dense student, and in his inability to learn from Jesus' many miracles he reveals the impotence of Christian teaching. So, too, does *Andreas* reveal the potential hollowness of Beowulf's boasts. He pays particular attention to Beowulf's speech before Wealhtheow:

> *Ic þæt hogode,   þa ic on holm gestah,*
> *sæbat gesæt   mid minra secga gedriht,*
> þæt ic anunga   eowra leoda
> willan geworhte   oþðe on wæl crunge
> feondgrapum fæst.   Ic *gefremman sceal*
> eorlic *ellen,*   oþðe endedæg
> on þisse meoduhealle   minne gebidan. (632–8, italics added
> throughout to highlight parallels)

(I intended, when I set out to sea, sat down in a ship with my band of men, that I would completely accomplish the wishes of your people or fall in battle, trapped in the enemy's grip. I shall accomplish a heroic exertion or experience my final day in this mead-hall.)

For the moment a good pupil of his heroic model, Andrew repeats the beginning of Beowulf's boast in his own attempt to rally the troops during a sea-storm:

> *Ge þæt gehogodon,   þa ge on holm stigon,*
> þæt ge on fara folc   feorh gelæddon,
> ond for dryhtnes lufan   deað þrowodon (429–31)

(You intended, when you set out to sea, to carry your life to hostile people and to suffer death for the love of the Lord.)

Andrew underscores the echo of Beowulf's speech a few lines later by introducing the story of Jesus calming the storm with 'Swa gesælde iu, þæt we on sæbate' (so it happened long ago, that we in a ship) (438). Still, in reminding his men of their willingness to be martyrs and, indeed, of their lord's remarkable control of wild waves, Andrew acknowledges their fear. Their bravery has already faltered, as has his own, their promises shallow.

Much later, Christ appears again to buttress Andrew's strength before his three days of torture: 'Scealt ðu, Andreas, ellen fremman!' (Andrew, you shall accomplish a heroic exertion) (1208). Once again, Andrew only follows part of the lesson, enduring stalwartly for two days, then complaining about his suffering on the third. In writing his drama of instruction, the *Andreas* poet breaks up one Beowulfian boast into two Christian teaching moments, scenes that draw attention to students' ultimate vulnerability despite their bold intentions. Appropriately, variations on *ellen fremman* only appear in these two poems, the third instance being the famous introduction of the Spear Danes in the first lines of *Beowulf*, those princes who '*ellen fremedon*' (3). The reliably ironic poet of *Andreas* may have sensed the disappointment in that line too.

***

The side of the ship made an opaque belt of shadow on the darkling glassy shimmer of the sea. But I saw at once something elongated and pale floating very close to the ladder. Before I could form a guess a faint flash of phosphorescent light, which seemed to issue suddenly from the naked body of a man, flickered in the sleeping water with the elusive, silent play of summer lightning in a night sky.

Joseph Conrad[19]

Intimacy coalesces on the edges of things. It glimmers on the borders between land and water, life and death. No wonder that the poet of *Andreas* introduces Mermedonia as an 'igland' (island) (15a) and a 'mearcland' (borderland) (19a). In the poem's analogues, the home of the cannibals is simply a city. North and Bintley note the seeming contradiction between these two descriptions, explaining that 'Mermedonia is a borderland because it is on the fringes of human society and experience, like Grendel's mere in *Beowulf* and the

Crowland hermitage in *Guthlac*.'[20] *Andreas* understands that shores are sites of encounter, both with dangerous strangers and with mortality itself.

Marginal spaces are also where *Andreas* connects to *Beowulf*, using the older poem's moving shore scenes to highlight the instability of Andrew's hagiographical mission. The *Andreas* poet borrows boldly – as has often been noted – from the description of Scyld Scefing's funeral ship:

> Þær wæs madma fela
> of feorwegum   frætwa gelæded.
> Ne *hyrde* ic *cymlicor   ceol* gegyrwan
> hildewæpnum   ond heaðowædum,
> billum ond byrnum;   him on bearme læg
> madma mænigo,   þa him mid scoldon
> on flodes æht   feor gewitan.
> Nalæs hi hine læssan   lacum teodan,
> Þeod*gestreonum* (36b–44a)

(There were many treasures, precious things, brought from distant ways. I never heard of a ship more beautifully adorned with war-weapons and battle-clothes, with swords and coats of mail. On his chest lay a multitude of treasures which were to go far with him into the water's possession. Nor did they provide him with lesser gifts, with treasures of the people.)

When Andrew sits next to the disguised Christ in his boat, the narrator of *Andreas* pays his heroes an epic compliment:

> æfre ic ne *hyrde*
> þon *cymlicor   ceol* gehladenne
> heah*gestreonum*. (360b–362a)

(I never heard of a ship more beautifully laden with costly treasures.)

This parallel has often been noted as evidence for *Andreas*'s borrowing from *Beowulf*, and not without controversy. The narrator's remark seems at first an inappropriate description of holy men, though at second glance it elegantly captures the spiritual worth of Christ and his saint.[21] Critics have not noted, however, the dark shadow that *Beowulf* casts on *Andreas* here. Two ships set off, one bearing its treasure-laden corpse to parts unknown, the other carrying a hesitant hero to a cannibal land. Indeed, the ship Andrew has boarded carries a dead man too, one who has disguised himself as a seafarer for the time being.

Dividing lines are where recognition happens; sometimes the basis for intimacy is a fence after all. After the sea voyage, angels gently lay Andrew and his men on the sand ('greote') (847a) outside the Mermedonian city walls. The poet describes sun, clouds, and city in a scene of Boethian illumination original to the narrative, but thickly made up of borrowings from *Beowulf*. Indeed, this is the densest agglomeration of unique parallels to *Beowulf* that I find in the entire poem:

> leton þone halgan   be herestræte
> swefan on sybbe   under swegles hleo,
> bliðne *bidan*   burhwealle *neh*,
> his niðhetum,   *nihtlangne fyrst*,
> oðþæt dryhten forlet   dægcandelle
> scire scinan.   *Sceadu sweðerodon,*
> *wonn under wolcnum*;   þa com wederes blæst,
> hador heofonleoma,   ofer hofu *blican.*
> Onwoc þa *wiges heard,*   *wang sceawode,*
> fore burggeatum;   *beorgas steape,*
> hleoðu hlifodon,   ymbe *harne stan*
> tigelfagan trafu,   torras stodon,
> *windige weallas.*   Þa se wisa oncneow
> þæt he Marmedonia   mægðe hæfde
> siðe gesohte,   swa him sylf bebead,
> þa he him fore gescraf,   fæder mancynnes. (831–46)

(They left the saint sleeping in peace by the high way, under the sky's covering, to await joyful close to the city wall and his deadly enemies, for the space of a night, until the Lord allowed the day-candle to shine brightly. The shades withdrew, dark under the clouds. Then came the sky's flame, bright heavenly light, shining over the dwellings. The war-hard man then awoke, looked at the land before the town gates. Steep mountains, cliffs towered, around the grey stone stood tile-adorned buildings, towers, windy walls. Then the wise man realized that he had sought the people of the Mermedonians from far, just as the Father of Mankind himself, who had appointed him before, commanded him.)

Andrew has much to recognize after this passage: who the captain of the boat was, his own error of faith, the city of Mermedonia. But the poem's readers are also prompted to wake up from their beachy slumber and note that they are no longer in a sub-Roman province but somewhere in Scandinavia. They might begin in Heorot, waiting for a night for Grendel ('nihtlongne first nean bidan') (528), move through the sea with Beowulf, as the waters calmed and he could see the land's windy walls ('brimu swaþredon / þæt ic sænæssas geseon mihte, / windige weallas') (570b–572a). They might think to the night falling on Heorot again, the shapes of shadows stalking, dark under the clouds ('scaduhelma gesceapu scriðan cwoman / wan under wolcnum') (650–1a), or be transported to Beowulf's ship, the men finally sighting the sea-cliffs and steep hills ('brimclifu blican, beorgas steape') (222). Or they could be transported to the battle of Sigemund, that man hard in war, with a dragon under a hoary rock ('syþðan wiges heard wyrm acwealde ... under harne stan') (886, 887b). Or that grey rock might be the one Hrothgar saw as he scanned the unfriendly landscape for Æschere's head ('wong sceawian ... ofer harne stan') (1413b, 1415a). *Andreas* echoes phrases that *Beowulf* likes a lot, so these lines might also recall the wind and walls of 1224a, the clouds of 1374a, or the grey stones of 2553b and 2744b. And just as Andrew recognizes that he had sought a city, as the Lord had ordained for him, so the poem's audience might realize they had sought a remembered place through those many allusions, one ordained for them by the author. On the Mermedonian shore, between water and city walls, under a sky shifting from night to day, two poems intertwine.

***

The shadowy, dark head, like mine, seemed to nod imperceptibly above the ghostly gray of my sleeping suit. It was, in the night, as though I had been faced by my own reflection in the depths of a somber and immense mirror.

Joseph Conrad[22]

Likeness can be easier to find in death, or just near it. This may be due to the workings of empathy, which allow us brief glimpses of a stranger's humanity when we watch them suffer. It may be the way darkness masks identifying details; in a world of shadows, all souls are clothed in the same tenebrous hue. Or it may be that in the process of dying, we are so often reduced to our bare components of blood and muscle and bone, universal and unremarkable.

The hero of *Andreas* suffers three times, on three days, in imitation of Christ. The descriptions of his bloody torture echo each other and, thickly, *Beowulf*'s scenes of death. *Andreas* borrows *Beowulf*'s vocabulary of gore, connecting to the earlier poem through the raw materials of life and death. It uses the language of suffering to render stranger what is already an unusual saintly passion. Unlike typical pain-resistant saints, who smile or crack jokes as their bodies are viciously disassembled, Andrew really hurts. He hurts so much, in fact, that on the third day of his trial he complains about the extremity of his punishment, notes that Christ complained on the cross after only one day of torture, and wishes for death, hinting that he has been abandoned by his protector (1401–28). But *Andreas* gives its cowardly saint epic treatment. Take, to begin with, a passage describing Andrew's body during the first day of his trial:

> Wæs þæs halgan lic
> sarbennum soden,   swate bestemed,
> banhus abrocen;   *blod yðum weoll,*
> *haton heolfre.* (1238b–1241a)

(The saint's body was afflicted with sore wounds, soaked with blood, the bone-house destroyed. Blood flowed in waves, with hot gore.)

A space later, Andrew's second torment echoes the first:

> Swat *yðum weoll*
> þurh bancofan,   *blod* lifrum swealg,
> *hatan heolfre;*   hra weorces ne sann
> wundum werig.   Þa cwom wopes hring
> þurh þæs beornes breost (1275b–9a)

(Blood flowed in waves, through the bone-chamber, blood poured in gushes, with hot gore. The body did not cease suffering, exhausted from the wounds. Then came a ring of tears, through the man's breast.)

Both passages feature versions of the half-line 'hatan heolfre', as well as 'blod' and 'weallan'. In using a common vocabulary of surging waves of hot blood, Andrew's first two days of torture both recall the dark lake in which Grendel dies:

> Ðær wæs on *blode*   brim *weallende*;
> atol *yða* geswing   eal gemenged
> *haton heolfre*   heorodreore *weol*. (847–9)

(There the water surged bloodily, a scary swirl of waves all mixed up with hot gore bubbled with sword-blood.)

Andreas paints Andrew's saintly passion with the burgundy tones of a blood-stained lake, as if the murky water were staining his hagiographic set piece, as if Grendel's mere had entered Andrew only to be bled out again. In using this particular cluster of words twice, it reminds us that *Beowulf* does so too. After the Danes discover Æschere's head, they gaze at the horrifying lake again: 'Flod *blode weol* – folc to sægon – / *hatan heolfre*' (The water surged with blood – the people looked on – with hot gore) (1422–3a). The intimacy between the two poems takes place in the substance of suffering bodies, in the hideous similarity between apostle and Danish warrior and kin of Cain as their bone-houses are destroyed. Andrew's tortures do other work as well. The hot welling blood that soaks him recalls the mere, but the combination of destructive heat and bones recalls two moments connected to the death of Beowulf. One occurs as the dragon bites into him:

> <u>hat</u> ond heaðogrim,   heals ealne ymbefeng
> biteran <u>ban</u>um.   He ge<u>blod</u>egod wearð
> sawuldriore;   <u>swat yðum weoll</u>. (2691–3)

(hot and battle-grim, it surrounded the entire neck with sharp teeth. He was imbued with life-blood. The blood surged in waves.)

Later, at his funeral, the flame consumes Beowulf's body, 'oð þæt he ða <u>banhus</u> ge<u>brocen</u> hæfde / <u>hat</u> on hreðre' (until it had broken the bone-house, hot in the heart) (3147–8a). Both of these moments trace the undoing of Beowulf's body, appropriate sources for the physical unmaking of Andrew.

Richard North has noted the ways in which Andrew is a response to Beowulf, joining the older hero's epic qualities to the happy possibility of Christian redemption. Andrew, put differently, wins his battles, his *banhus* does not stay *gebrocen*. Still, the close lexical relationship between *Andreas* and *Beowulf* underscores intimacies within the older poem. Andrew's tortures allusively join Beowulf's death to Grendel's and Æschere's, suggesting the horror of all death, unconcerned with heroism, monstrosity, or sanctity. What the *Andreas* poet finds in *Beowulf* are bones breaking, hot gore, waves of surging blood.

***

> And byd him that, on alle thyng,
> He take up Seys body the kyng,
> That lyeth ful pale and nothyng rody.
> Bid hym crepe into the body
> And doo it goon to Alcione
> The quene, ther she lyeth allone,
> And shewe hir shortly, hit ys no nay,
> How hit was dreynt thys other day;

And do the body speke ryght soo,
Ryght as hyt was woned to doo
The whiles that it was alyve.

Geoffrey Chaucer[23]

The insomniac narrator of Chaucer's *The Book of the Duchess* reads the story of Ceyx and Alcyone to while away the night. He finds in Morpheus's encounter with Alcyone while inhabiting Ceyx's drowned body a scene of multiple intimacies: the committed love of husband and wife, meeting once again at night, albeit only in seeming; the uncanny closeness of a god creeping into a corpse and speaking with its voice. This vision is embedded in a scene of reading, in the narrator's bedtime encounter with a marvellous 'romaunce' (48). The old fables written in this book provoke wonder in the narrator: in reading them he also experiences a dark encounter with a zombie text speaking from the past. *Andreas*, too, is haunted by both bodies and texts. Its story is populated by the walking dead. Christ appears inhabiting the body of a seafarer, the stone angel orders Abraham, Isaac, and Jacob to rise from their graves and proclaim the Lord, and drowned Mermedonians are raised up to life again. The revivified dead in both *Andreas* and *Duchess* stand for the way a writer can make an old text live again by using it as a source, retelling it, just as Chaucer retells the story of Alcyone from Ovid, or the *Andreas* poet recalls Cynewulf and *Beowulf*. Chaucer's take on this motif reminds us that the use of sources has an affective component, ironic, satirical, distanced, loving, awed, or desiring. Above all, the encounter with a zombie is one of wonder, in its full medieval sense of marvelling and horror.[24]

The stone angel in *Andreas* is not dead per se, but it is a thing miraculously made to move and enliven the dead. In doing so, it not only awakens buried patriarchs who figure the dead letter of the Old Testament, it also animates the monsters of *Beowulf*. When Jesus commands the stone angel to search out the graves in Mamre, the line describing his command recalls the curse of Cain:

Gewat he þa feran,   swa him frea mihtig,
scyppend wera,   *gescrifen hæfde*,
ofer *mearc*paðu (786–8a)

(He went travelling then over the path through the march, just as the powerful lord, the creator of men, had appointed to him)

Line 787 forms a unique parallel to *Beowulf* 106, 'siþðan him *scyppen forscrifen hæfde*' (since the creator had condemned him), describing

Grendel's banishment to the fens. The poet of *Andreas* slyly changes the negative *forscrifan* (to condemn, proscribe) to the more ambivalent term *gescrifan* (to judge, assign, appoint; to shrive, censure),[25] but he reinforces the connection to Grendel, the '*mearc*stapa' (wanderer or stepper in the borderlands) by having the stone angel walk on the '*mearc*paðu' (march-path). The parallel suggests that walkers of the marches are dangerous, even – or perhaps because – they have been appointed to their liminal spaces by God. *Andreas*'s description of the rising of the dead patriarchs is haunted by *Beowulf* too, if only by extension. The introduction of Grendel is followed by an awakening, the 'eotenas ond ylfe ond orcneas' (giants and elves and monsters) (112) that arose or 'onwocon' from Cain's crime against Abel.

The wonder of the stone angel scene in *Andreas*, one that prompts the Jews observing it to accuse Jesus of witchcraft, lies partly in its reincarnation of Beowulfian monsters. The angel embodies Grendel as it steps along borderlands, but even before it begins moving it recalls the dragon and its treasure:

> Ne dorste þa forhylman   hælendes bebod
> wundor fore weorodum,   ac of wealle ahleop,
> *frod fyrngeweorc*,   þæt he on foldan stod,
> *stan fram stane*. (735–8a)

(The wonder before the multitudes did not dare then to leave the Saviour's command uncompleted, but it leapt from the wall, the wise ancient work, so that it stood on the earth, stone from stone.)

This stunning scene echoes another awakening near stone, as the dragon in *Beowulf* is interrupted from his sleep by the theft of his treasure:

>   frea sceawode
> fira *fyrngeweorc*   forman siðe.
> Þa se wyrm onwoc,   wroht wæs geniwad;
> *stonc* ða æfter *stane* (2285b–2288a)

(The lord examined the ancient work of men for the first time. Then the dragon awoke, quarrel was renewed. It sniffed along the stone)

A few lines earlier, the dragon is 'wintrum *frod*' (wise in winters) (2277a), strengthening this cluster of light echoes. The angel that commands dead bodies to rise and speak also carries in its matter and its movement the creatures of *Beowulf*, especially as they appear in scenes of animation, awakening, incitement. The sculpture that comes alive moves with the decisiveness of a cursed descendant of Cain, with the smell of an old dragon. *Beowulf* slips into the textual body of *Andreas* in uncanny ways, animating its stones and its corpses with inhuman energy.

✱✱✱

> Sitting on the floor with her arms round Mrs. Ramsay's knees, close as she could get, smiling to think that Mrs. Ramsay would never know the reason of that pressure, she imagined how in the chambers of the mind and heart of the woman who was, physically, touching her, were stood, like the treasures in the tombs of kings, tablets bearing sacred inscriptions, which if one could spell them out, would teach one everything, but they would never be offered openly, never made public. What art was there, known to love or cunning, by which one pressed through into those secret chambers? What device for becoming, like waters poured into one jar, inextricably the same, one with the object one adored? … for it was not knowledge but unity she desired, not inscriptions on tablets, nothing that could be written in any language known to men, but intimacy itself, which is knowledge, she had thought, leaning her head on Mrs. Ramsay's knee.
>
> Virginia Woolf[26]

Certain Old English poems show how the intimacy of a relationship can be felt, and remembered, through the body's gestures. When the main speaker of *The Wanderer* falls asleep, he recalls a physical proximity to his lord at once formal and childlike: 'þinceð him on mode þæt he his mondryhten / clyppe ond cysse ond on cneo lecge / honda ond heafod' (it seems in his heart that he is embracing and kissing his liege lord, and laying his hands and head on his knee) (41–3a). Knees suggest familial or tribal relation in old Germanic languages.[27] In *Andreas*, the Jewish high priest at the Temple claims that he knows that Christ is no divinity, but a person born in this land, among his relatives or 'cneomagum' (knee-relatives) (685b). Like shoulders, knees join people to one another in social and affective relations.

But there are other ways to express intimacy of the soul through the body. Reading each other is one of them, looking into the tablets of the heart, decoding the inscriptions of another person's character or soul. Hrothgar does this when he looks at the hilt Beowulf brings him and explains Beowulf to himself. 'Oferhyda ne gym' (do not be intent on pride) (1760b), he says to a man who will fall prey to that very sin, and he warns him of all the ways he might go on to die. While examining the mysterious letters ('runstafas') (1695a) on an old work of giants ('enta ærgeweorc') (1679a), Hrothgar in fact reads the young warrior standing before him, swelling in his victory.[28]

The *Andreas* poet shapes his material into just such a scene of double-reading. It occurs late in the poem, after Andrew is visited in prison by Christ, who miraculously restores the apostle to physical health following three days of brutal torture. The poet interjects at this point to describe the process by which he has composed the poem, complaining of the difficulty of telling the story of these heroic deeds. The narrative flashes back into the prison, where Andrew sees columns by the wall, which, like the hilt in *Beowulf*, are the ancient work of giants ('eald enta geweorc') (1495a). Andrew addresses one of the columns, asks it to release a flood to destroy the Mermedonians, and tells it that God inscribed his ten laws on it, described as 'terrible mysteries' ('recene geryno') (1511a). Andrew finally prompts the column to understand itself: 'þu scealt hræðe cyðan / gif ðu his ondgitan ænige hæbbe' ('you will quickly demonstrate if you have any understanding of him') (1520b–1521). The column responds silently, but fatally. It opens and lets out a stream that visits horror and death on the Mermedonians.

In other versions of Andrew's story, there is no authorial interruption. The column has no mysterious writing on it, nor is it particularly ancient. A statue on top of the column opens its mouth to let out the flood when commanded by Andrew, but there is no suggestion that either the column or the statue could be readable. In the moment when Andrew suggests a reading of the column, the *Andreas* poet prompts his audience to re-read *Beowulf*. The authorial interruption and the description of Andrew's gaze and address to the column have multiple unique borrowings from *Beowulf*, with a particularly thick cluster at lines 1487–95.

What does *Andreas* read inscribed in *Beowulf*? Unsurprisingly, pride and failure. Or perhaps not so unsurprisingly. So often *Andreas* is described as telling a saint's life in English heroic language, as if the vocabulary of heroism were an obvious good in the Anglo-Saxon period, a sweet sugar coating around the bitter pill of a Christian story. The passage mentioned above echoes a number of single lines in *Beowulf*, but also three small clusters, and these are more telling. A man wise in the law should recall the hardship of grim battles ('grimra guða') (1487a), says the narrator, adding that it is an old story how he suffered a great number ('weorna feala')

(1490a) of torments. The reader might recall the story of Andrew from its Latin source at that moment, and might just as well remember Unferth's exchange with Beowulf, in which Unferth suggests that Beowulf's previous success at 'grimre guðe' (527a) will not be repeated, and Beowulf accuses him of speaking a bit too much, 'worn fela' (530a), about Breca.

Another memory surfaces, of an older Beowulf, weaker but still boastful. After the authorial interruption, the imprisoned Andrew sees columns standing by the wall: 'He be wealle geseah ... stapulas standan ... eald enta geweorc' (1492a, 1494a, 1495a). It is a clear echo of Beowulf's approach to the dragon's barrow, when he sees stone arches by the wall: 'Geseah ða be wealle ... stondan stanbogan' (2542a, 2545a). This is more than a borrowing. Beowulf sees not only the stone arches, but also a hot burning stream that keeps him from approaching the hoard (2545–9), dividing him from the gold he has just sworn to obtain or die ('gold gegangan') (2536a). Listeners who did remember the scene from the older epic might have picked up on the *Andreas* poet's little joke.[29] 'Læt nu of þinum staþole streamas weallan' (let streams flow forth from your foundation now) (1503), Andrew says to the stone column, 'ðu golde eart, / sincgife, sylla' (you are better than gold or a gift of treasure) (1508b–1509a). There is no internal reason for Andrew to tell the column it is better than treasure or gold, unless in reading it, he reads Beowulf. He reminds the audience of the folly of a king who left his people to search for gold, was willing even to risk his own life for that treasure, and was stopped temporarily by a stream coming from a stone.

Andrew in prison also summons a scene of death, the end of the boast:

> Ða se æðeling giong
> þæt he *bi wealle*   wishycgende
> gesæt on sesse;   *seah on enta geweorc*,
> hu ða stanbogan   *stapulum fæste*
> ece eorðreced   innan healde. (2715b–2719)

(Then the prince went, so that he sat on a seat by the wall thinking wisely. He looked on the work of giants, how the stone arches, firm in their columns, held the earth-hall perpetually from the inside.)

Here, *Beowulf* echoes itself, repeating the image of a man near a wall, gazing at old architectural features, but this time sitting to contemplate his pyrrhic victory.

Andreas thus recalls three moments from *Beowulf* in lines 1487–95: the hero's youthful debate with Unferth about the extent of his brave deeds; his entry into the dragon's barrow; and his final, dying gaze at that same earth-hall. This passage is a riddle that, for a while, might be resolved as Beowulf or as Andrew. Perhaps the audience was meant to see the superiority of the saint, his power over deadly streams, his endurance in closed spaces filled with the crafted but foreboding old work of giants. Still, the audience might have seen something else too, the visual echo between Andrew, in his prison cell, nearly killed but now with terrifying destructive energy at his command, and Beowulf in the dragon's lair, vanquished by a monstrous power he could not, ultimately, control. Perhaps it is appropriate that the *Andreas* narrator's elaborately humble interjection quotes Wiglaf, the man who views the wreckage of Beowulf's community.[30] The story of the saint is 'ofer min gemet' (over my capacity) (1481a), says the narrator, just as Wiglaf helped his kinsman 'ofer min gemet' (2879a). *Andreas* communes with *Beowulf*'s monstrous heroes and hidden places of devastating liquidation. It also resonates with its observant, critical voices, with Unferth and Wiglaf, men who understand the limits of heroism.

***

> We grow closer through distance, through a gap of time or space or context across which we are somehow better able to apprehend connection than if that which we seek were directly at hand.
>   Stacey D'Erasmo[31]

Does absence make the heart grow fonder because the loved one's blemishes and peccadilloes are out of sight? Or is it something deeper, the fear of death that might arrive at any time, the knowledge that, in a flash, a temporary separation could become permanent? Does intimacy reside in distance or in reunion? In matching scenes of reconnection, *Beowulf* and *Andreas* convey the sweet familiarity of seeing a beloved friend or leader. When Beowulf fights Grendel's mother in the mere, the Scyldings see the blood mingled with water and write him off for dead. His own troop awaits him faithfully, however, staring at the water and hoping he will emerge. When he does so, their greeting is almost maternal in its relief:

> Eodon him *þa togeanes,* *Gode þancodon,*
> ðryðlic þegna heap, þeodnes gefegon,
> *þæs þe hi* hyne *gesundne* *geseon moston.* (1626–8)

(They went then to meet him, the mighty band of thanes, thanked God, rejoiced in their chief, that they might see him unhurt.)

Andreas could not resist connecting to this moment of connection. Here is Matthew's reaction when he sees that Andrew has come to him in the Mermedonian prison:

> Geseh þa under swegle   swæsne geferan,
> halig haligne;   hyht wæs geniwad.
> *Aras þa togenes,   Gode þancade*
> *þæs ðe hie onsunde   æfre moston*
> *geseon* under sunnan (1009–13a)

(He saw there under the sky his dear companion, saint saw saint. Hope was renewed. He rose then to meet him, thanked God that they might ever see each other under the sun.)

Andreas transforms the reunion of military band and lord into an encounter between two friends and equals, and transposes it, momentarily and figuratively, outdoors. Intimacy, this moment seems to suggest, is recovery, it is the hope of vanquishing death, it is a step into the light.

What does *Andreas* achieve by moving towards *Beowulf*, then? Here is a poem obsessed with bringing back the dead, with its stone angel that awakens patriarchs from their graves and its wayward saint who brings back his dead teacher. *Andreas* teaches that miracles can recall the deceased, but memory does too; after all, Andrew's education throughout the poem is to understand what he can achieve by remembering Christ's power. The poem brings back *Beowulf* too, but at the level of style. It is filled with allusions to the previous epic, miniature riddles that could be solved with Beowulfian scenes. As long as Beowulf is a question, he still lives. Perhaps this is why *Andreas* draws so heavily on Beowulf's encounter with the dragon. It seems interested in fixing its readers in that precise moment when the Geatish hero is poised on the edge of death. By weaving the poetry of *Beowulf* into its narrative, *Andreas* proves that style is never dead, that its history can always be rewritten. *Andreas*'s imitation of *Beowulf* is creative misreading, wry criticism, and intimate reawakening.

Notes

1 Virginia Woolf, 'Montaigne', in Andrew McNellie (ed.), *The essays of Virginia Woolf*, vol. 4 (London: Hogarth Press, 1994), p. 71.

2 Anita R. Riedinger, 'The formulaic relationship between *Beowulf* and *Andreas*', in Helen Damico and John Leyerle (eds), *Heroic poetry in the Anglo-Saxon period: studies in honor of Jess B. Bessinger, Jr.* (Kalamazoo, MI: Medieval Institute Publications, 1993), pp. 283–312; Anita R. Riedinger, '*Andreas* and the formula in transition', in Patrick J. Gallacher and Helen Damico (eds), *Hermeneutics and medieval culture* (Albany, NY: State University of New York Press, 1989), pp. 183–91; Alison M. Powell, 'Verbal parallels in *Andreas* and its relationship to *Beowulf* and Cynewulf', PhD thesis, University of Cambridge, 2002; Julius Zupitza, 'Zur Frage nach der Quelle von Cynewulfs Andreas', *Zeitschrift für deutsches Altertum und deutsche Literatur*, 30 (1886), 175–85; Hans Schabram, 'Andreas und Beowulf. Parallelstellen als Zeugnis für literarische Abhängigkeit', *Nachrichten der Giessener Hochschulgesellschaft*, 34 (1965), 201–18; David Hamilton, '*Andreas* and *Beowulf*: placing the hero', in Lewis E. Nicholson and Dolores Warwick Frese (eds), *Anglo-Saxon poetry: essays in appreciation for John C. McGalliard* (Notre Dame, IN: University of Notre Dame Press, 1975), pp. 81–98; Paul Cavill, '*Beowulf* and *Andreas*: two maxims', *Neophilologus*, 77 (1993), 479–87; Claes Schaar, *Critical studies in the Cynewulf group* (Lund: C. W. K. Gleerup, 1949), pp. 261–97; Leonard J. Peters, 'The relationship of the Old English *Andreas* to *Beowulf*', *PMLA*, 66.5 (1951), 844–63; Andy Orchard, 'The originality of *Andreas*', in Leonard Neidorf, Rafael J. Pascual, and Tom Shippey (eds), *Old English philology: studies in honour of R. D. Fulk* (Cambridge: D. S. Brewer, 2016), pp. 331–70.

3 For *Andreas*'s sources and parallels, see Franz Blatt (ed.), *Die lateinischen Bearbeitungen der Acta Andreae et Matthiae apud Anthropophagos* (Gießen: Alfred Töpelmann, 1930); Robert Boenig, *The acts of Andrew in the country of the cannibals: translations from the Greek, Latin, and Old English* (New York: Garland Publishing, 1991); 'Πράξεις Ἀνδρέου καὶ Ματθεία εἰς τὴν χώραν τῶν ἀνθρωφάγων', in Constantin Tischendorf (ed.), *Acta apostolorum apocrypha* (Leipzig: Avenarius and Mendelssohn, 1851); Richard Adelbert Lipsius and Maximilien Bonnet (eds), *Acta apostolorum apocrypha* (Leipzig: Hermann Mendelssohn, 1898); R. Morris (ed.), *The Blickling Homilies*, Early English Text Society (London: Oxford University Press, 1967), pp. 228–49; James W. Bright and James R. Hulbert (eds), *Bright's Anglo-Saxon reader* (New York: Holt, Reinhart and Winston, 1963), pp. 113–28.

4 Martha A. Malamud, *A poetics of transformation: Prudentius and classical mythology* (Ithaca, NY: Cornell University Press, 1989), p. 37.

5 Richard North, 'Meet the pagans: on the misuse of *Beowulf* in *Andreas*', in Marilina Cesario and Hugh Magennis (eds), *Aspects of knowledge: preserving and reinventing traditions of learning in the Middle Ages* (Manchester: Manchester University Press, 2018), pp. 185–209.

6 Quotations from *Andreas* are from Richard North and Michael Bintley (eds), *Andreas: an edition* (Liverpool: Liverpool University Press, 2016) and are cited in the text by line number. Translations are my own.

7 Quotations from *Beowulf*, with occasional minor changes, are from R. D. Fulk, Robert E. Bjork, and John D. Niles (eds), *Klaeber's Beowulf*, 4th edn (Toronto: University of Toronto Press, 2014) and are cited in the text by line number. Translations are my own.

8 See also R. M. Lumiansky, 'The contexts of O.E. "ealuscerwen" and "meoduscerwen"', *JEGP*, 48.1 (1949), 116–26.

9 North, 'Meet the pagans'.

10 Ibid., p. 205.

11 North and Bintley, *Andreas*, p. 64.

12 Joseph Conrad, 'The secret sharer', in *Heart of darkness and the secret sharer* (New York: Bantam Books, 1969), p. 151.

13 See, for example, John Niles's analysis of 'The Wife's Lament' and 'The Husband's Message' alongside other enigmatic texts in John D. Niles, *Old English enigmatic poems and the play of the texts* (Turnhout: Brepols, 2006). On the more expansive riddle tradition, see Andy Orchard, 'Enigma variations: the Anglo-Saxon riddle-tradition', in Andy Orchard and Katherine O'Brien O'Keeffe (eds), *Latin learning and English lore: studies in Anglo-Saxon literature for Michael Lapidge*, vol 1 (Toronto: University of Toronto Press, 2005), pp. 284–304.

14 George Philip Krapp (ed.), *Andreas and The Fates of the Apostles: two Anglo-Saxon narrative poems* (Boston: Ginn and Company, 1906), p. xxxv; Jason R. Puskar, '*Hwa þas fitte fegde*? Questioning Cynewulf's claim of authorship', *ES*, 92.1 (2011), 1–19.

15 David Clark, *Between medieval men: male friendship and desire in early medieval English literature* (Oxford: Oxford University Press, 2009), p. 35.

16 Andy Orchard, *Pride and prodigies: studies in the monsters of the Beowulf-manuscript* (Cambridge: D. S. Brewer, 1995), pp. 32–3.

17 Geoffrey Chaucer, *The book of the duchess*, in Larry D. Benson (ed.), *The Riverside Chaucer* (Boston: Houghton Mifflin, 1987), pp. 329–46, ll. 749–57.

18 See Amity Reading, 'Baptism, conversion, and selfhood in the Old English *Andreas*', *Studies in philology*, 112.1 (2015), 1–23, at 20; Irina Dumitrescu, *The experience of education in Anglo-Saxon literature* (Cambridge: Cambridge University Press, 2018), pp. 90–128.

19 Conrad, 'The secret sharer', p. 142.

20 North and Bintley, *Andreas*, p. 82.

21 David Hamilton, 'The diet and digestion of allegory in *Andreas*', *ASE*, 1 (1972), 147–58, at 155.

22 Conrad, 'The secret sharer', p. 146.

23 Chaucer, *The book of the duchess*, ll. 140–51.

24 Dennis Quinn, '*Me audiendi … stupentem*: the restoration of wonder in Boethius's *Consolation*', *University of Toronto quarterly*, 57.4 (1988),

447–70; Caroline Walker Bynum, 'Wonder', *The American historical review*, 102.1 (1997), 1–26.

25 Joseph Bosworth and T. Northcote Toller (eds), *An Anglo-Saxon dictionary* (London: Oxford University Press, 1898), s.v. 'forscrifan', 'gescrifan'.

26 Virginia Woolf, *To the lighthouse* (New York: Harcourt Brace Jovanovich, 1955), pp. 78–9.

27 Rosemarie Lühr (ed.), *Etymologisches Wörterbuch des Althochdeutschen*, vol. 5, *iba–luzzilo* (Gottingen: Vandenhoeck and Ruprecht, 2014), s.v. 'kniuwento'.

28 See also Seth Lerer, *Literacy and power in Anglo-Saxon literature* (Lincoln, NE: University of Nebraska Press, 1991), pp. 158–94.

29 On the humour pervading *Andreas*, see Jonathan Wilcox, 'Eating people is wrong: funny style in *Andreas* and its analogues', in Catherine E. Karkov and George Hardin Brown (eds), *Anglo-Saxon styles* (Albany, NY: State University of New York Press, 2003), pp. 201–22.

30 For more on Wiglaf, see Mary Dockray-Miller's chapter in this volume, pp. 304–18.

31 Stacey D'Erasmo, *The art of intimacy: the space between* (Minneapolis, MN: Graywolf Press, 2013), p. 112.

13

Beowulf, Bryher, and the Blitz: a queer history[1]

Peter Buchanan

The novel *Beowulf*, an account of a London tearoom during the Blitz, occupies a curious and somewhat embarrassing place in early medieval literary studies. The first notice that early medievalists took of it is a brief entry in Donald Fry's bibliography of the Old English poem: 'Bryher, Winifred. *Beowulf*: A Novel. NY, 1956. No relation to the poem.'[2] This entry poses several interesting questions about the nature of bibliographic inquiry because it explicitly distances itself from the subject of the bibliography in which it is included. Much like a Wikipedia disambiguation page or Alec Guinness on a desert planet, this entry exists solely to let serious scholars of Old English literature know: this is not the *Beowulf* you're looking for. Fry's encyclopaedic zeal led him to include an entry for Bryher's novel in spite of its apparent irrelevance to the topic, although I am left wondering how often bibliographies of major literary works include similar entries – presumably Skelton scholars don't feel a need to carefully distinguish the sixteenth-century author from the twentieth-century comedian. Fry includes the entry due to the singularity of the name and its clear association with a certain type of literature, an association that is apparent even outside of scholarly study. The two reviews available for Bryher's *Beowulf* on Amazon make this clear. The earliest review, from a disgruntled reader expecting something different, aside from making a hash of the book, notes, 'This is not about the Beowulf [*sic*] you might think it is', while the later reviewer offers a much more accurate and sympathetic review, highly recommending the book 'as long as you're not in the market for Viking swords and gore'.[3] These statements, both scholarly and not, exist to temper expectations and prevent readers from being misled. Fry's 'no relation', a phrase more commonly seen as a journalistic parenthetical, lets scholars of the period, who may have incidentally heard mention of the novel, know that there is nothing to see, nothing to look into, and nothing of interest, at least as it relates to the study of the poem. It's a different sort of blood running through the veins of the two works. But relations are tricky, as are bibliographies. Rather than distancing study of the novel from study of the poem, Fry's entry calls attention to itself by its very distinctiveness. A close investigation of the novel suggests much more consanguinity than expected and in fact challenges our conception of what it means to relate to the past, a past in Bryher's novel that very explicitly includes the Old English poem. Rather than bearing an incidental titular similarity, the two works share several related concerns: courage in the face of violent attack; the creation of community through the sharing of food and drink; the role of women in public life; the mediation of past, present, and future amid upheaval. All this is to say nothing of similarities between the Beowulf of poetic tradition and the ugly plaster bulldog bearing his name in Bryher's novel, nor of some explicit discussion of the poem within the novel. This speaks to a certain scholarly hubris about the kinds of interpretations that the poem affords and our ability to parse works that adapt without being adaptations. Bryher's *Beowulf* is a queer, feminist masterpiece of documentary realism and modernist whimsy in which the Old English *Beowulf* plays a pivotal and underappreciated role, and whose marginalization within the field of early medieval studies is a consequence of a masculinizing ethos that often goes unchallenged, even in feminist scholarship on the poem.

Throughout this chapter, I will argue that Bryher's *Beowulf*, while overtly a historical novel about the London Blitz during the Second World War, also practises a unique kind of queer historiography, layering multiple times and perspectives to demonstrate the fundamental instability and idiosyncrasy of interpretation. First, I will provide a brief account of Bryher's life – given her relative obscurity outside of historical studies of modernism – in which I will pay special attention to her relationship with H.D., the modernist poet and 'since 1919 [Bryher's] companion, sometime lover, and always friend',[4] and the French bookseller Adrienne Monnier, to whom the novel is dedicated. H.D. and Monnier represent the nodes of queer community around which Bryher's life revolved, and understanding their relationships is critical to understanding Bryher's under-studied role as both patron and producer of art. Further, H.D. is the source of my own queer critical attachment to Bryher and her projects, as it was through my passion for H.D.'s work that I became aware of Bryher and her use of early medieval themes.

Next, in analysing the nature of Bryher's queer historiography, I will draw on Carolyn Dinshaw's queer touch across time and Elizabeth Freeman's argument for a queer writing of embodied intimacy. I will also draw on H.D., whose poems inspired by the London Blitz use the concept of the palimpsest as a metaphor for a queer, feminist historiography of ancient mythologies. These different modes of queer historiography all shape my understanding of Bryher's distinctive mode of intimacy and community in the novel to shape engagement with tradition and the place of women in a world that can be hostile to them. Bryher's *Beowulf* shows readers the Blitz through the eyes of the owners and patrons of the Warming Pan, a tearoom run by Selina Tippett and Angelina Hawkins, who seek to empower women and create community. Both women embody the contradictions of an awareness of the past with a desire for new futures that meet in a tumultuous present, and these contradictions come to a head in the figure of Beowulf, a plaster bulldog that Angelina Hawkins buys with the grocery money, intending it as a symbol of English resilience and resistance in the face of attack. The bulldog's very garishness draws the eye and provokes thought about the interpretation of the past in ways that are as multiple as the people who look upon it.

Finally, my analysis will focus on developing the queer relation between poem and novel, situating Bryher's work within subsequent feminist scholarship in early medieval studies. The women of the London tearoom and their relationship to the past as represented by the plaster bulldog will lead into an analysis of the women in *Beowulf*, particularly Wealhtheow. I will posit a certain resonance between tearoom and mead-hall, in which communities are created and strengthened by the words and deeds of women. I will argue that scholars of Old English literature have too often taken the history of women's reception of the literature for granted and that we need to value the creative work of adaptation performed by Bryher's novel, which can and should shake up orthodoxies of interpretation that have a corrosive effect in our field. That *Beowulf* is a story by, about, and for men is too often taken for granted, and Bryher offers an opportunity for scholars to reconsider Wealhtheow's speeches in the mead-hall in a new light, one that both critiques the limits of the community that women created in early medieval life but that also adapts it to new purposes.

Much to the chagrin of bibliographers such as Fry and the creators of library catalogues who are generally uncomfortable with mononyms, Bryher is the entirety of the author's chosen name. She was born in September 1894[5] as Annie Winifred Ellerman, the daughter of the shipping magnate John Ellerman, one of the richest men in England.[6] As a young woman, she was deeply influenced by the poet Hilda Doolittle, whose first publication launched the imagist movement and gave her the abbreviated name H.D. by which she would become known. H.D. had given Ezra Pound one of her poems to read, upon which he wrote 'H. D. Imagiste' before sending it straight to Harriet Monroe's then new and avant-garde magazine *Poetry*.[7] H.D.'s book *Sea Garden* captured the imagination of the young Bryher, well before she knew the identity of its author:

> There will always be one book among all others that makes us aware of ourselves; for me, it is *Sea Garden* by H. D. I learned it by heart from cover to cover ... I began the morning and ended the day repeating the poems. It was not until some months later that I discovered ... that H. D. was a woman and American.[8]

In 1918, at the age of 24, Bryher was given H.D.'s London address. H.D. invited Bryher in, and while Bryher 'was waiting for a question to prove my integrity and the extent of my knowledge', H.D. asked the kind of question that guarantees lifelong love and companionship: 'I wonder if you could tell me something ... have you ever seen a puffin and what is it like?' Bryher responded, 'They call them sea parrots and there are dozens of them in the Scillies. I go there almost every summer, you must join me next year.'[9] In fact, Bryher's chosen name was taken from the name of one of the Scilly Isles, located off the south-western coast of Cornwall.[10]

The start of the following year, 1919, was a time of great turmoil. Both H.D. and her then husband, the writer Richard Aldington, had been pursuing other romantic entanglements, and H.D.'s led to a pregnancy; during her convalescence, she contracted Spanish influenza.[11] When Bryher visited, she was shocked to find H.D. on the brink of death. Her landlady bluntly asked Bryher, 'Do you know the woman? She is going to die. Can you pay the funeral expenses?'[12] Bryher dedicated herself and her money to H.D.'s care, and in spite of the grim predictions of H.D.'s landlady and doctor, both she and her child, Frances Perdita, survived. This marked the beginning of their lifelong companionship. The trio travelled frequently, including trips to Greece and Egypt that would prove significant in H.D.'s later writing. H.D. felt immense gratitude to and concern for Bryher, due to suicidal tendencies that stemmed from Bryher's discomfort with a rigid gender binary, identifying at some points more as a man than a woman.[13] Although the two were lovers only 'comparatively briefly', they were close for the rest of their lives, writing letters while apart.[14]

In adulthood, Bryher became increasingly assertive in using her fortune to act as patron to a growing circle of modernist writers and artists, but by no means including H.D.'s former fiancé Ezra Pound, whom Bryher both disliked and was disliked by, as strong a point in favour of her personal character as any that could be imagined. In 1927 Bryher married H.D.'s lover, Kenneth MacPherson, funding a magazine on cinematography, *Close Up*, as well as appearing together with H.D. in MacPherson's 1930 silent film, *Borderline*, which starred Paul Robeson and employed experimental methods to mine the sexual drama of an interracial love triangle.[15] MacPherson and Bryher became adoptive parents to Perdita and made their home with H.D. in Switzerland, though travelling frequently to London, Paris, and Berlin.

In Paris, Bryher became a strong supporter of the expatriate community of writers and artists on the Left Bank, particularly those swirling around the milieu of Sylvia Beach, the American founder of the English-language bookshop *Shakespeare and Company*, and her romantic partner Adrienne Monnier, owner of the French bookstore and lending library *La Maison des Amis des Livres*. Bryher's introduction to Beach and Monnier came from her first husband, Robert McAlmon, whom she met while travelling in America with H.D.[16] Concerning her introduction to Bryher, Beach wrote,

> Then, one day, a great day for Shakespeare and Company, Robert McAlmon brought her in – a shy young English girl in a tailor-made suit and a hat with a couple of streamers that reminded me of a sailor's ... Bryher, as far as I can remember, never said a word ... So McAlmon and I did the talking, and Bryher did the looking. She was quietly observing everything in her Bryhery way, just as she observed everything when she visited 'The Warming Pan' teashop in the London blitz days – and, as *Beowulf* proves, nothing escaped her.[17]

Bryher's quiet shyness belied her deep engagement with the avant-garde community, and she would offer crucial financial support to Beach in lean times, providing her with enough financial stability to write her memoirs.[18] As a result of her personal shyness and her multifaceted role behind the scenes in promoting art and literature, Emily Wojcik notes that

> Bryher can be hard to locate within primary accounts of her time, in part because she appears to have been so willing to recede into the background, silencing herself in ways that are themselves culturally

significant … This personal and professional reticence has also, unfortunately, resulted in a critical invisibility that is only now being undone.[19]

However, it was Monnier with whom Bryher would develop the closest friendship. Of their first meeting, Bryher notes, 'I was shy with Adrienne Monnier at first, my British accent got in my way and I also knew directly I looked at her round forehead and deceptively placid blue eyes that she was a thought reader.'[20] Monnier used her clairvoyant talents to recommend exactly the books Bryher most needed to read, and Monnier and Beach's home became a place of fine food and conversation with 'some of the finest minds in France', although Bryher's silent observation continued, such that she would later write, 'I never spoke unless I was spoken to and so they forgot sometimes that I was a foreigner. Sylvia, of course, had been adopted by them all.'[21] Through Beach and Monnier, Bryher would become acquainted with writers, artists, and thinkers including Gertrude Stein, Tristan Tzara, Man Ray, and Walter Benjamin, whose escape from Nazi Germany to Paris Bryher aided.[22]

Bryher's social circle established intimacy through meals eaten together, books shared, and writings dedicated to one another. The English edition of Bryher's *Beowulf* is dedicated 'To *Sylvia Beach* and the memory of *Adrienne Monnier*'. In Beach and Monnier, we glimpse a model for women as both owners of businesses and as creators of fellowship through food and drink, like the women who own the Warming Pan in *Beowulf*. But the dedication also speaks to the importance of Beach and Monnier to the publication of the work. Initially published in a French translation, Bryher's novel found its first serious critic in Monnier, who wrote an introduction to it. Monnier's introduction helps situate the novel, revealing the journalistic eye that Bryher brought to the work of building her characters, among whose number we should include the setting of the novel, the Warming Pan itself. Bryher relied on observations of actual people and places during the Blitz and adapted them to the shifting narrative of her novel. For Monnier, Bryher's work deserves comparison to 'the admirable documentary films that were shown to us a bit after the Liberation', but is also elevated by 'the art of the novel, that is to say, a transposition into a domain that is more plastic and more rich in spiritual values'.[23] It is also from Monnier that we gain a glimpse of the relationship of the novel to the poem from which it derives its name: 'Bryher has given to her book, in a manner that is half humorous, half serious, the name of the hero of the Anglo-Saxon epic.'[24]

If scholars of early medieval England are interested in studying the reception of pre-Conquest English literature, then we must begin by not dismissing works as irrelevant to our study if they approach their adaptation and use with an ironic and humorous intent. We must begin by recognizing that adaptation often puts old things to new uses, transforming the hero of an Old English poem set in Scandinavia into a tacky plaster statue symbolizing English resistance, and that this kind of adaptation is not strange or impermissible but is a natural result of living together with the past and approaching it not merely with reverence but with the full range of emotion.

In addition to dedicating her books to members of her social circle, Bryher was also a dedicatee, and of a book also spawned by the experiences of the Blitz, the first volume of H.D.'s *Trilogy*, *The Walls Do Not Fall*, whose dedication reads like a poem of time and place:

To Bryher
for Karnak 1923
from London 1942[25]

H.D.'s dedication signals her preoccupation with the past, connecting her own experience of the Blitz to her travels undertaken with Bryher nearly twenty years before to the archaeological site of Karnak in Egypt, whose connection to the past informs H.D.'s approach to the present. Nor is this the only dedication to Bryher, who is also featured in the dedications of a translation of Euripides' *Ion* and H.D.'s novel *Palimpsest*.[26] In *The H.D. Book*, Robert Duncan argues that in these dedications Bryher emerges as a patroness modelled after late medieval art patrons, at once steadfast and unidealized.[27] This dedication came after a lifetime spent together, and in Duncan's words:

> The dedication of *The Walls Do Not Fall* in 1942 is not a propitiation. In a lifetime, the poetess and her patroness had come to the understanding of old companions, living in some recognition of their differences. But it is perhaps a payment of a kind, 'for Karnak', a gift in return for the gift of 1923. A return.
>
> And the poem itself begins as a letter from H. D. in London to Bryher, who was still in Switzerland in 1942.[28]

The dedicatory communities created by H.D., Bryher, and Monnier create a rich historical context for the reception and transmission of the works, which have taken a long time to receive widespread recognition.[29]

H.D.'s *Trilogy* figures queer, feminist history in terms of a metaphor derived from manuscript culture, the palimpsest. Palimpsests are manuscripts where one layer of text has been scraped away so that the parchment may be used for a new purpose. Palimpsests are of immense historical significance, as the first layer of text may preserve an important witness to texts that may be poorly represented in extant manuscripts from the time. For H.D., the palimpsest becomes an important metaphor for both the recovery of old truths and the writing of the new. Early in *The Walls Do Not Fall*, H.D. imagines a chorus of derisive mockery for her attempts to poetically investigate representations of divine women, too often characterized as 'old flesh-pots' and the difficulty of 'scratch[ing] out // indelible ink of the palimpsest / of past misadventure'.[30] This reveals the dual nature of H.D.'s palimpsest, her attempt both to read under words that have been passed down to 'recover old values',[31] and also to scratch out received tradition to make room for her own writing.

For H.D., the materiality of writing and its connection to violence is revealed all too readily in war. The instruments of writing, 'the stylus, / the palette, the pen, the quill endure' through their association with the masculine figures of Thoth and Hermes, even while 'our books are a floor / of smouldering ash under our feet'.[32] But not only are the books wantonly destroyed in this senseless way. There is also still demand for books: 'yet give us, they still cry, / give us books, // folio, manuscript, old parchment'. However, this demand is driven not by a desire for the word but to undo these materials, to rend and cut them into containers for something other than words, as they 'will do for cartridge cases'; and the poem ends with the wry observation that 'Hatshepsut's name is still circled / with what they call the *cartouche*', punning on cartouche's double meaning as both a paper cartridge containing ammunition as well as the oval figure in Egyptian hieroglyphics that encloses the name of a powerful pharaoh and woman.

H.D.'s poetic ruminations on the materiality of writing serve as the launching point for her consideration of the past, impelled by the horrors and destruction of the Blitz, rooted in the observation that something yet remains – 'Still the walls do not fall'[33] – prompting H.D.'s 'search for historical parallels, research into psychic affinities', according to the 'peculiar intricate map' of her own 'way of thought'.[34] *Trilogy* delves in its three volumes into historical parallels in Egyptian, Greek, Persian, and Judaeo-Christian mythology, culminating in an extended reflection on the figures of Mary Magdalene and Mary the mother of Jesus as seen through the eyes of Kaspar, who is ascribed the gift of myrrh. H.D.'s historical method is, by her own poetic admission, idiosyncratic, drawing on puns, anagrams, and historical resonances to limn the outlines of a recovered place for women in the hierarchies of the divine, with consideration for the fragility of life and the life of words in her historical present.

It was through my love of H.D. that I first encountered Bryher, first as H.D.'s lover and companion, and then as an author in her own right. The *Trilogy* stands with the Old English *Beowulf* as my two favourite poetic works, and so, inevitably, I find myself reading Bryher's *Beowulf* through the queer historical method of H.D., driven by the search for psychic affinities, for reading the sedimentation of historical experience through the metaphor of the palimpsest. As I introduce the characters of Bryher's novel and explore its connection to the Old English poem, it will be with an eye to the interpenetration of different historical epochs and the rich layering of literary history with the experiences of Londoners in the Blitz.

Bryher's *Beowulf* explores the comings and goings of characters around the Warming Pan tearoom, focusing especially on its two proprietors, Selina Tippett and Angelina Hawkins. The point of view of the narrative shifts throughout the novel, and as a result characters (including both the plaster bulldog Beowulf and the Warming Pan itself) are composite images refracted through individual perspectives. The initial perspective is that of Horatio Rashleigh, an elderly artist whose craft never developed beyond Victorian paintings of sailboats for calendars.

Rashleigh's gentlemanly misogyny serves as an introduction to the gender politics of the novel as well as the tension exhibited throughout between desire for the past and change in the present. Disturbed by the sound of one of the other boarders early in the morning, Rashleigh reflects to himself,

> In a well-ordered world, girls would not tear down the stairs to business, clattering like a fledgling man-at-arms in a leather coat without even the pretence of a cap on short, smooth hair. ... Forty years ago Eve would have been taught to creep past his door had a necessary errand called her forth early in the morning.[35]

It is hard as a reader not to delight in Eve's exuberant morning clatter and her refusal to pay heed to feminine fashion norms loosened and undone in the disorderliness of the Blitz. Rashleigh's desire to enforce gender norms and the impotency of his private grumblings to effect their restoration within the world of the Warming Pan render him a figure at once sad and comic, yet affectionately drawn. In one of her memoirs, Bryher noted, 'People complained that [Rashleigh] was a conventional figure when they read *Beowulf*. He was, but I did not invent him. If we had met, I should have shocked him profoundly.'[36] Rashleigh's venial grousing sets the stage for a novel that is often concerned with capturing how people complain about one another, and yet Bryher writes in a whimsical tone that accepts gossip and complaint as an inescapable part of humanity.

The central focus of the novel is Selina Tippett, often referred to simply as the Tippett. Our first introduction to Selina is through the eyes of Rashleigh: 'Poor woman, she was one of nature's less successful drawings, a little sketch scribbled on a telephone pad, and he chuckled, of superimposed O's from rump to chin.'[37] However, the denigration of Rashleigh's observation is contrasted with Selina's first appearance: 'Selina Tippett, who ought to have been called Madge, trotted down the stairs.'[38] What a world of characterization can be packed into a name, even one that doesn't properly belong to a character! Selina is a figure of uncommon good sense, the name Madge conjuring a figure who is solid and respectable but also quick about her business, rather unlike Rashleigh's sketch. She started the Warming Pan with Angelina out of frustration with other tearooms, in which 'she had never found "the toast, the temperature, and the tea" ... all together',[39] and because 'Tearooms had had a special meaning for Selina. She associated them with freedom. Only those people, she thought, who lived obedience for six and a half days of the week knew what liberty was.'[40] Selina is acutely aware of her position as a woman living under societal constraints, and tearooms in her world become a space in which women especially have something to themselves: a moment of their own. While Selina's role as proprietor of a tearoom aligns her with a certain brand of English traditionalism, she revels in the new opportunities available to women, especially young women, and conceives of herself as a facilitator of that freedom. Prompted by a consideration of her own childhood full of motherly disapproval, Selina reflects, 'Dear me ... how the world has changed since I was ten. Changed for the better, too, in spite of the raids. Nobody questioned a girl like Evelyn about her friends.'[41] If Rashleigh grumbles about Evelyn (and Selina) in private, who's to know, except for the readers.

Selina is a portrait of contrasts to Angelina, the other proprietor of the Warming Pan. While Selina runs the tearoom itself, 'Angelina looked after the staff and the purchases, but her heart was really with the courses that she was always taking to improve, as she said, "the future of us women"'.[42] Angelina is impatient for further change, although her approach to taking courses is scattershot, moving from Eastern philosophy, which at least had the benefit in Selina's eyes of encouraging her 'to control her temper', to politics, which has led Angelina to cultivate a scornful attitude towards the customers, whom she has begun referring to as the 'stupid bourgeoisie'.[43] Angelina's mercurial intellectual energy and ability to deal with people outside the tearoom sets her apart from Selina, but also leads her into passionate undertakings that Selina doesn't always understand, and it is this aspect of her character that is the catalyst for the introduction of the titular character of the novel, the plaster bulldog named Beowulf.

The scene of Beowulf's introduction is a comedy of interpretation, with characters vying with each other to determine the symbolism of the plaster bulldog and where to place it.

> Angelina set her burden carefully on the floor and stood up, smiling at her audience. Beside her sat a plaster bulldog, almost life size, with a piratical scowl painted on his black muzzle.
>
> 'Don't scold me', she appealed to the room, 'wouldn't he be lovely as a stand for bulletins? And I do think these days symbols are important.' ...
>
> 'What about standing him in the fireplace?' Mrs. Spenser suggested, watching the Tippett's embarrassment with delight. 'Where did you find him?'
>
> ... 'In a salvage sale, opposite the Food Office. I can't keep a dog, I know, in the raids, but it's so cheerless without one. I was afraid at first that you might be tempted to call him Winnie, but then I thought, no, here is an emblem of the whole of us, so gentle, so determined ...'
>
> '... and so stubborn.'
>
> Angelina glanced up suspiciously, but Mrs. Spenser appeared to be perfectly serious. 'Stubborn! Oh, I see what you mean, we don't leave go, whatever happens. I should have thought that a better word was resolution. He must have a name, though. I shall call him Beowulf.'
>
> 'How gallant, Miss Hawkins, but I'm sure he is a gallant dog.'
>
> Angelina glared at Horatio, whom she loathed. Plaster is such bad

taste, his mind was saying. 'I bought him', she retorted, 'not as a symbol of gallantry but of common sense.'

An ugly woman, Horatio thought, and how she bullied her conscientious little partner, but at his age it was essential to keep upon friendly terms with everyone. 'Ah, but you must not grudge us poor artists the luxury of dreaming about happier, courtlier days.'

'I am sure Beowulf's monster wasn't courtly', she sniffed, bending down to lug the plaster object into the fireplace. An old fool like that would not know his history nor that Beowulf, unlike Drake, could be accepted by the proletariat. Had he not fought the dragon (merely a symbol no doubt for Viking dictatorship) to save the whole people? 'You are right, Mrs. Spenser, the fireplace is just as good as a kennel.' They all giggled at her little joke. 'You know, I envy, I positively envy, that ribbon in your hat to make a collar for him.'

... The preposterous bulldog that should have been simply vulgar really gave the bleak, dingy room an air of gaiety.[44]

This passage is astonishing in many ways, not least to an early medievalist for what is one of the earliest Marxist interpretations of Beowulf, in which he is transformed into a hero ready for acceptance by a proletariat oppressed by the dragons of both English government and German bombardment. Angelina's enthusiasm for the plaster bulldog and the early medieval hero suggests the mercurial affections inspired by her educational courses and, in someone obsessed by the creation of new orders, an interesting attachment to traditions of the past. Adrienne Monnier sees in the politics of the present's relationship with the past something powerful that is often taken up by new movements: 'I admire that Bryher has noted in Angelina's character that the social and literary avant-garde always rediscovers the totems of primitive clans, while conservatives are content with a much more recent past, the past of which they are the direct heirs.'[45] Angelina's attempt at literary interpretation is amateur, a term that often attracts derision, but one that Carolyn Dinshaw has argued is in need of reconceptualization, linking *amateur* with *queer*:

> amateurs – these fans and lovers labouring in the off-hours – take their own sweet time, and operating outside of regimes of detachment governed by uniform, measured temporality, these uses of time are queer. In this sense, the act of taking one's own sweet time asserts a queer force. *Queer*, *amateur*: these are mutually reinforcing terms.[46]

Dinshaw argues for a queer understanding of temporality focusing on asynchrony: 'different time frames or temporal systems colliding in a single moment of *now*'.[47] Dinshaw's concept of asynchrony and the amateur reader creating new kinds of attachment to medieval texts provides a useful way of thinking through how Bryher's *Beowulf* comments upon the Old English poem. It is vital that studies of reception focus not only on the work of adaptation but also on the work of folk commentary by which the polysemous nature of medieval texts comes into focus.

Throughout the passage, the plaster bulldog is described in a multitude of ways by different speakers. He possesses 'a piratical scowl'; he is 'an emblem of the whole of us, so gentle, so determined', but also 'so stubborn'. He is full of 'resolution' and is also 'gallant'. He is a symbol of 'common sense'. He is courtly, according to Horatio, and definitely not courtly according to Angelina. He is 'preposterous' and 'vulgar' and yet brings 'an air of gaiety'. The entire passage is a tussle over the meaning of symbols, and particularly over the intervention of the past in the present. Speakers develop different affective relationships with the bulldog that reveal attitudes towards and various ways of cultivating or resisting intimacy with the past. One of the greatest contributions of queer studies to the analysis of literature is in the development of what Dinshaw has termed the queer historical touch across time, as when writers and historians use 'the body in unusual, nonnormative ways, in order to make loving relations across time'.[48] This deployment of touch and affect as an important part of queer historiography has been further developed by Elizabeth Freeman, whose work, rather than seeking 'a fully present past, a restoration of bygone times', focuses instead on an 'erotohistoriography' that 'does not write the lost object into the present so much as encounter it already in the present, by treating the present itself as hybrid. And it uses the body as a tool to effect, figure, or perform that encounter.'[49]

In both Dinshaw's and Freeman's work, the queer historical impulse is figured through the metaphor of non-normative sexual desire, but that is one thing that is notably lacking in Bryher's *Beowulf*. It is tempting to read Selina and Angelina as lesbians, but this reading depends on interpolating Bryher's actual community of queer and lesbian women and shop owners into the text as well as reading between the lines of the relationship of the owners of the Warming Pan. Throughout the book, Selina and Angelina are frequently referred to as partners and occasionally as colleagues (although Angelina has to regretfully admit that whatever else she may be, '"comrade" simply didn't suit Selina').[50] And yet the intimate nature of their relationship is revealed at several points throughout the text. Prior to owning the Warming Pan, the two women were companions to a Miss Humphries, who is put into a bad temper by the idea of Selina spending time with Angelina, 'of whom she was so jealous', to the extent that they sit 'in [Angelina's] bedroom with the door open, in case Miss Humphries should call'.[51] While the question of whether or not the two women had a sexual relationship is left open by the text, the intimacy that they share deserves its own queer historiography, worked out not in bodily relations but in the sharing of food and gossip, achieving 'the temperature, the toast, and the tea' all together in a place that admits multiple temporalities swirling together in the constitutive chaos of the Blitz.

Food acts throughout the novel not only as a catalyst for affective relationships between people, but also as something that affects people themselves, a truth that is recognized in many ways. Early in the novel, Horatio Rashleigh thinks, 'He would feel better, he always did, after he had had a cup of tea.'[52] Selina takes pride in the capacity of the Warming Pan to influence not only customers, but many more, 'For if clients came in to lunch and went off cheerfully afterwards, they, in turn, would affect their relatives and their maids. It was inspiring really, especially on such a cold, dreary morning, to think how much one solitary woman could do in defence of her native land.'[53] Selina and Angelina even reflect on the capacity of food to change each other's personalities. Selina believes, 'If Angelina would only eat more, she would be less restless and talk less strangely',[54] while Angelina feels that Selina 'was dominated by her appetite'.[55] The power of food to affect people, both in ways that they can predict and that they are wholly unaware of, argues for what Jane Bennett refers to as the agency of edible matter, which 'includes the negative power to resist or obstruct human projects, but ... also includes the more active power to affect and create effects'.[56] Bennett's theory of materiality explores matter's capacity to act with and upon the human, and the importance of food in the context of the tearoom suggests how the desiring bodies of the Warming Pan create their own thick temporalities. The queer historiography of *Beowulf* is not located in a desire to touch other bodies but derives instead from the intimacy created by bodies desiring and sharing food together. The capacity to affect and be affected by one another comes first from the capacity of the body to be acted upon by food. Rashleigh, in desiring a cup of tea, also desires the effect that it produces in his body. When Selina imagines her ability to radiate influence throughout London, it is premised upon the good feelings created when customers lunch at the Warming

Pan, and this capacity to act in concert with edible matter is gendered
in the context of the tearoom. Using food to influence others without
their even being aware of it becomes a powerful tool for cultivating
affective relationships, one that is applicable as much to the early
medieval mead-hall as the London tearoom whose fireplace is guarded
by a plaster bulldog with an Old English name.

In proposing this connection, I don't mean to suggest a direct
correspondence between mead-hall and tearoom, nor that Bryher
was engaged in a straightforward adaptation of one historical context
into another. Instead, I want to return to the metaphor of the historical palimpsest introduced by H.D. as a way of understanding the
temporal hybridity of the two *Beowulfs*. I am proposing that we
read the text of the poem as if it had been written over by the text
of the novel, the words still legible, even though the story is different.
Like Selina Tippett, Wealhtheow, the wife of Hrothgar, is a woman
who understands the importance of edible (or drinkable) matter.
In her first appearance in the poem, she distributes drinks to the
men in the hall after Beowulf has sworn to kill Grendel:

> Eode Wealþeo forð,
> cwen Hroðgares   cynna gemyndig,
> grette goldhroden   guman on healle,
> ond þa freolic wif   ful gesealde
> ærest East-Dena   eþelwearde,
> bæd hine bliðne   æt þære beorþege,
> leodum leofne;   he on lust geþeah
> symbel ond seleful,   sigerof kyning. (612b–619)[57]

> (Wealhtheow went forth,
> Hrothgar's queen, mindful of customs;
> adorned with gold, she greeted the men in the hall,
> then that courteous wife offered the full cup
> first to the guardian of the East-Danes' kingdom,
> bid him be merry at his beer-drinking,
> beloved by his people; with pleasure he received
> the feast and cup, victorious king.)[58]

After sharing the cup with the hall,

> hio Beowulfe,   beaghroden cwen
> mode geþungen   medoful ætbær;
> grette Geata leod,   Gode þancode
> wisfæst wordum   þæs ðe hire se willa gelamp
> þæt heo on ænigne   eorl gelyfde
> fyrena frofre. (623–8a)

(the ring-adorned queen, of excellent heart,
bore the mead-cup to Beowulf;
she greeted the Geatish prince, thanked God
with wise words that her wish had come to pass,
that she could rely on any earl for relief
from those crimes.)

Scholarly interest in scenes of communal drinking and women's
role in passing mead-cups has been central to the analysis of women
in early medieval culture, and in *Beowulf* in particular, in the role of
peace-weavers.[59] One of the central debates concerns whether the
role of peace-weaving is passive or active, whether Wealhtheow and
other women need to 'surmount the passive peace-weaver role in
order to influence political and dynastic decisions', as Shari Horner
argues, or whether peace-weaving itself requires that we 'redefine
the place traditionally allotted to the domestic world within a heroic
ethos ... and recognize women as central forces, rather than marginal
supports, in the production of social order', in the words of Stacy
Klein.[60] In this passage the tension between these two conceptions
of women's place in society comes out clearly. While Wealhtheow
speaks, it is in indirect discourse, and as she shares mead from
her cup with each person present, she does so *cynna gemyndig*, a
phrase which the *Dictionary of Old English* translates as 'mindful
of what is fitting, proper behaviour' or possibly even 'mindful of
social distinction'.[61]

The bracketing of Wealhtheow's speech in indirect discourse
on her first appearance in the poem stands in marked contrast to a
pair of speeches that she delivers in close succession to Hrothgar
and Beowulf after the slaying of Grendel. Like Selina Tippett
in her tearoom, Wealhtheow knows the value of a beverage. She
begins her speech to Hrothgar, 'Onfoh þissum fulle, freodrihten
min, / sinces brytta' (Take this cup, my noble, courteous lord, /
giver of treasure!) (1169–70a), before exhorting her husband, who
is on the verge of adopting Beowulf as his own, to be mindful
of the futures of their two sons. Her speech to Beowulf follows
a similar tack, buttering him up with gifts and kind words,
urging him to think well of her sons, before showing steel at the
very end:

Her is æghwylc eorl   oþrum getrywe,
modes milde,   mandrihtne hold;
þegnas syndon geþwære,   þeod eal gearo;
druncne dryhtguman   doð swa ic bidde. (1228–31)

(Here each earl is true to the other,
mild in his heart, loyal to his liege-lord,
the thanes united, the nation alert,
the troop, having drunk at my table, will do as I bid.)

Wealhtheow yet again recognizes the capacity of the mead she serves
in the hall to produce an effect, binding the thanes to one another,
to Hrothgar, and also to her. It is a moment of bared steel in defence
of her (male) children that foreshadows the impending ravages of
Grendel's vengeful mother and exacerbates the problem of interpretation: is Wealhtheow going off-script in claiming the loyalty of the
thanes or is she acting within a well-defined role for women in
Germanic legend?

This question is complicated by Wealhtheow's singularity as a
speaking woman in the poem. The Bechdel test, introduced by
Alison Bechdel in the 1980s in her comic *Dykes To Watch Out For*
and then popularized in feminist film criticism in the 2000s, helps
clarify the problems of the representation of women in media. The
test has three parts: 'One, it has to have at least two women in it
who, two, talk to each other about, three, something besides a man.'[62]
Beowulf passes the first test, with six women – Wealhtheow, Hygd,
Hildeburh, Freawaru, Thryth/Modthryth/Fremu, and Grendel's
mother – but it falters at the second. Whether restricted to a legendary
past recounted by scops or to the social confines of the mead-hall
or to a monstrous exile, in spite of scholarly desire to bring the
women into dialogue with another, they actually have little to say.
Wealhtheow's two speeches are addressed to Hrothgar and Beowulf
and concern her sons, Hrethric and Hrothmund. The women in
the poem are defined by their relationships with men, something
that even scholars arguing for the centrality of women to the production and maintenance of social order admit, as Dorothy Carr Porter
does at the end of her anthropological study of women in *Beowulf*:
'Though they are all defined by the men that they are close to,
either sons, fathers, or brothers, none of the women in *Beowulf* are
marginal or excluded.'[63] Given the first half of Porter's sentence,
if they are not marginal or excluded, the women in the poem are
still subordinated to men.

The subordination of the women in the poem to men is a problem
for scholars to deal with, even feminist scholars seeking to challenge
how we understand gender in the poem. Thus, Gillian Overing
notes, 'We certainly do not need feminist theory to tell us that
Beowulf is a profoundly masculine poem',[64] and Clare Lees begins

her interrogation of masculinity with the statement, '*Beowulf* is an Anglo-Saxon poem about men – male heroes, warriors, kings.'[65] Even when scholars suggest the opposite, it can come in the form of a joke; when Paull F. Baum joked that *Beowulf* was written by a woman, he was motivated by what Shari Horner has described as 'twentieth-century essentialist views of femininity, his suppositions that women are typically unconcerned with gore and battles, sympathetic to other women's plights, and given to talking too much – simply because they are women'.[66] Although Baum's dated views on gender at least served as a prompt to Horner to think seriously about women in the poem, she does so as a means of thinking about how 'we can better understand how *Beowulf* normalizes and regulates femininity',[67] rather than considering what it would mean to make space for women as authors of *Beowulf*.

The space for women as readers is further problematized in James Earl's moving account of a dream he had concerning the poem:

> I dreamt about a little girl who had a fascinating, unusual doll, every part of which – arms, legs, head, torso – seemed to be made from other dolls, all of different colors and proportions. I knew where it had come from: the little girl's brother had collected all the old, broken dolls he could find ... then he had made a single doll out of all their parts, and had given it to his little sister. Far from thinking it was junk, she thought it was beautiful and loved it ... The doll, of course, is *Beowulf*; I am the little girl, and the poet is her brother.[68]

Earl's dream about the creation and transmission of the poem sticks with me, in part, because the first time I read it I thought it laughable as scholarship; but as I returned to the essay, it grew on me more and more because it points to the absence of serious studies of subjective response to early medieval literature. In this dream, Earl discovers himself not as a scholar of the poem and its era but as a child enraptured by its beauty, as a reader who cherishes the work, both in spite of and because of its seemingly incongruous parts. However, Earl's identification with the subject of the dream, the little girl receiving the poem from her brother, once again points to the problem of the subordination of women, now as readers. In his dream, Earl genders the reader of the poem as a girl in an 'attempt at compensation, though necessarily condescending ... since the poem so strongly marginalizes the female reader already'. However, this female reader is an abstraction, and one of the pleasures of Bryher's *Beowulf* is that, almost unlooked for in the field of Old English studies[69] but already hiding in plain sight, we have a record not only of a female reader of *Beowulf* adapting it to an entirely unexpected use, but also a fictionalized female reader in the character of Angelina, whose progressive spirit nonetheless encompasses an ability to respond sympathetically to the poem along class lines.

In fact, Bryher's novel anticipates debates about the role of women within our field decades before they occurred. In Selina, we find an affirmation of women's capacity to influence others through her role as hostess, securing the future for new generations, as Wealhtheow seeks to do for her sons, though Selina's efforts are focused more on the future of the young women who come to her tearoom, maintaining and producing social order in a time of uncertainty. However, in Angelina, we find a progressive impatience with patriarchal tradition and the tendency of traditional gender roles to restrain and regulate women's place in society; and yet Angelina is also the one who cultivates a nostalgia for the deep past and sees in *Beowulf* something deeply appealing. The polyphonic nature of Bryher's work allows for multiple perspectives to develop in dialogue with and against each other and questions the very notion that there is something uniquely feminine about women's voices while reaffirming their necessity.

Nor should we accept the fiction that Bryher's relationship to the early medieval past was purely incidental. In addition to her memoir and the novel *Beowulf*, Bryher was best known for her historical novels, including *The Fourteenth of October*, which concerns the life of a boy in the time of upheaval of the Norman Conquest. In a brief essay included on the back of the dust jacket, Bryher reflects on her own understanding of the past, rooted both in her deep reading of history (including reading Edward A. Freeman's multi-volume *History of the Norman Conquest* at the age of 15), and in a less academic knowledge gained from her travels in the English countryside, connecting the early medieval past to her war-torn present:

> I stood on the battlements and looked across the deep green meadows towards the place where perhaps the destiny of Saxon England was really decided. Dunkirk was fresh in our minds, but who remembers the Great March when the housecarles tramped three hundred miles in thirty days, along the rough track of a road, without transport and with little organized supply in the way of food? ... How long ago it seems, the fight on the hill; yet I drove through Battle once again this past April, and it was as if it had been yesterday. History did not repeat itself in 1940, but by how narrow a margin! Will it repeat itself?[70]

Bryher's engagement with the past was deep, and if amateur rather than scholarly, she brought to it all the love that *amateur* etymologically implies, and she was just as invested in exploring the psychic affinities of the past in the present as H.D.

Part of the secret of Bryher's queer, feminist embrace of the medieval past lies in her refusal to take it simply as it is. Much like Earl's dream-doll constructed from the broken-down remnants of other dolls, the titular character of her novel is an entirely unexpected and, in his own way, quite marginal figure, a plaster bulldog so ugly that an assistant at Harrods would, after the war, assure Bryher 'that they had never stocked anything so vulgar'.[71] Furthermore, the appearance of Beowulf excites comparisons not to heroic men, but to women, with the plaster bulldog compared to Selina both as a measure of similarity and difference. Angelina views it as similar to Selina: 'Of course, a plump face like Selina's was never meant for leadership. Oddly enough, it reminded her of Beowulf, the Tippett so resembled a ladylike and gentle bulldog.'[72] However, Eve draws the opposite conclusion, noting that Beowulf's 'wrinkled jaw precisely matched the chin of a woman sipping tea at the adjoining table', causing her to exclaim, '"It's so unlike Tippett." The black muzzle was too smug and restful; for Selina acted, if she did not look, a lady with a past.'[73] What a contrast to other depictions of Beowulf, in which he invariably appears as a humourless hulk, inexplicably fighting Grendel in his birthday suit.[74] Bryher's Beowulf is of an unfixable nature, by turns ladylike and gentle, but unsuited to leadership, or like a woman sipping tea, smug and restful and without a past. The indeterminacy of Bryher's *Beowulf* is a useful corrective to an understandable scholarly failing: the desire to fix a text's meaning.

Although the little plaster bulldog is a marginal figure, exiled to the fireplace, it still never fails to draw the eye and attract contradictory comment. Moreover, Beowulf's arrival coincides with the puncturing of the thick temporality of the British tearoom, past, present, and future all colliding in a rupture that was all too common in the Blitz. As the characters retreat to a nearby air-raid shelter, Selina returning to drag Rashleigh from his garret with moments to spare, the Warming Pan is destroyed:

> A bomb had hit the corner next to the restaurant, and as a result the Warming Pan was simply not there. The staircase that Eve had run up and down so many times had disappeared except for the bottom flight of steps. Her room was air. All that remained was a table, upright, with two plates on it and Beowulf standing quietly under the mantelpiece.[75]

This image cannot help but recall the barrow gazing out upon the wreck of history at the end of the Old English poem. In the closing pages of the novel, the characters reflect on what has been lost: Eve's desire for 'the anonymous liberty of thought that her room and old Selina's cheerfulness had given her'; Angelina's delight in discovering Beowulf unharmed and her unabashed rush 'into the future'.[76] Selina sits among the wreckage, still feeling concussed from the bombs, and yet upon hearing that Beowulf has been dressed up in a Union Jack, wryly reflecting, 'You can't imagine the Germans taking a nasty dog seriously, can you? It would shock them.' The whimsical nature of Bryher's queer historical palimpsest surfaces even in the depths of tragedy, and while the Blitz has revealed the fleeting temporality of the space afforded by the Warming Pan, the voices of its women striving to achieve freedom according to their own desires creates a community that brings the women of the legendary past and the fictionalized present into dialogue with Bryher's circle of writers and readers. While the legendary *Beowulf* ended with a desire for praise, Bryher's *Beowulf* fittingly ends with a bashful acknowledgement of a universal truth by Selina: 'Oh dear … I do think it is very embarrassing to be bombed.'[77]

Notes

1 This essay would not have been possible without the encouragement, support, and suggestions of many people: Kenneth Irby, Daniel Remein, Erica Weaver, Tyler Caroline Mills, Jennifer Lorden, Claire Battershill, and especially Renée Buchanan.

2 Donald K. Fry, *Beowulf and the Fight at Finnsburh: a bibliography* (Charlottesville, VA: University Press of Virginia, 1969), p. 26. Fry's bibliography also gives the mistaken impression that Bryher is her last name. The only other references to Bryher's novel are also bibliographical: Hans Sauer, with Julia Hartmann, Michael Riedl, Tatsiana Saniuk, and Elisabeth Kubaschewski, *205 years of Beowulf translations and adaptations (1805–2010): a bibliography* (Trier: Wissenschaftlicher Verlag Trier), p. 82; and John William Sutton, 'Beowulfiana: modern adaptations of Beowulf', University of Rochester, The Robbins Library, https://www.library.rochester.edu/robbins/beowulfiana (accessed 5 June 2019). Sauer has 'only distantly related to *Beowulf*' and Sutton, 'a fairly obscure Modernist novel'.

3 vladimir998, 'This is not the Beowulf you might think it is', review of *Beowulf: A Novel*, by Bryher, Amazon.com, 9 May 2007, www.amazon.com/Beowulf-Novel-Winifred-Bryher/dp/0394416678 (accessed 5 June 2019).

4 Helen Carr, *The verse revolutionaries: Ezra Pound, H.D., and the Imagists* (London: Jonathan Cape, 2009), p. 37.

5 Bryher, *The heart to Artemis: a writer's memoirs* (Ashfield, MA: Paris Press, 2006), p. 1.
6 Carr, *The verse revolutionaries*, p. 873.
7 Ibid., p. 1.
8 Bryher, *The heart to Artemis*, p. 216.
9 Ibid., p. 217.
10 Sylvia Beach, *Shakespeare and Company* (1959) (Lincoln, NE: University of Nebraska Press, 1991), p. 100.
11 Carr, *The verse revolutionaries*, pp. 872–4.
12 Bryher, *The heart to Artemis*, p. 223.
13 Carr, *The verse revolutionaries*, p. 875.
14 Ibid.
15 Bryher, *The heart to Artemis*, p. 289. *Borderline*, directed by K. MacPherson, in *Paul Robeson: portraits of the artist* (1930: Criterion Collection, 2007), DVD. H.D., credited as Helga Doorn, plays Astrid, with whom Robeson's character has an extra-marital affair, while Bryher is the hotel manageress.
16 Bryher's marriage to McAlmon in 1922 was platonic: 'We were divorced in 1927 but could have got an annulment just as easily except that this was a longer and more expensive procedure.' Bryher, *The heart to Artemis*, p. 239. See also Beach, *Shakespeare and Company*, p. 101.
17 Beach, *Shakespeare and Company*, pp. 100–1.
18 Noël Riley Fitch, *Sylvia Beach and the Lost Generation: a history of literary Paris in the twenties and thirties* (New York: W. W. Norton, 1983), p. 374.
19 Emily Wojcik, '"Their own privately subsidized firm": Bryher, H.D., and "curating" Modernism', *Jacket2*, 28 September 2011, http://jacket2.org/article/their-own-privately-subsidized-firm (accessed 5 June 2019). See also Jayne E. Marek, 'Toward international cooperation: the literary editing of H.D. and Bryher', in her *Women editing Modernism: 'little' magazines and literary history* (Lexington, KY: University Press of Kentucky, 1995), pp. 101–37.
20 Bryher, *The heart to Artemis*, p. 247.
21 Ibid., p. 248.
22 Bryher in fact dedicated a third of her money to aiding her extended circle of friends. See Fitch, *Sylvia Beach and the Lost Generation*, p. 397.
23 Adrienne Monnier, *The very rich hours of Adrienne Monnier*, trans. Richard McDougall (Lincoln, NE: University of Nebraska Press, 1996), p. 174.
24 Monnier, *The very rich hours of Adrienne Monnier*, p. 174.
25 H.D., *Trilogy* (New York: New Directions, 1998). The original volumes in H.D.'s *Trilogy* are *The walls do not fall* (Oxford: Oxford University Press, 1944), *Tribute to the angels* (Oxford: Oxford University Press, 1945), and *The flowering of the rod* (Oxford: Oxford University Press, 1946). All quotations in this chapter are taken from the collected New

Directions edition, and citations of poems are to volume and poem number.
26 In *Ion*, the dedication reads: 'For B. Athens 1920/ P. Delphi 1932', where B. stands for Bryher and P. Perdita, H.D.'s daughter. H.D., *Euripides' 'Ion'* (Boston: Houghton Mifflin, 1937). See also H.D., *Palimpsest* (Paris: Contact Editions, 1926).
27 Robert Duncan, *The H.D. book*, ed. Michael Boughn and Victor Coleman (Berkeley, CA: University of California Press, 2011), pp. 219–20.
28 Ibid., p. 248.
29 Duncan's *H.D. book* circulated in bits and pieces for decades before receiving full publication in 2011. I was fortunate to be loaned Kenneth Irby's self-assembled copy as an undergraduate in 2005.
30 H.D., *The walls do not fall*, p. 2.
31 Ibid., p. 2.
32 Ibid., p. 9.
33 Ibid., p. 43.
34 Ibid., p. 38.
35 Bryher, *Beowulf*, pp. 10–11.
36 Bryher recorded her affection for Rashleigh: 'I loved my characters, especially Rashleigh, Ruby, and Selina'; Bryher, *The days of Mars: a memoir, 1940–46* (New York: Harcourt Brace Jovanovich, 1972), p. 15.
37 Bryher, *Beowulf*, p. 11.
38 Ibid., p. 21.
39 Ibid., p. 25.
40 Ibid., p. 24.
41 Ibid., pp. 21–2.
42 Ibid., p. 26.
43 Ibid., p. 29.
44 Ibid., pp. 65–7.
45 Monnier, *The very rich hours of Adrienne Monnier*, p. 177. In spite of Monnier's assessment, reactionary conservative movements are all too ready to selectively embrace the medieval. See Dorothy Kim, 'Teaching medieval studies in a time of white supremacy', *In the middle*, 28 August 2017, http://www.inthemedievalmiddle.com/2017/08/teaching-medieval-studies-in-time-of.html (accessed 5 June 2019).
46 Carolyn Dinshaw, *How soon is now? Medieval texts, amateur readers, and the queerness of time* (Durham, NC: Duke University Press, 2012), p. 5.
47 Ibid.
48 Carolyn Dinshaw, *Getting medieval: sexualities and communities, pre- and postmodern* (Durham, NC: Duke University Press, 1999), p. 46.
49 Elizabeth Freeman, *Time binds: queer temporalities, queer histories* (Durham, NC: Duke University Press, 2010), p. 95.
50 The use of the term partner occurs on the following pages: 22, 28, 55, 65 (2x), 66, 68, 93, 98, 101, 163, and 199; colleague: 31 and 94; and comrade: 94.

51 Bryher, *Beowulf*, pp. 67, 25.
52 Ibid., p. 18.
53 Ibid., p. 23.
54 Ibid., p. 30.
55 Ibid., p. 101.
56 Jane Bennett, *Vibrant matter: a political ecology of things* (Durham, NC: Duke University Press, 2010), p. 49.
57 All quotations from *Beowulf* are from R. D. Fulk, Robert E. Bjork, and John D. Niles (eds), *Klaeber's Beowulf*, 4th edn (Toronto: University of Toronto Press, 2008).
58 All extended translations refer to Roy M. Liuzza (ed. and trans.), *Beowulf*, 2nd edn (Peterborough, Ont.: Broadview Press, 2013).
59 L. John Sklute, 'Freoðuwebbe in Old English poetry', *Neuphilologische Mitteilungen*, 71 (1970), 534–41; repr. in Helen Damico and Alexandra Hennessey Olsen (eds), *New readings on women in Old English literature* (Bloomington, IN: University of Indiana Press, 1990), p. 208. See also Michael J. Enright, *Lady with a mead cup: ritual, prophecy, and lordship in the European warband from La Tene to the Viking Age* (Dublin: Four Courts, 1996); Stacy S. Klein, *Ruling women: queenship and gender in Anglo-Saxon literature* (Notre Dame, IN: University of Notre Dame Press, 2006). On mead-sharing as peace-weaving, see Jane Chance, *Woman as hero in Old English literature* (Syracuse, NY: Syracuse University Press, 1986), p. 5, although Megan Cavell sounds a cautionary note in 'Formulaic friþuwebban: reexamining peace-weaving in the light of Old English poetics', *JEGP*, 114.3 (2015), 360–1.
60 Shari Horner, *The discourse of enclosure: representing women in Old English literature* (Albany, NY: State University of New York Press, 2001), p. 77; Klein, *Ruling women*, p. 104.
61 Angus Cameron, Ashley Crandell Amos, and Antonette diPaolo Healey (eds), *Dictionary of Old English: A to H* (Toronto: Dictionary of Old English Project, 2016), s.v. *cynn*, adj.
62 Alison Bechdel, 'The rule', in *Dykes to watch out for* (Ithaca, NY: Firebrand Books, 1986), p. 22; also available on Bechdel's website, http://dykestowatchoutfor.com/the-rule (accessed 11 September 2019).
63 Dorothy Carr Porter, 'The social centrality of women in *Beowulf*: a new context', *The heroic age*, 5 (2001), www.heroicage.org/issues/5/porter1.html (accessed 5 June 2019).
64 Gillian R. Overing, *Language, sign, and gender in Beowulf* (Carbondale, IL: Southern Illinois University Press, 1990), p. xxiii.
65 Clare A. Lees, 'Men and *Beowulf*', in Clare A. Lees (ed.), *Medieval masculinities: regarding men in the Middle Ages* (Minneapolis, MN: University of Minnesota Press, 1994), pp. 129–48; repr. in Eileen A. Joy and Mary K. Ramsey (eds), *The postmodern Beowulf: a critical casebook* (Morgantown, WV: West Virginia University Press, 2006), p. 417.

66 Shari Horner, 'Voices from the margins: women and textual enclosure in *Beowulf*', in Horner, *Discourse of enclosure*, pp. 65–100; repr. in Joy and Ramsey (eds), *The postmodern Beowulf*, pp. 467–500, at 467. See also Paull F. Baum, 'The *Beowulf* poet', *PQ*, 39 (1960), 389–99; repr. in Lewis E. Nicholson (ed.), *An anthology of Beowulf criticism* (Notre Dame, IN: Notre Dame University Press, 1963), pp. 353–65.

67 Horner, 'Voices from the margins', p. 493.

68 James W. Earl, '*Beowulf* and the origins of civilization', in his *Thinking about Beowulf* (Stanford, CA: Stanford University Press, 1994), pp. 161–88; repr. in Joy and Ramsey (eds), *The postmodern Beowulf*, pp. 268–9.

69 However, recent scholarship has done a better job of examining female readers of Old English. See Clare A. Lees, 'Women write the past: medieval scholarship, Old English, and new literature', *Bulletin of the John Rylands Library*, 93.2 (2017), 3–22; and Mary Dockray-Miller, 'Mary Bateson (1865–1906): scholar and suffragist', in Jane Chance (ed.), *Women medievalists and the academy* (Madison, WI: University of Wisconsin Press, 2005), pp. 67–78.

70 Bryher, 'How I came to write *The fourteenth of October*', in *The fourteenth of October* (New York: Pantheon Books, 1952). This brief essay appears in its entirety on the back of the dust jacket.

71 Bryher, *The days of Mars*, p. 13.

72 Bryher, *Beowulf*, p. 101.

73 Ibid., p. 133.

74 This is unfortunately the case both in Robert Zemeckis's animated film adaptation and in Santiago García and David Rubín's graphic novel adaptation. Santiago García and David Rubín, *Beowulf*, trans. Joseph Keatinge (Berkeley, CA: Image Comics, 2016).

75 Bryher, *Beowulf*, p. 189.

76 Ibid., pp. 190, 199.

77 Ibid., p. 201.

14

Dating Wiglaf: emotional connections to the young hero in *Beowulf*

Mary Dockray-Miller

Wiglaf, the young warrior who helps Beowulf kill the dragon at the end of the poem, offers a new definition of heroic masculinity for a post-Beowulf (not post-*Beowulf*!) world. The premise of the *Dating Beowulf* collection allows an examination of Wiglaf's affective and emotional contributions to the poem as a whole. When the critical focus turns to Wiglaf, moving Beowulf and the other Geats into ancillary roles in Wiglaf's narrative, we see that his performance of heroism includes emotional association, understood as expressions of affection and caregiving, as well as more typical masculine skills of speech making and monster killing. Most unusually, Wiglaf's heroism assumes feminine-coded forms when he nurses and then mourns Beowulf in the aftermath of the dragon fight. By the end of the poem, Beowulf's heroism is quite literally burned out, and Wiglaf's innovative heroic masculinity is in tenuous ascendance.

Lexical and connotative analysis of the vocabulary and phrasing referring to Wiglaf in the final third of the poem reveals the ways in which the poet creates an emotional connection between Wiglaf and the poem's audience. As Wiglaf demonstrates loyalty to his lord, participates in battle, and then enacts a traditional and cross-cultural ritual of mourning, he completes his emotional growth and assumes the role of primary male and hero. Wiglaf's masculine appeal and social status are enhanced by his grief in such a way that his performance realigns the poem's definition of heroic masculinity away from military expertise and towards emotional association.

A review of the critical literature reveals that Wiglaf has received surprisingly little attention in *Beowulf*'s extensive secondary corpus. The current edition of *Klaeber's Beowulf* remarks only that 'a suitable counterpart to the aged king of the Geatas, the young retainer Wiglaf also cannot fail to remind one of the youthful Beowulf as portrayed in the Grendel episodes'.[1] When mentioned at all, Wiglaf is usually discussed as a minor representative of a larger theme such as heroic loyalty or the transitoriness of life.[2]

Most criticism focused on Wiglaf tries to place him definitively within the kin structures of the poem.[3] The poet refers to him seven times in variations of the phrase 'Weoxstanes sunu' or 'byre Wihstanes' (Weohstan's son) (2602, 2752, 2862, 2907, 3076, 3110, 3120) and once as 'leod Scylfinga' (prince of the Scylfings) (2603), terms that present Wiglaf as a Swede, a tribe feuding with the Geats. But Beowulf calls Wiglaf 'endelaf usses cynnes / Wægmundinga' (the last of our Wægmunding kin) (2813–14a), placing them in the same extended family. Scholars have tried to reconcile these seemingly contradictory identifications: how can Wiglaf be both a Swedish prince and a kinsman to the Geatish King Beowulf? Potential answers include relationships as disparate as uncle/nephew (specifically mother's brother/sister's son), extended cousinship, or even honorary rather than biological kinship.[4]

These suggestions extrapolate a hypothetical relationship from the ambiguous references in the poem; ultimately, an exact definition of the specific biological relationship is less important to them than the question of whether Wiglaf can take Beowulf's place on the Geatish throne. To use Michael Drout's terminology, Wiglaf has a good but not ironclad claim to that throne based on both 'blood and deeds'.[5] Wiglaf has performed a heroic deed (helping Beowulf in his time of need to kill the dragon), and he is related to Beowulf by blood (although we are not sure exactly how). While earlier scholars seem to have assumed that Wiglaf would follow Beowulf as king of the Geats, more recent work has cast substantial doubt on that assumption, emphasizing Wiglaf's disappearance from the poem during the funeral preparations and the absence of a statement (from Beowulf, Wiglaf, or anyone else) declaring his succession.[6]

These sorts of arguments elucidate Wiglaf within the structure and narrative of the poem, but they tend not to analyse his character beyond the question of his fitness to rule. The recent affective turn in medieval studies in general, and in early medieval English studies in particular, facilitates a more multivalent analysis of Wiglaf's emergent heroism, one that includes the interrogation of emotion in interpersonal relationship as well as the more usual military and political endeavours.[7] The 2015 publication of *Anglo-Saxon Emotions* decisively marked a turn towards the study of emotion in Old English texts and culture; three of the essays in that volume focus specifically on *Beowulf*, but none mentions Wiglaf.[8] Wiglaf's heroism, however, stems at least in part from his emotional growth, his loyalty and grief, at the poem's close.

After Beowulf, Wiglaf is the main character at the end of the poem; he is referenced in line 2599 and then formally introduced in line 2602. From his entrance, Wiglaf is consistently defined as 'geong' (young); he is the 'geongan cempan' (young champion) (2626a), the 'geongum garwigan' (the young spear-warrior) (2674a and 2811a), 'se maga geonga' (the young kinsman) (2675a), and 'ðam geongan' (the young man) (2860a). Wiglaf is not 'young' in the sense of awkward or ignorant; 'geong' is praiseworthy in these instances, modifying favourable nouns. While the poet tells us that 'Þa wæs forma sið' (it was the first time) (2625b) that Wiglaf had gone into battle with Beowulf, he also states that Wiglaf's father had waited to pass on heirlooms 'oð ðæt his byre mihte / eorlscipe efnan swa his ærfæder' (until his child could perform earl's-deeds like his forefather) (2621b–22). His father's gift implies that Wiglaf has some but not extensive experience in battle before he follows Beowulf into the dragon's lair. Wiglaf's youth, then, is positively connoted throughout the episode. Rather than inexperience, his youth implies strength and enthusiasm – excellent traits for an emerging hero.

Throughout the episode, Wiglaf expresses and enacts deep loyalty to and affection for Beowulf as lord and king, another indication of his heroism. His speech to the cowardly retainers invokes the debt they owe Beowulf as their lord and ring-giver: Wiglaf says that Beowulf 'us ðas beagas geaf' (gave to us these rings) (2635b) and he 'usic garwigend gode tealde' (thought us good spear-warriors) (2641). Only Wiglaf, of course, turns and enters the battle; the rest run away. When he addresses Beowulf directly, Wiglaf calls him 'Leofa Biowulf' (beloved Beowulf) (2663a). Beowulf responds with the same terminology, addressing him as 'Wiglaf leofa' (beloved Wiglaf) (2745a) after the dragon is dead; the verbal echoes here reinforce the emotional nature of the bond between the warrior and the king.[9] This verbal exchange is a notable and direct contrast to the poet's reference to the cowards as 'unleofe' (unloved) (2863b) after Beowulf's death. Wiglaf continues to use this terminology after Beowulf's death as he speaks to the Geats about the 'leofne þeoden' (beloved lord) (3079b) and 'leofne mannan' (beloved man) (3108a). Similarly, Wiglaf declares to Beowulf as he enters the battle that 'ic ðe fullæstu' (I will support you) (2668b). In this speech, delivered directly to Beowulf and presumably out of earshot of the departed cowards, Wiglaf does not mention rings or oaths or reciprocity. He merely states his intention to support the 'leofa' one at a time of great need.

The poet's diction throughout the dragon fight and Beowulf's death thus stresses the depth of the emotional bond between Wiglaf and Beowulf. Wiglaf's actions and gestures similarly emphasize this bond, as Wiglaf acts as assistant, colleague, and finally nurse and mourner as the episode comes to a close. While Wiglaf has stated that he enters the battle to support Beowulf, his first action is to clamber 'under his mæges scyld' (under his kinsman's shield) (2675b) when Wiglaf's wooden one is incinerated by the dragon's fire waves. The diction here emphasizes their kinship again ('mæges'), even as Wiglaf is receiving more help than he is providing at this particular moment. Presumably, the two are then huddled under the shield together, since Beowulf had the special shield made 'eall irenne' (all of iron) (2338a) expressly for this battle, and the only relatively safe space in the literal firestorm is under or behind this iron shield. At this moment, the two kinsmen experience the intensity and physical intimacy of this decidedly martial and heroic space.

They both move away from this protection, however, in a coordinated attack that demonstrates their alliance and cooperation. Beowulf strikes at the dragon's head; the dragon bites Beowulf in the neck; Wiglaf strikes the dragon in the belly or at least in the lower part of its body; Wiglaf's hand is burned; Beowulf then 'forwrat' (carved) (2705a) the dragon through its body. Although these events take place over the course of twenty lines (2688–708), they combine to form a quick, precise sequence in a systematized and successful attack that seems more spontaneously organic than consciously planned. The poet's diction again emphasizes their bond with the word 'begen' (both): 'hi hyne þa begen abroten hæfdon' (they both then had destroyed it) (2707). Despite his youth, Wiglaf has performed well in his first battle for Beowulf: he has demonstrated clear, strategic thinking and he has endured and ignored pain 'þær he his mæges healp' (when he helped his kinsman) (2698b). Like the speeches and descriptions that precede and follow it, the actual sequence of action demonstrates Wiglaf and Beowulf's emotional and affective bond.

That bond is made even more clear by the poet's use of a hapax legomenon, 'sibæðelingas' (kin-princes) (2708a) to bind Wiglaf and Beowulf together lexically as well as thematically and militarily. *Sibæðelingas* is unique not just to *Beowulf* but to the entire Old English poetic corpus.[10] John M. Hill calls *sibæðelingas* a 'constructed honorific' that 'embraces them both as they mutually achieve a costly victory', even as (in Hill's analysis) their biological kinship remains relatively remote.[11] It is the only *sib-* (kin-) compound in the poetic corpus that includes connotations of aristocratic social class (contrast with *sib(be)gedriht* [kin-band], *sib(b)lufan* [kin-love], or the redundant compound *sibgemagas* [kin-relatives]). As such, *sibæðelingas* unites Wiglaf and Beowulf, even somewhat eliding their differences in age and fame, by emphasizing instead their shared aristocratic nobility.

Other phrases similarly emphasize this bond between the young and old kinsmen. In a foreshadowing of the victory to come, the poet tells us that the dragon discovered that Wiglaf's spirit was strong 'syððan hie togædre gegan hæfdon' (after they had come together) (2630). The plural pronoun-phrase 'hie togædre' here refers to Beowulf and Wiglaf, working in tandem against their common enemy.[12] Wiglaf also binds himself to Beowulf through his use of the first-person plural pronoun *urum* when he reproaches the cowardly Geats, separating the cowards from himself and Beowulf when he says 'urum sceal sweord ond helm, / byrne ond beaduscrud, bam gemæne' (we must have sword and helmet with both mail-coat and battle-clothes) (2659b–60). The heroic and affective bond is thus also lexical.

During the dragon fight, the diction of the poem promotes Wiglaf away from youth and into full maturity, using terms and descriptors of success and accomplishment. The diction shows Wiglaf to have become a fully adult male *eorl* immediately after Beowulf has been bitten in the neck in the second part of the dragon fight: 'ða ic æt þearfe gefrægn þeodcyninges / andlongne eorl ellen cyðan' (then I heard at the need of the nation-king, the earl made known [his] courage throughout) (2694–5). Similarly, the anonymous Geatish messenger of the end of the poem refers to Wiglaf as an *eorl* as Wiglaf holds something of a vigil over Beowulf's body: 'Wiglaf siteð / ofer Biowulfe, byre Wihstanes, / eorl ofer oðrum unlifigendum' (Wiglaf, son of Weohstan, sits over Beowulf, [one] earl over the other un-living) (2906b–8). This diction shows that Wiglaf has fully matured as he has been tested in battle.

Another indication of Wiglaf's new, higher status is the poet's use of the celebratory adjective 'sigehreðig' (victory-glorious) (2756a) to refer to Wiglaf during the interlude after the fight but before Beowulf dies. Forms of *sigehreð* are used only four times in *Beowulf*; one reference is to God (94), two to Beowulf (490 and 1597), and the last to Wiglaf (2756). Wiglaf is *sigehreðig* as he passes into the dragon's den to collect treasure for Beowulf to view; as Beowulf is dying, the diction of victory moves from the old king to the new hero, affirming Wiglaf's new power in the narrative.

At the same time, however, Wiglaf's ascendant heroism takes a decidedly non-masculine turn when he becomes the chief nurse and mourner for the dying Beowulf. While there is ample analysis available of the connections in early medieval British culture between mourning and feminine performance,[13] 'nursing' as in 'caring for the sick and dying' seems to have received hardly any attention, probably because the act of nursing is not featured in the Old English corpus.[14] Scholarship on early medieval medicine tends to focus on the medical texts rather than on the people engaged in medical practice, and the very little extant work discusses doctors (who diagnose illness and prescribe treatment) rather than nurses (who care for the sick more generally).[15] Such work of general caring tends to be invisible in the historical record; however, Montserrat Cabré has described how 'women's significant contribution to healthcare can be mapped out by looking at the domestic space that is largely left outside the histories of medieval medicine'.[16] Cabré's analysis of 'the medieval health-care system' shows the difficulties for historians in differentiating among various types of women's work in the household, so that care of family members (both healthy and sick), preparation of food, cleaning of clothing, objects, and interior space all merge into the 'domestic space' as general women's work rather than as distinctive tasks attached to an 'occupational label' (nurse, cook, laundress, etc.).[17] Cabré's sources (including some fascinating home-remedy recipes) come from late medieval Iberia, but she suggests 'that perhaps the essence of [her] argument could be valuable for other Western European regions', especially since 'the household was the primary locus of the medieval provision of health care'.[18] Cabré, like other medical historians, focuses more on diagnosis and treatment of illness than on general care of the sick; in other words, she examines more closely what modern culture would term 'a doctor's work' rather than 'a nurse's work'. To further her argument about women's medical work enfolded in and thus made invisible by their daily work of care in the household, I would like to suggest here that Old English seems to have had no word for 'nursing' (apart from the very specific act of wet-nursing an infant) because care of the sick and dying was embedded in daily household work, work presumed to be appropriate to the female role and enacted almost exclusively by women.[19]

Wiglaf's care of Beowulf in the aftermath of the dragon fight, then, could not be described as 'nursing' in the language of the poem, but Wiglaf does indeed nurse the dying Beowulf in the sense that he tries to alleviate his lord's pain and suffering as much as he is able. After the dragon is definitely dead, Beowulf realizes that he too is dying; at that point, Wiglaf 'winedryhten his wætere gelafede' (washed his lord with water) (2722) and 'his helm onspeon' (unfastened his helmet) (2723b). Neither of these actions will stop Beowulf from dying, but they may make him more comfortable in the process; washing and (un)dressing, of course, are services that women have traditionally tended to perform for children or for incapacitated people (or for the dead, in fact). Any potential Christological association also feminizes Wiglaf, as it is *mulieres* (women) who proceed to the tomb to tend to the body of Christ (Luke 23.55–24.1).[20] Wiglaf actually washes and refreshes Beowulf with water twice more, performing these feminized activities as part of his heroism and service to his lord. After Wiglaf follows Beowulf's orders to explore the dragon's hoard and retrieve treasure for Beowulf to look at as he is dying, 'he hine eft ongon / wæteres weorpan' (he began to cast water on him again) (2790b–1a), continuing to keep Beowulf as comfortable as possible. Finally, the cowardly Geats return to the scene to see Wiglaf denying Beowulf's death by persisting in his use of water to comfort the dying (now dead) man: Wiglaf 'wehte hyne wætre' (would have roused him with water) (2854a).[21] There may be some quasi-baptismal or last rites overtones to this repeated washing, especially since it is remarked upon three times in this relatively short sequence of 132 lines. But it also illustrates an unusual level of tender caregiving, and its reiteration shows that this nursing is an important part of Wiglaf's character; his loyalty to his lord includes not just the willingness to fight to the death but also to care for the body of the dying. Wiglaf thus adds a new and unusual dimension to the poem's intertwined definitions of masculinity and heroism.

This emotionally charged caregiving metaphorically wounds Wiglaf in a way that the dragon could not. Perhaps reinvigorated by Wiglaf's ministrations, Beowulf begins his directions to Wiglaf for the construction of his tomb, and his words break apart Wiglaf's 'breosthord', literally his breast-treasure, metaphorically his heart, his thoughts, his mind: 'he hine eft ongon / wæteres weorpan, oð þæt wordes ord / breosthord þurhbræc' (He began again to cast water upon him, until the spear-point of a word broke through [his] heart) (2790b–2a). Bosworth-Toller defines *ord* as 'the point (of a weapon)', not as the 'point' or main idea of a phrase.[22] Beowulf's following speech (2794–808) wounds Wiglaf emotionally, penetrating his emotions ('breosthord þurhbræc') in a way that the dragon could not penetrate his body. In this surprising image, the poet deepens our understanding of Beowulf and Wiglaf's bond as physically embedded in their heroic bodies. That heroic focus on the body is embedded in the poetic diction of the scene as well. The poet tells us, just before the third reference to Wiglaf using water to soothe Beowulf, that 'He gewergad sæt, / feðecempa frean eaxlum neah' (he sat wearied, the foot-soldier, near the shoulders of his lord) (2852b–3); the description suggests that Beowulf's head may be in Wiglaf's lap in an emotionally charged, physically intimate posture.[23] The imagery here as well implies that Wiglaf and Beowulf are metaphorically two parts of one body, Wiglaf the feet ('feð') and Beowulf the shoulders ('eaxlum'); their assignments here roughly correspond to the spots where each stabbed the dragon's body a few lines before. Their military, biological, and emotional closeness is reinforced in the unifying bodily diction of the image, even though at this point in the narrative Beowulf is dead.

All of these close readings point to a role for Wiglaf as the ascendant young hero, ready to take over as the old hero dies and enters the realm of posthumous fame and glory. Wiglaf is young, loyal, brave, skilled, intuitive, and nurturing. Beowulf himself, however, seems not to see Wiglaf as a fully worthy successor. As noted above, scholars have engaged in extended discussion about the exact nature of Beowulf and Wiglaf's kinship; that discussion has included reference to Beowulf's bequest of his war-gear to Wiglaf, since Beowulf has no biological son. After the poet has resoundingly and uniquely defined them as 'sibæðelingas', and before Beowulf sends Wiglaf into the dragon's lair to collect treasure, Beowulf says that:

Nu ic suna minum   syllan wolde
guðgewædu,   þær me gifeðe swa
ænig yrfeweard   æfter wurde
lice gelenge (2729–32a)

(Now I would give to my son [my] battle-gear, if there to me had been given any heir belonging to my body that remained after [my death])

However, Beowulf does not immediately give the items to Wiglaf. Wiglaf has to wait approximately eighty lines before Beowulf makes

the seemingly logical next step to follow his statement above, that
since he has no biological son he will treat Wiglaf as a worthy proxy:

> Dyde him of healse   hring gyldenne
> þioden þristhydig,   þegne gesealde,
> geongum garwigan,   goldfahne helm,
> beah ond byrnan,   het hyne brucan well:
> 'Þu eart endelaf   usses cynnes,
> Wægmundinga;   ealle wyrd forsweop
> mine magas   to metodsceafte,
> eorlas on elne;   ic him æfter sceal.' (2809–16)

(The glory-minded lord did give to the thane, the young spear-warrior,
the golden ring from his neck, the gold-decorated helmet, ring, and
mail-coat, ordered him to enjoy [them] well. 'You are the last of our
Wægmunding kin. Fate has swept away all of my kin to the measured
end, those earls in courage; I must go after them.')

Beowulf actually undercuts the bond between him and Wiglaf twice
in this sequence. First, he hints that Wiglaf will inherit the war-gear
since Beowulf has no biological son, but does not then immediately
follow through on that suggestion. Instead, he makes Wiglaf gather
treasure from the dragon's barrow (2752–91), then gives thanks to
God (2792–800), and then provides tomb-building instructions
(2800–8) before he fulfils the implied promise in the earlier lines
and gives his war-gear to Wiglaf since he has no biological son.

Second, even as that transfer takes place, Beowulf seemingly
contradicts himself and somewhat delegitimizes Wiglaf, at first
affirming that Wiglaf is the last 'usses cynnes' (of our kin) but then
lamenting that 'ealle … mine magas' (all my kin) (2813b–15a) are
dead. Hill differentiates between connotations of *cynnes* and *magas*
in this sequence, reading *cynnes* as implicitly more distant that
magas, which Hill translates as 'personal kinsmen'.[24] Even if the
terms have different emotional valences, however, Beowulf still
bemoans his lack of kin while he has a young, strong, loyal kinsman
right next to him, diminishing the relationship that the narrative
has just established. Wiglaf seems not be offended by this deathbed
slight; he remains seated by Beowulf's corpse, sprinkling it with
water in a futile gesture of hope.

While scholars have focused on Beowulf's (somewhat grudging)
gift of his war-gear to Wiglaf, none has remarked that Wiglaf does
not need the gift, either practically or metaphorically. Wiglaf has
already participated in the iconic ritual of receiving arms from his
(biological) father. Beowulf needs a son to receive his war-gear, but

Wiglaf does not need a father or more weapons and armour. Wiglaf has his father's 'bill ond byrnan' (sword and mail-coat) (2621a) as well as more generalized 'guðgewæda / æghwæs unrim' (countless of each [kind] of battle-articles) (2623b–4a). He holds his family's ancestral property (2607). He has an unclear but important biological relationship with the Swedish royal family, enough of one that Wiglaf is called 'leod Scylfinda' (a prince of the Swedes) (2603b) when he is introduced. Once Beowulf is dead, the Geats need Wiglaf more than he needs them. As noted above, critics have parsed the end of the poem in an attempt to determine whether Wiglaf succeeds Beowulf as king of the Geats, but they have proceeded on the assumption that Wiglaf would want that succession. Hill emphasizes the ways in which Wiglaf's loyalty to Beowulf is that of a retainer to a lord; Wiglaf's loyalty is to Beowulf the individual, not to the Geats as a nation or tribe. Once Beowulf is dead, that bond of loyalty disappears, since it is a bond of homosocial intimacy rather than one mediated by any larger entity of tribe or group or nascent nation. Throughout the poem, Wiglaf expresses no loyalty to the Geats, who after Beowulf's death will endure the terrors prophesied by an anonymous woman at Beowulf's pyre:

>   sæide geneahhe
> þæt hio hyre heregeongas   hearde ondrede,
> wælfylla worn,   werudes egesan,
> hynðo ond hæftynd (3152–5)

(she said earnestly that she feared harsh army-attacks, a multitude of abundance of the slain, horror of the war-host, loss and captivity)[25]

The Geats may see Wiglaf as a potential and attractive new king, but his disappearance at the very end of the poem indicates instead that Wiglaf, like many heroes before and after him, sets off into the unknown. The poet does not permit the audience a glimpse into his future; that future does not lie within the bounds of the poem's narrative and geography.[26]

Part of Wiglaf's attractiveness for the audience is his status as one of the few dynamic characters in Old English poetry. In the course of the dragon fight and its aftermath, he has grown from a young to a mature man. While he does not necessarily become king of the Geats, he certainly assumes command, even if temporarily, once Beowulf is dead. After Beowulf's death, Wiglaf gives orders, with the poet twice using forms of the verb *hatan* (to command) to describe his actions. Wiglaf 'heht ða þæt heaðoweorc to hagan biodan' (then ordered that the battle-work be proclaimed to [those in] the enclosure) (2892) after he castigates the cowards who deserted Beowulf. His order is promptly followed, as an anonymous Geat announces Beowulf's death and predicts future devastation following line 2900. Similarly, the Geats act as he orders them to build Beowulf's funeral pyre:

> Het ða gebeodan   byre Wihstanes,
> hæle hildedior   hæleða monegum,
> boldagendra,   þæt hie bælwudu
> feorran feredon (3110–13a)

(Then ordered the son of Weohstan, the war-brave man, to command the many heroes, the bold-actors, that they from afar bear the firewood)

The poet reinforces 'het' (ordered) with 'gebeodan' (to command), emphasizing the subordinate position of the Geatish 'hæleða' and 'boldagendra' in relation to Wiglaf. These two instances of reaction to Wiglaf's speech stand in marked opposition to the reaction to his first speech, which takes place before the dragon fight (2633–60). In that first speech, he reminds his companions of their debt to Beowulf; they ignore his exhortation, and then they run away. After the dragon fight, in contrast, the Geats do what he tells them.

The poet as well realizes that Wiglaf has changed through the course of the narrative. The text's final reference to Wiglaf is as 'se snotra sunu Wihstanes' (the wiser son of Weohstan) (3120).[27] The poet refers to Wiglaf as Weohstan's son both at his introduction (2602) and his exit (3120), but much affective growth and expansion have been layered on top of that patronymic identification in the intervening lines. While translators tend to ignore the comparative form 'snotra' at 3120 (translating it simply as 'wise' or 'sage'),[28] Wiglaf is indeed 'wiser' on his departure from the text than he was at his entrance.[29] He speaks with authority and wisdom. He has experienced battle against a monstrous creature. He has nursed his king, watched him die, and mourned that loss. All of these activities play into the meaning of his name: Wig-laf, battle-remnant.[30] Wiglaf's wisdom comes from the experience of battle and from its aftermath. In these processes, Wiglaf has performed an affective, masculine intimacy that constitutes a distinct alternative to Beowulf's static, heroic masculinity.

Because of his range of emotional experience and emotional growth, the poem's audience can identify with Wiglaf in a way we could not with Beowulf. Beowulf's experiences in the poem consist almost entirely of heroic deeds and boasting speeches; his emotional range is narrow.[31] Wiglaf's range of emotion and experience, in contrast, is much broader and also more nuanced; in fighting and speech making, he is somewhat like Beowulf, but he also nurses, mourns, and becomes wiser through all of these experiences. His experiences, even as narrated in the elevated diction of heroic poetry, are 'common' in the sense that all humans mourn the death of a 'leofa' (a loved one), and all humans change in response to that grief. His process of mourning and subsequent growth into leadership creates an appealing and sympathetic character, a new kind of hero to end the epic. Wiglaf excels in stereotypically masculine performance: he remains loyal to his king as they fight together to kill the dragon. He also excels in more stereotypically feminine performance: he nurses, he mourns, he prepares a funeral. In his association with death and its aftermath, Wiglaf performs a heroism that encourages empathy and imitation – or, in short, intimacy. Members of the poem's audience will probably never have a chance to kill a dragon, but all will mourn loved ones.

This affective connection endows Wiglaf with emotional attractiveness; ironically, his masculine appeal and social status are enhanced by his grief in such a way that Wiglaf's performance realigns the poem's definition of heroic masculinity away from military stoicism and towards emotional association. As such, the final hero is Wiglaf, the empathetic, emotional, dynamic, and multidimensional man. While the Geats do not have a new king at the end of the poem, the audience has a new, more intimate definition of heroism.

Notes

1 R. D. Fulk, Robert E. Bjork, and John D. Niles (eds), *Klaeber's Beowulf* (Toronto: University of Toronto Press, 2008), p. 252. All quotations from the poem are from this edition; all translations are my own and attempt to be literal rather than poetic. Throughout, I have used the online *Bosworth-Toller Anglo-Saxon Dictionary*, ed. Joseph Bosworth and T. Northcote Toller, compiled by Sean Christ and Ondřej Tichý, Faculty of Arts, Charles University in Prague, 19 July 2010, http://www.bosworthtoller.com.

2 For example, see R. M. Lumiansky, 'Wiglaf', *College English*, 14.4 (1953), 202–6, at 205; Stanley B. Greenfield and Daniel G. Calder (eds), *A new critical history of Old English literature* (New York: New York University Press, 1986), p. 142; Kenneth Sisam, *The structure of Beowulf* (Oxford: Clarendon Press, 1965), p. 53; Dennis Cronan, 'Wiglaf's sword', *Studia neophilologica*, 65 (1993), 129–39, at 137; Edward Irving,

Rereading Beowulf (Philadelphia, PA: University of Pennsylvania Press, 1989), p. 111.

3 A generally historicist turn in literary criticism went to an extreme in Richard North's claim that *Beowulf*'s Wiglaf is a reference or homage to King Wiglaf of Mercia in *The origins of Beowulf: from Vergil to Wiglaf* (Oxford: Oxford University Press, 2006); it should be noted that Michael Lapidge refers to North's thesis as 'the mother of all crackpot theories' in his review of *The origins of Beowulf*, Reviews in History 617, http://www.history.ac.uk/reviews/review/617 (accessed 5 June 2019).

4 For examples, see Rolf H. Bremmer, 'The importance of kinship: uncle and nephew in *Beowulf*, *Amsterdamer Beiträge zur älteren Germanistik*, 15 (1980), 21–38; Norman E. Eliason, 'Beowulf, Wiglaf and the Waegmundings', *ASE*, 7 (1978), 95–105; Stephen O. Glosecki, 'Beowulf and the wills: traces of Totenism', *PQ*, 78 (1999), 15–47; John M. Hill, *The Anglo-Saxon warrior ethic: reconstructing lordship in early English literature* (Gainesville, FL: University of Florida Press, 2000).

5 Michael D. C. Drout, 'Blood and deeds: the inheritance systems in *Beowulf*,' *Studies in philology*, 104.2 (2007), 199–226.

6 For examples, see Irving, *Rereading Beowulf*, pp. 75–6; Hill, *Anglo-Saxon warrior ethic*, pp. 42–4; Frederick M. Biggs, 'Beowulf and some fictions of the Geatish succession', *ASE*, 32 (2003), 55–77; Frederick M. Biggs, 'The politics of succession in *Beowulf* and Anglo-Saxon England', *Speculum*, 80.3 (2005), 709–41.

7 In addition to the Jorgensen collection, for work on emotion in medieval culture more generally, see Barbara H. Rosenwein (ed.), *Anger's past: the social uses of an emotion in the Middle Ages* (Ithaca, NY: Cornell University Press, 1998) and her *Emotional communities in the early Middle Ages* (Ithaca, NY: Cornell University Press, 2006).

8 Alice Jorgensen, Frances McCormack, and Jonathan Wilcox (eds), *Anglo-Saxon emotions: reading the heart in Old English literature* (London: Routledge, 2015); the three essays that concentrate on Beowulf are Stephen Graham, 'So what did the Danes feel? Emotion and litotes in Old English poetry', pp. 75–90; Kristen Mills, 'Emotion and gesture in Hrothgar's farewell to Beowulf', pp. 163–76; and Erin Sebo, '*Ne sorga*: grief and revenge in *Beowulf*', pp. 177–92.

9 These echo the other uses of *leofa* in the poem, which is used exclusively in intergenerational address. It occurs in direct address from Wealhtheow to Beowulf (1216), Beowulf to Hrothgar (1483), Hrothgar to Beowulf (1758 and 1854), and Beowulf to Hygelac (1987).

10 J. B. Bessinger (ed.), *A concordance to the Anglo-Saxon Poetic Records* (Ithaca, NY: Cornell University Press, 1978), p. 1055.

11 Hill, *Anglo-Saxon warrior ethic*, pp. 32–4.

12 It is possible but not likely that *hie* could refer to the three combatants (Beowulf, Wiglaf, and the dragon) as they 'come together' in battle.

However, the subject of the sentence, *se wyrm*, makes its discovery after the two previously separated humans 'come together' to oppose the dragon.

13 For analysis of the identification of mourning as a female activity in pre-Conquest England, see Helen Bennett, 'The female mourner at Beowulf's funeral: filling in the blanks / hearing the spaces', *Exemplaria*, 4.1 (1992), 35–50; and Patricia Clare Ingham, 'From kinship to kingship: mourning, gender, and Anglo-Saxon community', in Jennifer C. Vaught and Lynne Dickson Bruckner (eds), *Grief and gender: 700–1700* (New York: Palgrave Macmillan, 2003), pp. 17–31. On mourning as a male activity in *Beowulf*, see also Robin Norris' essay in this volume, pp. 210–26.

14 Translations of *nutrix* into Old English cluster around words for fostering and feeding children: *cild-fostre, fostre*, etc. See *An Anglo-Saxon dictionary online*, www.bosworthtoller.com. I am indebted to Monica Green for her insights about medieval medical history in general and the dearth of information about medieval nursing practices in particular.

15 See, for example, the primary overview: M. L. Cameron, *Anglo-Saxon medicine* (Cambridge: Cambridge University Press, 1993). Chapter 3 is entitled 'Physician and patient'. Cameron's index does not include 'nurse' or 'nursing'. Monica Green has addressed the issue more generally in 'Integrative medicine: incorporating medicine and health into the canon of medieval European history', *History compass*, 7.4 (2009), 1218–45, at 1221–2.

16 Montserrat Cabré, 'Women or healers? Household practices and the categories of health care in late medieval Iberia', *Bulletin of the history of medicine*, 82 (2008), 18–51, at 18.

17 Ibid., 23–6, quotation at 23.

18 Ibid., 24–5.

19 I am indebted to Craig Davis for his insight in this analysis of nursing as feminized work in pre-Conquest culture. Davis suggested (via personal email 2 February 2017) that some men must have cared for the sick in a monastic context; the *Regularis concordia* does indeed direct both monks (*seruitores*) and laymen (*famulorum*) to aid monks in the infirmary; Dom Thomas Symons (ed. and trans.), *Regularis concordia / the monastic agreement* (London: Thomas Nelson, 1953), ch. 12, p. 64.

20 In the Gospel of Mark, these women are specifically identified as Mary Magdalen and Mary, mother of James and Salome (Mark 16:1).

21 The editors of *Klaeber's Beowulf* suggest following Alfred Bammesberger's argument ('Old English *wœteres weorpan* in *Beowulf*, 2791a', *American notes and queries*, 19.1 (2006), 3–7) that *wehte* here is a preterite subjunctive (258).

22 'Ord', *An Anglo-Saxon dictionary online*.

23 This posture would then be an inversion of the imagined scene in *The Wanderer*, wherein the speaker lays his head and hands on his lord's knees (41–4).

24 Hill, *Anglo-Saxon warrior ethic*, p. 35.

25 Much of this section is conjectural due to manuscript damage; see the description and discussion of this folio in *Klaeber's Beowulf*, p. xxviii as well as Bennett, 'Female mourner'.

26 Approximately 1,000 years after the *Beowulf* manuscript was made, Wiglaf's story was retold and then continued by Rebecca Barnhouse in *The coming of the dragon* (New York: Random House, 2010) and *Peaceweaver* (New York: Random House, 2012).

27 Although Wiglaf is *eahta sum* (3123), one of the eight in the group to go into the dragon's barrow, he is not specifically identified by name or patronymic at that point; he is not mentioned again, directly or indirectly, in the remaining fifty-nine lines of the poem.

28 For instance, R. D. Fulk uses 'sage' in Fulk (ed.), *The Beowulf manuscript*, Dumbarton Oaks Medieval Library (Cambridge, MA: Harvard University Press, 2010), p. 291; Frederick Rebsamen, 'young', in Rebsamen (ed. and trans.), *Beowulf: an updated verse translation* (New York: Harper Collins, 1991), p. 99; Michael Alexander, 'in his wisdom', in Alexander (ed. and trans.), *Beowulf* (New York: Penguin, 1973, repr. 1986), p. 150. Translators who use 'wise' include Howell D. Chickering (ed. and trans.), *Beowulf* (New York: Anchor Books, 1977), p. 237; Seamus Heaney (trans.), *Beowulf* (New York: Farrar, Straus, and Giroux, 2000), p. 209; Roy Liuzza (ed. and trans.), *Beowulf*, 2nd edn (Peterborough, Ont.: Broadview Press, 2013), p. 148; Burton Raffel (ed. and trans.), *Beowulf* (New York: New American Library 1963), p. 119; J. R. R. Tolkien, *Beowulf: a translation and commentary*, ed. Christopher Tolkien (New York: Houghton Mifflin, 2014), p. 104.

29 I am indebted to Stephen J. Harris for grammatical expertise about the form of *snotra*.

30 I am indebted to the Manchester University Press reviewer for the suggestion to incorporate the implications of Wiglaf's name into this argument.

31 While Gillian Overing does not use the phrase 'emotional range', she does delineate the 'masculine economy' of *Beowulf*, in which she sees 'a continual need for resolution – the hero says, I will do *x* or I will die – and the notion that choice is heroic, inescapable, and reducible to simple binary oppositions'. Gillian R. Overing, *Language, sign, and gender in Beowulf* (Carbondale, IL: Southern Illinois University Press, 1990), p. xxiii.

Index

EU authorised representative for GPSR:
Easy Access System Europe, Mustamäe tee 50,
10621 Tallinn, Estonia
gpsr.requests@easproject.com